# Cognition and Cognitive Psychology

# Cognition and Cognitive Psychology

Anthony J. Sanford

Basic Books, Inc., Publishers    New York

This book is dedicated to my daughter Bridget

# Contents

# Contents ix

# Foreword

This book is intended to provide a general introductory coverage of cognitive psychology, with a bias in the direction of broader 'cognitive science'.

The detail of the discussions varies from topic to topic. The assumption is that perception and memory are generally treated in specialist courses and, accordingly, the discussions of these topics are somewhat rudimentary. A number of excellent books are available on these subjects which may be used to supplement the text in hand. Other topics of general importance are not usually treated in special courses, and these are dealt with in more detail: schema theory and various aspects of language and thinking are covered here in depth, partly because there are few books of an introductory kind offering amenable and balanced treatments. In the view of the author, aspects of these problems are also important because they fit together and provide a unifying theme which is absent from many works.

Many of the discussions reflect the views and interests of the author, of course, but professors seldom rely exclusively on the views expressed in one text, and it is hoped that where my statements differ from the views of other individuals, the conflict will provide a stimulus to the student rather than cause confusion. Some of the Chapters have 'evaluations' appended which bring some of the author's biases and omissions to the surface.

In any general book of this kind, the order of presentation of the material poses a further problem. Traditionally, cognitive psychology texts move from the 'peripheral' to the 'central', starting with topics in perception, going on to attention, and ending with memory, language, and thinking. One problem which this raises is the discovery, over the life of the subject, that perception is intrinsically bound up with memory, that attention is bound up with perception and memory, and that language is bound up with memory, perception, and attention. After much heart-searching, it was decided to order the material here in a more-or-less conventional way, although this means that the earlier topics receive a more shallow treatment than the later ones.

The problem of ordering leads to two particularly noticeable discontinuities in flow, kindly brought to my attention by the series editor, Alan Baddeley. Towards the end of the sections on memory, the complex role played by memory in the processes of understanding leads to a discussion of semantics (a major aspect of meaning) which goes beyond that normally found in introductory books, and which is liberally illustrated with examples of language understanding.

When the book moves on to language per se, readers will find themselves dealing with some elementary process models of syntax. To some readers, this may appear to be a step backwards from the relatively 'high-level' considerations of understanding discussed in the earlier chapters. For such readers, the second language chapter, which deals with *discourse* (language in use) jumps back again to what are traditionally considered to be 'high-level' aspects of understanding. In fact, the discontinuities are a natural consequence of the author's way of thinking. Language processing is presumably aimed at manipulating the state of mind (memory) of the user. Since this is obviously a problem of the control of memory, the sequence of the book begins with the relationship of language to memory. But it is equally apparent that the order of words used and the rules of word order (syntactics) play an essential role in the use of language – even its very nature according to linguistics. As a consequence, this topic is examined as the first 'pure language' chapter. Equally obviously, language utterances are produced in rich perceptual and linguistic contexts – and this aspect is taken up in the second language chapter. Language is a huge topic, and only the most elementary sketch is provided here, but chapter notes serve to provide pointers to the broader field.

A second major discontinuity for some readers might be the placement of the chapter on *imagery* at the end of the book. But the reader should ask himself where a chapter on this important topic might truly belong. Is it part of perception? Yes. Is it part of memory? Yes, there have been many studies of memory which are related to imagery. It is the author's belief that imagery is not really separable from the act of building and manipulating models of the world, and a great part of this book provides the infrastructure for readers who are unfamiliar with cognition to understand what such modelling might mean. Besides this obvious reason for the ordering chosen, it is not so long ago (maybe half a century) that images were considered to be subsets of thoughts, and so the chapter's placement does not seem unnatural to the author, though some might wish to argue this point. Imagery is at best a thorny problem but I see no reason to exclude aspects of its study from an introductory book.

Apart from omissions through the bias of the author, and those accounted for in occasional chapter notes, there are more serious omissions which require comment at the outset. Virtually nothing has been said of traditional work in the area known as 'human performance', including work on the impact of environmental stress. An even greater omission is that there is little discussion of skill and its acquisition – a topic which does indeed play a central role in modern as well as earlier conceptions of the mind. These were omitted for reasons of space and simplicity. Similarly, there is very little discussion of the relation of brain architecture to information processing: cognitive neuropsychology is a rapidly expanding field. Once again, the omission is not an indicator of lack of importance, but is rather one of simple expediency given the volume of material being covered. Indeed, in the final appendix, the important journal *Brain and Behavioural Science* is quoted as an essential source for ongoing discussions of work in this field.

It would be somewhat tardy to continue my apologia beyond the necessary; I hope that as it stands the volume will give students food for thought and generate in their minds the kind of questions which are the mainsprings of scientific inquiry.

The author is grateful to a large number of people who have helped shape his views and who have provided critical and supportive comment. They include my close colleagues and friends Simon Garrod, Hana' Al-Ahmar, Jim Mullin, Ian Bushnell, Bob Leiser, Linda Moxey, Angela Lucas and Tony Anderson. I am also grateful to those undergraduates who cast a critical eye over various drafts, with a view to eliminating unintelligibility. Special thanks are due to Sheena Bryson who turned scribbles into pages of text, to the series editor Alan Baddeley for helpful comments, and to Muriel McGeechan who helped me keep writing when the going was rough. Any failures in judging content and style, and any inaccuracies, rest with me.

A.J. Sanford
Glasgow

*February 1984*

# Acknowledgements

I wish to thank the following individuals and organizations for permission to reproduce the following figures and tables:

Figure 2-9(b)

Sanford, A.J. (1971), 'Effects of changes in the intensity of white noise on simultaneity judgements and simple reaction time', *Quarterly Journal of Experimental Psychology*, 23, pp. 296–303.
© Experimental Psychology Society.

Figure 2-12

Rabbitt, P.M.A. and Vyas, S.M. (1970), 'An elementary preliminary taxonomy for some errors in laboratory choice RT tasks', *Acta Psychologia*, 33, pp. 56–76.
© North-Holland Publishing Co., Amsterdam.

Figure 2-13

Eriksen, C.W. and Collins, J.F. (1967), 'Some temporal characteristics of visual perception', *Journal of Experimental Psychology*, 74, pp. 476–84.
© American Psychological Association.

Figure 2-14

Adapted from Sperling, G. (1963), 'A model for visual memory tasks', *Human Factors*, 5, pp. 19–31.
© The Johns Hopkins University Press.

Figure 3-6

Adapted from Tulving, E., Mandler, G. and Baumal, R. (1964), 'Interaction of two sources of information in tachistoscopic word recognition', *Canadian Journal of Psychology*, 18, pp. 62–71.
© Canadian Psychological Association.

Figure 7-5

Adapted from Collins, A.M. and Quillian, M.R. (1972), 'How to make a language user', in E. Tulving and W. Donaldson (eds), *Organization and Memory*, Academic Press: New York.
© Academic Press.

Figure 7-9

Redrawn from Rumelhart, D.E. and Ortony, A. (1977), 'The representation of knowledge in memory', in R.C. Anderson, R.J. Spiro and W.E. Montague (eds), *Schooling and the acquisition of knowledge*, Lawrence Erlbaum Associates: Hillsdale, N.J.
© Lawrence Erlbaum Associates.

Figure 11-1

Silver, E.A. (1981), 'Recall of mathematical problem information: solving related problems', *Journal for Research in Mathematics Education*, 12, pp. 54–64.
© National Council of Teachers of Mathematics.

Table 10-1

From Thorndyke, P.W. (1977), 'Cognitive structures in comprehension and memory of narrative discourse', *Cognitive Psychology*, 9, pp. 77–110.
© Academic Press.

Figure 11-4

Simon, H.A. and Reed, S.K. (1976), 'Modelling strategy shifts in a problem-solving task', *Cognitive Psychology*, 8, pp. 86–97.
© Academic Press.

Figures 11-5 and 11-6

Adapted from Newell, A. and Simon, H.A. (1972), *Human Problem Solving*, Prentice-Hall: Englewood Cliffs, N.J.
© Prentice-Hall.

Table 13-1

From Smedslund, J. (1963), 'The concept of correlation in adults', *Scandinavian Journal of Psychology*, 4, pp. 165–73.

Figure 13-2

Adapted from Johnson-Laird, P.N., Legrenzi, P. and Sonino-Legrenzi, M. (1972), 'Reasoning and a sense of reality', *British Journal of Psychology*, 63, pp. 395–400.
© British Psychological Society.

Figure 14-3 (a and b)

Redrawn from Metzler, J. and Shepard, R.N. (1974), 'Transformational studies of the internal representations of three-dimensional objects', in R.L. Solto (ed), *Theories of Cognitive Psychology: The Loyola Symposium*, Lawrence Erlbaum Associates: Hillsdale N.J.
© Lawrence Erlbaum Associates.

# 1 Cognition and cognitive psychology

One pervasive and traditional pre-experimental view of the mind is that it divides into three domains: conation (the action of the will), affect (the actions of the emotions) and cognition (the actions of the intellect). By and large, it would be true to say that cognitive psychology and the associated discipline of cognitive science have at their core the study of the actions of the intellect. A typical course on cognitive psychology will consist of treatments of perception, memory, understanding, problem-solving, using language, decision-making, and other topics which we would ascribe in our everyday language to the intellect. This is not to say that cognitive psychologists are not concerned with the emotions or with motivation (a concept which has tended to replace conation), but rather to say that these issues have been less well treated in cognitive psychology than cognition itself.

One might well say that if these other facets of mind could be included in cognitive psychology, then does it not just boil down to *psychology* with no adjectival qualification? In a way it does, but on one reading 'cognitive psychology' denotes a particular philosophy of approach to the subject. This approach is termed the *information-processing* approach, and it has several important characteristics. First, it views those activities which make up mental events as reflecting a flow of information. When one acts in a particular way as a result of seeing something (such as calling for help if there is an accident), the entire sequence of events is seen as a flow of information: data are received by the senses, interpreted with the aid of what is stored in memory, translated into a goal to produce a certain response, and then the goal is realized by recourse to mechanisms responsible for appropriate language production. Secondly, such an approach implies a rather mechanistic view of the mind: it is seen as an automaton. The complexity and flexibility of that automaton is very great, greater than the most flexible of modern computers, which many see as analogous to the mind. In many ways, computers are tools made by man which capture a little of man's flexibility. Some people find this approach a little distasteful at first: how can man's mind be a machine? It is worth reflecting upon this. We all accept that the *body* is a complex machine: the metaphor has held good for centuries, and has replaced magic with medicine and physiology. Perhaps if we knew more about the mind viewed as a machine, psychiatry would not be in the sad state it is at present. Beyond this, we must remember that as cognitive psychologists we are seeking to *understand* mental life, and not to grasp some ultimate reality. Thinking in terms of automata is really a tool to aid exploration, and it is the most effective that we have to date. Another point is that 'automaton' is a technical term, not to be confused with a cigarette machine or a clock. An automaton is the term used for a *rule-governed system*, so if we reject its use in psychology, we may as well give up hope of expecting any regularity in human behaviour.

All of this is rather theoretical, but cognitive psychology is a practical subject as well. Studies of the practical aspects of memory and learning, decision-making, and intuition carried out by cognitive psychologists are giving people a better picture of what they are like, why things go wrong – even of what it is fair to expect of one's fellow human beings (Norman 1982; Sanford 1983). At present, the cognitive (or information-processing) approach is a veritable growth industry in psychology, and as theory becomes more and more technical, so the gap between what the layman expects of psychology and what he gets is in fact narrowing. There is still far to go, of course. The human mind is immensely subtle and adaptable, and we are struggling to understand its adaptability. If we understood it better, we could build more adaptable machines. Anyone who has used a computer system which is not sensitive to the user can imagine what a boon that would be! Almost all cognitive psychologists believe that this is an exciting time for psychologists, and it is hoped that readers will find things in this book to excite them too.

The cognitive approach is relatively recent in psychology for reasons which are briefly described below. Although cognition was studied at the birth of experimental psychology, it waned somewhat with the behaviourist revolution. Now that it has re-emerged, it has become very much part of mainstream psychology.

## 1 Behaviourism

All histories of psychology detail the rise of behaviourism in reaction to the earlier approaches which seemed to rely upon introspection, and which ascribed to the mind properties which could not be checked publicly. While the ensuing behaviourist period brought about the establishment of a wide range of experimental techniques of great value, and an understanding of control in psychological experimentation, it had a detrimental effect on the study of cognition. Since events 'within the organism' could only be inferred indirectly, the dominant pursuit of experimental psychologists was to study the correlation between the conditions and stimuli presented to animals and their subsequent behaviour, in a search for general laws. This valuable exercise says nothing about the *mechanisms* which mediate the behaviour. Of course, some psychologists, including the Gestalt psychologists and workers such as Frederick Bartlett (1932), continued to be concerned with these internal mechanisms. But missing from their explanations always was a detailed description of the chains of events in a language which did not smack of mentalism. In the author's view, the development of such a language was a necessary precondition for the development of an adequate cognitive psychology. Another facet of behaviourism was its laudable but restricting code of experimental control. One consequence was a tendency for many research psychologists to concentrate their efforts on the study of animals other than humans. Animals can be reared as required, brought up in controlled conditions, and presented with experimental situations in a *totally controlled way*. This is not possible with humans – a fact which, for many behaviourists, made humans inferior experimental subjects.

The shift to the current situation in which many more pieces of research are done with humans than with animals is at least partly explained by practical forces. The Second World War brought numerous necessary technological advances, and along with them the problem of how to make the machine fit the man (or the opposite!). The question became one of assessing, understanding, and improving the efficiency of the 'human operator'. Previously banned mentalistic concepts like attention, mental load, and cognitive strategy gradually infiltrated the increasing number of studies of human performance. Human-performance research was a direct precursor of modern cognitive psychology. In the age of technology, it is still a staple element of psychological research.

One might suppose that new studies of cognition must still suffer the problems of the old. How can it be any better than it was when superseded by behaviourism? It is, largely because of the development of theories of information processing, which have provided non-mentalistic language for the analysis of mental activity. The background to this part of the story lies in a number of different but related pieces of work which have blossomed from immediately before the Second World War right through to the present day.

## 2  Information research

The growth of the communications industry from the 1930s onward led to a great deal of research into how much information communication channels, such as telephone lines, could carry in a given time. The problem is straightforward: how many separate messages can a cable, for instance, carry? It soon became obvious that there was a limit, and that the more messages that were sent simultaneously, the more degraded (or noisy) any particular message became. Add to this extraneous agents producing noise in the system, and one has a fair idea of a general communication problem. The result was the development of a mathematical treatment of the information content of signals, and what it takes to differentiate signals from noise. Today, one of the main impacts of this work on psychology is in the theory of signal detection, a perception problem. During the 1950s, however, many psychologists working in the human performance area saw people as 'communication channels', taking messages from the world (percepts) and acting on them, classifying or otherwise using them. The application of information theory was only partly successful, but represented an important step in that researchers began to think of people as limited-capacity information-processing systems.

Later developments along these lines in psychology left the mathematical theory (except in certain areas), and began instead to differentiate the *flow* of information within the brain. This partitioning into stages and information flow routes is an extremely important way of representing the component processes and devices used in the brain in carrying out specific tasks. For instance, in later chapters we will discuss the flow of information from perceptual analysers towards recognition units and on into memory. This way of thinking owes a great debt to information theory and the study of communication.

A further important element came from another engineering-related subject, *cybernetics*, or the study of control. Research in this area was pioneered by mathematician Norbert Wiener (1948). One contrast between the early introspectionist psychologies and behaviourism revolved around causality. Using terms like intention and goal as explanations of behaviour was characteristic of early psychology, yet the standard model of science requires *causal* explanations – how events at time t bring about events at times after t. The looseness and apparent unscientific nature of teleological terms like intention and goal ran contrary to this, and they were not used as concepts by behaviourists. But cybernetics, the science of control, concerned itself with the theory and design of systems which could modify their own behaviour. Consider a thermostat. It keeps temperatures constant by monitoring the consequences of its condition. If the temperature is too high, it switches off the heating, and the room cools down. If the temperature is too low, it switches on again. Such behaviour is *goal oriented* ('keep temperature constant') yet results from a machine which is based in causal mechanisms. Many such control mechanisms are found in physiology, and much of human behaviour itself can be construed in such a way. The impact of cybernetics on psychology was to show how notions of goal and purpose are not inconsistent with causal explanations, and that human behaviour could be represented as the behaviour of a cybernetic machine.

## 3 The significance of computation

Computation is naturally associated with doing arithmetic although, in fact, calculation is a better name for that. Computation is a far more general term for all kinds of *symbol manipulation*. The theoretical study of symbol manipulation is called *symbolic logic*, and it was with the study of logic that the modern conception of computation began, largely in the work of Alan Turing (1950). Turing is responsible for the development of an account of the limits of computation: that is, on the basis of a given set of *rules* or admissible operations, and a set of symbol statements, what kinds of statements can possibly be derived? These limits are expressed in terms of classes of operations which have to be allowed to achieve the desired result, and their study is called the theory of automata. It would be out of place to go into these matters in an introduction, but these ideas are used in chapter 9 on language.

The practical scientific outcome was the development of general-purpose symbol-manipulating machines called digital computers. Any rule-governed process could be implemented in a computer which was a sufficiently complex (powerful) automaton. For Turing (among others), if human behaviour and cognition is rule governed, then it can be expressed in terms of automata theory, and so implemented in a computer progam. A very interesting paper by Turing (1950) lays out some of these arguments, in a non-technical way, and disarms most of the more obvious counter-arguments. With developing technology, emergent electronics, and so on, we end up with the situation which we have today: computers that can play chess, hold dialogues, solve problems, and so on. It is worth reflecting on the fact that as early as 1956, a program called 'Logic Theorist' could work out logic proofs in a way which seemed to match the descriptions given by logicians of how they did it.

Many people saw the brain as like a large flexible general-purpose computer. This has had several consequences. First of all, attempts to write computer programs to mimic intelligent human behaviour, such as understanding or solving problems, reveal to the person writing the programs the full complexity of the problems. Indeed the psychologist's conception of what must happen in the mind has been heavily influenced by attempts to mimic some of that activity. Research into developing such complex programs is called 'Artificial Intelligence'. Although the design of such programs and the study of the principles behind intelligent programs is a study in its own right, it has fairly obvious implications for the study of mind. It is difficult to write programs which mimic essentially human activities without at the same time studying how humans do things, and it is foolhardy to devise theories of human cognition without considering the computational implementation of the theory. In fact, a growing number of researchers now call themselves 'Cognitive Scientists', and believe that the only way to understand human cognition is through the study of computation, psychology and various ancillary subjects, rather than through the study of any one of them (see Norman 1982).

One of the great advantages of the computational metaphor of the mind is that computational theories have to be very explicit, otherwise they would not work in program implementation. Another is that it provides a language for talking about mental processes which is not merely mentalistic, but which has a significance in terms of general information-processing theory. Let us consider a very simple example. One of the mental-processing acts which we can all do is to answer a question like 'What is four plus five?' Now reflect on how you did it. You would probably say that you 'just knew it', or answered without any thought. Just knowing it is a typical mentalistic turn of phrase. You might grace it with a fancy name, like 'immediate apprehension of the answer', but what happened?

Now consider a simple computer program, which has some memory entries and some procedures. Suppose the memory entries are as follows:

$$1+1=2 \quad 2+1=3 \quad \ldots \quad 9+1=10$$
$$1+2=3 \quad 2+2=4 \quad \ldots \quad 9+2=11$$
$$1+3=4 \quad 2+3=5 \quad \ldots \quad 9+3=12$$
$$\cdot \qquad\qquad \cdot \qquad\qquad \cdot \qquad\qquad \cdot$$
$$\cdot \qquad\qquad \cdot \qquad\qquad \cdot \qquad\qquad \cdot$$
$$\cdot \qquad\qquad \cdot \qquad\qquad \cdot \qquad\qquad \cdot$$
$$1+9=10 \quad 2+9=11 \quad \ldots \quad 9+9=18$$

To answer a query like 'What is $4+5$?', a procedure something like this would be required:

1 Find expression $4+5$ on left-hand side of one of the columns.
2 Read answer from right-hand side.

The answer is 'automatic' because the memory already has the complete expression in it. The problem is thus one of how the system finds the appropriate left-hand expression.

If you ask a small child who is learning arithmetic the same question, he will not answer so automatically. Suppose he knows how to count. This would be equivalent to having the following, somewhat different, data in memory:

Ascending numbers: 1, 2, 3, 4, 5, 6, 7, 8, 9

To answer '4 + 5' using *this* database, an appropriate procedure would be:

1   Break 4 + 5 into '4', '+', '5'.
2   Locate 4 in the ascending numbers' table.
3   On basis of '+', select to count from left to right.
4   Move 5 places from 4, to the right.
5   You are at answer. Assert it.

These are two very different ways of producing the same answer. The differences spring from what is in memory, and the procedures which have to be used to get the right answer. In fact, the two capture something of the difference between adults and children. To demonstrate this is an empirical and psychological problem.

## 4  Back to psychology

Of course, merely to illustrate how task performance might be conceptualized computationally does not do any justice to much of cognitive psychology. We could take a thousand tasks, and come up with several thousand such descriptions. At root, the problem is to discover principles of organization which constrain the possible variety of such programs. The only way cognition will be understood is if there are generalizations which can be made about such constraints. Fortunately, psychological studies have revealed a number of these which seem to crop up over large numbers of tasks. For example, many cognitive activities seem to be limited in scope because they are funnelled through a system called 'working memory', which can only operate upon a limited amount of data at a time.

Our task is thus twofold: on the one hand, we wish to understand how human beings are able to perform such an astonishing range of intellectual activities, and on the other, we have to search for generalities in processing patterns. A good analogy is to suppose that the brain has a number of special devices in it, each of which is used for a particular job. Any task will use some or all of these devices. The problem is to establish what they are.

One final word about scope is in order. Mental activity is immensely complex and difficult to study, and the idea that all is solved by the computational metaphor must be dispelled. A very large part of studies in both artificial intelligence and psychology is at the natural history level – simply discovering phenomena. This is the normal precursor of true theory in science, and is the characteristic of cognitive psychology in its present state. One might draw an analogy with biology: before the theory of evolution, biology was largely in a natural history state. The theory provided a basis for a deeper understanding of biological phenomena, and, of course, it rested upon what had been learned from the natural history. There are cognitive scientists who believe that the information-processing approach, particularly the automata-theory aspects, represent a theory of a high order in cognition (Newell 1981): it is a little early to tell. One thing is clear, although we have learned much about our own minds, we still have a long way to go.

# 2 Accrual of stimulus information

A great deal of human information-processing is instigated or controlled by events in the world. Given this self-evident truth, it is scarcely surprising that perceptual phenomena have an important role to play in the study of cognition. Of course, perception studies represents an almost independent subarea of psychology in its own right, and the treatment given here is complementary to treatments given in perception, and should not be considered a summary of research in that field. Despite this, perception is important to us here because when we analyse cognitive activity, much of it is intrinsically bound up with perceptual processes. Furthermore, many of the most central problems in perception recur in other guises in cognition, and this commonality is part of the foundation of an integrated view of human information-processing.

The basic perceptual problem can be expressed very easily: it is to explain how physical events in the world become represented in a useful form in the nervous system. In a frog, for instance, the useful aspect of a dark blob travelling rapidly across the visual field is that it may be an insect, which is food for the frog. Accordingly, the frog's visual system appears to be geared towards the detection of just those blob movements which are most likely to constitute food. Many simple creatures seem to have visual systems which specialize in the detection of those patterns of light which are biologically useful to it, but to very few others. Of course, in human beings, the picture seems more complex, and may be of a different order. Our conscious impressions are of pictures of an integrated 'world', or of meaningful sounds, from which we select or focus upon those aspects which are most useful to us at any given time (see Marr 1982 for a discussion of intra-species visual mechanisms). Yet to both human and to more humble creatures, the basic problem is one of representing important patterns of stimulus energy, or energy change.

One of the principal characteristics of human perception is the rapid, unconscious recognition of objects and forms. We have little trouble in recognizing things for what they are unless the angle of vision is extremely unusual. It is almost as if the objects themselves were 'in our heads'. Despite these naive impressions, studies of perception show that the recognition of objects depends upon many cues being extracted from energy patterns in the world, and, by using these cues as 'evidence', deciding that the object is indeed there and is what it is. The extraction of these cues, and the integration of them, is an essentially probabilistic process. This is an important idea and a main theme of the next two chapters; it is also a general point. The idea of combining information providing evidence for something is important in perception, attention, memory and thinking.

To begin with, we shall consider the simpler problem of detecting the presence of the most easily described stimuli. All physical stimuli consist of changes or differences in energy, and the simplest stimulus of all is one in which there is simply an energy change with everything else held constant, for instance, presentation of a tone of a particular frequency, or increasing the brightness of a light. We shall begin here. Even the representation of these simple events is fairly complex, however, and two sections of this chapter are devoted to the problem of how one decides that a simple energy-change stimulus has been presented. Although this may seem a small start in a book which promises to introduce the reader to problems of memory, thinking, language and so on, it is in some ways a good place to start, for much of what has been learned about the detection of simple stimuli forms the basis of ideas about more complex things.

Later in the chapter, more complex stimuli are considered. In particular, stress is put on the process by which decisions on whether a stimulus is one configuration or another are made – in other words, stimulus recognition is introduced. How we recognize objects in the world, and scenes, is a difficult issue. In the present chapter, we are concerned with the recognition of much simpler stimuli – mostly alphanumeric. Chapter 3 continues this theme in more detail, and goes on to discuss some work on the perception of objects and scenes.

## A  Signal detection theory

Hearing or not hearing a signal appears to be a very straight-forward affair at first sight; either the signal is perceived or it is not. Furthermore, it might be supposed that all tasks involving the detection of a signal would have a processing stage in common – the stage responsible for perception. After perceiving the signal, a subject could say he heard or saw the signal, or, as in a simple reaction task, press the button as quickly as possible. This is an oversimplification, however, even in the very simple case of determining the presence of a change in stimulus intensity.

Traditionally, the 'threshold' was an expression used to indicate the value that a stimulus must take to be detected. Imagine listening for a very quiet stimulus over silent headphones. The minimum amount of sound energy necessary for hearing is termed the *absolute threshold* of hearing. Of course, in experiments aimed at estimating this, many readings have to be taken and given statistical variability for any given energy level; subjects will sometimes report hearing a signal and sometimes not. In practice, absolute threshold is that value at which the subjects make 75 per cent correct detections. The same arguments apply to judging whether one stimulus is louder than another when both are above absolute threshold. The difference at which the subject judges correctly on 75 per cent of occasions is called the *difference threshold*. Behind these estimating techniques of classical psychophysics is the simple view that there is a threshold. Above the threshold, detection has taken place; below it, it has not. There are a number of difficulties with this point of view, one of which can be illustrated through the subjective experience of taking part in threshold determination tasks. Around threshold values, be they absolute or difference thresholds, one experiences great uncertainty about whether one did or did not actually hear or see the stimulus. Under such circumstances, there is a degree of arbitrariness about saying one did or did not believe the signal to be present. Such experiences are not easily reconciled with the view that either one does or does not detect the stimulus – in fact, often one can more readily express a degree of confidence that one has detected a stimulus then one can make a categorical yes/no statement.

The general approach towards signal detection problems rests upon two rather different issues. The first is the group of theories which address the problem of how signals are *represented* in the brain, while the second group is aimed at the problem of what response a subject decides to make in the face of uncertainty associated with a representation, such as that described above. While the first group of theories classically belong to the subject areas of sensory psychology and physiology, the latter, issues of decision-making, rest squarely within cognitive psychology.

### 1 The statistical nature of signal information

It is misleading to think of a simple signal, such as a burst of white noise, as being discretely represented in the nervous system. Auditory intensity is represented in the nervous system as the rate of firing of the bundles of neurones which make up the auditory pathway. The greater the amount of firing per unit time, the more intense the stimulus (see, for example, Stevens 1970). But such neural activity is not restricted to situations in which there is a stimulus present. Some *spontaneous* firing of nerve cells occurs continuously, even in the absence of an external stimulus; such firing is generally referred to as 'neural noise'. Furthermore, in the intact organism, the movement of blood in blood vessels around the sensory receptors can serve as a 'stimulus', contributing further to the neural activity. In this way, the distinction between a stimulus and background becomes somewhat blurred.

What is the difference between noise and stimulus? We can think of it as essentially the degree of firing of neurones in the sensory nerves. For example, clearly audible signals will induce a mean level of firing which is much higher than the mean level normally associated with noise. In contrast, very weak signals will not produce a mean firing level which is so clearly differentiated. At around 'threshold', then, detection difficulties may arise because there are insufficient grounds to decide whether a mean firing level is caused by noise alone, or whether there is a signal there.

According to signal detection theory, decisions as to the presence or absence of a stimulus are made on the basis of *statistical* considerations. In our example, we can think of the statistical decision as being based on the properties of firing rates. Figure 2-1 (a) shows three distributions. The left-most distribution shows a hypothetical firing rate associated with 'noise' in a perceptual system. One should imagine that the distribution was obtained by sampling the firing rate associated with noise on a very large number of occasions. Obviously the firing rate will not always be the same; rather, a distribution (shown here as normal) will be obtained.

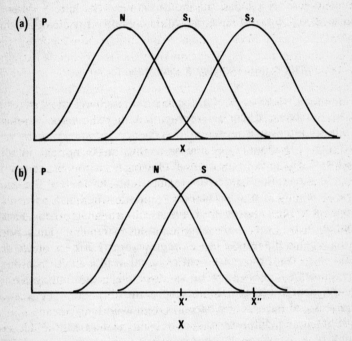

*Figure 2-1.* (a) Distributions of evidence (X) based on assumed neural activity. N, the noise distribution, covers lower values of X than does a weak signal (S₁), while a stronger signal covers much higher values of X. (b) For a given signal and noise distributions, there will be overlap which is a function-to-noise ratio. In the figure, suppose that a value of X′ is the sensory evidence on a particular trial. Is this part of N or S? It could be either. On the other hand, a level as great as X″ clearly comes from S. (In both figures, P is probability density.)

The other two curves show similar distributions for two signal intensities; the right one being more intense than the left. The average values of firing (X) differ in these two cases, X being higher for the more intense stimulus. The firing which results from a stimulus being present can be thought of as being added to the noise firing level.

Signal detection theory assumes that whenever a subject is asked whether a signal has been presented, an X value is obtained for that trial, and the subject is effectively in the position of having to decide whether the value of X comes from the noise distribution (in which case there is 'no signal'), or from the signal distribution. Consider figure 2-1(b), for instance. Suppose that on a particular trial of an experiment, the value of X obtained from the sensory pathway was X'. Does this value come from the N (noise) distribution, or from the S + N distribution? Obviously, in this case it is equally likely to come from either. Now suppose the value on a trial to be X''. This time the value is sufficiently extreme for it to make sense to assume that it comes from the S (signal) distribution. Indeed, X'' is a value which is far more *likely* to come from the S distribution. The point is that there is a range of uncertainty over which it is unclear whether the value is representative of a signal or merely of noise.

Similar arguments apply to detecting an increment in the intensity of a background noise. Obviously, if the increment is small enough, this can be extremely difficult. In terms of our present argument, the problem is to decide whether a particular value of X obtained from an observation belongs to the background distribution or background-plus-increment. Thus both absolute and difference thresholds can be treated in much the same way. The subject is construed as making a choice based on tacit knowledge of S and N distributions, and a current X value: is current X more likely to come from S or N?

It is clear that this way of representing a signal means that a subject who is making decisions for signals around threshold has to make a choice in the face of uncertainty – a statistically based choice. One way of thinking about making such choices is to assume that a subject has to decide what is the minimum value of X above which he will call all events 'signal present'. The consequences of some of the options are illustrated in figure 2-2.

Suppose that a subject adopts a criterion (criterion 1) throughout an experiment, as shown in figure 2-2(a). This means that all values of X which are greater than criterion 1 are treated as though they meant a signal had been presented. The subject will correctly say 'signal' given a signal at a rate defined by the area labelled P(c) on the diagram. He will *also* say 'signal' when there is no signal at a rate defined by the area labelled P(FA); that is, he will make a false positive response.

Figure 2-2(b) shows what happens if an attempt is made to reduce the false positive rate by setting the criterion to a higher value of X (criterion 2). While P(FA), the false alarm rate, will go down, so too will P(c), the correct detection rate!

The important point about this way of treating detection situations is that P(c) and P(FA) are shown to be *monotonically related*. As P(c) goes up, so too does P(FA). In fact the curve for the relationship, assuming normal distributions, is as shown in figure 2-3. Any change in criterion will just produce a new point defined by P(c), P(FA).

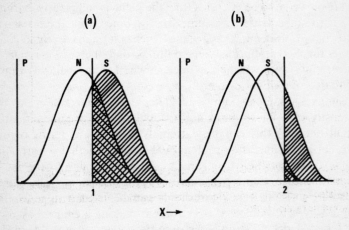

*Figure 2-2.* The effect of criterion setting on P(c) and P(FA). (a) With criterion 1, a certain area of the curve for S comes into the 'yes' response zone, to the right of 1. But so too does a certain area of the curve for N. Responding 'Yes' for X values beyond 1 will produce a certain value for P(c), but also one for P(FA). (b) With a more conservative criterion (value 2), P(FA) is reduced, but *so too* is P(c).

This curve is known as a Receiver Operating Characteristic (ROC), and is concave-downward and symmetrical about line P(c) = 1.0,  P(FA) = 1.0 when the underlying distributions are normal and of equal variance. The line labelled 'chance diagonal' is the ROC for a situation where the N and S distributions simply lie on top of one another. If the overlap between the N and S curves is reduced, as would be the case with stronger signals, then although the ROC will still have the same general characteristics, it will bow further out from the chance diagonal. In fact, a whole family of curves can be generated, one for each signal intensity, as shown in figure 2-3. What this means is that for stronger signals, a relatively high P(c) can be obtained at the cost of a relatively low P(FA).

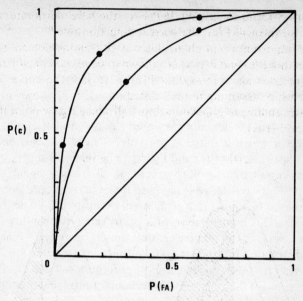

*Figure 2-3.* Idealized ROCs for a detection task. The left-most curve is for a signal-to-noise ratio which is greater than that for the right-most. The points are generated by adopting three different criterion settings. P(c) bears a concave-downwards relation to P(FA).

## 2 *Psychological studies of the ROC*

Early in the development of signal detection theory (see Green and Swets 1966), experiments were carried out using stimuli at around threshold to establish whether people actually conformed to the theory. The experimental requirements for the standard signal detection theory to be applied are that it should be possible to get a good estimate of P(c) and P(FA) for any signal strengths of interest. This means a large number of trials, usually hundreds, using only one intensity of stimulus. Subjects are then systematically encouraged to use various subjective criteria for deciding whether or not to say 'signal present' or 'signal absent' on each trial.

What could cause different settings in the criterion to be adopted? Broadly speaking, there are three main methods: *instructions, signal probability*, and *cost-pay off manipulation*. In the case of instructions, one might tell subjects to say 'signal present' on any given trial only if they were *absolutely sure* one was present, which would put the criterion of value high on the X dimension. To the value lower, one could ask them to say 'signal present' if they are *reasonably sure*. To move the value lower still, one might ask them to say 'signal present' if they *think one may have been present*.

In the usual signal detection case, half of the trials will be ones in which no signal is actually presented ('noise' trials), and half will be ones in which a signal is presented ('signal' trials), enabling optimal estimates of $P(c)$ and $P(FA)$ to be made. But suppose the subject knows that on 80 per cent of all trials a signal will be present. This knowledge is likely to make him say 'present' more often than if he knows that signals will occur in only 20 per cent of the trials. This manipulation of a priori signal probability is thus another way of manipulating the subject criterion. Finally, a reward structure may be set up favouring correct detections or the avoidance of false positives. For example, subjects would be expected to set their response criteria differently under conditions 1 and 2 where:

Condition 1 – For each hit, subject gets 2p. For each false alarm, subject loses 2p.

Condition 2 – For each hit, subject gets 10p. For each false alarm, subject loses 2p.

By carefully manipulating payoff conditions, a whole range of criterion settings is possible.

Finally, a very useful technique is simply to ask people to indicate on a confidence scale the degree to which they are certain that a signal was present, or absent in each and every trial. $P(c)$ and $P(FA)$ can then be found for each confidence category, resulting in points on an ROC.

All four methods have been used in various experiments (see Green and Swets 1966; McNichol 1972). Invariably, ROCs are produced which are very similar to those predicted by signal detection theory. This is true for both visual and auditory perception, and for absolute threshold and discrimination tasks.

## 3 The threshold concept and alternative ROCs

There was nothing inevitable about the way in which human subjects produced ROCs consistent with signal detection theory.

The earlier notion of absolute thresholds, in which stimuli are either heard or not heard, or seen and not seen, can also handle false positives, but does it in a different way. According to *classical threshold theory*, either a subject is in a 'detect' state or he is not, and neural noise is considered to be so low on the X dimension that there are no false positives in the sense discussed above. A false positive on the classical theory arises if the subject has not actually detected a signal, but decides in any case to say 'signal present' for one reason or another – let us say he 'guesses' that a signal might have been present.

Investigators were aware of guessing behaviour early in the history of psychophysics. In a standard detection task, investigators would include 'catch trials' on which no signal was actually presented. As we have seen, this will normally enable false positive responses to be detected, but within classical threshold theory they are handled in a completely different way, by the application of a 'guessing correction'.

It is quite easy to derive an ROC for the classical threshold model. Quite simply, the *true* P(c) for a subject for a signal of a given S/N ratio is the *observed* P(c) where there are *no* false positives, and the purpose of the guessing correction is to enable *true* P(c) to be calculated.

First, an *observed* P(c) will consist of two components, *true* P(c), which arises from the subject being in a 'detect' state, and saying 'Yes, the signal was there' and, added to this, a *false* P(c), a contribution to correct detections arising from trials on which a signal *was* present but the subject was *not* in a detect state, yet he *guessed* a signal was there. This can be written as a very simple equation:

$$Observed \ P(c) = True \ P(c) + False \ P(c) \quad\ldots\ldots\ldots\ldots\ldots\ldots\ldots \quad (1)$$

*False* P(c) can only arise if the subject was not in a detect state, and the probability of this happening is:

$$1- True \ P(c) \quad\ldots\ldots\ldots\ldots\ldots\ldots\ldots\ldots\ldots\ldots\ldots\ldots\ldots\ldots \quad (2)$$

Suppose that when this occurs, the subject guesses that a signal was present on g per cent of occasions. This *false* P(c) is given by:

$$False \ P(c) = g \ (1- True \ P(c)) \quad\ldots\ldots\ldots\ldots\ldots\ldots\ldots\ldots \quad (3)$$

The guess rate, g, can be directly observed. On the classical threshold theory, all false positives are the result of guessing, and so:

$$g = P(FA) \dots\dots\dots\dots\dots\dots\dots\dots\dots\dots\dots\dots\dots\dots\dots\dots\dots \quad (4)$$

This can be substituted in (3):

$$False\ P(c) = P(FA)\ (1-\ True\ P(c)) \dots\dots\dots\dots\dots\dots\dots \quad (5)$$

Finally, this can be substituted into (1), giving:

$$Observed\ P(c) = True\ P(c) + P(FA)\ (1-\ True\ P(c)) \dots\dots\dots \quad (6)$$

This equation is useful because the only unknown in it is *true* P(c), which we want and which can be determined by the following simple rearrangement of (6):

$$True\ P(c) = \frac{Observed\ P(c) - P(FA)}{1 - P(FA)}$$

This is called the *guessing correction*.

In order to make an ROC for the classic threshold theory, first notice that equation (6) above has *observed* P(c) on one side, and P(FA) on the other. The two are in fact related through this equation, in a linear fashion, and produce an ROC of the type shown in figure 2-4. For various values of P(FA), different values of *observed* P(c) can be produced, assuming a constant *true* P(c).

The important thing to notice is that the ROC produced is *linear*, in contrast to the ROC based upon signal detection theory which is a *curve*. As we have seen, ROCs produced by human subjects fit the signal detection model, and do not fit the classical model at all. Although there are complications over the signal detection model itself it is fair to say that in almost all situations the signal detection models give the best approximation to human performance which we have at present.

### 4 Signal detection indices of task performance

The index of sensory efficiency in the classical threshold framework is *true* P(c). In figure 2-4, *true* P(c) is the intercept of the ROC on the P(c) axis. Of course, for signal detection theory, there is *no true* P(c), so no version of P(c) can be used as an index of sensory efficiency.

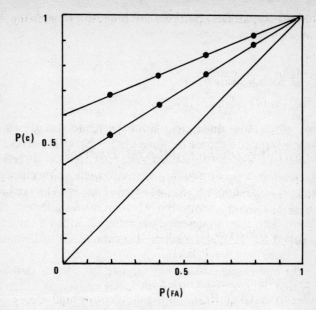

*Figure 2-4.* Idealized ROCs for the classical high-threshold theory. The upper curve is for a signal of higher signal-to-noise ratio than the lower. In contrast to signal detection theory ROCs, P(c) is linearly related to P(FA). The points represent different values of g.

The sensory efficiency index most widely used in signal detection theory is called d′ (d-prime). To understand its use, we have to go back to the different distributions of X obtained under noise and signal plus noise conditions at various intensities. The meaning of d′ is indicated in figure 2-5. It is the distance between the means of

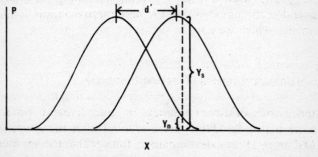

*Figure 2-5.* d′ is the difference in means of N and S distributions. β is the ratio $y_s/y_n$, measured at the criterion point.

the S and N distributions, expressed in terms of standard deviation units. In terms of a simple equation,

$$d' = \frac{\text{Mean } S - \text{Mean } N}{\sigma_N}$$

where $\sigma_N = \sigma_{SN}$. It is quite clear from the figure that $d'$ will be greater for a larger difference between the S + N and N curves.

*Regardless* of where the subject sets his criterion, $d'$ reflects sensory efficiency. Very often, apart from knowing how efficient a subject is, it is desirable to know whether he is being risky or cautious in the decision criterion which is being adopted. The index most often used to describe the criterion which a subject is using is called $\beta$ (beta), and is simply the ratio of the ordinates, as shown in figure 2-5.

The most interesting lesson to be learned from signal detection theory is that even a simple stimulus is not registered within the nervous system as an all-or-none affair. Being able to detect a stimulus depends upon an evaluation of the neural evidence that it is there, and this evidence has been characterized here as lying on a continuum of neural activity. The decision to be made is thus a statistical one, and the final outcome of any trial of a detection task will be a result of *criterion setting* as well as the *sensory information available*. According to signal detection theory, the quality of the information available (reflected in $d'$), and the criterion setting (reflected in $\beta$) are not directly related to one another; $d'$ and $\beta$ can be independently manipulated. Although we will refer to $d'$ and $\beta$ again, the most important point for this chapter is that sensory information regarding the presence of a stimulus is not all-or-none.

## 5  Signal detection theory in perspective

Our discussion above indicates how signal detection theory may be applied to simple detection problems. In order to make the theory concrete, we considered the dimension X as reflecting neural firing rate. At this point, it is appropriate to indicate that the application of signal detection theory does not really require us to identify X with firing rates. X can be considered as *any* dimension along which two things are being compared – the only requirement is that the values taken by those two things have distributions on X. For example, the theory is quite applicable to recognition memory tasks. In such tasks, subjects may be given a list of words to learn. Later, they are presented with (say) single words, some of which were on the list ('old' words), and some of which are 'new' words. The subject has to decode whether each of the single words is old or new. Quite clearly, under these circumstances, the subject will produce a proportion of *correct* judgements, responding 'old' to an *old* item, but subjects may also respond 'old' to a new item; a so-called *false recognition*. These two responses are directly analogous to P(c) and P(FA) in detection theory.

Signal detection theory has been applied to memory studies of this type (e.g. Kintsch 1970). Receiver operating characteristics (sometimes called Memory Operating Characteristics) can be produced by a variety of techniques, such as instructing subjects to respond 'old' only if they are *sure* that the stimulus is old, or on other occasions to respond 'old' if they *suspect* that they have seen the stimulus item before. When this is done, ROCs resembling those produced in sensory experiments are obtained.

Clearly the suggestion is that judgements are based on values of X, but what is X? It has been called 'memory strength', or 'familiarity'. Given a particular value of X (familiarity) resulting from an item on a particular trial, the problem is to decide whether it is in the familiarity range of 'old' items, or whether it is so low as to be in the range associated with 'new' items. This is directly analogous to the detection problem discussed above.

The point is that we do not need to know what X is in order to apply the theory. Nobody really knows how familiarity is represented in neural terms. Of course, this does not alter the argument that stimulus intensity affects firing rates, and that these rates are behind the X values in simple signal detection (Luce and Green 1972 offer a sophisticated treatment of this point of view). In the next section, we shall treat clearly detectable signals in terms of firing rates.

## B  Dynamic aspects of signal detection

While the signal detection theory, as described above, is applicable to difficult discriminations where reasonable levels of misses and false alarms are observed, as it stands it cannot be applied so readily to obviously detectable, or clearly suprathreshold, stimuli. Present someone with a clearly audible sound and they are not going to miss it. Similarly, if two bursts of sound are presented for comparison, and one is clearly louder than the other, then there will be no (or few) errors in indicating which one was the louder. When one considers clearly audible stimuli in this way, signal detection theory as we have described it is apparently inapplicable. And yet the basic argument that loud stimuli produce an increase in the rate of neural firing holds good for suprathreshold stimuli. While clearly detectable signals do not allow the calculation of a measurable $d'$, there are other results which give uniformity to our view of the detection of simple stimuli. In particular, the continuum of evidence idea is reflected in the *time* taken to detect stimuli rather than in the *probability* of detecting them.

## 1 Reaction time to simple stimuli

A simple reaction-time task is one in which a subject waits for a stimulus of some sort to occur (a burst of noise, a flash of light), and presses a microswitch as soon as he or she has detected its presence. The point at which the stimulus is presented is rendered unpredictable by varying the interval between a warning stimulus which precedes the test stimulus, the interval usually being known as foreperiods or preparatory periods. A diagram of the sequence of events is set out in figure 2-6.

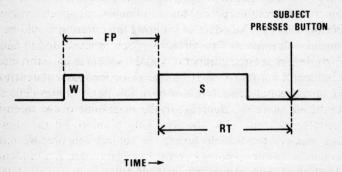

*Figure 2-6.* Sequence of events in a simple reaction-time task. The period FP is the foreperiod, and is measured from the onset of the warning signal, W, to the start of the 'reaction' stimulus, S. Reaction time is measured from the onset of S to the point where the subject presses the button.

One of the earliest findings concerning simple reaction time was that the time taken to press a button was shorter for more intense (louder, brighter) stimuli. This result is somewhat unsurprising – loud stimuli make you react more quickly – but it has been used as one source of evidence to suggest that percepts or representations of stimuli do not arrive in the brain instantaneously, but rather are gradually accumulated over time.

A very simple explanation of the intensity-reaction time effect was suggested by Grice (1968), and similar explanations have been given by many other researchers (e.g. LaBerge 1962; McGill 1963; Murray 1970; Sanford 1972). The essence of the idea is that discovering the presence of a signal depends upon the *accumulation* of neural evidence that a signal is indeed present, that what is accumulated is a running total of neural impulses, and that the accumulation occurs in some sort of neural counter. Detection of a stimulus is presumed to occur when the impulse count passes a certain criterion level. A simple version of the model is illustrated in figure 2-7 (a).

The model accommodates the qualitative effect of intensity on reaction time, because weaker stimuli will result in less neural activity per unit time, hence less impulses accumulated within any given time, so that weak stimuli will take longer to pass the criterion level.

There are various predictions which this simple model and its variants make, one of which concerns the criterion. Rather than being fixed, for instance, the criterion can be changed to accept more or less evidence depending upon the task. It may be that if a subject was well prepared for a stimulus, a lower evidence criterion was set. The effect of lowering the criterion would be to *reduce the magnitude of the intensity effect*, as illustrated in figure 2-7 (b). In fact, a large number of variables seem to have this effect on reaction-time patterns. If incentives or feedback of reaction-time performance are given, not only do reaction times decrease overall, but there is a decrease in the magnitude of the intensity effect (Henricksen 1971; Murray 1970). Similarly, if the stimuli occur at more predictable times, the subject can prepare more adequately; faster responses occur, but again there is a reduction in the size of the intensity effect (Kellas, Baumeister and Wilcox 1969). 'Blank' trials – those in which a warning signal is given, but no stimulus occurs, and so the subject does not respond – have a similar effect (Murray 1970). In some ways a blank trial

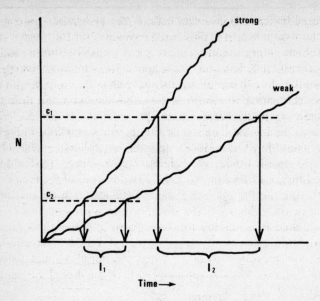

*Figure 2-7.* A hypothetical illustration of a neural counter. Impulses (N) are counted cumulatively over time. The accumulation rate is assumed to be roughly linear, and to be higher for a strong signal than a weak one. If some criterion level of N is passed, the signal is detected. $C_1$ is passed, the signal is detected. $C_1$ shows a high criterion, $C_2$ a lower one. It is clear from the geometry that the effect of intensity due to a high criterion, $I_2$, is greater than that for a low criterion, $I_1$, in terms of times for detection to occur.

corresponds to a noise trial in the standard detection task, and blanks enable a priori signal probability to be manipulated. Results indicate that the higher the proportion of blanks, the longer the reaction times in a series, and the *greater the intensity effect*. All in all, each of these manipulations are in qualitative agreement with the counter model.

## 2  Reaction and detection

Section B1 illustrates some rather basic ideas about the detection of simple suprathreshold stimuli. We must now, however, scrutinize the whole notion of stimulus detection. Most of the literature on simple reaction time has tended to equate passing a criterion level of activity with detection, since once this stage is passed, a signal can be passed from the detection device to a device concerned with response production: key pressing in most cases. This two-stage model is illustrated in figure 2-8. But suppose that the subject is not asked to press a key. Suppose instead that on being presented with one stimulus, a judgement of whether it occurred before or after *another* stimulus was required? Obviously, this situation also requires that the stimulus has been detected. Is it the output from the same detection mechanism which would enable such a task to be performed? If it is not, then there would have to be more than one way to detect a stimulus! The question is important, because so many tasks have stimulus detection as an element.

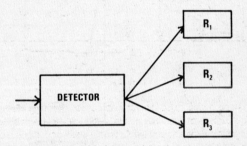

*Figure 2-8.* A theory which maintains that detection is a unitary process. After detection in the 'detector', reactions $R_1$, $R_2$, $R_3$, etc., become possible. $R_1$ may be pressing a button, $R_2$ saying 'I heard it', etc. On this model, similar intensity effects should hold for all R, whatever the tasks are. This appears unfounded.

The most direct means of addressing this is to compare the effects of intensity in the two tasks mentioned above: simple reaction time and the perception of order (or the perception of simultaneity). One such study was carried out by Sanford (1971). Subjects were required to watch a graduated clock-face, over which a pointer passed at a rate of one 360° sweep per second. At the same time they listened through headphones for an increment in a white noise background. The increments constituted the signals and subjects were asked to indicate where the pointer was when the noise increment occurred. Following the logic of the earlier arguments, subjects should take longer to detect a smaller increment than a larger one. And so, if the increments actually occurred when the pointer was in the same place on each trial, they should believe that the point was *further on* in the case of the small increment. This is illustrated in figure 2-9(a). The results supported this contention; the smaller the increment, the less far on the pointer was judged to be.

In the next part of the study, the size of this intensity effect was compared with that obtained from a simple reaction-time task under similar circumstances. Subjects watched the pointer going around in exactly the same way, but used the sweep as a warning signal. When the stimulus occurred they pressed a button. Indeed,

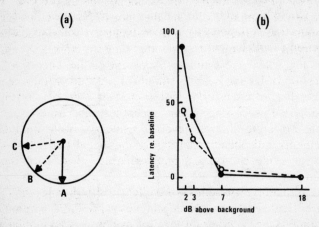

**Figure 2-9.** In the experiments of Sanford (1971), subjects watched a special clock-face. (a) Suppose that a sound stimulus began when the pointer was at A. Given perceptual lag, the subject might not detect it until it is at B. If it is a weaker stimulus, C might be the detection point. Comparing B with C gives a measure of the intensity effect on the task. (b) The result of comparing simple reaction time (solid line) with the clock task (dotted lines) over a range of stimulus intensity. *Baseline*, set at zero, is the latency for the loudest stimulus. The effect of intensity on the button-pressing task is greater.

in one version of the study, subjects pressed the key and made a pointer judgement in the same trials. The results showed a much larger intensity effect for reaction time than for pointer judgements, although the test conditions were identical.

This and other evidence from similar comparisons (e.g. Roufs 1963) suggests that there is not one evidence level for stimulus detection, but that the amount of evidence needed before a button is presssed or a pointer judgement made is task dependent. It is almost certainly not a question of shifts in the level of a single criterion (which of course explains different magnitudes of intensity effect) because in one of the studies the two tasks were performed simultaneously.

A similar issue arises when a somewhat different experiment is carried out. Sanford (1970) ran a straightforward simple reaction task, but after each trial, subjects were asked to indicate on a sheet whether their reactions were slow or fast on a four-point scale. They were aware of reacting more slowly to quiet stimuli. This alone is a problem for any simple model, because if they were *aware* of the stimulus, why did they not respond? However, by examining the mean reaction times within a particular speed-rating category, it was possible to show that they were not aware of the *entire* lag with quiet stimuli. Apparently, the latency of the impression of having heard a stimulus is dependent on intensity, but the effect of intensity on button-pressing is greater. It is likely that different processing systems accept a stimulus as 'detected' on the basis of quite different levels of evidence. Both simultaneity judgements and phenomenal impressions seem to require lower levels of evidence for a signal's presence than does button-pressing.

These findings present a broadly consistent and important picture. Evidence that a simple stimulus is present is accumulated over time. Once a criterion level of evidence is accumulated, it may be sufficient to be accepted by another mechanism as meaning 'stimulus detected', but that certain level of evidence will be a function of the task itself. In the case of simple reaction time, the required level of evidence appears to be under the control of the subject, and is modified by task variables, such as feedback, and temporal uncertainty.

## C  Evidence accrual in more complex situations

Our discussion to date has centred on the simplest of stimuli – changes in intensity. Cognitive psychology is concerned less with such simple stimuli and more with complex ones. In the remaining sections, we shall explore the idea of information accrual in progressively more complex situations, ending with some ideas about the recognition of alphanumeric characters. To begin with, we shall consider the problem of discrimination of clearly discriminable stimuli.

## 1 Discrimination reaction-time studies

Henmon (1906) carried out an experiment in which subjects were asked to decide which of two line stimuli displayed on a screen was the longer. He found that the larger the difference between the two lines, the faster the reaction time. Exactly the same result occurs in numerous other settings. Henmon himself, for instance, found similar results for pairs of tones differing in pitch, presented one after the other, and for patches of different colours. The principle is that the greater the physical difference between the stimuli, the faster the difference can be used in a discrimination experiment. Similar results have even been found with non-physical stimuli, and these will be discussed when we consider 'mental comparisons' (chapter 14).

Most existing models of the process generating reaction-time/discriminability functions are similar in many ways to the counter model described above for simple reaction time. For two-choice situations evidence is accumulated for the presence of one or other of the two possibilities, A or B. It is important that some critical level of evidence which enables the system to decide that an A or a B has, in fact, been presented should obtain. Figure 2-10 is based on a single decision mechanism which keeps a running total of evidence in favour of each possibility: the 'evidence line' moves towards A or B as evidence from the stimulus favours A or B on a moment-to-moment basis. A decision to press the button for A or B is made when the evidence function passes a critical criterion level. This model, known as a *random walk*, is thus sensitive to the *difference between* the amount of evidence favouring A and B (Laming 1968).

It may seem strange to suppose that as evidence from a presented stimulus is accumulated, it could be confused with evidence for another stimulus which was *not* presented. However, suppose you have to make a fast choice between the two letters P and R, and you do not know which will be presented. The kind of evidence being accumulated may be a straight vertical, a right-convex semicircle, etc. In other words, much of the evidence for a P is the same as the evidence for an R (the only evidence *discriminating* the two is the foot on the R). This is elaborated in chapter 3. Without going into further detail, models of this type are convenient for the interpretation of a range of phenomena. For instance, it is obvious that stimuli which are perceptually

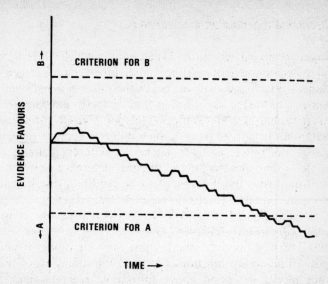

*Figure 2-10.* Representation of evidence collection in a two-choice task. The solid line shows the evidence focusing alternative 'A' or 'B' as it is collected. When the line crosses a boundary, shown as dotted lines, identification is assumed to have occurred.

similar (lines of similar length, close hues, etc) will have so much in common that the rate of evidence accumulation favouring one over the other will be relatively slow.

A related and very important idea is that if the criteria are fixed so that reactions take place on the minimum of evidence then high error rates should result. An illustration of this, using the random-walk model, is shown in figure 2-11. The prediction in general is straightforward: faster overall reaction times should be associated with a greater probability of making an error. Indeed, a number of researchers have plotted a systematic relationship between speed of response and accuracy; this is known as the speed-accuracy function, or the latency operating characteristic. In general, for discriminably different stimuli (where d' is so large as to be unmeasurable), faster responding is associated with higher error rates.

Speed-accuracy functions may be obtained in a number of different ways. For instance, a plot could be made by taking different subjects, and plotting the probability correct against the mean reaction time for each person. Vickers, Caudrey and Wilson (1971) did this, and found that slower responders made fewer

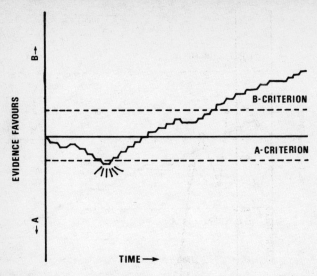

*Figure 2-11.* When the criteria are minimal, there is a high likelihood of the evidence accumulation function crossing the wrong boundary.

errors. Or subjects can be asked or induced to respond at different speeds at various points during an experiment. Each block of trials will then provide a point on a speed-accuracy function which is defined by the mean reaction time and the probability correct for that block. By a judicious manipulation of ranges of reaction times, a complete function can be obtained (Wilding 1982). A speed-accuracy tradeoff is shown in figure 2-12.

The existence of such smooth functions is consistent with the idea that the identification of a stimulus consists in part in *the accrual over time of evidence to determine what that stimulus is*. Consistency with a theory, however, does not rule out other explanations. Errors occur when people are responding quickly. Suppose that, in their efforts to respond quickly, people sometimes *guess*, at random, rather than wait until they know what a stimulus is. This too would produce a speed-accuracy tradeoff, but for a completely different reason. In many ways, the distinction resembles that made earlier between the significance of false positives in signal detection theory terms and in terms of classical threshold theory.

The idea that *fast guesses* may account for the whole thing does not appear likely, although they may occur under some circum-

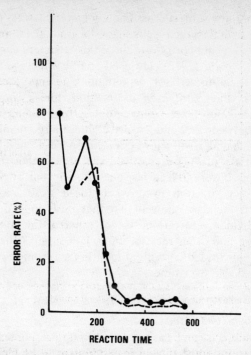

*Figure 2-12.* A speed-accuracy tradeoff function from a two-choice reaction experiment. The solid line results if the stimuli are presented at a fixed rate, and the dotted line, if stimulus comes on after the subject has responded to a prior stimulus. *(From Rabbitt and Vyas 1970.)*

stances. One example of a study which suggests that fast guessing is not the whole story was carried out by Pachella (1974). His reaction-time study required subjects to decide whether pairs of letters were both consonants or not. Some of the stimulus pairs were the same in class only (e.g. P and Q, which are both consonants). Others were the same in class *and* in name (e.g. Q and q, upper and lower case). Subjects did not know in advance which type of pair they would get. Pachella found somewhat different speed-accuracy curves for those two types. Pairs of the P–Q type showed a steeper rise in error rate as reaction times decreased than did pairs of the Q–q type. Furthermore, with pairs like Q and Q, which are physically identical, the increase in error rate with faster reaction times was even slower. Now if the errors were due to guessing alone, the increase in error rate with faster reaction times should follow the same course in all cases, since in pure guessing, the subject is assumed *not to know* what the stimuli are. Rather than this, the results suggest a gradual accumulation of information. Further corroboration of this argument comes from a study by Swensson (1972). He used stimuli which were hard to discriminate, and forced fast responding. One important aspect of his data was the *distribution* of reaction times. There were a number of reaction times below about 250 msec, almost no reaction times between 250 and 280 msec, and a large number higher still. This remainder still showed a clear speed-accuracy tradeoff. Using a variety of measures, Swensson argued that those times below 250 msec were indeed fast guesses, but that by obtaining a speed-accuracy function even when these were excluded, he claimed that the data showed that there was indeed a gradual accrual of evidence favouring one or other of the stimuli. As it stands, these and other reaction-time data support the idea that speed-accuracy tradeoffs result at least in part from the accrual of stimulus evidence over time.

## 2 The masking technique

The simplest and most fundamental message to be gleaned from the studies being described here is that it takes time to accrue evidence that something is present, or to determine what that something might be. Rather than rely on reaction-time data alone, another technique must be considered. The basic idea is to terminate the flow stimulus information by stopping the stimulus after a certain exposure time, and to determine what the subject knows about the stimulus after that exposure. Following the evidence accumulation notion, we would expect that the subject's knowledge of the characteristics of a stimulus would increase with increased stimulus duration. This is true, broadly speaking, but the situation is complicated by certain very interesting facts. If one presents a few letters very briefly on a screen (50 milliseconds, say), and simply removes them from display after that time, it appears that the stimulus has been registered in some sort of sensory memory store within the subject, so that the characteristics of the stimulus can still be read off from the store over a further (but short) period. Sperling (1960) produced one of the best-known demonstrations of this (for vision) although earlier work pointed to a similar conclusion (see Vernon 1952). Sperling's subjects were given brief views of only 50 msec duration of a matrix of letters. Then, some time just before or just after the offset of the physical stimulus, subjects were cued with a tone to report the content of one of the three rows. A high tone meant report the top row, a medium tone the middle row, and low tone the bottom row. Now suppose that the stimulus display left a trace in a transient memory. This would mean that some time after the stimulus was switched off, it should be possible for a subject to 'read off' what was in memory. By probing unexpectedly for a read-off from the top, middle, or bottom line, Sperling was able to check on just how much of the original display was available in transient memory. Although the amount of the display available to a subject is maximal when the stimulus is still present, it does not suddenly plummet when the stimulus is switched off. Rather, it declines uniformly reaching its low point after about one second. This indicates that a record of the stimulus is preserved after the stimulus itself is terminated; the record is known as *iconic* or *sensory memory*.

A somewhat different way of demonstrating this persistence rests upon the *integration* of two meaningless displays to form a meaningful one. Eriksen and Collins (1967) presented subjects with brief exposures of two dot patterns, one after the other. Although each dot pattern was meaningless, if they were super-imposed, a somewhat noisy nonsense syllable could be seen (figure 2-13). By varying the delay between the offset of the first stimuli pattern, and the onset of the second, it was possible to estimate how long a usable memory of the first stimulus persisted, simply by seeing how well subjects reported the nonsense syllables. The results showed a maximum percentage correct with a zero inter-stimulus interval, and again a steady rather than a sudden decline up to about 300–500 milliseconds.

Clearly there is a persistence of stimulus in a memory – iconic memory – after termination of the physical display itself. Similar results hold for auditory stimuli (cf. Crowder and Morton 1969; Darwin, Turvey and Crowder 1972) where the store is variously known as echoic memory (Neisser 1967) and precategorical acous-tic storage (Crowder and Morton 1969). The characteristics of both types of memory are that they appear to be a similar representation to the stimulus itself, preserving form, spatial location, etc., and that they are both relatively shortlived, the information decaying quite rapidly. Current estimates suggest that

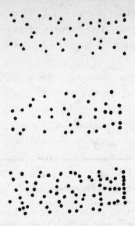

*Figure 2-13.* When the top line of dots is superimposed on the middle line, the syllable VOH becomes visible. By varying the delay between the top and middle, it is possible to estimate visual persistence. *(After Eriksen and Collins 1967.)*

the decay rate is somewhat faster for the visual than for the auditory store.

The presence of iconic and echoic stores is interesting in its own right, and will be considered again in chapter 3. However, our main purpose in introducing it here is as a *complication* in tracking the course of information accrued by presenting stimuli only briefly. The solution lies in interfering with the icons (iconic memories) by a procedure known as *masking*. The idea is straight-forward. When a stimulus has been displayed for as long as required, rather than simply switch it off, it is switched off and a second stimulus of some sort is presented. This makes the iconic memory as unusable as possible. This second stimulus, the *masking stimulus*, is typically random visual dot patterns, termed visual noise.

To demonstrate the accrual of information over time, the technique is to present a stimulus briefly and follow it with a noise mask. The subject is then required to report on the stimulus which was presented. Sperling (1963) presented sets of letters varying in number from two to six with delays of the mask from the *onset* of the first stimulus from 0 to 60 msec. His results, shown in figure 2-14, clearly demonstrate an increase in accrued information over time. The results of reaction time and masking tasks are in broad qualitative agreement: information is accrued over time.

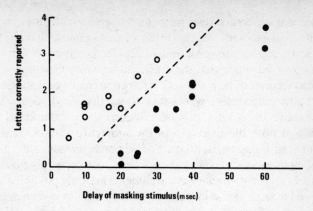

*Figure 2-14.* The number of letters correctly reported as a function of delay between exposure and mask. Solid dots show results when a noise field was presented beforehand as well and open dots result when the initial field was dark. The points are not joined because they come from a number of different initial conditions. The dotted line shows a rate of one letter per ten milliseconds. *(Adapted from Sperling 1963.)*

## D  Summary and comments

The earliest accounts of the detection of simple stimuli took the view that energy changes at low signal-to-noise ratios were either detected or not. Detection depended upon passing some threshold. Since then, psychophysical work has shown that such a formulation is inappropriate. According to modern signal detection theory, the evidence that a signal-event has or has not occurred is continuous with noise in the system. The problem on an observation trial is to establish whether a given level of evidence is more likely to be a signal or simply noise. Studies of correct responses and error rates enable the predictions of both classical threshold and statistical decision models to be checked. The statistical decision model fits the data more satisfactorily.

Quite apart from the technical and practical value of signal detection theory, we can glean an important general theoretical point. When detecting stimuli, the problem is one in which evidence for the signal is accumulated up to some limit. This is a simple but important point, and contrasts with the naive impression that a signal is simply 'there' or 'not there'. The work on simple reaction time provides an easy way to see how the same argument applies even to easily detected stimuli. The evidence for a signal event is accrued over time, and when a satisfactory level of evidence is obtained, we can think of the signal as having been 'detected', and so later processing becomes possible. While this is a gross oversimplification, the argument provides us with a simple baseline account of how the act of detection might be understood.

As a slight digression, we went on to see that the detection stage may require different levels of evidence to be completed as a function of both the readiness of the subject to respond, and the kind of task being carried out. For instance, simultaneity judgements seem to require less evidence than button-pressing tasks. It is important to notice that such arguments are only possible if they are based upon a model in which stimulus evidence is seen as being accrued over time.

In the later parts of the chapter, we went on to apply the same idea to the recognition and discrimination of more complex stimuli. The result is an explanation (not the only one, but a likely one) of the speed-accuracy tradeoff. This tradeoff is of the greatest importance, not just for theory, but also for practice. Latencies or errors, for instance, are often used as measures in psychological tasks. Theory and practice are not unrelated: investigators have to ensure that the interpretation of latency differences is not confounded by differences in accuracy resulting from criterion or other differences.

Apart from measuring how long people take to make judgements, it is also possible to present information for various brief durations and use accuracy as a dependent variable, as with the masking procedure. The fact that exposure duration influences accuracy in a systematic way provides further evidence for the view that information for presence of and nature of a stimulus is accumulated over time. Finally, in discussing this process, the masking procedure illustrates how basic sensory data is stored for a brief period in a *sensory memory*. Sensory memory will be reintroduced at various points in chapters 3 and 4.

# 3 An introduction to some aspects of visual pattern recognition

In chapter 2, we concentrated on demonstrating that evidence for the presence of a stimulus was gathered over time, albeit over a very short time in the circumstances considered. In the case of the detection of simple stimuli (energy change), the story was made concrete by the proposal that 'evidence' could be viewed as neural impulses, and that decisions as to the presence of a new stimulus could be made on the basis of changes in neural impulse rate. This means that at least the basic element of a stimulus, energy level, could be thought about in a concrete way. When we moved on to more complex stimuli – line lengths and letters – we gave little indication of what sort of evidence might be accumulated. When we deal with visual forms, even simple ones like line length or letters, the stimulus information is more complicated. Indeed, it is so complicated that psychologists and others are still actively engaged in trying to establish precisely what information is accrued from such forms to enable us to know that they are indeed what they are. How does a pattern or a shape come to be recognized? Being able to say that an A is an 'A' or a 3 is a '3' is so easy and automatic for human beings that it hardly seems like a problem at all. But of course it is; it is known as the problem of *pattern recognition*.

Unfortunately, the further one proceeds into the subject of pattern recognition, the more the whole problem starts to grow into one of perception as a whole. This book is not aimed at the study of perception, and it must be appreciated that short measure is given to many worthy topics and ideas in perception. Nevertheless, the aim is to provide a skeleton outline of some of the issues which have a special bearing on general aspects of cognitive psychology.

## A  Basic computational approaches to pattern recognition

A great deal has been learned about pattern recognition by trying to write computer programs to recognize patterns. There are many practical reasons for doing this – automatic letter-sorting, for example, could be done on the basis of post-codes if a machine was able to recognize handwritten numbers and letters. A similar sort of problem is encountered in the automatic checking that computer components have been put together in the correct positions on the boards by having a machine read the codes on the components, and match these against the desired plan. There are many, many such applications. Through the practical expedient of designing machines to do this, the nature of pattern recognition is being thoroughly explored. In this section, two elementary approaches to the problem will be discussed. Our interest in the approaches is in the light they cast on the nature of the problem in general, and in the way in which they might relate to pattern recognition in human beings.

### 1  Template-matching

The simplest view of recognizing an A as an 'A' (for instance) is to suppose that the perceptual stimulus is matched against a number of 'templates' stored in memory. The template which gives the best fit is then the class assigned to the stimulus. For instance, with upper-case alphanumeric characters, there would be a template for each of twenty-six letters and for ten digits. Machines working on this principle have some sort of light-sensitive matrix, on to which characters may be projected. The pattern of activity on the matrix is then checked against the set of patterns until one which matches is found. This is depicted in figure 3-1. Machines of this type can and have been made (see Selfridge and Neisser 1960 and Uhr 1963 for a discussion), and are extremely reliable for *invariant* character sets.

The idea of invariance is important. Look at the variety of letter shapes in the samples shown in figure 3-2. Quite apart from the different shapes and details, there are also different sizes. The variability in stimulus shapes which can be called 'As', 'Bs' or 'Cs' etc is enormous. It is great for printed letters, but it reaches mammoth proportions in the case of normal handwriting. Pattern-

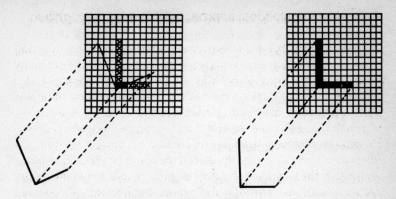

*Figure 3-1.* The letter 'L' projected on to a template matrix. In the left-hand illustration, because it is rotated, the L fails to match to the appropriate part of the matrix (indicated by Xs). In the right-hand illustration, the match is perfect. It is not difficult to see how minor variations in stimulus orientation, size and character would cause a template to fail.

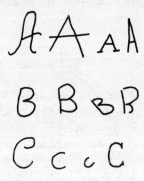

*Figure 3-2.* Some handwritten characters. The variability poses a serious pattern-recognition problem.

recognition devices based on template-matching are simply not able to cope with such variety. Indeed, they cannot even cope with sizes which differ from that specified by the template, or with shifts in orientation of any significant degree, even when only standard stylized upper-case characters are used.

A somewhat different approach to the problem relies upon the idea that characters are made up of a number of *features*. For instance, a B is made up of a vertical straight line I, and two left-convex curves ∃; a Z is made up of two horizontal straight-lines, ⁼, and a top-right/bottom-left diagonal /. *Precisely* which sets of features might be useful for artificial character recognition, let alone which human beings might use, is not very clear, but it is possible to distinguish standard shapes on the basis of such features. Consider a well-known computer program written for character recognition which makes use of feature-matching rather than template-matching.

## 2 Selfridge's Pandemonium

Selfridge (1959; Selfridge and Neisser 1960) developed the Pandemonium system for the identification of hand-printed characters (originally it was designed for the automatic recognition of Morse code). The basic system consists of a series of stages, each characterized by the operation of what the designers called *demons*.

The architecture of the information flow within Pandemonium is shown in figure 3-3. At the input end, the first stage of the system

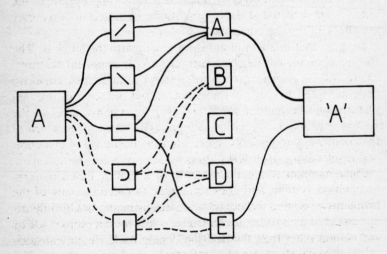

*Figure 3-3.* Simplified pandemonium-like system. Four levels are depicted, going from left to right. Image demon, feature demons, letter demons and decision demon. Feature demons are sometimes the image for the feature they represent. If a match is found, they become active. Letter demons receive activity from the feature demons which are relevant to the description of a particular letter. The solid lines represent currently active pathways. Both 'A' and 'E' are active, but 'A' is more so, because it has more inputs from the feature demons. The decision demon therefore accepts that 'A' is the pattern.

is an artificial retina, on which the stimulus display itself is represented: an electronic representation of the shape of the stimulus. It clearly corresponds to iconic memory as described in chapter 2. The image display is systematically tested by a group of computational demons, each of which consists of a program which runs tests for a *particular* visual feature. For instance, there may be one which tests for a vertical line, one which tests for a left-concave semicircle, one for a horizontal line and so on. Each works independently, in parallel with the others. The outcome of this level of analysis is that any demon may or may not find the feature which it is searching for.

The next layer of demons are 'cognitive demons'. Suppose the program was set for the recognition of alphanumeric characters (A, B, ... Z; 0, 1 ... 9). One particular cognitive demon would be set up to check for one particular member of this set, so that there would be one demon for A, one for B, and so on. Each cognitive demon carries out computations on the output from the feature demon level. What this means is that an A demon has access to a list of features which describe an A. If features appropriate to the letter A are detected at the computational demon level, then they are check off by the computational A demon.

Suppose that Pandemonium is presented with the letter R. The feature demons will detect a certain set of component features. These will be relevant to the interests of a number of cognitive demons (P, R, I, L, M, N for instance), but the score of relevant features will be highest for P and R. The topmost level of the system consists of a 'decision demon'. This determines which of the cognitive demons has accumulated the best level of evidence, and results in a categorical output.

Pandemonium is a good example of a feature-based pattern-recognition system, and goes some way to meeting many of the problems associated with template-matching methods. One important aspect of the system, for example, is that the decisions made by any demon other than the decision demon itself are not categorical. If the characters are not perfectly formed with respect to the feature set of Pandemonium, a feature demon may not be 100 per cent satisfied by the evidence available. It would then produce an output which was below its maximum level. In the end, the decision demon itself applies a 'best-bet' principle to the evidence which *it* gets from the cognitive demons and bases its decision upon which cognitive demon is producing the best output.

## B  Evidence relating to feature-analyser systems

A considerable research effort has gone into looking for feature analysers in the perceptual systems of humans and other animals. In humans, the work has been largely psychological, while in other animals it has been mostly neurophysiological. Quite obviously, if one is to construct a theory of perception in humans based on feature analysis, then it is necessary to discover what these features might be. In this section, we review some of the evidence.

### 1  Physiological evidence relating to feature detectors

One direct physiological approach to questions of pattern perception has been to examine the kinds of stimuli to which individual cells at different points in the optic system are sensitive. Such micro-electrode studies have been carried out on a variety of species. The general technique is to present patterned stimuli of various types to the animal's retina, and measure the electrical responses of particular cells to these stimuli. There is ample evidence to suggest that specific cells respond to specific types of stimuli. Cells sensitive to specific patterns have been found at the *retinal* level in certain organisms. For instance, in the frog, cells responsive to the movement of small dark patches were found (Maturana, Lettvin, McCulloch and Pitts 1960). The frog, because it catches small moving objects which are detected in this way, is sometimes called the 'bug' detector.

In higher organisms, such retinal-level specificity is rare or non-existent. However, cells responsive to very specific stimulus aspects have been found further up in visual systems. Perhaps the best-known examples come from Hubel and Wiesel's (1962) work on the visual system of the cat. In the cat's visual *cortex*, they found cells sensitive to moving slits of light, bars, or edges, of specific orientations and cells sensitive to line segments, ends of lines, and corners. Lower down in the visual system, cells are found which respond to local brightening and dimming. These authors worked out an explanation of how the various cells relate to one another. Up to the level of the cortical cells, the organization of the cells appears to be hierarchical, the properties of the cells receptive to local dimming and brightening supporting the responses of the more complex cells. Such a hierarchical structure is obviously analogous to the early parts of Pandemonium. Detailed discussions of Hubel and Wiesel's work can be found in the original papers, and in several standard cognitive psychology textbooks (e.g. Lindsay and Norman 1977; Reynolds and Flagg 1983).

The discovery that specific cells respond to specific pattern fragments has been used to argue that there is some physiological support for the idea of feature detectors, and indeed it can be interpreted that way, although not many specific pattern-sensitive cells have been found. However, there is a limit to how far the argument can go. This is normally described as the 'grandmother cell' or 'yellow Volkswagen' problem – the idea of a cell which responds only to one's grandmother, or to a yellow Volkswagen. Weisstein (1973) has argued that such things are unlikely to be found, while Marr (1982) has argued that the discovery of such a cell would be unlikely to tell us much about vision because one would not know how or why such a thing could be constructed from the output of simpler cells.

From our point of view, it is quite interesting that detectors sensitive to edges and orientations have been found, because they clearly fit the prescription of detectors required by feature theory.

## 2 Psychological evidence related to feature detectors

One straightforward prediction of feature theory is that shapes (letters) should be confused with each other sometimes, especially if the letters are displayed only briefly. But the confusions should not be random; rather, letters which are recognized by acting upon some of the same feature detectors should be confused. Thus it might be possible to confuse C and G; or P and F, and so on, but G and F should not be, since in any reckoning of simple features, G and F would not trigger the same responses.

Investigations have been carried out in which letters have been presented briefly, and matrices have been drawn up to indicate which letters were wrongly classified, and what they were classified as. Such *confusion matrices* do indeed produce non-random patterns of errors. One study (Kinney, Marsetta and Showman 1966) showed the following major confusions between alphanumeric stimuli (from most frequent to least frequent):

C called G
B called 8
8 called B
O called G
G called 6
C called 0
(there were others of lower frequency)

Similar confusion patterns have been obtained by Rumelhart (1971) using highly stylized letters made up of seven possible segment types.

A more indirect line of evidence comes from a number of studies carried out by Neisser and his colleagues (Neisser 1963; Neisser and Beller 1965; Neisser and Lazar 1964). They used a *visual-search procedure* in which subjects were presented with lists consisting of blocks of letters, and asked to scan these lists as quickly as possible for a certain target. Some examples are shown in figure 3-4. As soon as the subject finds the target, he presses a

| (i) | A E F L K | (ii) | P S U D B |
|-----|-----------|------|-----------|
|     | M N K T V |      | G O C U R |
|     | F V L K N |      | D S U C O |
|     | E H I F L |      | D G Q S U |
|     | K Q N A K |      | G J C B U |
|     | M L V T F |      | S R J C D |

*Figure 3-4.* Short lists similar to the longer ones used by Neisser. It is easier to detect a Q in the left list than in the right one.

button. Notice that list (i) consists of letters made up entirely of straight line segments, while (ii) consists mainly of curved segments. The interest in this study lies in the ease with which searches for letters made up of curved segments (e.g. Q), or straight line segments (e.g. Z), may be made within each of the three types of list. Indeed, Neisser and Beller (1965) showed that searches for Z are much slower in a list like (i) than in a list like (ii). Conversely, searches for Q are much slower in type-(ii) lists than in type-(i) lists. The results thus show that if the target character has very different features from the background, then it is easily found. You might find this unsurprising, arguing that the distinctive letters 'stand out' more. However, to make use of this, people must be able to concentrate on the distinctive features alone. To do this, there must be distinctive features to concentrate on, which of course means that people have detectors for these features. For instance, the discovery of *one* feature in a non-target letter which is not a feature of the target would serve as grounds for a decision that the non-target is indeed a non-target. Quite obviously, curvature could be used as such a clue when searching for a Z in a set of curved letters. Thus, such a search would be relatively fast when compared with searching for a Z in a background of letters made up of straight lines. This explanation also fits the observation made by subjects in such a task that in the easy condition the background items appear 'fuzzy', while the critical item 'stands out'.

The results of these experiments seem quite consistent with a featural model of letters and number recognition. Other methods have also been used which have a bearing on feature models. One such method is the psychological technique of *adaptation*. The idea is that if neural feature detectors actually exist, then it should be possible to *fatigue* them by constant stimulation; such fatigue is a well-known property of neural systems.

Thus, continued exposure to a horizontal set of contours should produce adaptation in horizontal feature detectors, leading to an increase in their thresholds. Furthermore, the degree of adaptation should be independent of the display in which the contours appear. For instance, closely spaced contours should produce the same adaptation as widely separated contours, and the effect should be independent of colour or direction of movement. By and large, however, this does not occur. The amount of adaptation observed seems to depend on the overall similarity between adapting and test stimuli, and not on the presence of a single feature in both (cf. Spoehr and Lehmkuhle.

## 3  Difficulties with feature-based recognition systems

Having reviewed a little of the evidence for feature-detection processes, it is appropriate to step back and review the plausibility and difficulties with such accounts of pattern recognition.

We are familiar with a vast number of patterns, which can be seen from innumerable angles, in innumerable positions on the retina and are subject to many possible distortions, including rotation. It is implausible that we have templates in memory for all of these things. It is much more likely that objects are recognized with reference to critical elements – some sort of perceptually primitive units out of which they are built. The discussion of features indicates one approach to this problem. However, it is much more of a problem to decide what these features might be.

We began by introducing notions of simple features, like lines of various orientations, curves, etc., with exclusive reference to alphanumeric characters. A little thought will indicate that the recognition of disconnected features of this type is not enough for even the simplest of stimuli. If one uses such features as primitive building blocks, then it is essential to test for connectivity. The pattern ⊐ is simply *not* the pattern D. Tests for features must include tests for connectivity. The other thing is that there are constraints on the tolerances of connectivity. Thus while A is clearly an A, △ is not, nor is ∧. A fully developed theory based on features must accommodate these facts.

Some degree of distortion and size variance in standard patterns will be handled reasonably well by the Pandemonium type of model. For instance, Lindsay and Norman (1977) argued that: 'the feature demons collect information from line detectors which are themselves insensitive to the length of the lines. Right angles are still right angles, and acute angles are still acute angles, regardless of the size of the letter.' However, this seems like a gross oversimplification. Orientation is more difficult to deal with. If one posits such feature detectors as slant-line detectors, then it is clearly necessary to posit a detector which can relate to the main axis of the figure. This means establishing a main axis from the pattern *prior to* the operation of an orientation-specific line detector.

Quite apart from these problems with simple feature notions, it is patently clear that the number and kind of features will be considerably more complex for the recognition of visual scenes, rather than stereotyped alphanumeric characters. Add this to the fact that different lighting conditions and different vantage points produce very different images (intensity patterns), and it becomes quite clear that simple feature theories are likely to be quite inadequate (Marr 1982).

Despite these complications, feature theory enjoys a prominent place in most introductory books on cognitive psychology. To some extent this is understandable. It is almost certainly the case that the perception of an object or a scene depends upon the recognition of more *primitive* perceptual elements; the problem is to know what those are. Furthermore, there is evidence that whatever these elements are, their utilization depends upon non-sensory factors, such as context and expectancy. It is to these issues that we turn next, particularly with respect to alphanumeric stimuli.

## 4 Predictability and character recognition in word strings

Words consist of letters. It is therefore natural to think that the recognition of words logically consists of combining the results of some letter-recognition mechanisms, even if their output is imperfect. After all, the mental description of the physical characteristics of a word could just be an ordered letter sequence. However, it has been known for nearly a century that things may not be that simple. Cattell (1885; 1886) discovered that subjects can report letters from briefly exposed individual *words* much better than they can from *random strings* of letters. Such an effect could come about for a number of reasons. One explanation could be based on *memory*. It is well known that it is easier to remember a 'meaningful' string of letters for a few seconds than a meaningless one (chapter 5). Perhaps subjects in Cattell's study could simply remember the letters better if they were words. Another possible explanation is that the effect is due to *guessing*. If all letters were not recognized fully in the two cases, word and non-word, but an equal *number* of letters were recognized in the two cases, then perhaps it is easier to guess the remaining letters. For instance, what would you guess the missing letters to be in mem_r_ and tde_t_? The first case is much easier.

More recently, studies by Reicher and others have shown these explanations to be quite inadequate (Reicher 1969; Spoehr and Smith 1975; Wheeler 1970). Reicher's subjects were presented with a fixation spot, then a four-letter string which was presented briefly (50 milliseconds), then a masking field with two letters clearly marked on it (figure 3-5). The letter string could be either a word, such as WORK, or a non-word such as ORWK. The mask then obscured the letter string but two letters appeared at the same time at a certain position relative to the four stimulus letters. The subjects' task was to decide which of the test letters actually occurred in the display in this position. The interesting thing about

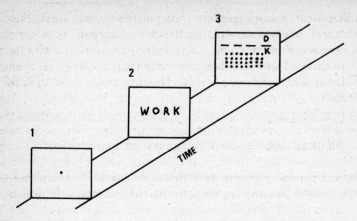

*Figure 3-5.* The sequence of events in the Reicher experiments (after Reicher 1969).   1 A fixation spot.   2 A four-letter string, displayed for 50 msec.   3 A masking field with response alternatives shown.

Reicher's materials was that in the word condition, *either* letter would yield a word. Reicher found that letter-recognition accuracy was still higher in the word condition than in an exactly equivalent non-word condition. Clearly, the results can have nothing to do with memory: the subject only has to make a choice, not report back the string. Furthermore, the results cannot be explained by guessing.

Subsequent studies (cf. Wheeler 1970) ruled out a number of other more sophisticated arguments to the effect that the results were an artefact of the particular procedures employed for its demonstration, and it appears as though the phenomenon is due to the visual characteristics of words and non-words, and not to any response biases or guessing. This is important, because it means that word recognition is not achieved by the accumulation of features associated with the individual letters which make up words. It also involves the idea that perhaps words are treated as *whole* patterns in some way.

One property of words is that they display what is called *redundancy*. First, some letters in a given language, say English, are more likely to occur than others in certain spatial positions in words. For instance, more words begin with T than K (Mayzner and Tresselt 1965). This is generally known as positional (or spatial) redundancy. A second type of redundancy is the *sequential* type. Letters which occur together in English words (or words of other written languages) are not randomly distributed. For instance, U always follows Q, and, with the exception of N, the only letters which follow M have a vowel sound associated with them.

Both types of redundancy are important for word recognition (Mason 1975; Thompson and Massaro 1973), and appear to facilitate the report of individual letters. It is therefore quite conceivable that whole words, or at least word parts, are analysed as a whole by pandemonium-like units, rather than words being synthesized directly from the output of individual letter units. Although we shall use the word 'feature' in what follows, we must be careful to recognize that this is simply a shorthand way of speaking of potentially complex relational perceptual information.

## C Context in word perception

With the processes described up to now we have concentrated on what are called *bottom-up* or *data-driven* processes. This is only half of the story of pattern recognition. In this section we shall introduce *top-down* or *concept-driven* processes. The success of pattern recognition is normally the outcome of an interaction between the two types of processing.

Top-down processing in pattern recognition utilizes *context* to facilitate computation. Consider, for instance, the recognition of the last word of the sentence 'The cat sat on the *mat*'. Suppose the complete sentence were written in rather poor handwriting, so that 'mat' was not very clear. Perhaps the word 'mat' would be recognized quite well, because of its predictability from context. The same principles apply to other aspects of perception, but we shall begin in this section with some phenomena associated with word recognition.

### 1 The role of context in word recognition

There are numerous examples which show that context enters into perceptual processes; an early example is found in a study carried out by Tulving, Mandler and Baumal (1964). They displayed target words briefly in a tachistoscope, and the subject's task was to report back what the word was. The duration of the flash was manipulated systematically so that as a consequence the probability correct (the measure used) was varied. Apart from flash duration, varying degrees of context were used. Each target word (a noun) could belong to a sentence. Subjects saw either the preceding eight, four, two or zero words of the sentence before making a judgement on the target. Thus both sensory information and context were independently manipulated. The results of the experiment are depicted in figure 3-6. Both increased stimulus

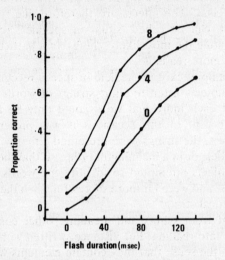

**Figure 3-6.** The joint effect of exposure duration and number of context words (zero, four or eight) on proportion of words correctly recognized. *(From Tulving, Mandler and Baumal 1964.)*

duration and increased context lead to a greater probability of recognition. Context clearly facilitates recognition.

In a similar sort of study, Morton (1964) asked subjects to fill out missing words in sentence frames with a word missing. Obviously, context constrains choices, and depending on the consistency of subjects' responses, Morton was able to class particular words in particular contexts as having high, medium or low probabilities of occurrence. He went on to show that if the 'context' is first presented, and then a target word is displayed briefly on a tachistoscope, then it is more likely to be recognized if it has a high rather than medium probability of occurrence; similarly, medium probabilities of occurrence facilitate recognition more than low probabilities of occurrence.

In situations like this, predictability can depend upon several

things, two of which are *grammatical class* and the *word itself.*
Consider, for instance, the two sentences:

(a) The car skidded on the ice.
(b) The car skidded on the banana.

Although both ice and banana are nouns, *ice* is more likely to be
a single word continuation than banana. Because of syntactic
constraints, Morton's experiment effectively controlled for likely
grammatical class. The effects are therefore due to a brand of
context which can be called 'situation specific': recognition of
words designating the most likely 'things' in a particular situation
are rendered more readable.

Parallel examples exist in the field of speech recognition. Miller
(1962) had subjects listen to short strings of words, mixed with
noise so that each individual word could only be identified on
about 50 per cent of the occasions it was presented. In the
word-string test, the strings were presented either with the words
in random order, or in a meaningful order, so that they made up a
sentence. Subjects attempted to identify the words under these
circumstances, and were far more successful when the words made
up a grammatical string.

Quite apart from syntax and meaning, other contextual constraints enter into reading. For instance, written words are highly
*redundant*, in the sense that they contain elements which are not
necessary for them to be understood. This can be illustrated by
replacing some letters of a sentence by an X: the result does not
greatly detract from its intelligibility:

Thxs ix an inxtanxe of whxt wx mexn.

The point of this demonstration is not only to show that
language is written in a redundant way, but also that it may not be
necessary for the perceptual system to carry out a full analysis of
the individual letters in order for us to be able to recognize or
make use of the words. Indeed, it is highly unlikely that in normal
skilled reading a complete analysis does occur. Top-down processes can provide enough information to make it unnecessary to
complete a bottom-up analysis.

Proofreading provides a good illustration of the incompleteness
of stimulus analysis which occurs during normal reading. Normal
skilled reading of a passage – reading for meaning – is a much
faster process than proofreading, say for spelling mistakes. The
letter information is not completely analysed, and it is a very easy

matter to miss a misspelled word, even an obvious one. In fact, proofreading and reading for meaning seem to require quite different processing acts: for most people, the major goal of looking at words is to read for meaning, and this process must be actively inhibited by a novice proofreader. Sometimes it is better to proofread the material backwards!

Word recognition is facilitated by the likelihood of a word occurring in a given context, but some words are simply more likely than others to occur in the language – that is, the set of words has a distribution of frequency. Word frequency too influences the ease of recognizing a word: the higher the frequency of occurrence, the shorter the duration for which it has to be exposed in order to reach some criterion level of correctness (Solomon and Postman 1952).

With all of these studies, the effect of context can be thought about in two ways:

(1) If the subject cannot recognize the stimulus on the basis of perceptual (perhaps 'featural') information alone, he will guess. His guesses will be particularly successful if the context is very restricting.

(2) Context directly influences the representation of the pattern presented. Guesses do not come into it. For instance, context may somehow influence the feature-analysis process so that analysis is more efficient for common or expected stimuli.

To this, unfortunately, we must add the possibility that perhaps (1) and (2) give the right account in different circumstances, or even that (1) and (2) both might operate. However, before taking up this question, we turn towards another line of evidence on context effects.

A series of papers by Meyer and his colleagues (e.g. Meyer and Schvaneveldt 1971; Meyer, Schvaneveldt and Ruddy 1975) contain reports of two interesting techniques for the investigation of contextual effects by two means. One method requires that the subject reads out words as they appear, on a screen. Typically, pairs of words, such as the following, are used:

NURSE–DOCTOR
BREAD–BUTTER
NURSE–BUTTER
BREAD–DOCTOR

Notice that the first two pairs are associated with one another in meaning. A typical procedure used by Meyer and his colleagues is to present the words of each pair successively, requiring the subject to read the words aloud, as quickly as possible, as they appear.

By these means it was established that the second word of a pair is pronounced more rapidly if it is preceded by an *associate* (as in the first two cases), rather than by an unassociated word. This effect is generally called *semantic priming*, and has been amply replicated.

The other method is slightly more complicated. Consider the letter strings shown below:

NURSE–DOCTOR          (word, associated word)
BREAD–DOCTOR          (word, unassociated word)
WINE–PLAME           (word, non-word)
PLAME–WINE           (non-word, word)
PABLE–REAB           (non-word, non-word)

The introduction of non-words, made by changing one letter of a word, results in a *lexical-decision task*. This time, subjects are asked to decide whether each string is a word or a non-word by pressing one of two keys. If two words are presented, then the second 'yes' response will be faster if the first word is associated with the second, again showing a semantic priming effect. This result has also been amply replicated. In each case, the priming effect is of the order of 40–50 msec.

One interesting manipulation with this task is to degrade the quality of the second stimulus by introducing visual noise in the form of random dots, as shown in figure 3-7. The net effect on

STIMULUS      STIMULUS

*Figure 3-7.* Random-dot noise can be used to degrade a stimulus without making it unrecognizable.

reading time or on lexical decision time is to slow it down. Such a view is consistent with the idea that the rate of sensory information extraction is reduced by the presence of the noise. Now given the two effects of priming and noise, it is possible to see how they act *together*. Meyer, Schvaneveldt and Ruddy (1975) carried out just such a study, and discovered that when the second stimulus was related to the first, the effect of noise was reduced, as shown in figure 3-8. What this means is that the detrimental effect of visual degradation is compensated for by contextual (associative) support.

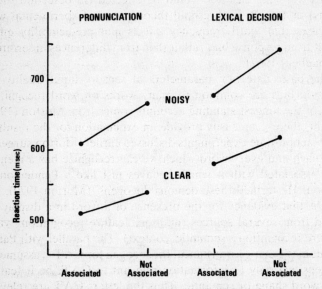

*Figure 3-8.* Joint effects of visual noise and priming (Association versus No Association) on reaction times in a pronunciation task (left) and a lexical decision task (right). *(From Meyer, Schvaneveldt and Ruddy 1975.)*

## 2  Mechanisms underlying context and word recognition

In contrast to latency experiments, in detection experiments the subject's situation is clearly analogous to the simple detection situation described in chapter 2. The subject could make a correct response on the basis of two sorts of information: by having enough *stimulus* information, or by making a judgement on the basis of inadequate evidence which turns out to be correct. One version of this (analogous to classical threshold theory) would be that if he does not *know* what the stimulus is on the basis of sensory analysis, then he will simply guess. His guesses will tend to be better if the word is a common one, or if it is very strongly constrained by context. This sort of explanation ascribes the advantages of context to *response bias*, β in signal detection theory, or g, the *guess rate*, in threshold theory. The alternative is that context influences the efficiency of the sensory process, so that (say) features are extracted more rapidly from high frequency items, or from items supported by context. It might be argued that if this were the case, d' would be affected (in detection theory terms) or true $P_c$ in threshold theory terms. Experimental work indicates that word frequency effects and predictability effects result from response bias rather than from differences in sensitivity (Broadbent 1967).

The basic detection parameters of sensory input quality and decision bias are common to many works on word recognition. One of the longest-standing accounts comes from Morton (1964), and his theory can easily provide an explanation for the results of the reaction-time experiments discussed earlier. Morton suggested that each and every word which we can recognize has a memory unit associated with it which behaves just like a Pandemonium demon. He termed these demons 'logogens' (Morton 1970). The idea is that evidence for the presence of a word in a display can come from several sources (auditory feature recognition; visual feature recognition; 'semantic' context). The parallel with Pandemonium is exact – for instance, the logogen for CAT is assumed to be sensitive only to information relevant to CAT, be it featural and word shape or semantic. Thus the letters CAT are relevant, and so is the context: 'Sleeping before the fire was a large black _____.' Logogens are assumed to possess an activation level, normally low, but increased by relevant evidence. Furthermore, they are assumed to have a threshold, so that when the degree of activation exceeds the threshold, the word is *recognized*. In Morton's more exact terminology, the word's name becomes available in an *output buffer*. A simplified block diagram of Morton's system is shown in figure 3-9.

An individual logogen is thus an evidence accumulator, which produces an output when its threshold is reached. The model has been used to account for a wide range of phenomena, and provides a good baseline for a discussion of alternative theories. But let us return to the observation that the effects of visual degradation on a word are less if the word has been primed. We can explain this in the familiar terms of evidence accumulation process, within Morton's general framework (e.g. Sanford, Garrod and Boyle 1977; Seymour 1979). Suppose that the test word of interest is DOCTOR. When it is presented, the activity level of the

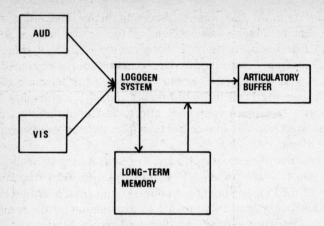

*Figure 3-9.* Morton's mark 1 logogen theory was based on this information-flow idea. AUD designates an auditory pattern analyser, VIS a visual one. Evidence for particular words comes from these and is accumulated by individual logogens in the logogen system. From there, words can be named, in which case their articulatory code is fed to the output buffer, and their meanings reached in long-term memory. Meaning (context) is also a source of information which is used by individual logogens.

logogen for DOCTOR will increase as relevant featural information is discovered. So too would logogens for DOCK, PROCTOR, etc., since these also share relevant features; however, the DOCTOR logogen will accumulate the most relevant evidence. If the word is visually degraded, it will simply take longer to reach threshold. If DOCTOR is preceded by NURSE, then the NURSE logogen will first reach threshold, and will activate a network of semantic associations. As a result, the logogens for all words semantically related to NURSE (for example, HOSPITAL, UNIFORM, DOCTOR, etc.) will receive an increment in their activation. Figure 3-10 shows the changing states of activation in the DOCTOR logogen when it is presented in *degraded* or *clear* form, following on from either NURSE or BREAD as an initial stimulus. The diagram is a simple geometric representation, rather like those used in the exposition of the counter model of simple reaction time. It is clear from the geometry of the model that in reaction-time experiments, noise effects will be smaller with primed materials.

This adaptation of Morton's model is only one way of explaining the interaction of context with the quality of the visual stimulus,

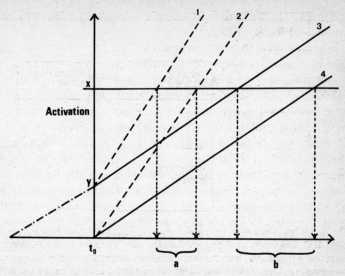

*Figure 3-10.* Hypothetical effects of degradation and priming on the state of an individual logogen. The logogen is for a word presented at $t_0$. The vertical axis is the degree of activation in the logogen, and the horizontal axis is time. If an associated word (or other relevant context) occurs before $t_0$, the logogen gains in activity up to point y. If an unassociated word is presented, there is no activity. At $t_0$, featural information becomes available over a period of time. If the stimulus is clear, the rate of gain of activity is fast (lines (1) and (2)). If the stimulus is degraded, the rate of gain is slow (lines (3) and (4)). When the logogen threshold (x) is exceeded, the word is 'recognized'. It is clear that the effect of priming on clear materials (effect *a*) is smaller than the effect of priming on degraded materials (effect *b*), the result found by Meyer et al.

but it serves to illustrate one way in which top-down processes (due to context) and bottom-up processes (influenced by stimulus quality) can be brought together. A fuller treatment is given in Morton (1969), where the issues concentrated upon are slightly different. Other theories of this type have been put forward in different variants by a number of researchers, and a number of references are given in the chapter notes.

We now turn to a way of describing the interactions of bottom-up and top-down processing in a general way. The class of theories are called 'blackboard' models, and are currently enjoying favour with a number of psychologists (e.g. Lindsay and Norman 1977; Rumelhart 1977); furthermore, blackboard models are the basis of a number of working computer programs, which are capable of utilizing context in order to recognize patterns (Lesser, Fennell, Erman and Reddy 1974).

When applied to word recognition, the idea is that incoming sensory (featural) information provides one basis for obtaining data that a particular word is present in a display. But as a message unfolds, so other predictive information, for instance *syntactic* information, comes into play. If a sentence begins 'The cat jumped on . . .', then although there is a wide range of possible things the cat could have jumped on, they will all be described by *noun-phrases*, which restricts the possible set of words. The possible things are also likely to be *concrete* objects of the kind cats can jump on – also restricting information. Finally, some things are more likely to be jumped on by cats than others, which will further restrict the search set. In fact, the restriction will be even more complete if the sentence appears in a fuller context, for instance:

A mouse ran across the floor the other night. The cat jumped on . . . .

In this case, the remainder of the sentence is likely to introduce a term which designates the mouse in some way: it might be 'it' or 'the mouse'. There are thus many constraining influences which might help us to recognize the next word(s) in a sentence. The same can be true of many other situations. For instance, suppose that one is playing a game of chess, and the game has reached a certain point. If one announces the next move, it will not be a *random* move: it will be one of a small number of moves likely to be useful in the game. An opponent of similar skill will be able to utilize his knowledge of which moves you are likely to make as an aid to recognizing your utterance.

Finally, top-down processing is sometimes *essential* to recognize a message. Lindsay and Norman (1977) cite as an example the following speech pattern: 'noo display'. Such a sound pattern could *either* be 'nudist's play', or 'new display' (on the American side of the Atlantic). How it is heard will depend entirely, and critically, upon the context in which it occurs!

Blackboard models thus assume that there are a large number of expert 'demons' at work when a message is coming in. Each demon is concerned with only a limited task, so there might be demons for feature extraction, likely letter clusters, syntactic class, likely candidate words as a function of what is understood up to now of the message, and so on. In a pandemonium-like way, each demon can be thought of as gathering evidence for the support of a particular hypothesis – and entering the hypothesis on to a 'blackboard'. The total array of working hypotheses, along with which demon is doing what, is assumed to be overseen by another specialist demon called the 'supervisor'. The supervisor is assumed to be capable of redirecting the efforts of the other demons to ensure that promising hypotheses are not ignored.

Such a general organization embodies several specific assumptions about the nature of processing procedures. First, it assumes that a great many individual activities occur at the same time, in parallel. Second, it assumes that the relative dominance of the contribution of a particular demon will vary depending upon the current demands of the situation. For instance, if stimulus input is good, recognition may occur through 'feature' demons more or less unaided, but if it is bad, then top-down demons may predominate.

This particular view cannot easily be tested directly, and it is important to understand that it has evolved from a number of considerations, including the following:

1   Many simpler models were found to be inadequate: either they do not fit all of the available data, or they are too limited to accommodate a sufficiently wide range of phenomena.

2   Pattern recognition in humans is extremely flexible, and experiments have demonstrated that many types of contextual information can be utilized. The blackboard models reflect this richness.

3   Blackboard models are broadly consistent with a wide range of work on selective attention (chapter 4), and so provide a uniform conception of the earlier stages of human information-processing.

4   Blackboard models can be implemented as computer programs, which are more successful than some other approaches at recognizing complex patterns. For instance Reddy, Erman, Fennell and Neely (1973) have implemented a blackboard system called HEARSAY which plays chess with a human being. The blackboard is used to represent data from both the *voice* of the human opponent (who plays by speaking his moves) and the current state of the game.

Against these advantages one must pit the fact that a blackboard model is hard to test experimentally. Indeed, it is more appropriate to think of the model as a *framework* rather than a detailed exposition of processing. However, more detailed theories within the framework are possible, and these at least can be tested more easily.

## D  The perception of more complex scenes

This book steers clear of the knotty problems of perception in general. However, it is appropriate to indicate that the kind of reasoning described above is not limited to letter and word recognition. In the sections which follow, we shall take a very brief look at the more complex questions of object and scene perception.

### 1  Scenes containing line-drawn objects

For some years, computer scientists have been interested in the recognition of objects within fairly complex visual displays, ranging from the recognition of everyday objects, geometrical shapes, and so on, right through to such things as the interpretation of X-ray photographs and the images produced by medical scanning procedures. The range of techniques available is very large indeed (see Ballard and Brown 1982 for a comprehensive introduction). Among the various things studied by artificial intelligence methods are line-drawn objects; the best-known work in the field is that of Guzman (1968), Waltz (1975) and Winston (1970).

Consider the block stimuli depicted in figure 3-11. There is no problem in segmenting the line display into recognizable 'objects' – a prism, a pyramid, a cube, etc. From a computational (and hence from a processing) point of view, however, the problem is very great indeed. Quite obviously, if simple template-matching is inadequate for recognizing naturally occurring letters, then it is clearly even less adequate for the present purpose. Imagine how different the visual scene depicted in figure 3-11 would be if the 'world' were rotated, yet unless one of the 'objects' was almost obscured, recognition of each of them would still be fairly easy.

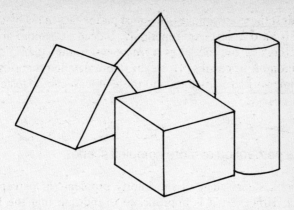

*Figure 3-11.* Line drawings that depict three-dimensional objects.

Once we reject the idea of template-matching, we come face to face with the problem of *segmentation*: how to break down the mass of lines in such a way as to correctly ascribe their presence to a set of individual objects. Notice that this process will be complicated by the fact that many lines must be *supposed* to continue, because some lines are obscured by the implicit solidity of some of the objects.

Guzman (1968), among others, suggested that a process similar to feature extraction might be used, and in his program (SEE) he concentrated on matching various *vertex* types to the line-drawing images. The vertex types are depicted in figure 3-12. The program begins by identifying the occurrence of vertices in the patterns presented. By comparing the geometry of adjacent vertices, it becomes possible to determine whether a particular vertex is concave or convex. This process relies upon natural constraints in vision – for instance, it is not possible for a convex edge at one junction to become a concave edge at a neighbouring junction. Finally, from these constraints, edges and surfaces can be identified. A complete study of the constraints on possibility in the line-drawing world by Waltz (1975), which also included 'shadow' information, showed that the problem was quite tractable. 'Objects' can thus be segmented within line drawings of prismatic solids.

This artificial intelligence approach, which brought together feature-like primitives and knowledge of what is possible in a miniature visual world, was clearly successful. Is what is possible in

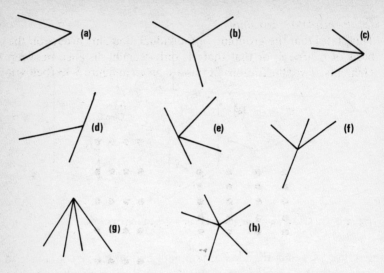

*Figure 3-12.* Types of vertex identified by Guzman as important in determining objects in line drawings.

the miniature world of line-drawn prismatic structures also possible for natural-world scenes? The segmentation problem there is much more complex and requires a rather different approach (see Marr 1982 for a full discussion).

Which primitive elements are used when and how in interpreting the visual world is clearly a very complex problem. Some of the complications associated with the segmentation process, and with how it comes about, are described in the next section.

## 2 Gestalts and organization

The Gestalt psychologists were especially interested in the principles by which individual elements become organized into meaningful wholes (i.e. segmented) and carried out important work on this in the 1920s. They discovered a number of important dimensions of organization which have stood the test of time and experimentation. A relatively recent Gestaltist exposition of this work, including a full discussion of 'Gestalt principles', can be found in Wertheimer (1958). Let us enumerate some of these principles.

*(a) Principle of proximity*
This states that the grouping of individual elements occurs on the
basis of nearness, or that there is only a small distance between
elements. Two illustrations of this are given in figure 3-13 (below).

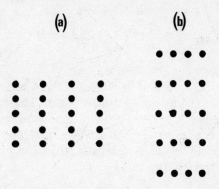

Each figure consists of a 5 × 4 dot matrix. But (a) looks like four
columns of five dots (which is how it would normally be described),
while (b) looks like five rows of four dots. Thus field (a) segments
into four objects, while (b) segments into five.

*(b) Principle of similarity*
If the elements of a display are similar in form, then they will tend
to form a segment. This is illustrated in figure 3-14 (below).

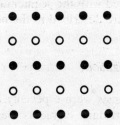

*(c) Principle of common fate*
Elements may be grouped together because they share a common
pattern of motion. For instance, in figure 3-15 (overpage), dots
(a) and (b) would not normally belong to the same group. However,
if they moved up and down to points a and b, they would be grouped
together because of common motion.

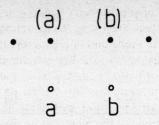

(d) *Principle of good continuation*

Elements will be perceived as wholes if the wholes produce few interruptions or changes in continuous lines. Thus, in figure 3-16 (below), it is possible to describe (a) as four wavy lines originating from O, but it is more likely that (a) will be perceived as two wavy lines which cross at O. Similarly, (b) looks like three wavy lines of dots which intersect at O.

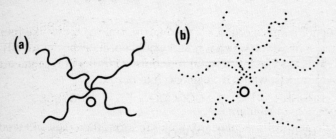

(e) *Principle of closure*

Organization tends to take place around closed figures, regardless of similarity or proximity. This is illustrated in figure 3-17 (below). While it could be described in many ways – for example, as a diamond with two rectangles with squares out butting on to it, it seems to be perceived as two overlapping rectangles.

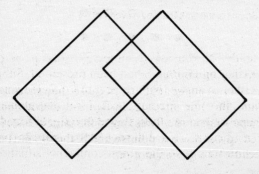

These Gestalt principles are very general, and illustrate another layer of the problems resulting from trying to ascertain the primitive elements of scene and object perception. For instance, a number of investigators have asked whether global (*gestalt*) or local (element) information is used first in pattern analysis. One study addressing this issue was carried out by Navon (1977). His technique was to set local and global elements of stimuli into opposition: an example of the materials he used is shown in figure 3-18.

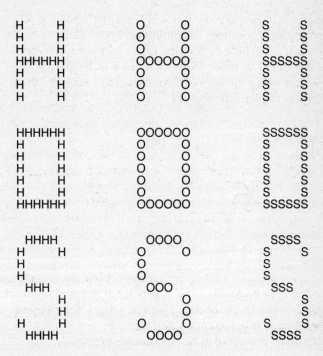

*Figure 3-18.* Stimuli of the type used by Navon (1977).

In one study, Navon asked subjects to decide as quickly as possible whether an H or an S had been presented. Subjects were instructed either to answer with respect to *local* elements or *global configuration*. In some circumstances, local and global elements were the same letters, in others they differed. He found that with the *local* instructions, a conflicting global pattern produced a longer reaction time than did a non-conflicting situation. Global information thus seems to be extracted very quickly. In contrast, no such conflict effect emerged for *global* instructions.

Does this then mean that global evidence is processed more quickly, or even as quickly, as local evidence? And if it does, out of what is the global evidence obtained? Kinchla and Wolf (1979) repeated Navon's studies, but used displays of different sizes (visual angle). They successfully demonstrated that when the global character is quite large, subtending a large visual angle, the *local* letters are easier to respond to. It appears, therefore, that forms having an optimal size (in visual angle terms) are processed most quickly. One likely possibility, discussed by Kinchla and Wolf, is that pattern perception begins with an analysis of low spatial frequency components of a visual display. Low spatial frequency analysis means that individual small characters are initially no more than 'blobs', the blobs being elements out of which global form emerges. Higher frequency analysis, allowing detail to be extracted from the 'blobs', is a slower process, possibly dependent on the first.

Finally, there is an interesting parallel between word recognition and line-drawing recognition. In word recognition, we saw how the individual letters of a word are recognized more easily if they appear in a word, an effect which could be attributed to the likelihood of one letter appearing next to another, and so on. In the case of objects, there is a similar effect, called *object superiority*. Weisstein and Harris (1974) compared the ease with which people could detect a line of a particular position and orientation during a brief tachistoscopic presentation. If the line was embedded in a line drawing of a real three-dimension form, then detection of it was better than if it was embedded in a less coherent set of connected or unconnected lines. Such a result suggests that general form extraction precedes specific local feature extraction.

## E  Overview and conclusions

We began this chapter by asking what kind of evidence is accumulated when we recognize a visual pattern of some sort. Feature theories have enjoyed great popularity in various guises in both psychology and in artificial intelligence. There is even some physiological evidence for the existence of neural systems which resemble feature-analysers. It is only by looking at the proposed processes in detail that the inadequacies of simple feature theory become apparent.

Feature accounts are certainly 'right' in the sense that visual stimuli are not handled as wholes in the nervous system. Whatever a percept is, the information enabling one to come about is rooted in detectors of intensity gradients and intensity changes. And it would appear that in the initial stages of pattern analysis, relatively low spatial frequency analysis takes place, higher spatial frequency analysis taking more time. Whichever way one looks at it, the process will take time, and is thus in some way analogous to evidence accumulation, which plays an important role in more general psychological accounts of perception, attention and memory. The big problem is to say just how and when various types of 'primitive' information are used in processing.

Word perception constitutes a special case in that it is dedicated to the recognition of artificial stimuli – after all, writing systems are a human invention. In this chapter, we have treated word perception in a very general and rather shallow way. In particular, the many aspects of word perceptions in the speech modality have been omitted. Nevertheless, some important points about processing have been introduced. First of all, contexts of various sorts have been shown to play a role in word perception, and of letters within words. This makes sense in processing terms. It is the case that q is always followed by u in English, and that certain words are likely to follow other words. It would be incredible if the human processing mechanism did not make use of these facts. As it does, one can distinguish between bottom-up or data-driven processes, and top-down, or concept- (or context-)driven processes. However, recognition of this distinction does not explain *how* the interactions of the two take place. One general way of thinking about it is that top-down processes *constrain* the possible outcomes of bottom-up processing.

Some very elegant work is being carried out in the field of word recognition, but one very general criticism can be levelled against the approaches described in the present chapter, and that is their concentration on the *explicit* recognition of individual words. It may make a real difference to our models of word recognition if we remember that we normally need to recognize words in the *continuous reading of text*. It is not even necessary to recognize the occurrence of each and and every word as it appears. In fact, some readers may not have noticed that there were two 'ands' in the previous sentence. A concentration on individual word recognition may mislead us in constructing detailed process models of perceptual aspects of reading.

# 4 Attention and processing resources

One of the key notions of attention is that it operates *selectively*: for instance, if one is at a party, and people around are chatting away, it is somehow necessary to *pay attention* to the particular conversation in which one is engaged. This appears to have the effect of screening out the other conversations to some extent. What is equally obvious, apart from this screening effect, is that we do not appear to be able to process more than one conversation at a time to any significant extent: we do not appear to be able to listen to two conversations simultaneously. Research on selective attention has been concerned with how this screening process works. Given all of the information impinging on the senses of a person, at what point(s) in the processing chain does selectivity play a role? What happens to 'unattended' information? These questions are tackled in section A of this chapter.

A second notion of attention is another consequence of this selective principle. Why do we need to be selective? Why do we appear to be unable to listen to three, four or more conversations at the same time and still understand them perfectly? One possible answer is that there is a *limited processing capacity system* in which sensory input can be analysed and worked on. One might say that a selective mechanism is necessary so that this limited capacity system does not become overloaded. Following this line of thinking, we might say that everything which leads up to the attention restriction may be of *effectively unlimited capacity*, while that which is attended to is processed in the limited-capacity system.

We know the sense in which a bottle's capacity is limited, but in what sense could an information-processing system be limited? There are, in fact, many possible ways of thinking about this. Take, for instance, a computational analogy. All computer systems are limited in terms of memory, and, in general, for any particular operating system the available memory will be partitioned and each partition allocated to certain functions. Thus most of the memory might be allocated to information storage, and a relatively small part of it kept aside working on material with the current program. Another variant on this theme is to suppose that it is quite possible to perform two tasks simultaneously, provided they do not use the *same* processing mechanisms at the *same* time.

This chapter contains two main sections. The first is concerned with a generation of attention theories which began with Donald Broadbent's famous filter theory (Broadbent 1957). Although Broadbent conceived of his theory as having a potentially wide range of applications, it has been most closely related to work on what may be called *selective perception*, for instance, selecting which of two messages to listen to. The set of arguments leading to the rejection of the theory as originally postulated is a fascinating story. Equally fascinating are the capacity and effort notions of attention (section B). Many current writers believe that the latest in this line of theories can explain much of the data of selective perception studies, and put the earlier explanations of the data into a reasonable perspective. The reader should be warned that the study of attention raises questions of processing which are relevant to all aspects of cognition. Doubtless, the fullest understanding of attention will depend upon a rather full understanding of cognition and information-processing in general.

## A  Studies and theories of selectivity

### 1  Broadbent's filter theory

Modern studies of selective attention effectively began in the 1950s and the earliest work was undertaken by electrical engineer Colin Cherry and experimental psychologist Donald Broadbent. One of the main experimental tasks used required people to listen to (attend to) one of two messages which were being presented to them at the same time. One specific variation on this task, the so-called *dichotic listening task*, was an arrangement in which one message was presented to one ear, and one to the other. Such an arrangement relies upon an important feature of perception: if a message is presented to the right ear alone, it is interpreted as if it is coming from a source on the right. Similarly, if it is presented to the left ear, it seems as though it is coming from a source on the left. Thus presenting different messages separately to each of the two ears is very much like having one person speak on your left, and the other on the right.

Broadbent (1954) carried out one of the earliest experiments using this technique. He presented three different digit sets to each of his subjects' ears at the same time, for instance:

|        | Left ear | Right ear |
|--------|----------|-----------|
| pair 1 | 7        | 3         |
| pair 2 | 4        | 2         |
| pair 3 | 1        | 5         |

The digit pairs were presented with half a second interval between them, and subjects were asked to respond by recalling the digits in any order they wished. First, subjects tended to recall those presented to one ear, then those presented to the other ear. Overall performance levels were such that about 65 per cent of the lists were correctly recalled. This indicates a preference for recalling from one source first, and then from the other. Indeed, another condition required subjects to attempt to recall the digits in their order of presentation, first pair 1, then pair 2 and so on, rather than by ear. Performance under these circumstances was especially poor, subjects recalling only about 15 per cent of lists correctly.

Two interesting aspects of this experiment are that it suggests that the ear is a perceptual channel, and that once a particular channel is being attended to, it takes time to switch back to the other one. So, with only half a second between stimulus pairs, there is not enough time to shift from the first selected channel to the second before the next stimulus comes in. The result is that the stimuli from one channel (ear) are processed together, followed by the stimuli from the other channel. To account for this, Broadbent (1957; 1958) suggested that unattended stimuli can be held in a 'pre-attentional store' for a very limited time period, and that they are not processed further until attention is shifted from the attended channel. This is illustrated in figure 4-1. The pre-attentional store is clearly necessary with this account of attention, otherwise the stimuli would not be available for processing following processing of the first batch. Obviously, this model is critically dependent upon the notion that attention can only be switched from channel to channel at a particular rate. In fact, Broadbent (1954) showed

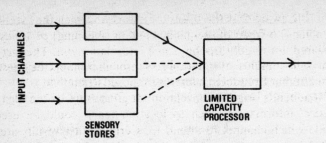

*Figure 4-1.* Attention construed as a selection mechanism mediating between a number of sensory input channels and a subsequent limited-capacity processor. In the figure, selection is on Channel 1. The sensory memory stores are essential to account for the fact that unattended data can be retrieved, but the stores are considered to hold information only briefly; they correspond to the sensory stores discussed in chapter 2. This diagram exemplifies the filter theory of Broadbent (1958); the selector corresponds to Broadbent's filter.

that if the stimuli were presented more slowly, with a two-second interval between pairs, then performance improved such that subjects managed to recall some 50 per cent of the stimulus sets.

This model, known as the *filter theory*, was the first of a new generation of theories of attention, and now has the status of a conceptual benchmark. Subsequent research indicates the inadequacies of the theory, but it stands as an important point of reference. One of the techniques which provided some early data contrary to Broadbent's position is known as *shadowing*. In a shadowing task (devised by Cherry 1953), subjects listen to a message, and at the same time repeat it, staying as close to the message, in time, as possible. This furnishes some sort of guarantee that subjects are indeed paying attention to the relevant channel, because it is a formidable task unless one is highly practised. To make shadowing into a classic dichotic listening task, one simply presents the message to be shadowed on one ear, and another message on the other. Messages are typically long tracts of prose.

The technique has been used to investigate three major aspects of selective attention (Broadbent 1971): what is known about irrelevant messages by the listener, what cues are used in determining *what it is* that is being attended to, particularly physical cues and, finally, the effect of message content on selectivity.

Moray (1959), using this technique, established that subjects could not recall the content of the unattended message, but were obviously aware that there *was* a message to which they were not attending. So while the semantic content (meaning) of a message appeared not to get through, some information did. The fact that even *some* stimulus information gets through prompts the question: what is it that Broadbent's filter is supposed to stop?

Broadbent's original conception set great store by the idea that *physical* information, such as location (ear), could be used to decide which channel to attend to. Certain other results are not entirely contradictory to Broadbent's view: Cherry's (1953) discoveries that subjects could listen selectively to a female or a male voice, for instance, and that they could recognize the sex of the speaker on the unattended channel lend support to his position. These constitute physical cues along the lines Broadbent originally and rightly supposed would be used as a basis for selecting a message as the attended one. Indeed, in a very early study, Cherry (1953) had already shown that if a listener was presented with two messages in the *same voice* on the *same ear* then it was extremely difficult to shadow just one of the messages.

## 2 Treisman's attenuator model

The problems with the filter theory began with the discovery that certain aspects of unattended (unshadowed) messages could 'break through' the filter, although these aspects would normally be considered as requiring processing late in the cognitive system. In one instance, Moray (1959) found that subjects sometimes reported hearing their own names on the unattended channel if they were presented as part of the to-be-ignored message. Is one's own name a special exception for the filter? Probably not. Suppose that the following messages are coming through the headphones:

Right headphone – 'I saw the girl song was wishing . . .'
Left headphone – 'Me that bird jumping in the street . . .'

Notice that if the subject attends to (shadows) the right ear, the message makes sense through the sequence 'I saw the girl', but the next part, 'song was wishing', does not follow on meaningfully. On the other hand, if the subject were to switch to the left ear midstream, the message would follow on (I saw the girl jumping . . .). Treisman (1960) found that if the messages were arranged in this way, shadowing responses shifted channels, so that subjects might say 'I saw the girl jumping ...'. Of course, the whole point of the shadowing instructions is that the subject should avoid such shifts. Such effects are not easily handled by the filter theory. If one supposes that the filter operates after the meanings of the two messages have been analysed, then it is necessary to accept that considerably more processing goes on before the filter comes into play than Broadbent supposed. In fact, it is difficult to see precisely what the filter is filtering in such cases.

Treisman (1969) offered a somewhat different model from that of Broadbent, based on data like those discussed above. Her argument was that the filter was intended to shut out the irrelevant information completely, on the basis of minimal physical cues, and this was invalidated by the data. Rather, she suggested, irrelevant information was *attenuated* in some way. A commonly presented analogy is that information on the unattended channel is subjectively quieter, or less intense (e.g. Reed 1982). However, we have already encountered enough theory to put forward a slightly more technical version. In chapters 2 and 3, a case was built up that the perception of stimuli is not an all-or-none affair, but depends upon the accumulation of evidence over time for the presence of a stimulus. Furthermore, it was argued that the recognition of a stimulus is dependent upon some device which was sensitive to evidence for that stimulus. Treisman's model relies upon such ideas. Her view is that part of memory contains 'dictionary' units (exactly the same as Morton's logogens), and that the operation of a *selective attenuator* is to reduce the quality of the evidence reaching the dictionary units. Of course, physical cues such as ear or voice would be used to attenuate the appropriate message. The effect is thus similar to degrading the quality of the stimulus, hence the term 'attenuation theory'. Each dictionary unit (like a logogen) has a threshold which must be exceeded if the word is to be used in some way. And, like the logogen, the thresholds or extant activation levels of dictionary units are assumed to be a function of context. Thus, if an input is 'Mary had a little ...', the threshold of the unit 'lamb' is assumed to be lowered. Now this argument will accommodate the 'meaning breakthrough' phenomena in the following way: if one is shadowing 'Mary had a little ...' on one ear, then the dictionary unit for 'lamb' will have a threshold reduction. If 'lamb' comes in through the unattended (attenuated) channel, there may still be enough input to raise the 'lamb' unit above threshold, and so shadowing can switch to 'lamb'. The essence of the attenuation theory, then, is that rather than block out information pertinent to word recognition, an attenuator merely reduces the quality of the information: it still passes through to a dictionary unit system, but is simply attenuated. This account will handle cases like recognizing one's own name, since the dictionary unit for one's name could plausibly be assumed to have a low threshold.

Broadbent and Gregory (1963; also Broadbent 1971) report an experiment using the signal detection theory measures of d′ and β in a dichotic listening task, the results of which, they claim, conform more to Treisman's theory than to the original filter theory. They presented six digits to one ear, and a burst of auditory noise to the other ear. The noise contained a weak tone on some trials, and not on others. In one case, subjects had to attend to and report back the digits. In the other, subjects had to ignore the digits. In both cases they also performed the same detection task. The interest lies in the tone-detection performance, analysed in terms of d′ and β.

If signal information is attenuated by being unattended, then a lower d′ value is predicted for the case where subjects attend to the digits. Treisman's theory makes this prediction. However, the same drop in d′ would be expected according to the filter theory, since this would correspond to absolute attenuation. The difference in the two theories lies in the values of β which would be expected. Broadbent and Gregory argued that β would be greater for unattended signals than for attended ones, on the filter theory. If signals convey little information to a subject, then few correct detections *or* false positives, which are the conditions for high values of β, would be expected. The results of the experiment indicated a clear drop in d′ in the unattended case, but no change in β. Broadbent and Gregory concluded that the results were more consistent with Treisman's theory than with the original Broadbent theory. Similar results have been obtained by Treisman and Geffen (1967), and Moray and O'Brien (1967).

According to Broadbent's original theory, filtering occurs at a very early stage, on the basis of minimal information: where the voice is coming from, or some other simple feature, such as the acoustic characteristics of a particular voice. The evidence of later studies showed a number of ways in which other information could get through on the unattended channel, however, so that even the meaning of words could influence the partitioning of attention in shadowing tasks. Quite clearly, in some way the message is getting through and Broadbent's original conception is flawed.

Treisman argued that when messages are encountered, a series of tests can be applied to them. The earliest tests distinguish between inputs on the basis of sensory qualities alone (e.g. male or female voice; location of message source). Later tests can make distinctions based on syllabic patterns or specific sounds and individual words. And a final series of tests can make distinctions based on meaning and syntax. Thus, if an early test is sufficient to distinguish between two inputs, Treisman supposed that *attenuation* (not complete blocking) occurs from that stage on. Thus Treisman suggests that the *locus of selective attention is variable*, and that it is certainly not necessarily as early as Broadbent proposed. As an illustration of the variable-locus notion, consider a dichotic listening task described by Treisman (1964). Subjects were required to shadow a message in one ear. Two types of messages were presented to the other ear. *Either* the message was in a *different* voice (permitting early selection) or in the *same* voice, in which case early characteristics of voice could not be used as a basis for selection. Subjects were much better at shadowing in the first case.

These arguments lead to the point where we might ask whether attention is being looked at in quite the right way. The emphasis began with screening operations on the crude physical characteristics of auditory information. Subsequent experiments suggested that selective processes could operate much later, and may not be all-or-none in any case. Rather, Treisman suggested that non-attended information may simply be attenuated or reduced in quality. Other investigators, for instance Deutsch and Deutsch (1963), and, later, Norman (1968), have even suggested that attenuation is unnecessary. Norman, for instance, introduces the notion of 'pertinence', which is his term for top-down processes operating on incoming evidence. So, for instance, it is possible that selectivity may *not* require attenuation but only that 'irrelevant' messages never have components which are sufficiently pertinent.

The point is reached where the problems of selective attention are so obviously linked to those of pattern recognition that it is necessary to treat the two together (Lindsay and Norman 1977). For instance, the processes involved in pattern recognition represent a long and complex series of steps. The importance of various aspects of the process appears to depend upon the context in which the sensory information is accumulated. As various people have suggested, it may be better to view selectivity as a process of biasing the deployment of the underlying analytical mechanisms to fit the demands of the situation. Potentially, selective effects may then be demonstrated at many levels, depending on the situation. It is to such an approach we now turn.

## B  Resources and capacity theories of attention

The studies and theories in section A mark the first wave of an attack on attention in the revival of studies of cognition. They are essentially *bottleneck* models, the idea being that because the processing system cannot cope with all inputs, some are selected for 'further processing', while the others are not. Paying attention, on these accounts, is this act of selection. The underlying principle in terms of general processing is one of *time-sharing*: only one 'task' can be carried out at a time and if it appears that two tasks have been carried out at the same time, this is really the result of switching back and forth from one task to the other. This corresponds directly to the computational principle of time-sharing. When more than one user is communicating with a computer at the same time, in fact only the work associated with one user is being dealt with at any given moment, with an executive time-sharing system deciding what has priority when. Unless two such 'tasks' require the system to be dedicated for a considerable time, rapid switching back and forth is possible, and the users are unlikely to notice that things are happening a little more slowly than they would be on a single-user basis.

A somewhat different view of attention is the *resource* family of accounts. Moray (1967; 1969) suggested that an appropriate way of thinking about attention is in terms of the amount of processing resources dedicated to the activity in question. On this view, mental processing of any type is assumed to draw upon a limited number of resources in the processor. It is assumed that the resources can be flexibly allocated to a wide range of tasks, even to two or more tasks at the same time. It will only become impossible to do two tasks at the same time if the resources required surpass the limit of what is available. Furthermore, resources required will depend critically upon the conditions of the task itself. For instance, with the simple task of detecting a stimulus in noise, it may very well be the case that to perform at some maximal level of, say, reaction time, more resources are needed for signals of low signal-to-noise ratios than high signal-to-noise ratios.

In this section we shall develop some of the arguments about attention from this point of view. The framework is much broader than those related to the filter and attenuation class of models, and allows for a much wider range of possibilities as to how processing might come about in any particular situation.

## 1  Attention, task performance and effort

It is a truism that the harder one tries at a task, the better one does, up to a point. Such improvements can be sudden and dramatic if the subject 'puts more effort' into a task or 'pays closer attention' or 'concentrates'. Although in some circumstances one might suppose that paying closer attention means not paying attention to other things (such as daydreaming), we are all familiar with the way in which just by trying harder – by somehow concentrating – we can improve. A good example of this is the simple reaction-time task. Subjects are always instructed to 'react as fast as possible', but do not always do so. Figure 4-2 shows the results of giving a subject these instructions in an auditory simple RT task, and then intervening after the first fifteen reactions, and simply saying to him that he was not doing his best. Although reaction sixteen was slow (after the intervention), the next ten were remarkably fast. Clearly the subject was able to concentrate more, and perform better, perhaps by making greater use of predictability in foreperiod information, or whatever; certainly by allocating more processing resources to the task.

Such a dependence of performance on effort would appear to have its limitations, however. There is a considerable body of evidence to suggest that with great efforts to improve performance, it can actually deteriorate. To understand something of this, we have to introduce the notion of *arousal*.

Arousal is meant to describe some interface between the general (often physically manifest) aspects of an organism, and the quality of the organism's performance on a given task. One usage treats arousal as referring to the physical state in which one is alert, excited, and keenly aware of the environment. At various times, a

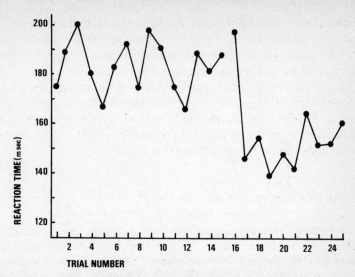

*Figure 4-2.* Data from the first twenty-six reactions of a single subject to a medium-intensity tone. Although the subject was initially instructed to react as quickly as possible, intervention by the experimenter re-instructing the subject at trial fifteen produced a considerable improvement by trial seventeen which was maintained for a period. Such results are commonplace during the instruction phase of simple RT tasks, and illustrate the degree of control over effort and resources which subjects have. *(Sanford unpublished data.)*

whole range of conditions of the organism have been put forward as influencing arousal (cf. Broadbent 1971; Duffy 1962; Kahneman 1973). But first, the *point* of the arousal concept in the present discussion is the supposed relation of arousal to performance of the so-called 'inverted-U' function, as depicted in figure 4-3. This curve was first formulated by Yerkes and Dodson (1908), and is often termed the Yerkes–Dodson Law. The essential idea is that for any given task, there will be an optimal level of arousal. Below this level, performance will be poor, and above it, it will deteriorate. The idea is important for both practical and theoretical reasons, and an astonishing range of questions have fallen under the umbrella of studies of arousal. As an introduction, we will list some of the situations which have been tied to arousal at various times.

*(a) The motivational state of the organism*
In the original Yerkes–Dodson study, the motivational state of the

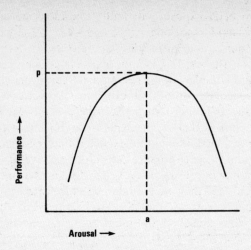

*Figure 4-3.* The 'inverted-U' function of arousal and performance. At low and high levels of arousal, performance is poorer than at some intermediate levels. There is a maximum performance level at the optimal level of arousal. The optimal level is considered to be a function of task complexity. Both performance and arousal are in arbitrary units.

animals was manipulated by strength of shock in a learning task. They found that fewer errors were made in learning when the shock was of 'medium' intensity, rather than being higher or lower. Parallels in humans include changing motivation by knowledge of results, which is assumed to be arousing, and which can counteract the effects of agents assumed to reduce arousal (see (c) below).

*(b) The personality characteristics of the subject*
These are important in terms of the Eysenckian dimension of introversion-extraversion (e.g. Eysenck 1963). According to one picture, extraverts are supposedly chronically under-aroused, hence they seek 'arousal' situations; conversely, introverts are chronically aroused, and so seek 'quiet' situations. In his early work, Eysenck and his colleagues sought a detailed justification of this point of view.

*(c) Extraneous 'stress' variables*
Since the early 1950s, psychologists have been interested in a number of stress conditions in work settings. The best studied of

these have been exposure to loud continuous noise (above 95 decibels), sleep loss for one or two nights (see Broadbent 1971 for a good account), and shiftwork cycles and circadian rhythms (see, for example, Blake 1971; Colquhoun 1971). One much-favoured interpretation of many of the results is that noise increases arousal, sleep loss decreases arousal, and that arousal varies as a function of circadian rhythm. An attractive aspect of this way of thinking about stressors is that it can explain certain interactions among them. For instance, it might be expected that noise would cause a deterioration of performance on tasks, as would sleep loss. Deprive someone of sleep, and then let them work in a noisy environment, and they are bound to be worse than ever. Not so. In a variety of task settings, the noise stress appears to counteract the sleep loss, thus cancelling out the detrimental effects on performance (e.g. Wilkinson 1965).

*(d) Task-induced arousal*
Some tasks which people have to do are notoriously under-stimulating, and concentration is thus rendered difficult. A much-studied and important task of this type is *watchkeeping*. Specific examples include performance on monitoring radar screens or sonar displays. Such tasks have been said to be under-arousing and may even border on sensory deprivation (Broadbent 1971). Almost always, decrements in performance occur after a short period on such tasks. Provided the tasks do not involve high signal rates, continuous loud noise can actually improve performance. This has been explained in terms of the arousing nature of noise (Broadbent 1971).

This list is by no means exhaustive. The most common interpretation is that the optimality of performance depends upon the level of arousal of the subject, which critically depends upon a whole range of variables.

One important aspect of the notion of arousal is that it links the psychological issue of processing efficiency with physiological states. In general, cognitive theories have tended to bypass this question, concentrating on the computational aspects of processing. Yet one does not have to carry out laboratory studies to appreciate a bodily aspect to mental work. For instance, working on a difficult problem can result in physical tiredness, in sweating, in holding one's breath in anticipation, and so on. Of course, there have been a large number of laboratory studies of just such variables in the field of psychophysiology and indeed a considerable part of the literature on arousal has been aimed at investigating the relationship between task performance and physiological indices of activation. Such indices have been numerous and include muscle tension, skin resistance and conductivity, electroencephalographic measures, heartrate and regularity of heartrate, breathing rates and patterns, and so on. The picture which emerges is complex, because not one of these indices can be considered *the* index of arousal, but in many cases, correlations exist between them and performance (e.g. Duffy 1962). But the picture is complicated by specific problems.

From our point of view, regardless of the details and complications of arousal theories, the general picture is cited as a reminder of the fact that mental effort occurs within the medium of a physiological machine, and that it is quite wrong to conceive of attention without taking this point seriously. If effort at a task consists of giving more 'computational' resources to the performance of that task (a typical cognitive position), then we must not forget that such resource allocation alters the finely balanced equilibrium of the whole physiological system. It seems entirely plausible that there will be an upper limit to the amount of resources which can be allocated over a given period on a task for purely physiological reasons. This type of argument is not very well understood, but it is known that extreme effort on a processing task seems to be quite shortlived. A task as straightforward as simple reaction time can be used as an illustration.

It is well known that subjects react more quickly in simple reaction-time settings if they can predict approximately when the stimulus is going to occur (e.g. Klemmer 1956). A typical processing explanation of this is that the subject lowers his evidence detection criterion at the right moment to be able to respond on a minimal amount of evidence (Sanford 1972). But it is equally well known that preparation cannot be kept at the maximum for very long, and that subjects usually control (modulate) the points at which they prepare maximally (Loveless and Sanford 1974). It is not clear why such modulation is necessary, but it is worth pointing out that subjects alter their breathing patterns when they are preparing, typically holding their breath, and that complex changes in heartrate occur (Callaway 1965; Lacey and Lacey 1958). The task is being carried out by the biological organism, and its state of balance is disturbed by preparation. Limitations on mental effort may well be accounted for by the degree of disturbance which the body finds acceptable but nobody really knows at present.

## 2 Kahneman's attention-allocation model

Kahneman (1973) presented a rather full account of a capacity theory of attention which incorporated the idea of arousal and effort. His view typifies the general characteristics of most capacity-based explanations of attention. His assumptions are that there is an upper limit to the total amount of resources available at any given time, and he supposes that this amount is dependent on arousal. Generally, the higher the level of arousal, the more resources are assumed to be available, up to some limit as specified by an inverted-U principle. Adequate task performance is assumed to occur if enough resources are made available for it; this will depend upon both arousal and a *current allocation policy*. Allocation policy is Kahneman's rather useful term for some mechanism which determines *how* resources will be allocated to tasks at hand. If there are enough resources to allocate to two tasks at the same time, then performance on the two tasks will be good. If there are not, then either both will be done badly at the same time, or the allocation policy may favour one task over another. On Kahneman's conception, in principle, resources may be allocated *flexibly* depending on what the situation demands.

In one series of experimental studies, Kahneman (1973) reports the use of *pupil diameter* as an index of effort. This psychophysiological index is one of a number thought to vary with arousal and, in Kahneman's studies, was related systematically to performance on a dual task. The study is particularly interesting because it enables the time-course of performance on the two tasks to be plotted, along with the time-course of changes in pupil diameter. A great advantage of using pupil diameter as a measure is that changes in it can be detected very readily; it also has a fast response latency so it is useful for tasks where the time-course is important.

Subjects were presented with four digits in the auditory modality, at the rate of one per second. After hearing them, they had to add one to each of them, and report back the answers. This was the primary task. As a secondary task, they simultaneously

monitored a screen which displayed letters individually and successively, with instructions to check for the occurrence of the letter K.

The results are shown in figure 4-4. First, note that pupilary
dilation, the index of arousal and effort, increases during the
listening phase to a peak in the middle of the report phase.
Kahneman's claim is that this reflects an increasing demand for

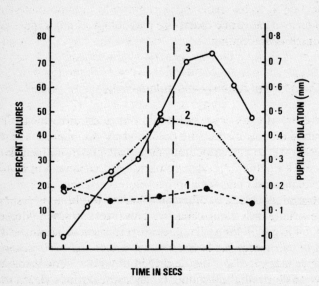

Figure 4-4. Performance on digit transformation (1), letter detection (2), and
pupilary response (3) as a function of time, centred on presentations of the letter
K. (From Kahneman 1973, figure 2-3.)

resources as the task proceeds, leading to increased effort. Secondly,
performance on the primary task was more or less constant over
the duration of an experimental trial. However, performance on
the letter-detection task fell steadily during the 'listen' phases, and
began to improve again only at the end of the report phase.
Kahneman's explanation is that subjects always allocated more
effort to the listening task (the primary one). As more and more
effort had to be allocated to this, so less was available for the
secondary task.

This is a neat but typical demonstration of the relations of effort
to the performance of two tasks. It is broadly consistent with
Kahneman's account, in that it requires the concepts of effort,
arousal, and a flexible allocation policy. But one can see problems

with this type of account, not the least of which is that it is insufficiently detailed to characterize the ranges of possible performance. For instance, were subjects making a *maximum* effort? If they could and did make more effort, would the secondary task show no decrement during the time-course of a trial? What would happen if they made less effort? Some of these issues are discussed in section 4. Kahneman's book represents an important synthesis of ideas from varied parts of psychology, and is part of our recommended reading.

## 3  Questions of capacity and automaticity

There are two obvious and important questions which relate to capacity models of the sort described by Kahneman. The first is whether all cognitive operations draw upon resources, and the second is whether all tasks draw upon the same pool of resources. These questions are not unrelated to each other.

First of all, like any other mechanism, the brain is assumed to have a finite processing capacity. This assertion says nothing at all about the problems at hand, however, because it can be shown that by fairly acceptable criteria, some tasks seem to require very little capacity in the sense described up to now. An anecdote will serve to illustrate the argument. When one begins to learn to drive a car, all of one's resources seem to be taken up in the act of driving itself. To have a conversation at the same time is a near impossibility: pupils at a driving school are often incapable of hearing a message like 'second on the left' when they are driving for the first time. With practice all of this changes: skilled drivers listen to the radio, dictate while driving, and apparently have very little processing capacity dedicated to driving itself! However, in difficult driving conditions, even skilled drivers can soon reach a capacity limit as they have to bring more resources to bear on the act of driving.

There are many other examples of this kind, some of which have been the subject of direct enquiry by psychologists. Well-practised subjects can perform quite complex tasks simultaneously with little or no decrement. For instance, people can type while shadowing or reciting, and play music while reading out loud (Allport, Antonis and Reynolds 1972; Shaffer 1975). Such tasks seem to be 'automatic', where automaticity comes with very substantial practice. Without a high degree of practice, performance on each of two tasks is usually more difficult than it is in the case where they are performed separately.

The development of automaticity does seem to result in a dramatic reduction in processing demands, but what then is the difference between an 'automatic' and a resource-demanding task? Recently, a number of psychologists have taken an interest in this question (e.g. Shiffrin and Schneider 1977; Shiffrin and Dumais 1981). One possibility is that early on in practice at a task, the component elements involved in the task have to be brought together and ordered. To begin with, this will be *arbitrary* from the point of view of the processor. For instance, the sequencing of brake, gears, mirror, accelerator, clutch and so on in starting a car is arbitrary, defined only by how the car is built, how the roads are designed to be used, and so on. However, with repeated practice, the sequence of events becomes learned as a unit. Now suppose that as the sequence is more and more used, it becomes stored as one of a library of programs which can be used under the appropriate circumstances. There is no need to go through the business of assembling the program again after that. It is automatic in the sense of being established and stored for later use. The reason it was not automatic in the first place is because the unit had to be built up out of many components in the correct sequence. (In chapter 5 we shall look at this idea in some detail.) This picture is consistent with a suggestion made by Shiffrin and Dumais (1981), that 'automatic' sequences tend to reoccur as complete units which are difficult to modify. For instance, if you learn to play a passage on the piano, and make a wrong note consistently, it is extremely difficult to correct it. The picture is one in which processes which are capacity consuming are open to modification, while automatic processes are not.

It is thus argued that it may be possible to perform two tasks together if they are sufficiently automated, or if one of them is. This is obviously a special case of the argument that if there are only so many resources to go around, then provided the demand does not exceed this limit, no difficulties will emerge. However, there is another argument which also has to be considered in relation to the resource picture, and that is whether resources are a common pool of general-purpose facilities, or are special purpose. To illustrate an obvious limiting case, it is patently obvious that we cannot verbalize two different messages at the same time because we only have one articulatory system (resource). Allport, Antonis and Reynolds (1972) and McLeod (1977; 1978) have argued that some of our resources may very well be special purpose. If a task requires the use of one of these special-purpose resources, then another task cannot use it at the same time. Conversely, if two tasks use entirely different resources then there is nothing to stop the two tasks being performed together as easily as they could separately. Driving and listening to the radio, for instance, may use entirely different resources.

## 4  Data and resource limitations

In 1975, Norman and Bobrow published a paper which attempted to pull together a number of aspects of attention, including selective attention to input, a problem which we have left rather in the air. They introduced some new ideas, but part of their paper delivered important criticisms of the general interpretation of many results in attention studies.

These authors make an important distinction between *resource limitations* and *data limitations*. Performance on a task is said to be resource limited if not enough resources are being given to it to perform it optimally. A typical test for resource-limited performance is to see whether performance improves if more effort is put into the task. If it does, then the task is resource limited. If it does not, then resources are no longer a factor limiting performance. At this point, tasks are said to be *data limited* in that any improvement in performance must come from the data sources being dealt with. For example, a person might be putting maximum effort into a signal detection task. However, if the stimulus quality is poor, the only way performance can improve is by increasing the signal-to-noise ratio. This is a signal-data limitation. Similarly, if you are performing with maximal resources on a memory task, but do not have the required information in memory, then performance is memory-data limited.

This may seem fairly obvious but the consequences are far-reaching. First of all, for some single tasks, subjects may very easily be able to allocate a small amount of resources, sufficient to make the task only data limited. For instance, in a signal detection task, this limit might be reached very easily; so easily that no effort limitation would normally be observed in an experimental setting.

Other tasks may show a considerable improvement with effort. In theory, they may still show improvement over that point where the subject can or is prepared to go. Such tasks will not reach the point of pure data limitation.

Figure 4-5 illustrates such states of affairs. The shaded portions represent parts of the 'effort' curve which are unlikely to be discovered in any experiment. Subjects always make some effort,

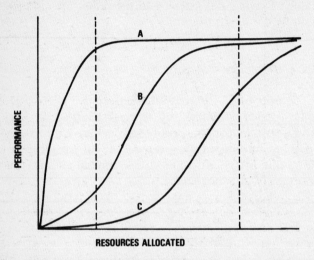

*Figure 4-5.* Hypothetical resource-performance functions for three tasks. The shaded regions represent areas unlikely to be detected in any experiment, either because the resources are below minimum effort or above maximum effort. Task A is at a data-limited point right over the observable range. Task C is resource limited. Task B shows a transition from being resource limited to being data limited at the upper extreme of the observable range. *(From Norman and Bobrow 1975.)*

and there is a limit to the effort which they are prepared to make; consequently, in any given experiment, the range of the effort-performance function which can be obtained will be somewhat restricted, and in the figure is represented by the centre zone.

The way in which resource-performance functions are important for divided attention or dual-task performance can be illustrated with a simple diagram (figure 4-6). For the sake of argument, assume that there are 100 resources of various types which can be brought into play for carrying out one or more tasks. In the figure, task 1 requires 20 units of resource to reach the point where it is data limited (hence optimal). Task 2 requires 50 units of resource to reach a similar point. So, provided a subject uses effort to the extent of 70 units, both tasks could be performed as well *together* as separately. However, if an effort of only 50 units were used, then one or both tasks would suffer. In a dual-task paradigm,

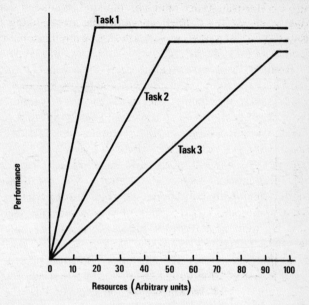

**Figure 4-6.** When two tasks are carried out together, the resource account suggests that whether there is a decrement on one or even both tasks depends upon their underlying resource-performance functions. If only 70 resource units are used by a subject, then tasks 1 and 2 could be carried out together with no apparent decrement, since both become data limited on a total of 20 + 50 = 70 resources. However, task 3 cannot be combined with either 1 or 2 without a decrement. Such considerations indicate how difficult it is to answer the question 'Can two tasks be done at the same time without decrement?'. To answer the question, the resource-performance functions of each component task would have to be known, as would the limit on resources which subjects can, or are prepared to, make available.

under the 50-unit circumstance, one might be inclined to think that both tasks cannot be performed together although, of course, in the 70-unit circumstance one would draw no such conclusion. Task 3, a more complex task, requires 95 units of resource to reach the optimal (data-limited) level. Combining it with task 2 or even task 1 would be impossible without some drop in performance. The argument is thus a simple one, though if one is trying to predict performance on two tasks at a given level of resource allocation to each, one would need to know the exact shape of the resource-performance functions.

Norman and Bobrow use the resource argument to explain a number of findings from the kind of experiments on selective attention with which we began. A particularly interesting case is the resolution of the apparently contradictory findings of Treisman and Geffen (1967) on the one hand, and Lawson (1966) on the other. Both of these investigators used shadowing as the main task, and had a secondary task in which subjects had to listen for target items in *either* channel. In the Treisman and Geffen study, the items were specially selected words. They found that subjects missed many of the items on the secondary channel, a finding consistent with the attenuation theory. Lawson's targets were rather different, consisting of pure tones which were clearly audible under normal listening conditions. The result was that even under shadowing conditions, with high-level performance at shadowing, subjects could detect the tone on the secondary channel. Norman and Bobrow suggest a resource explanation handles the apparent discrepancy. A high level of shadowing consumes many resources, so that few are left for the secondary task. In the case of tone detection, they claim that few resources will be required, and so tone detection can get into the data-limited region even with a high level of performance at shadowing. In contrast, word recognition, they say, requires more resources than are available, so unless shadowing suffers because fewer resources are allocated to it, the detection of target words will suffer.

It is clear that resource explanations of selective attention are quite different from the original filter explanations. Indeed, it is debatable whether it makes much sense to ascribe selectivity to any particular processing stage at all. However, Norman and Bobrow do suggest that more resources have to be spent on organizing responses than on detecting stimuli. They base this view on observations by Moray (1974; Moray and Fitter 1973) and others, that when subjects are not required to make responses, they seem able to monitor signals arriving simultaneously on different channels without any apparent interference. It is also possible to justify such a view when one considers the unnatural-ness of the response component of many laboratory tasks. For instance, pressing a button in response to a tone does not constitute a natural part of a person's repertoire of activities. It is likely that many laboratory tasks have response components which are not sufficiently automated to be in a low-resource region.

Clearly, Norman and Bobrow's account is both plausible and very different from earlier views of selectivity. The problem is that it is difficult to test. In fact, it is really a framework for *thinking about* specific problems of divided and selective attention. It offers a way of developing specific models of resource allocation in situations where more detailed investigations enable resources to be identified. Finally, Norman and Bobrow do not deny that resources may not be an undifferentiated 'pool'. What they call 'structural interference' could still occur between tasks requiring use of the same resources even if the resources available in total, relative to those demanded by the two tasks, are large.

## C  Summary and conclusions

We have illustrated two major aspects of attention: selectivity and capacity. Studies within these areas are numerous, and there have been a variety of theoretical positions. There is little doubt that Norman and Bobrow raise problems of interpretation for many of these studies, and offer a useful framework for the development of detailed theories of specific situations. It is also clear that in order to understand attention, it is necessary to understand the precise way in which the particular tasks being monitored are carried out. It is difficult, perhaps impossible, to explain or predict the ranges of performance on two tasks unless the resources used by each of them are known, and that is a tall order. Of course, if this is impossible, it will not prevent progress as developments like the Norman–Bobrow account prove. But it does not have the satisfying feel of a detailed process model.

Some investigators have used very simple stimuli, such as pure tones, possibly on the assumption that the underlying processes will be fairly simple (e.g. Moray 1969); it is possible that some success may be forthcoming through that strategy. However, the interest in attention is much broader than that. Putting it boldly, division of attention in the broadest sense means the division of labour among all usable processing resources, which rest upon an understanding of what those resources *are*; the solution to that problem is a major brief of cognitive science! Similarly, if effort is the allocation of resources, then to know what effort *does* in a wide range of cases requires that we know what the resources *are* again. Of course, cognitive psychologists (and cognitive scientists in general) are trying to meet this objective. We may look forward to a greater refinement in theories of attention as the processing details of families of tasks become better known.

On the positive side, a great deal has been learned about the nature of selectivity in the *natural history* fashion. Furthermore, studies of effort have the valuable effect of reminding us that the processing system is *biological*, and that attending is intrinsically linked to the general physiological state of the organism. This is extremely important, because, while information-flow models may be good for depicting the programmatic elements of how a task is performed, they have not been related convincingly to bodily function.

# 5 Memory 1 : Preliminary aspects

The involvement of memory in the processing systems described up to now is fairly obvious. The assemblies of procedures for pattern recognition are part of memory, for example. It may sound a little strange to call such things memory, but it is not: in the case of alphabetic characters, for example, the shapes have to be learned and remembered at some stage. The reality of this is easily tested by trying to learn a new alphabet, such as the Islamic or Cyrillic. Furthermore, we have encountered examples of temporary storage, for instance with echoic and iconic memory. Over the next few chapters, we shall develop the notion of memory considerably, but some warnings are in order. While memory is ubiquitous in processing, even a simple act like understanding and remembering a straightforward instruction relies upon numerous processes which fall under the headings of memory research. Suppose, for example, someone tells you 'Don't forget to go to the bank as soon as possible'. A very incomplete list of some of the things which doing this entails illustrates something of the range of memory phenomena:

1   Understand the sentence. For instance, think about the phrase '. . . as soon as possible'. As a mobile person, this could literally mean *right now*; but as it is *understood*, it means something like 'at your earliest convenience'. To know this, the language processing system has to have access to many things in memory: social conventions, ways in which you normally deal with such requests, and so on. Yet access is so rapid that the fact that it happens will go unnoticed unless there are problems.

   Understanding the sentence also requires that the pattern of sounds are matched against recognition procedures, and that words are recognized and meaning accessed.

2   Remember the instruction. The instruction itself has to be stored in memory but this does not mean just the sound of the utterance. It is *at least* the meaning of what was said, and aspects of the context in which it occurred. For instance, if it was your girlfriend who said it, then you will almost certainly remember that she said it, roughly when she said it, and so on. Such contextual coding poses enormous problems for realistic theories of memory.

3   Retrieve the utterance (or the significance of it) at some suitable point during the day. Either something may remind you, or you may automatically remember it at some point. This process is somewhat mysterious too. You may even forget. How does forgetting occur?

4   If you do not forget, and carry out the sequence of actions necessary in order to go to the bank, you do not have to plan everything from scratch. You have done it before, so you retrieve the appropriate plans from memory. What are these plans? How are they retrieved?

Memory crops up everywhere. Having illustrated memory phenomena around a particular example, it is also appropriate to illustrate some of the alarming but fascinating varieties of activities which constitute acts of remembering. It is advisable to try each activity:

1   *What was the registration number of Isaac Newton's car?*
The answer comes rapidly: he could not have had a car. Now think about the process which could lead to such an answer. Somehow, when a request is made to memory, the entailments of the request must be understood very rapidly, so search is not undertaken.

2   *How many names for flowers do you know? Give a figure.*
Most people can pull a figure out of the air. In fact, figures are given for far more serious questions than this on the basis of global assessments of what is in memory. The answers are often very inaccurate, and frequently underestimate what you *do* know.

3   *Make a list of all the flowers you know of.*
This is easy to begin with and then gets difficult. Even after an hour the chances are that you will still be able to think of others. The total will probably exceed the estimate given in 2 if you keep going. Furthermore, you will find yourself posing new questions, like Do I know any African/Indian/etc. flowers?

What did I see last time at the Botanic Gardens? In other words, the task becomes one of finding *sources* of information about flowers which you may know of.

4  *What were you doing on the first Tuesday of November three years ago at 10 a.m.?*

This one sounds difficult, but most people can come up with an answer. However, there is much inference-making. You may, for example, have been at school, and on Tuesday mornings you may have had a maths class. Specific details may even become available. But are they *true*?

5  *Read the following sequence once, and then repeat it with your eyes closed: AZRPDLSZBNTV.*

It is impossible, but QNRVLS is quite possible. It seems to be only possible to immediately recall only a few individual letters.

6  *Read the following and then repeat it with your eyes closed: Mary went into the office and operated the faulty word processor.*

It is possible to immediately recall many words provided that they make sense.

7  *Which of the following words have appeared in this book up to now: cognition, underestimate, yclept, and, uranium?*

Are they all remembered in the same way? Can you remember where you *saw* the ones you said 'yes' to. In all probability, you can with *cognition*, but not with *underestimate*.

8  *Can you remember how to draw a circle? Draw one.*

Although you have a motor program in memory, you do not have access to it from a verbal point of view. Try describing how to draw a circle. Some memories are verbally accessible and some are not.

The complete study of memory is so intertwined with questions of general processing that it is necessary to divide the field. One of the earliest efforts to do this was made by Ebbinghaus (1885). He argued that memory could be investigated separately from other cognitive processes, and this view has had a considerable influence on the techniques used in the study of memory. His approach was to 'decouple' memory from the rest of cognition by using meaningless materials, requiring subjects to learn and retrieve such things as nonsense syllables (XOB, for example – a consonant-vowel-consonant trigram), so that the memory process would not be contaminated by those of understanding. Later research in this tradition used lists of unrelated words. There is an alternative tradition, which is to treat the cognitive system, including memory, as a whole – a tradition exemplified by the work of Frederick Bartlett (1932). This approach maintains that memory has evolved for biologically relevant purposes, and should be studied using materials normally important in human life, such as descriptions of things, discourse, visual scenes and the like. The approach stresses that problem-solving and understanding are intertwined with memory, which indeed they are. In practice, both approaches have much to offer, and by far the greatest advances in measurement technique and experimental control came from the Ebbinghaus tradition.

In this chapter and the next, we shall explore work from each of these traditions; in this chapter a rather mixed bag of topics is presented. We begin with a very general overview of some mainstream memory research, and then move on to the picture of the memory system which emerged as a result of early ideas on information processing. We then emphasize a particular aspect of the memory system, called short-term/working memory, which is of central importance to the way much cognitive processing is currently explained. Among the points throughout is the way in which interpretation (sometimes called 'encoding') relates to memory. This will be a major issue when we turn to the Bartlett tradition in chapter 6.

## A   Some basic aspects of memory and measurement techniques

In this first section, some of the more elementary aspects of memory will be discussed. The gap between the examples of the intricacies and variety of memory given above, and the work described, will be notable. Yet it is with issues such as those outlined below that the modern study of memory began, and it is through such studies that many elegant research methods were devised. All of the studies are in the Ebbinghaus tradition and, in most cases, use sets of relatively unrelated words as materials.

### 1  Phases of memory and relationships to techniques

Broadly speaking, memory processes may be broken down into three groups of operations. First of all, much of what is in memory is learned. The process of getting information into memory is called *the learning phase*, or *acquisition*, or *encoding*. What gets into memory is termed *stored*, so storage is the second stage. The third stage is termed *retrieval*: getting what is stored back out again. There are, of course, many tasks of retrieval with very different characteristics. Suppose that you have learned a list of words and someone wishes to test your memory. You may be asked to recall the words; perhaps you have to recall them in the order in which you were given them (so-called *serial recall*), or perhaps you just have to recall them in any order (so-called *free recall*). Alternatively, the experimenter may present you with a new set of words, and ask you to *recognize* which words had been presented, ticking the ones you had seen, and putting a cross by the ones you had not. Somewhere between recognition and recall lies *cued recall*: you may be given the first letters of some of the words, and then asked to say what they were, for example; or if you are expected to remember sentences, you may be given a word or phrase to initiate retrieval of the appropriate sentence.

These methods exemplify the principal retrieval tasks which are available in the study of memory. It must be appreciated that retrieval tasks provide the *only means* of deciding what the subject has stored as a result of learning something. Theories of what is stored are always tested through the results of retrieval tasks. However, it was discovered long ago that what can be retrieved seems to depend upon the particular retrieval task used. For instance, in terms of percentages correct, recall scores are almost always inferior to recognition scores, even under the same conditions of acquisition (e.g. Postman and Ran 1957). One might be tempted to draw different conclusions about how much information is stored following acquisition, depending upon which retrieval task was used, but this would be very naïve.

Tulving (1968) provides useful labels for discussing why it is that a word which can be recognized might not be recalled: he suggests that such a word is *available* in memory (i.e. is 'in store') but is not *accessible* through recall procedures. Kintsch (1970) and Anderson and Bower (1972) sought to explain this distinction by supposing that while recall involves two information-processing stages, recognition involves only one. Consider Kintsch's model. He proposes that when asked to recall words which have been presented, at the first stage a *search* of memory is implemented. This amounts to finding the items from the list among all the other things in memory. Once an item of some sort has been found, it then has to be *checked* to decide whether or not it was actually on the list. This process of checking, according to Kintsch, is the only process necessary for recognition memory. So one might say, on this formulation, that recall is search plus recognition. Kintsch assumes that in a recall test subjects typically try to use the 'meaning' of the words to assist search, but that this results in items which are similar to list items being retrieved. So a subject will be confused as to what is and is not a list item, and may reject items which *are* list items as not being list items. Kintsch argues that when subjects are expecting a recognition test, they do not bother to use the 'meaning' of words in remembering them. So there is less to be confused about, and higher scores will result under the appropriate circumstances.

Parenthetically, it is worth noting that the recognition process (or stage) can be looked upon as analogous to signal detection (chapter 2). Kintsch, among others, has suggested that when items are encountered in memory tests, they gain in familiarity. Now imagine a recognition test item with high familiarity. A subject might set a criterion value on familiarity, and if the item exceeds the criterion, class it as an 'old' item (thus recognizing it). In contrast, an item not in the original list should have low familiarity. The attraction of such a theory is that it brings in judgemental criteria, rather than making recognition an all-or-none thing.

## 2 Some phenomena of acquisition

The whole issue of what happens to representations of stimuli when they are registered in memory will be a major theme in both this chapter and the next, and will ultimately take the form of asking about the nature of understanding. In this section, we will just consider a handful of preliminary but very important phenomena.

Consider what you might do if you are told that your task is to remember a list of, say, twenty unrelated words. If the words are presented one at a time, you may simply *say* them to yourself. This is a relatively low-level activity and, depending on the physical conditions under which the stimuli are presented, there is a whole range of more elaborate things which are possible, and each has its own influence on subsequent memory performance.

Curiously, the procedures which improve memory performance

effectively require complicating the stimulus in some way. In one experiment, Mandler (1967) presented subjects with a hundred cards, on each of which a word was printed. They were then instructed to *sort* the words into conceptual categories, by piling up cards of a particular category in the same stack. Numbers of categories varied up to about seven. Subjects had to invent their own bases for categorization, and repeat the sort procedure until they had reached a consistent categorization. After that, the subjects were asked to recall as many of the words as possible.

Mandler made a number of interesting discoveries using this procedure. First of all, it made no difference whether the subjects who sorted knew that a memory test was coming up or did not know. Both groups on this contrast performed equally well. So it is the activity which the subjects perform at encoding which determines memory performance, and not mere intention to learn. To make a difference to memory, intending to learn would have to cause the subject to do something at the acquisition phase. The force of this generalization will become apparent later on. Secondly, in one experiment, Mandler ran a control group who were told that they had to learn the materials, but were not given categorization instructions. Instead, they simply saw the materials for the same length of time as the categorization groups, but did not sort the cards. This group performed more *poorly*: again, it is the activity at encoding, and not the intent to learn, which matters.

Further evidence for the importance of categorization comes from the fact that the greater the number of categories which subjects used, in the sorting condition, the better the recall performance. Also, the larger the category size (i.e. number of cards in a pile), the smaller the percentage of words recalled from that category. These two facts suggest that it is establishing distinctive properties of stimuli which is the important factor.

There are other studies which show powerful effects of encoding activity on subsequent memory performance. Among the best demonstrations are those which are the basis of mnemonic systems. There is a simple way of learning a list of ten words in strict serial order in one go (for instance, Hunter 1964; Miller, Galanter and Pribram 1960). First, one has to know the following rhyme:

- One is a bun, Two is a shoe, Three is a tree, Four is a door, Five is a hive, Six is sticks, Seven is heaven, Eight is a gate, Nine is wine, Ten is a hen.

Then as the first word in the list is encountered ('fire', say), the trick is to relate fire to bun. One way is to imagine a bun toasting in front of a fire, for instance. And so one proceeds, making a relationship with each until one reaches 'hen'. To *recall*, one begins with 'one is a bun', and from this, 'fire' is retrieved, and so on. Furthermore, with this system, serial order is built in. One could say what item *nine* was, for instance. Readers are advised to try it.

Similar results can be obtained using a rather different procedure called paired-associate learning. With this procedure, subjects see two words (or nonsense syllables) at a time and at the retrieval phase are presented with the first word, and have to provide the second. This is an interesting paradigm, and came into being because of the theory of associationism, in which the conditions under which two ideas are related to one another were a primary focus of interest. Consider a pair like COW–TREE. They are not essentially related. However, it is possible to actively invent a relationship, for instance, imagine a cow rubbing itself on a tree. The use of such relational efforts results in superior cued recall of the associate (e.g. Bower 1972). In this case, as in the mnemonic rhyme case, one is using information.

These three examples show some of the things which subjects are able to do with materials under the appropriate circumstances. Of course, if the stimulus materials are nonsense syllables, none of these would be readily usable, and yet even nonsense syllables are amenable to interpretation. XOB is a bit like YOB, for instance. Where interpretation of this sort is not possible, learning by *rote* can still take place, but it is a very slow process, and even there it is likely that subjects develop peculiar interpretations, reading meanings into the items. With words, especially related words, encoding becomes easier. Apart from using imagery, it may be possible to weave a narrative around a list of apparently unrelated words, if the conditions of testing allow it.

One might ask *why* these procedures result in improved performance. One possible explanation is that organization aids retrieval, perhaps by binding the stimulus items to readily available schemes. For instance, once the rhyme is retrieved in the 'one is a bun, two a shoe' case, the remainder will follow. It follows because the items have been related to the rhyme by the formulation of distinctive connexions.

## 3 Forgetting

Material in memory which can be retrieved at time t but cannot be retrieved some time after time t is said to be forgotten; but, of course, the assessment of what is forgotten is entirely dependent upon the means of assessing what cannot be retrieved. In fact, apparent forgetting could result from several rather different phenomena. For instance, what was previously in store may disappear in some way, or may simply become inaccessible for some reason. As it stands, there is no real evidence that anything which is stored in long-term memory is ever actually deleted. On the other hand, short-term storage of things, for instance the products of parts of calculations undertaken when doing arithmetic, does appear to be forgotten.

The classical theories of forgetting are somewhat global, attributing retrieval failure either to trace decay or to interference. Broadly speaking, trace decay means that the memory code degenerates over time, while interference means that it becomes impossible to retrieve the appropriate data because of other entries in memory which are similar (but different) and are perhaps stronger. Thus interference theories attribute forgetting to acts of information-processing. Short of suspended animation, it is difficult to test the idea of spontaneous decay. However, there have been experiments in which subjects have been tested after a period of sleep (reduced information-processing) and after normal waking periods of the same duration. Such studies show considerably more forgetting to have taken place after a waking period (e.g. Barret and Ekstrand 1972), suggesting that interference is a primary source of forgetting, but they cannot rule out decay.

Interference is well known as an agent in forgetting, and can be found in two basic varieties: retroactive and proactive. In the retroactive case, it is material learned *after* the test material which reduces performance. For example, if subjects learn a list, LIST 1, consisting of paired associates $A_1$–$B_1$, $A_2$–$B_2$, etc., and then learn a list with the *same* first terms but different second terms, $A_1$–$C_1$, $A_1$–$C_2$, etc., then subsequent performance at remembering the first list is substantially reduced (e.g. Webb 1917). McGeoch (1932) argued that the problem was one of response competition: the new response becomes available at recall, and thus *competes* with the other response. Melton and Irwin (1940) suggested that response competition was not the only thing which produced poor responding and that the original associations were *reduced in strength*. They termed this *unlearning*. To test this contention, they gave subjects a fixed amount of practice on an initial list, and gave subgroups varied amounts of practice on the second list. To estimate competition, they scored the number of *intrusions* from the second list which were given as responses to the first list. Although this increased a little with practice on the second list, with extended practice on the second list (more than ten trials) it dropped off. So while retroactive interference (RI) increased, intrusions, an index of competition, dropped off. They attributed the difference to *unlearning*.

Proactive interference (PI) takes place when previously learned materials depress the learning of new material. The importance of PI was made clear by Underwood (1957), who analysed percentage recall figures from a number of previously reported studies as a function of the number of previous lists which subjects had learned. The greater the number of previous similar lists, the smaller the amount of recall on the current list.

A great deal of work has been carried out on interference theories, and an excellent review is given by Baddeley (1976). Before leaving the topic, however, a comment is in order. Most of the studies on interference require subjects to remember not just words of nonsense syllables, but to be able to remember which *list* they belonged to. In other words, it is the items in context which have to be retrieved. In these circumstances, it is relatively easy to show RI and PI effects. However, memory is much broader than that: what about visual memory, or memory for facts (such as Paris is the capital of France). As Tulving (1972) has pointed out, it may be sensible to draw a distinction between *episodic* memory – memory for personal episodes (like remembering the act of learning list 1 or list 2, or what you had for breakfast) and *semantic* memory (memory for facts which have no personal tags). So far, there is no real evidence that semantic memory is susceptible to the same kinds of interference.

## B  The structure of memory: long- and short-term stores

Most of what has been described briefly above was work within the behaviourist tradition, and so had very little to say about information-processing mechanisms. During the 1950s, with the growth of interest in information-processing, a considerable shift of interest began and researchers started to look at the idea that there were functionally distinct processing mechanisms associated with different classes of memory phenomena.

One intuitively appealing account of memory posits two rather different *types* of memory, usually called short-term store (STS) and long-term store (LTS). For many years it has been known that if people are presented with short strings of unrelated items, such as letter strings or digit strings, then the longest string they are likely to be able to repeat correctly and immediately is about seven items. Indeed, in his famous review paper, Miller (1956) termed this 'the magic number seven, plus or minus two'. It is as though we can hold just about seven items as a block to repeat back. However, without study or repeated presentation, it is unlikely that the string could be retrieved after more than a few seconds.

Observations such as this suggest that a contrast might be drawn between STS and LTS. STS seems to be of limited capacity, LTS of effectively infinite capacity. Furthermore, to keep something in STS, it is most people's impression that they *rehearse* the sequence mentally (or even overtly); if they do not, they tend to forget it. In contrast, what is in LTS just seems to be there and no conscious attention seems necessary to keep it there. Indeed, William James (1890) called short- and long-term memory *primary* and *secondary* memory, and allied STS to a consciousness. This conscious aspect of STS seems to be a very good reason for supposing STS and LTS to be rather different sorts of store. But how should the difference be characterized? Traditional S–R psychology was little concerned with the distinction, but from the mid-1950s, investigations were aimed rather directly at examining it, and it became a central theme in information-processing psychology since it appeared to be a possible structural distinction. Perhaps the two kinds of memory phenomena were associated with different types of *stores* in the brain. To make such a claim, it is necessary to look at the evidence which indicates radically different properties.

## 1 Evidence cited for the two-store hypothesis

Brown (1958) and Peterson and Peterson (1959) quite independently presented evidence for what they viewed as a rapid 'decay' of information in STS. Their techniques were very simple: they

presented short sequences of items (three words, three consonants, three consonant-vowel-consonant trigrams, etc.) *once*
only, and found out how quickly they were forgotten. If rehearsal
is used, it is clear that subjects would be able to 'remember' them
for a very long time. To prevent rehearsal, they required subjects
to carry out a task of counting backwards by threes from some
arbitrary high number during the retention interval. Retention
intervals varied between three and eighteen seconds. Forgetting
was very rapid indeed. After only eighteen seconds, the chance of
correct recall was only 10 per cent; after only *three* seconds, the
chance had already dropped to 50 per cent! A typical decay
function is shown in figure 5-1. Both Brown and the Petersons
claimed that unrehearsed information *decays* rapidly in STS.

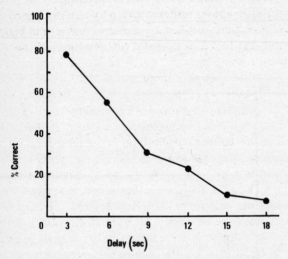

*Figure 5-1.* The short-term forgetting function obtained by Peterson and Peterson
(1959).

In contrast, information in LTS is 'lost' by *interference*. The
Petersons showed that the similarity of material in the rehearsal-
prevention task to the to-be-remembered material did not alter the
shape of the forgetting function, and claimed that interference was
not the cause of forgetting in STS. STS and LTS were therefore
thought of as being differentiable in terms of the mechanisms of
forgetting. Later evidence brought this assumption into question
(e.g. Waugh and Norman 1965) but by then, other evidence and

considerations had reinforced the utility of the STS/LTS distinction.

During the 1960s, a number of results emerged which supported the idea that short-term and long-term memory reflect quite different things. One important and general finding comes directly from the study of how well people remember lists of words which exceed memory span. Suppose you are given thirty words to remember, presented one at a time at a fixed rate. You only hear the string once, and are asked to recall it, in any order you like (termed *free recall*). It is most unlikely that all of the words will be recalled, no matter how long you have as a recall period. But what is forgotten is not just a random subset of the words: it depends upon how recently the words occurred in the list – the so-called *serial position effect*.

An illustrative experiment in the literature may be found in Murdock (1962), among others, and a schematic figure of the typical results obtained in such experiments is shown in figure 5-2. Such a curve has two characteristic features. First of all, on the

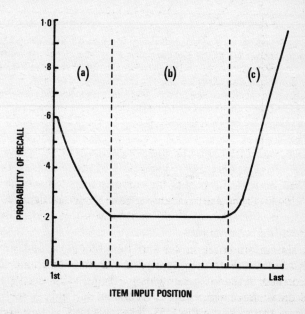

*Figure 5-2.* A schematic serial position curve. The vertical axis is the probability of recall, the horizontal is item input position, 'first' being the first item in the list, and 'last' the most recent. Region (a) is termed the *primacy effect* and region (c) the *recency effect.* For long lists, region (b) becomes flat, as shown.

extreme left, recall for the very first and sometimes the second item to be presented is better than the flat middle section. Second, after a relatively flat middle section, where the likelihood of recall is at its lowest, the last few items to be presented show an increase in likelihood of recall with serial position. The most recent item usually has a probability of recall approaching unity in a well-conducted experiment.

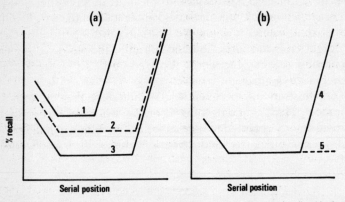

*Figure 5-3*. Schematic summaries of main serial position effects described in the text. Figure (a) shows two things; that the shape of the recency effect is unaffected by list length (1 versus 2 and 3), and that a high input rate (3) produces a lower central region than does a slow input rate (2), but the recency effect is not influenced by this variable. Figure (b) contrasts lists learned and then recalled with no intervening interference with lists learned and then recalled following an interference task. The recency effect disappears in the latter case (5 versus 4).

Let us concentrate on the right-hand part of the curve, the so-called *recency effect*. First, regardless of the lengths of the list which was learned, this part of the curve appears to have the same shape – the recency effect is constant, as shown in figure 5-3(a). This pattern of results was established by Murdock (1962) and has been replicated many times.

In a similar study, Postman and Phillips (1965) had subjects learn lists of words, but instead of asking for immediate recall, required them to count backwards by threes for a short period. The recency effect disappeared, as shown in figure 5-3(b). The conclusion from this is that the recency effect is the result of drawing upon short-term memory. By preventing rehearsal, the short-term memory trace decays, and so the recency effect vanishes. This view suggests a model of free recall for lists in which new stimuli are still represented in short-term memory, while old ones are only retained in long-term memory. The corollary is that the serial position curve is the outcome of searching in two memory stores.

Just as the STM component may be manipulated experimentally without altering the LTM component (the rest of the curve), so the LTM component can be manipulated without affecting the STM component. Murdock (1962) showed that stimuli presented at a slow rate (one per two seconds) produced higher recall from the flat part of the curve than stimuli presented more rapidly (one per second). On the other hand, the shape of the recency component was unaffected (figure 5-3(a)).

Thus the serial position curve takes its form because items can be recalled in one of two ways – either from short-term or long-term memory. The serial position curve thus constitutes a further piece of evidence for the existence of two separate memory systems.

A somewhat different approach supporting the two-systems notion comes from observations about the nature of coding in memory. If STM and LTM could be differentiated in terms of the way items are stored, then the distinction would be further reinforced. In carrying out studies of memory span for consonant sequences, Conrad (1964) observed that errors often occurred when the letters presented sounded similar (e.g. T,V,D,P,G etc.), even if they were presented *visually*. Similar patterns of error do not occur for visually similar stimuli. His results and subsequent analyses suggest that subjects were translating the letters from their visual form into an 'articulatory' form and that a main form of data storage in STS may well be articulatory.

Baddeley (1966) extended this observation, and tried to contrast it with coding forms in LTS. He reasoned that the main coding characteristic of LTS would be *semantic* for verbal materials: that is, items would be encoded in terms of their *meaning*. His experiment was designed to test the idea that this short-term storage would be more susceptible to inference effects of an acoustic kind, while long-term storage would be susceptible to semantic interference. His materials consisted of four types of list:

   (i)   Acoustically similar: man, mad, map ... etc.
  (ii)   Control, acoustically dissimilar: pen, day, rig ... etc.
 (iii)   Semantically similar: huge, big, great ... etc.
 (iv)   Control, semantically dissimilar: foul, deep, old ... etc.

Subjects were presented with lists of ten words of these types. Four presentations were given, and after each one was a brief twenty-second digit span task, followed by an invitation to recall. After this, a final invitation to recall was given twenty minutes later. In each case, all of the words were available to the subjects – their task was to say what was the *correct order*. Baddeley's results are shown in figure 5-4.

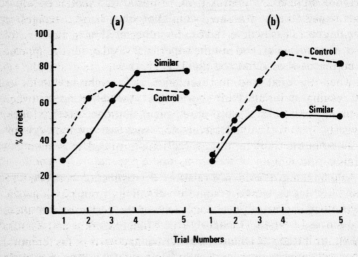

*Figure 5-4.* The influence of (a) acoustic similarity and (b) semantic similarity on memory for word order. (*From Baddeley 1966.*)

Acoustic similarity had no reliable effect on performance. However, similarity of meaning had an increasing effect as the number of trials increased, and was maintained on the twenty-minute retest. The semantic similarity of the items interfered with the recall of the order of the items – an effect which grew larger the more the materials were being recalled from the (hypothetical) long-term memory store. It appears, therefore, that while short-term retention of unrelated words is primarily articulatory in form, retention in longer-term storage is primarily semantic in nature. The results of this study provide more evidence for the view that there are two types of memory.

It seems a far cry from the lists of words of the Ebbinghaus tradition to the way in which intelligible discourse is retained. Yet Jacqueline Sachs (1967) carried out an interesting experiment which is compatible in certain ways with the observations made above. She had subjects listen to tape-recorded passages taken from factual articles. From time to time, the subjects were interrupted and shown a test sentence. They were asked to judge whether each test sentence was identical to one which they had heard in the passage, or different. 'Different' sentences were produced in a number of ways. Simple changes of word order, such as changes from active to passive voice, which preserved meaning were easily confused by subjects with sentences which had actually been presented. On the other hand, changes in *meaning* were easily detected by the subjects. Thus in memory for discourse, meaning, and not the superficial word ordering, appears to be the basis of LTM coding. This effect was greatest if the lag between the text and test sentences was eighty syllables of intervening material. With shorter lags, the difference between meaning and surface word-order manipulations was less. This suggests that surface characteristics, such as word order, are retained in the short-term, but that long-term coding is mainly in terms of meaning.

As a final line of evidence relating to a distinction between STS and LTS, let us consider some observations from physiological psychology and neurophysiology. One of the best known of these is the case of 'H.M.' (Milner 1970; Milner, Corkin and Teuber 1968). At the age of twenty-eight, H.M. had parts of his temporal lobe and hippocampus surgically removed (in an operation no longer used) in an attempt to control his epilepsy. The tragic result was that H.M. was left with a significant and substantial deficit in the ability to form new long-term memories. He could be introduced to the same person on several occasions, and yet be unable to recollect meeting the person before, even after relatively short time intervals. His case was frequently cited as supporting an account of memory in which STS was responsible for the essentially temporary storage of information for *transfer* to LTS. In H.M., transfer was not occurring.

Although H.M. seems to be the only patient to have suffered these particular effects of surgery, other patients show similar symptoms. In particular, there is a relatively large number of patients with Korsakoff's syndrome. This disease is usually caused by years of chronic alcoholism and poor nutrition, and appears to be mediated through the vitamin B metabolism, which is important to the hippocampus. The upshot is a cluster of complex symptoms, including a loss of ability to form new long-term memories.

Baddeley and Warrington (1970) carried out a number of memory tests on such patients, including one in which they studied their efficiency at immediate recall on ten-word lists. The resulting serial position curves showed a normal recency effect, but a substantial deficit over other parts of the function. Clearly, one interpretation of these curves is that information is not transferred from STS to LTS, supporting the dual-store-transfer theory.

Despite this apparent support, closer scrutiny of the performance abilities of both H.M. and the Korsakoff patients presents a much more problematic picture. In the first place, although H.M. had difficulty in learning certain things, there were others which he could learn. For instance, he showed steady improvement on perceptual-motor tasks, like moving through a finger maze, even though he could not remember practising. Similarly, Korsakoff patients could learn perceptual-motor tasks (Brooks and Baddeley 1976). Even more significant, perhaps, is the fact that although the Korsakoff patients performed poorly in Baddeley and Warrington's memory test, they tended to report a number of items as being in *current* lists which had in fact been presented on a *previous* occasion. These results suggest that memory 'transfer' had occurred, but that it was simply not organized appropriately for retrieval (e.g. Baddeley and Warrington 1973).

There are thus severe problems with the idea that information is strictly transferred from STS to LTS. Another clinical study makes the problem even more apparent. Warrington and Shallice (1969) reported a series of studies with a patient dubbed 'K.F.', who through injury had an unusual memory disorder. K.F. could recall nine out of ten paired-associates after three trials and a six-hour delay; and readily learn many new verbal and pictorial materials. Yet K.F. appeared to have an STM capacity of only *one* item! In a digit-span test, he could recall only two items; often only one. In serial position analyses, he showed virtually no recency effect. This patient and others like him (Saffran and Martin 1975) produce results which are absolutely inconsistent with the notion of transfer from STS to LTS, although STS and LTS appear to be functionally distinguished if K.F. and the amnesics are taken into account (Warrington and Shallice 1969).

## 2 The duplex theory and its problems

The basic assumptions underlying the duplex theory are schematized in figure 5-5. For verbal material, after pattern recognition in which letters, words, or numerals are identified, a small number of items can be held in a short-term store. Keeping them there depends largely upon rehearsal, and the code in which they are maintained is articulatory. Transfer from STS to LTS occurs, and its efficiency depends upon the length of time the material is in the short-term store.

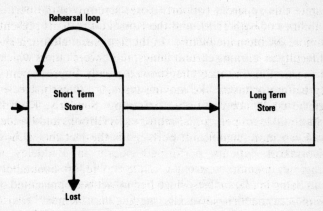

*Figure 5-5.*  The essential elements of the duplex model. The short-term store precedes the long-term in the input chain; if information is not rehearsed in STS it decays and becomes 'lost'.

These assumptions typify the kind of thinking behind what we will call the Duplex Theory. Of course, the amount of research on STS and LTS during the 1960s and early 1970s was substantial, and many psychologists did not accept all of the assumptions uniformly, but our characterization gives the general flavour of things. A more substantial account of the duplex theory, which is generally considered the classic formulation of the position, is given by Atkinson and Shiffrin (1967). For a similar view see Waugh and Norman (1965). In the basic formulation, we see a strategy of attempting to identify functionally separate mechanisms and stage-by-stage process as an explanation of memory performance.

While such a strategy typifies the approach which was taken in information-processing psychology, it is inadequate in many ways. In this section we shall concentrate on two, beginning with *scope*. One main characteristic of most experiments carried out in the framework of this theoretical effort was a great reliance upon unrelated verbal material, typically unrelated words, random numbers, random letters, or nonsense syllables. By concentrating on verbal materials, which are experimentally convenient, some of the results found may well be restricted entirely to verbal materials – take, for instance, the finding that STS uses articulatory codes. One might well ask what else one does to remember unrelated letters other than 'rehearse' them using an articulatory code, especially since we normally use letters as 'verbal' materials. What about the retention of visual scenes, of motor movements such as learning to move one's feet in a particular way in dancing? Is articulatory coding important there too? There is, therefore, a question of the process underlying other types of memory; there is also the problem of using unrelated materials. It has long been known that a person can remember many more than seven words if they form a sentence. Why? Whatever the reason, it is quite apparent that the kinds of material typically used in connexion with studies of the STS/LTS distinction focuses upon what is an artificial aspect of memory, or at least a very small part of typical memory activity.

Of course, it would be wrong to suppose that these other things have not been studied. There have been studies of visual memory, motor memory, and memory for meaningful materials. However, to a large extent, these studies are difficult to relate in any very great detail to the propositions of the duplex theory. Later, we shall consider some of these connexions.

Scope difficulties go even further than this. Many researchers were interested in the role short-term memory might play in a whole range of information-processing tasks – not just memory tasks, but in problem-solving, thinking, understanding language, and in other aspects of skilled performance. The verbally biased characterization of STS found in the duplex model was simply not sufficient to meet these needs.

Apart from scope, a second set of difficulties revolves around the arguments used to build up the duplex theory itself. Type of coding presents a problem. The original claim was that coding in STS was articulatory or acoustic, while in LTS it was semantic. However, there are studies which show acoustic coding in long-term memory, and semantic coding in short-term memory (Baddeley 1976). While such findings do not destroy the duplex model, they erode one of the pillars on which it stands. There have also been attempts to see whether the recency effect in serial position experiments depends upon acoustic or articulatory coding. There is some evidence for this, for instance, Shallice (1975) showed that when intrusion errors of recall occur in the recency component, they are sometimes associated with phonemically similar items. However, more investigators have failed to show such effects than have found them.

Finally, the work of Shallice and Warrington on patient K.F. rules out the role of an STS as the site from which information is transferred to LTS. While their work suggests that STS and LTS *are* separable systems, they do not represent two sequential stages in the acquisition of even verbal information.

A blow-by-blow account of the problems associated with the duplex theory is beyond the coverage of this book, and is not essential to what follows. The problems of scope associated with the theory are sufficient grounds to motivate a shift of emphasis towards broader issues. The framework offered by Craik and Lockhart, described below, leads the way towards a fuller consideration of memory in relation to information-processing in general.

## 3  Depth of processing and retention

In 1972, recognizing the discomfort many people felt with the duplex theory, Craik and Lockhart published a paper presenting an alternative way of thinking about long-term and short-term memory phenomena. Their suggestion was simple: memory should be viewed as an integral part of the whole information-processing system. Different tasks either demand or facilitate the treatment of stimulus materials in different ways by the entire system, and what is remembered depends upon how they are treated.

Specifically, Craik and Lockhart introduced the notion of *depth of processing*. The idea is that stimuli can be processed at different levels within the system. The shallowest levels relate to sensory analyses and pattern recognition. Deeper levels include stimulus identification and naming. The deepest levels include using knowledge to understand the meaning or significance of the stimuli. Imagine, for instance, that a list of ten words is used in a variety of tasks. Shallow processing would be used if the primary task were to count how many words contained the letter 'k', deeper processing would be used to check whether any of the words rhymed with a target word; and even deeper levels would be required for deciding whether any of the words were synonyms of a target word. There are many different ways in which a 'word stimulus' may be processed. Craik and Lockhart suggested that memory is a *trace of processing activities* carried out with respect to a given task and, further, that the traces of shallow processing are less durable, or less accessible, than the traces of deeper processing. This characterization addresses the problem of task description rather than structural architecture in memory. While it is important to identify structurally distinct 'units' in the brain, the point is that with the traditional duplex arguments, not enough is really known about how processing occurs on particular tasks to enable a satisfactory claim about structure to be made. Craik and Lockhart's view makes no structural assumptions.

Both before and after the paper was published, data were available that were consistent with the basic claim of the account. For instance, Craik and Tulving (1975) carried out a study in which people saw a number of words. The subjects were unaware of the fact that they were doing a memory experiment. Each group saw each word for 200 msec, but were asked to make different decisions about the words. One group decided whether the word was printed in capital letters, as quickly as possible. A second group decided whether the words rhymed with the word *weight*. The third decided whether each word fitted in the sentence frame 'He met a _____ in the street'. Each of these tasks was intended to use a different level of the memory.

After completion of the tasks, the subjects took part in a surprise recognition memory task. Subjects in the 'case' decision group correctly recognized only about 15 per cent of the words. Those in the rhyming group were correct about 50 per cent of the time, and the other group about 80 per cent. The *time* taken to decide whether a recognition item was one of the original words went up in proportion to the percentage correctly recognized, suggesting that the codes used for deeper tasks are more elaborate.

This result is typical of many which broadly conform to the depth-of-processing approach. Craik and Lockhart apply the argument to a broad range of phenomena, including those of divided attention experiments: for instance, the evidence for very rapid decay of unattended materials has usually been thought of as evidence for a short-term pre-attentive store. Craik and Lockhart suggest that the memory traces may simply be less durable because they have not been processed deeply. The same considerations apply to the short-term nature of short-term memory.

Rehearsing an articulatory code is not a very 'deep' level of processing. If digits can be processed more deeply, then long-term retention would become more likely. Typically, digits are *not* processed more deeply, but if they are, then retention *is* improved: this is discussed a little later.

The depth-of-processing framework is an attractive one, but makes the picture much more complicated, especially when additional necessary factors are considered. The most important of these involves the *spread of encoding*. With depth of processing, the idea is that processing can occur at different *levels* within a roughly sequential series of mechanisms, stretching from pattern recognition to using meaning. But think of carrying out any given task from the point of view of *resource deployment*. At any given *depth*, it may still be possible to deploy many or few processing resources. If one carries out complex encoding at one level, then memory retention may also be improved because a more complex code is produced (i.e. the 'trace' of processing will be more complex). By and large, it will be the case that shallow tasks will not really allow this: looking for upper or lower case words is a very simple process and it is difficult to see how it might be elaborated upon. In contrast, evaluating the meaning of words can be endlessly elaborated upon. Nevertheless, the potential for elaboration is presumably there, regardless of depth, provided the task requirements allow it.

The distinction between depth and spread looks reasonably clear, but some degree of caution must be exercised in accepting the good points of the story. First of all, depth and spread are not really independent dimensions of processing. As was the case with attention, to apply the Craik–Lockhart analysis one really needs to know precisely what kinds of things underlie the various tasks which bring about subsequent memories.

The Craik–Lockhart claim can be divided into several rather general assumptions:

(i)   Remembering is a function of processing because what is remembered is a trace of the activity of processing.

(ii)  Processing can be deep or shallow: deeper levels entail richer processing (or simply a greater number of processes) and are better remembered – the traces are more durable or accessible.

(iii) The concept of depth has to be supplemented by a concept of *spread* since at any given level it is possible that a greater or smaller number of processes may be used.

The problems with the account are obvious. It is difficult to obtain independent measures of depth, and of spread, so there is a very real danger of circularity. However, the value of the theory is that it forces rather different questions to be asked. In particular, it illustrates a clear need to specify exactly which processes are used in doing a particular task. It is simply not sufficient to think in terms of a subject trying to remember material, for a subject may remember different things with different degrees of efficiency because he carries out different kinds of processing operations in different settings.

Earlier on in this chapter, we drew a distinction between viewing memory as a subsystem which could be isolated, and viewing it as intrinsically bound up with other kinds of processing. In particular, the work on organization in memory clearly demonstrated that *how* the subject deals with the stimuli influences how much is remembered and how it is remembered. Craik and Lockhart's theory can be seen to bring this line of research into close contact with questions of the durability of memory traces, which is a key feature of the more structural duplex account. While many problems are far from being solved, two lines of attack (among others) have proven particularly useful. One is to look at general processing characteristics in relation to memory; this is discussed under the 'working memory' idea. The other is to study the detailed processing of input in relation to what is remembered in a particular situation. This has been studied widely and we shall look at memory for text (discourse) from this point of view in chapter 6.

## C  Working memory and grouping

The emphasis in the interpretation of short-term memory phenomena has transferred to a tendency to concentrate on looking on many aspects of memory as being functions of operations which are carried out on incoming data. While this does not really resolve any structural questions, it is obviously an important way to proceed. In this section we shall review some important generalizations about operations on incoming data, usually operations occurring in the context of memory and learning experiments. Regardless of the difficulties in interpreting the significance of STM, or of even defining it in any very clear way, the fact remains that early on in processing, limited-capacity operations are extremely important. Indeed, the picture which has emerged in recent years is one in which a limited-capacity processor which stores information only briefly is used to carry out coding operations on incoming material. This idea, which we shall term the 'working memory hypothesis', has a clear affinity to the STM/LTM model discussed above. However, it is not necessarily interpreted in the same way. Operations going on in working memory may be at various depths of processing, and so the probability of a durable memory trace may vary from task to task.

To begin with, we will consider some important data on learning which can be interpreted in terms of the working memory hypothesis. Then we will move on to more specific ideas which have been associated with the working memory concept.

## 1  Chunking of input and 'items' in STM

In his work on STM span, Miller (1956) concluded that the magic number was $7 + 2$ items. But then, what is an item? An item could be a letter, or a word. Indeed, if the words are related to one another, as they would be in a sentence, then the 'span' is vastly increased. It is obviously erroneous to think that what is meant by an item is clear.

From Miller onwards, a number of researchers have developed and used a concept known as *chunking*, in an attempt to clarify the meaning of an item, and so understand just what sort of capacity limit STM span indicates. Let us begin with Miller's original example, which concerns the retention of binary number strings. Try to remember the following string, and you will have a great deal of difficulty unless you know the trick:

001010110111000101011

With a little practice, one can easily learn to retain such sequences for short periods. The trick is first to learn the translation rule, which converts the binary digit code (0, 1) to an octal code (0, 1 ... 7). The translation code is as follows:

$000 = 0$; $001 = 1$; $010 = 2$; $011 = 3$; $100 = 4$; $101 = 5$; $110 = 6$; $111 = 7$;

Applying this rule to the original string of binary digits produces:

1　2　6　7　0　5　3

That is, it is *seven* digits only. Given enough time and practice, such a conversion can become quick and easy, as Miller (1956) reported.

The point of this demonstration is that what previously looked like twenty-one 'items' has been translated into only seven, which reduces the memory load to manageable proportions. The process has produced seven items, each of which can be unpacked into three items at recall. Each octal digit designates a *chunk*, consisting of three binary characters after unpacking. Finally, both chunking and unpacking use a rule which has first to be stored in LTM, but which can then be used on countless future occasions. The sections which follow will examine chunking in some detail. Miller's example seems quite artificial, but some theorists believe that chunking underlies much, if not all, learning behaviour (see, for example, Newell and Rosenboom 1982).

The range of possibilities for chunking is demonstrably enormous. Consider having to remember the following binary digit sequence:

0000011111

Would this best be accommodated by an octal conversion? Almost certainly not. This might best be remembered as 'five zeros, five ones'. Chunking has still occurred, but this time it depends upon the application of a Gestalt principle of grouping. Grouping of a different kind is evident in the following sequence:

4567123

Such chunking operations are much more natural than the one described by Miller in his illustration but are they really any different? Almost certainly not; in the case of the second example above, chunking depends upon a rule which is essentially arbitrary – the pairing of shapes of numbers within a sequence which we call ascending, and which at one time, in infancy, had to be learned.

These simple considerations suggest that there are two rather interesting sides to chunking: first, that it seems to be a process which gets around some short-term limit, and secondly, that it involves the interpretation of input through knowledge which is stored in long-term memory. The operation of working memory is conceived of as being an interpretation/chunking process, and will be invoked again and again throughout this book as we consider thinking, problem-solving, and language understanding.

Short-term memory limitations appear to be important only if interpretation and chunking are impossible. For instance, in one recent study, an investigation was carried out into 'skilled memory' (Chase and Ericsson 1982). In the memory literature, there are several well-documented cases of people who have apparently very large spans indeed (cf. Hunter 1968; Luria 1968). The mnemonists can remember tens of numbers for immediate recall, and we might well ask whether they are exceptions to the $7 + 2$ rule. Chase and Ericsson believe not. They report training a single subject over a period of two years (250 hours laboratory experience) on a 'digit span' task. Their subject, who began with an apparent span of about seven items, could report back no less than eighty after 215 hours of practice! This ability depended on a complex mnemonic system in which the subject associated number groups with athletic running times.

## 2  Grouping without meaning

Chase and Ericsson's subject made use of meaningful, or semantic, coding. Once the coding system was working efficiently, a single exposure to a digit display was enough to enable retention to occur. However, such strategies are not always used, and learning sometimes takes a considerable number of exposures. Nevertheless, grouping processes occur. Typical everyday examples of learning relatively meaningless sequences by rote include learning the alphabet as a child, learning new alphabets, learning the number sequence, and so on. There is also evidence that speeches may be learned by rote with little reference to meaning (Rubin 1977).

Muller (cf. Katona 1967), working at the turn of the century, noted that when subjects were attempting to learn sequences in fixed orders, they would tend to break up the material into groups. For instance, the sequence

3 6 2 5 9 4 7 3 6

might be broken up into:

(3 6 2) (5 9 4) (7 3 6)

One might say that the groups are sufficiently small to be separately manageable in short-term memory. There are several ways of determining the presence of such groups. One of the simplest is to have subjects rehearse the sequence out loud; this makes the groups recognizable through *pausing* and *clustering*, for instance:

3 6 2—5 9 4—7 3 6

Pause patterns can be induced by presenting items in pre-formed temporal groups (in the auditory modality), or pre-formed spatial groups (in vision). For instance, Wilkes (1975) presented subjects with twelve monosyllabic nouns, typed on cards to give a 3:3:3:3 spacing. During learning sessions, subjects read out these nouns, and Wilkes observed pausing at group boundaries. However, pause patterns also occur spontaneously – Wilkes, Lloyd and Simpson (1972) identified triplets as the most common, with doublets second, followed by quartets.

Such grouping facilitates short-term retention and recall, in that more material can be reported back correctly if it has been grouped by a subject. Furthermore, the best performance is usually found with groups of three or four (Wickelgren 1964; Ryan 1969). This is clearly less than memory span, however, and one must ask why. The effectiveness of three to four items in a group is found in other situations too. Consider the problem of copying strings of digits from one sheet of paper to another. Typically, people remember only a small group of digits, and write those down before going back to the source. Experimental work has demonstrated that these groups rarely exceed four items (Broadbent and Broadbent 1973). Why not seven? First note that span is defined as the length of strings which people will get right 50 per cent of time, and not recall perfectly. If groups exceeding three or four items were used, in a task such as copying, then there would be a substantial and undesirable chance of making an error. Groups of three or four guarantee short-term retention.

A number of studies show that the groupings used in a verbal learning task have a direct effect upon subsequent retrieval. As we have mentioned, Ryan (1969) found recall of sequences to be optimal if groups of three or four were used. Belmont and Butterfield (1971) demonstrated that the apparent increase in memory span during a child's development can be attributed to the failure of the youngest children to use a grouping strategy at rehearsal. If a grouping strategy is forced upon them, then span shows an apparent increase. It is also possible to show that experimental induced grouping patterns will lead to good long-term retention only if the groups used are kept *constant* (Winzenz 1972).

Much more direct relationships have been established between encoding groups and long-term memory and show that the groups seem to be present at retrieval, even after many years. The example we shall take is the alphabet, which for all of us was just an arbitrary string to be learned at one time in our lives. Other examples are discussed by Broadbent (1975).

Children often learn the alphabet as a pause- and intonation-defined structure, and certainly not as a uniform string. A typical grouping sequence might be:

(ABCD—EFG) (HIJK—LMNOP) (QRST) (UVW) (XYZ)

Readers may have a feel for their own 'groupings'. If, as an adult, one recites the alphabet very rapidly, it seems like a smooth flow, with no obvious signs of grouping. However, the presence of real groups may be revealed by other attempts to use the alphabet string. Suppose that you wish to look up a particular entry in the dictionary, say one beginning with R. You open the dictionary and find that you are at M. Which way do you turn the pages? To decide, you need to know whether R precedes or follows M, and sometimes such decisions are not automatic. Hamilton and Sanford (1978) carried out a laboratory analogue of this task, asking people to decide whether or not pairs of letters were close together in the alphabet. Decisions were slow and subjects reported 'running through' a few letters in their minds. For instance, given the pair PS, one subject reported imagining saying 'LMNOPQRS', and noticing that S followed P. Hamilton and Sanford showed that the number of 'items' in such reports was a linear predictor of reaction time, and that the process of running through seemed to account for most of the reaction-time variance in such a task.

The interpretation was as follows: first, the alphabet is learned as groups. Secondly, it is stored as a *motor program* for *saying* the alphabet. Thirdly, while it is possible to find which subprogram a particular letter sound is in, to retrieve order information, it is necessary to run through the program. On this view, the first letter of run-through should correspond to the group boundary. Subjects were therefore invited to indicate where they thought their group boundaries might be, which they did, and it was found that starting letters of run-through did correspond quite well with reported group boundaries.

Similar difficulties with order occur if subjects are asked to say which letter comes before a particular letter. For instance, what comes before 'U'? Again, run-through start point corresponds to group boundaries (Hamilton 1980). It appears, therefore, that even after many years, the alphabet is stored in memory in precisely the way it was learned, and that it is learned as groups of three of four items, which again appear as a 'working unit' in some sort of chunking operation. The particular patterns used do vary from person to person, however.

The work on grouping described in this section is quite clearly related to rehearsal, a process normally considered to be *articulatory*. In tasks where the grouping described above occurs, subjects typically use subvocal rehearsal as part of the learning process. Indeed, Baddeley and his co-workers (e.g. Baddeley, Thompson and Buchanan 1975) have offered a characterization of working memory as a kind of general-purpose computational area, used for coding and other computations, supplemented by an *articulatory rehearsal loop*. Baddeley, Thompson and Buchanan claim that the loop is limited not so much in the number of *words* but rather in the number of *syllables*, a fundamental unit of articulation. These researchers assess the limit of the loop being about one and a half second's worth of speech, which is about three words given the average complexity and length of words used in most span experiments. The articulatory loop hypothesis, as it has become known, sees the rehearsal loop as an independent means of holding information which is operated upon in working memory. Given the estimates of its capacity, as made by Baddeley, Thompson and Buchanan, it seems that this might well explain the natural tendency to group items into threes or fours in the kinds of studies discussed above. Of course, an account of this type does not describe the process by which the groups become represented in a way which is accessible in the long term.

## 3   Working memory and STM

When some stimulus event is presented to the subject for learning, the subject has the option of coding in various ways, from shallow phonological coding to deeper semantic coding. According to a general working memory hypothesis, it is in working memory that stimulus information is held while coding operations proceed. The idea of working memory is thus of a buffer which holds a small amount of data while they are being worked on. It is not *just* information which is to be remembered which is held there, however, but also data which are being mentally *manipulated*. A good example is working on arithmetic. If you add up two numbers in your head, say 436 + 543, you have to do two things: first, remember what the original numbers were and secondly add up each *column*, and remember the result. The more complicated the sum, the more you have to remember. If the sum is quite difficult, it may be necessary to *extend* working memory artificially, by using a pencil and paper. And of course, one does not wish to remember the details of all of this – short-term retention is quite adequate.

If there is a working memory (WM), then it would seem to have some of the properties of STM. The data in it are shortlived, and limited in quantity. Baddeley and Hitch (1974), proponents of the working memory idea, carried out a number of studies to establish how a notion like WM might relate to the earlier idea of STM.

Central to the idea of working memory is that because it holds temporary data generated during processing, there is actually *competition* between memory and processing itself. Working memory can be thought of as working *space* which may be flexibly divided between data storage and data manipulation. Baddeley and Hitch adopted a very simple strategy: they loaded STM by requiring subjects to remember some digits or letters, and then asked them to do tasks of reasoning or verbal learning. If reasoning or verbal learning involves data manipulation which competes for space with retaining the digits or letters, then this would be evidence for the WM notion, and would also imply a connexion, or possibly an equivalence, between WM and STM.

In one illustrative task, subjects were first given pre-loads of from one to six digits. They then had to check the truth or falsity of statements of the following form: A precedes B – BA (which is false); B is not followed by A – AB (which is true). This is a task of verbal reasoning. With one or two digits as a pre-load, there was little if any impairment of reasoning performance, either in terms of speed or accuracy of response. At six digits, however, there was a considerable decrement. Thus STM and WM are not *identical*, although it is possible that at full 'span', some of what is stored uses WM as well as STM.

Very similar results were obtained with other tasks, including memory load with a concurrent prose-reading task, and memory task, and memory load with a concurrent *list-learning* task. Once again, at high loads (six items), some degeneration of performance on the concurrent tasks was observed, but no dramatic effects. The list-learning task in particular was informative, in that a high load did not affect the recency component of the serial position curve for list recall. Note that this finding is quite embarrassing for the duplex theory. If STM is already full, then there should be no recency effect at all. In fact, partly as a result of this finding, Baddeley and Hitch (1976) carried out a study demonstrating that recency effects can be obtained in situations where it would be quite unreasonable to invoke STM as an explanation. Towards the end of a season of play, a rugby team were asked to remember as many of that season's fixtures as they could. More recent games were better remembered, thus producing a serial position curve. It is possible that recency has more than one origin, of course, but the results offer a clear warning against simplistic explanations.

The picture presented by working memory research, and by careful questioning of the original duplex hypothesis is thus complex. Present evidence makes Baddeley's theory very attractive: working memory is a limited capacity workspace which shares its resources between processing and storage. There is an articulatory loop which is used specifically for storage of verbal material in the short term. Full memory span may use both of these stores, and even LTM to a limited extent. A further question, not discussed here, is the possibility that there may be separable working memories for different *modalities*: one for verbal/acoustic material, one for spatial/visual material, and so on. In fact we shall see some evidence for this somewhat later on (chapter 14). The working memory hypothesis is exciting because it is clearly related to the questions of limited capacity discussed in chapter 4. However, in the author's view at least, to make the concept have any real content, it will be necessary to investigate it with respect to specific task settings which have some relation to tasks which people normally carry out (such as solving problems, learning skills, understanding language, and so on). Indeed, at present a number of investigators are taking this approach.

## D Overview

This chapter introduces many diverse issues and is intended as a starting point for the proper study of memory. From the general questions in section A, the chapter moved on to the duplex theory, which essentially posits two types of memory, STM and LTM, characterized as being different in terms of coding, capacity and permanence. In what is probably its most popular form, the duplex theory has an additional aspect: information is supposed to flow from STM to LTM. Later research indicated that such an account was not correct, and that much of the foundation for the STM/LTM distinction is not correct. Nevertheless, some information is available only over a short period, while other seems to be permanent. One way of accounting for this was suggested by Craik and Lockhart with their 'depth of processing' explanation. This too has problems, although something of the kind seems very reasonable. The crux of the arguments revolves around the idea that memory records are records of *processes* – such as interpretations, groupings, and so on. Clearly, interpretative processing has to take place in a memory space of some sort, and it has been suggested that there is a 'working' memory in which these operations take place.

While working memory is construed as a mental workspace in which things are only recorded in a temporary way, the work of Baddeley and his associates shows that this is not to be confused with the memory facilities used to hold span-sized lists of items. Indeed, Baddeley suggests a 'central executive' component of working memory together with another system which he terms the 'articulatory loop'.

The short-term and working memory area of research is a difficult one. This is unsurprising, since what is being investigated is really the temporary storage facilities associated with numerous types of processing. As was the case with attention, it is probable that a satisfactory theory of short-term retention will be related directly to the processing requirements of various tasks. So we get back to the point where it is necessary to investigate some of the *classes* of task which people carry out, in detail, in order to ascertain what kind of memory processes are implicated. Yet it is clear that rather severe limitations of temporary storage do constrain many activities. At the most general level, the notion of working memory is very similar to the notion of limited-capacity processing.

# 6 Memory 2: Memory for discourse and events

In this chapter we turn to studies of more 'naturalistic' aspects of memory. The focus is on the retention and retrieval of information gleaned from discourse (spoken or written text) and memory for events. In recent years, with the boom in cognitive psychology, these topics have become central areas of study. Although the fundamental questions about memory which were discussed in chapter 5 are pertinent to the study of naturalistic memory, studies of naturalistic memory emphasize other things too. In particular, there is an emphasis on the way in which what can be recalled or recognized depends upon the mental operations which take place at encoding. In the case of memory for written text, for instance, these operations are *reading* and *understanding*. These two activities are, of course, topics of study in their own right, and in later chapters will be covered as such. The discussion of discourse memory here is a kind of halfway house between the examination of memory per se and the examination of comprehension processes.

One important aspect of memory for naturalistic stimuli is that its study is of the greatest practical value. Quite clearly, it is of educational value to know which of two or more ways of writing an account of something – say the principles behind Linnaen classification – will result in the best understanding and retention. Similarly, it is important for a reader to be able to recognize how what a writer has said will influence the way he *remembers* what the writer actually put on paper. Because one infers a great deal about what writers 'mean', there is a tendency to confuse one's own perceptions of what a writer means with what was actually stated. It is possible to make this statement because of what is known about memory for discourse.

No less practical are the issues surrounding memory for events and actions. A critical example is eye-witness testimony in courts of law: a writer may be called upon to decide whether a particular detail of an accident actually occurred. The problem is that if it is plausible that the detail did occur, then the witness might not be able to discriminate whether it really did or did not happen. It is obvious that these questions treat memory as an integral part of a complete perception-understanding-retrieval system.

## A  Memory for discourse

Bartlett produced the earliest substantial treatise on memory for discourse (Bartlett 1932). One of his techniques was to read his subjects a story (a North-American Indian folk story called 'The war of the ghosts'), and ask them to recall as much of it as they could at some later point. The time-lags varied from very short delays to a matter of years. Two main findings struck him as particularly significant. First, subjects appeared to recall the *gist* of the passage best, and be somewhat poorer at recalling the details. This is fairly unsurprising in a way: we are all familiar with being able to remember the point of something, but not being able to remember all of the details. However, the psychologically important question is how does a subject 'extract' gist, and what precisely is gist in terms of information-processing operations? In recent years, the problem has been expressed in another way. How would one write a computer program to extract the gist of a passage, or of a story?

The second issue which Bartlett concentrated upon was the kind of errors made by subjects. In producing recall protocols, subjects not only omitted certain details, but also made errors of *commission*. Things which fitted in with the protocol which the subject was producing (and with the original story) appeared as details in the protocol, although they had not actually been mentioned in the original story itself. Furthermore, if a subject's recall was particularly sketchy, considerable embellishments might occur. These embellishments were used to fill out the protocols, and often had the characteristic of making sense with respect to stereotyped knowledge possessed by the subject, but again not present in the actual story. Thus, in one instance Bartlett quotes, the rather curious Indian folktale took on the character of a standard Wild West story in the recall protocol.

Bartlett claimed that all of these findings showed an 'effort after meaning' on the part of the subjects. When they first encountered the story, they tried to interpret it meaningfully, and when they came to recall, they tried to produce a meaningful and coherent piece of discourse in their protocols. In both cases, of course, it is necessary for the subjects to relate the story itself to what knowledge they have about the things and events being discussed. This is the central issue.

Bartlett's general results and sensitive observations have not only stood the tests of time and replication, but have led to numerous much more recent experiments and played their part in the development of modern theories. His account of his work is a classic of cognitive psychology, and should be read by every student of psychology. At the lowest level, his work shows that any account of text memory must be able to account for gist extraction and errors, and must therefore be related to comprehension itself. Both gist and errors are discussed in the following two sections.

It is important to realize the problems facing researchers who work with naturalistic materials. Imagine a very simple applied experiment in which you have two versions of a text describing some past event. As an applied psychologist, you have to find out which leads to better memory. It is unlikely that a score of verbatim recall, such as how many words that were in the text are recalled, would do as a measure. You would be more interested in how many of the *ideas* got through the reading-recall process. To compare the two texts, you would have to be able to analyse the text into idea units of some sort, and then see how many of these appeared in samples of recall. To get some feel for the problem, consider the sample passage shown below, and the recall protocols of two subjects attempting to remember it.

### Original

... John became increasingly afraid to go back to the house after the events of that evening in November. Everywhere he looked he imagined sinister relics of the horrific murder in every dark corner, under every chair, in every nook and cranny. Eventually he determined that he would sell the place ; perhaps someone from out of town would buy it if he sold without going through an estate agent. One thing he knew full well, if he kept returning, he would become completely obsessed. Yet already, despite his fear, he was drawn there as one is drawn to the edge of a cliff ...

*Protocol 1*

After these events, John became more and more afraid to go to the house, but he felt compelled to do so. When he was there, he imagined sinister relics of the terrible murder everywhere, in every dark corner. He thought he would have to sell to keep his sanity because he was becoming drawn to the house as if being drawn to the edge of a cliff. He would have to do it without using an estate agent.

*Protocol 2*

John was fearful of returning to the house after the murder had occurred there. He imagined evil lurking in every corner, under chairs, etc., and knew he would have to sell the house as he was no longer happy living there. He felt he would have to sell it without using an estate agent.

The two protocols both capture the gist of the original, but differ a great deal in detail, and faithfulness to the original wording. In fact, neither of them maintains the literal wording to any great extent. Protocol 2 introduces *the murder* right at the start: it is not out of place there, and is a key idea but it was not at the start in the original. One problem confronting research in text memory is that it is difficult to categorize and quantify these things. In section B1 below, we begin by describing one of a number of efforts to overcome this problem, by specifying what an *idea unit* is. On this foundation, it becomes possible to apply standard measurement methods, and so develop more detailed theories than is possible on the basis of qualitative observation.

## B  Propositions and text memory

One of the best-known frameworks for the investigation of text memory is that of Kintsch and his colleagues. Kintsch (1974) began a thorough and ongoing treatment of text memory by suggesting that a text can be broken down into idea units called *propositions*, the molecules of ideas in a metaphoric sense. He went on to suggest that people understand discourse in terms of propositions, and that propositions are an appropriate way of describing how discourse information is represented in memory.

Along with his co-workers, Kintsch has carried out many studies within this framework, culminating in a model (Kintsch and van Dijk 1978) which has the attractive property of combining discourse memory issues with some of the structural ideas about memory described in chapter 5.

## 1 The microstructure of text and propositions

The proposition is a technical concept imported into psychology from philosophy, logic and linguistics. Perhaps the most useful statement of what a proposition is, for our purpose, is this: a proposition is the simplest statement which is essentially capable of independent verification. Take the statement 'John is crying'. This is essentially capable of verification. One could check to see whether it is true or false under some imaginary set of circumstances. It is a proposition. Now consider the statement 'John is crying loudly'. This consists of *two* propositions: first, John is crying, and second, the crying is loud. Each of these can, in essence, be verified under some imaginary set of circumstances. According to Kintsch, the two propositions are two *idea units*.

It is convenient to represent propositions by means of a standard typographical format, known as Polish notation. In this notation, 'John is crying loudly' looks like this:

(CRY, JOHN) & (LOUDLY, CRY)

Each set of brackets embraces the elements of a supposedly separate proposition, and the position of the elements within the brackets indicates what kind of element each term is. There are two types of terms, called *predicators* and *arguments*, and the general description of a proposition is:

$$(\text{PREDICATOR, ARGUMENT}_1, \text{ARGUMENT}_2, \ldots \text{ARGUMENT}_n)$$

Various linguistic entities may play the role of predicators, including *verbs*, *adverbs*, *adjectives* and *conjunctions*. One way to think about this is that a predicator points to a series of *slots* which can be filled by arguments, and that each slot is a question which may be answered. For instance, the adjective 'heavy' is a predicator, and one might think of the slot question as being 'what?':

(HEAVY, ⟨what is heavy?⟩)

There are no other questions one could ask, and so HEAVY is considered a one-place predicator, taking one argument only, e.g.

(HEAVY, A₁); (HEAVY, BAG); (HEAVY, HEART) etc.

With verbs, things are a little more complex. Verbs generally depict states or actions, and with these one can envisage many slot questions. Take 'throw', for instance, as in 'John threw a stone':

(THREW, JOHN, STONE)

Both *John* and *stone* are arguments of threw. Verbs are n-place predicators, unless they are intransitive such as 'Mary fainted':

(FAINT, ⟨who?⟩)[1]
(FAINT, MARY)

Conjunctions are particularly interesting, since they can be used to join two propositions together. Consider 'and'. It is obviously a two-place predicator, having the general form:

(AND, ⟨something⟩, ⟨something⟩)

The 'something' can be propositions, as in the sentence 'John fainted and Mary cried'. There are two basic propositions to conjoin:

(FAINT, JOHN) and (CRY, MARY)

They are represented in the following way:

(AND, (FAINT, JOHN), (CRY, MARY))

The brackets preserve the integrity of the original propositions. As an expedient measure, sometimes such *embedded* propositions

---

[1] Tense is ignored in this introductory treatment.

are represented by symbols, such as greek letters, so the structure could be written as

(AND, $\alpha$, $\beta$)
(FAINT, JOHN) = $\alpha$
(CRY, MARY) = $\beta$

Although it is hoped that this discussion conveys the basic idea behind propositions, it should be pointed out that detailed analysis of this type becomes a minefield, and the reader should not be too worried if many questions about the proposition seem to be unanswered. However, we have covered enough to begin to look at Kintsch's use of 'propositional analysis' in relation to texts.

A text, according to Kintsch, is a connected structure which can be translated into a connected set of propositions. Connectivity is achieved in two basic ways, first, by *embedding*, as demonstrated with the conjunction example described above and, secondly, through term repetition. For instance, with the statement 'The skinhead shouted violently', we have the connected structure:

(SHOUT, SKINHEAD) & (VIOLENTLY, SHOUT)

because the SHOUT is the same term in each case. The adverbial proposition *follows* the verb proposition because it *depends* upon it. It makes no sense to assert that the shout was violent without previously asserting that the shout was there.

We can put all of this together, and show a complete tree structure and proposition list. Let our 'text' be 'Because the skinhead shouted violently, John fainted and Mary cried'. The structure is shown in figure 6-1. Kintsch's claim is that much more substantial texts may be represented as structures of the same type.

To illustrate that this analysis has some psychological utility, Kintsch (1974) undertook a number of interesting experimental studies. One issue was to show that propositional structure correlated with performance on a number of different tests; the other was to discover how propositional hierarchy relates to the intuitive notion of gist. In a now classic study, Kintsch and Keenan (1973 and Kintsch 1974) examined the effect of propositional structure

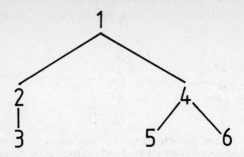

*Figure 6-1.* A tree structure based on the following propositions:

1 = (BECAUSE, $\alpha$, $\beta$)
2 & 3 = ((SHOUT, SKINHEAD) & (VIOLENTLY, SHOUT)) = $\beta$
4 = (AND, $\delta$, $\gamma$) = $\alpha$
5 = (FAINTED, JOHN) = $\delta$
6 = (CRIED, MARY) = $\gamma$

on reading time and on memory. For example, consider the following materials which Kintsch and Keenan used:

1   Romulus, the legendary founder of Rome, took the women of the Sabine by force.
2   Cleopatra's downfall lay in her foolish trust in the fickle political figures of the Roman world.

Material 1 contains sixteen words (including commas), but only four propositions. In contrast, while material 2 contains sixteen words, it is made up of no less than nine propositions by Kintsch's reckoning.

By using a variety of materials of these types, the investigators were able to show that the time which subjects spent reading a particular material was a roughly linear function of the number of propositions in the material, rather than being a function of the number of words. Kintsch and Keenan claim that this indicates that propositions are what people are encoding when they read a piece of text. The second part of the investigation was concerned with memory, and to understand it we must first look at the tree structure associated with sentence 2. It is depicted in figure 6-2, and is analogous to the example which was worked out earlier.

Note that the tree has four *levels*, with proposition 1, the basic causal proposition, at the top. Propositions at lower levels gener-

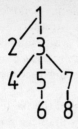

*Figure 6-2.* The propositional breakdown and tree structure for 'Cleopatra's downfall lay in her foolish trust of the fickle political figures of the Roman world'. *(After Kintsch and Keenan 1973.)*

1 (BECAUSE, $\alpha$, $\beta$)
2 (FELL DOWN, CLEOPATRA) = $\alpha$
3 (TRUST, CLEOPATRA, FIGURES) = $\beta$
4 (FOOLISH, TRUST)
5 (FICKLE, FIGURES)
6 (POLITICAL, FIGURES)
7 (PART OF, FIGURES, WORLD)
8 (ROMAN, WORLD)

ally represent more and more detail. In recall tests, Kintsch and Keenan found that when subjects did not remember the entire material, they tended to recall propositions from higher up, rather than lower down, the hierarchy. This is a result which is quite easy to replicate (cf. Kintsch et al. 1975 for an example using seventy-word paragraphs, for instance). The uppermost propositions of the hierarchy seem to be closer to the gist of the material than the lower propositions. Consider what might be reconstructed from a memory of only propositions 1, 2 and 3, for instance. The result would be something like 'Cleopatra's downfall lay in her trusting people'. Including lower-level propositions would only lead to more details of this rather basic statement. For these types of materials, at least, it would appear that Kintsch's analysis captures gist quite nicely. Presumably this is because the presence of lower-level propositions depends upon higher ones being there: as was pointed out, there is little point to having the lower-level propositions there without the higher-level ones upon which they depend.

Propositional analysis is useful. It goes some way towards providing a baseline for what an idea unit might be, and makes it easier to score a recall protocol in relation to a text. It is important to realize that a proposition is not just the original sentence represented a different way: rather, it is a template from which a number of sentences, all with similar meanings, might be constructed. For example, on the basis of the underlying propositions in figure 6-3, one could reconstruct the following text:

Cleopatra foolishly trusted the fickle political figures of Rome. Because of this, her downfall came about.

Although different from the original, most of the component propositions of this two-sentence version are essentially the same. Kintsch's methods are a great advance upon the more intuitive methods employed by Bartlett (although the author is not denying that great difficulties are associated with propositional analysis).

## 2  The Kintsch–van Dijk processing framework

Kintsch proposed that readers segment (or *parse*) text into propositions when they read it, and that the task is to connect the propositions appropriately as reading is taking place. It is the connected structure which is supposedly the memory for the text. More recently, Kintsch and van Dijk (1978) suggested a processing framework in which these operations might take place. Their paper contains wide-ranging issues, and here we shall restrict ourselves to the most central of them.

The model assumes that some sort of parsing process, which segments the text into propositions as it is read, takes place. This process is not part of the model itself. However, it is further assumed, quite reasonably, that only a part of the text is segmented as the reader proceeds through it. Suppose that the first three or four propositions have been discovered. It is assumed that these are entered into a short-term working buffer of limited capacity, of the kind discussed in chapter 5. The next part of the process is the *integration*, so far as possible, of these propositions. The mechanisms are assumed to be cross-checks within the buffer for term repetition. As connexions are discovered, a tree structure begins to form. If there are propositions which cannot be connected to anything, they remain in the buffer. Thus a continuous process of active search goes on within the confines of the working buffer. While propositions reside in the buffer, it is assumed that a record of them is made in long-term memory.

The buffer is filled with new propositions cyclically, but it is assumed that some propositions from cycle n are still in the buffer at cycle n + 1. This means that it is possible to check newly parsed propositions against certain old ones for potential connexion, using search procedures. As one reads through a text, then, the idea is one of a continuous search for connexion between propositions in the working buffer and, all the time, records of the propositions in the buffer are made in long-term memory.

Let us return for a moment to a proposition which has no connexion with anything else in the buffer. Once there is something in long-term memory, it is possible to search *there* for possible connexions as well. According to Kintsch and van Dijk, connexions are *first* searched for in the buffer, and *then* in long-term memory.

Given this general overview, we have to say something about propositions from earlier cycles being maintained in the buffer. How might a processor select appropriate or useful propositions to hold over? One selection principle suggested by Kintsch and van Dijk is based upon the degree to which they are already connected to other propositions. The argument is that a richly connected proposition is likely to be an important one – perhaps a main theme, or major point of reference for a large part of the discourse. Another selection principle is *recency*: not only is good retention of recent information a general property of memory, but recently mentioned propositions are more likely to be related to ones which come immediately afterwards than are more remote, earlier propositions. These two principles are indeed very important to any model of text processing, and figure in our discussion of discourse per se in chapter 10.

Having briefly outlined the bones of the encoding system, we turn now to memory. Kintsch and van Dijk assume that it is the number of cycles which a proposition spends in the buffer which determines its probability of recall. Once a proposition has become richly connected to other propositions, the likelihood of it being *kept* in the buffer for several cycles will be high if it is mentioned or used again. Consequently, well-connected ('thematic') propositions will be *better recalled* subsequently. In other words, the model extracts gist (although not in completely the same way as the Kintsch (1974) arguments suggest).

Kintsch and van Dijk have tested various texts in a computer simulation, adjusting the parameters of their model, and have shown that simulated recall can be made to approximate recall patterns produced by subjects trying to remember the same text. The model thus constitutes a reasonable part of a plausible process model. The authors discuss many other issues in relation to their model, some of which are alluded to in section C. Perhaps the most obvious unexpected aspect of their account is how parsing into propositions takes place. This is important not just for the adequate development of the Kintsch–van Dijk framework; if the parser does not deliver modular propositions in the way they suggest, then the foundation of the connexion searches is removed.

## C   Interpretation, inference and discourse memory

The discussion above shows how plausible a theory of text understanding based upon propositions as idea units appears to be. The efforts of Kintsch, van Dijk and others have given proposition-based theories a central position in current psychological views of how text is understood and remembered. The model of Kintsch and van Dijk has the added attraction of making assumptions about how the components of discourse are integrated which are both intuitively plausible and which rely upon a kind of working-memory system. Through the mechanism of the input buffer, the important phenomenon of 'gist' can be partly explained.

In this section, we introduce a rather different line of reasoning. As text is read and understood, the surface structure (exact wording) tends to be forgotten, and the 'meaning' retained. One might ask where the 'meaning' comes from. Of course, it comes from some mechanism by which the sentences of the discourse are checked against general knowledge for significance. This importation of general knowledge into the scene can be illustrated by Bartlett's early work, in which people sometimes produced 'elaboration errors', in which they 'remembered' plausible parts of a story which had not actually been presented, but which fitted the general gist of the story. This is in fact an issue which is at the heart of text memory, and which has been the subject of considerable experimentation.

The experiments described below show two things: first, that the ease with which a text is understood directly affects what can be recalled of a text and secondly, that precisely *how* the text was understood, what its significance was, influences the kind of errors which subjects make in recognition memory, the sort of errors made in recall, and the ease with which particular propositions in the text are recalled. The overall picture is one in which text memory is seen to result from two sources – the component utterances (elements) of the text itself, and aspects of general knowledge which are used to interpret the text. In fact, the two elements can become very easily confused by someone trying to remember a piece of discourse.

## 1 The general influence of comprehension on memory performance

One well-known illustration of the importance of understanding for discourse memory comes from the work of Dooling and Lachman (1971). They presented the following passage to two groups of subjects:

> With hocked gems financing him, our hero bravely defied all scornful laughter that tried to prevent his scheme. 'Your eyes deceive,' he had said. 'An egg, not a table, correctly typifies this unexplored planet.' Now three sturdy sisters sought proof. Forcing along, sometimes through calm vastness, yet more often over turbulent peaks and valleys, days became weeks as many doubters spread fearful rumours about the edge. At last, from nowhere, welcome winged creatures appeared signifying momentous success.

This passage is very difficult to recall as it stands. One of the two groups of subjects were presented with a *title* before receiving the passage, and this group performed very much better on a subsequent memory test. The title of the story is 'Christopher Columbus discovers America'. Without the title, the richness of the metaphor makes it virtually unintelligible, despite the fact that the component sentences are perfectly grammatical. The title, then, provides a key to interpretation by informing the reader of *what sort of knowledge* must be brought to bear on interpretation. Given a Christopher Columbus framework, it is an easy matter to interpret the passage.

The argument is that interpretation occurs at the time of

encoding. Is it possible that in the absence of the title the passage is *stored* in memory, but in literal or uninterpreted form, so that if a title were given at the *end*, interpretation would then be possible and so recall would be good? Dooling and Mullet (1973) carried out just such an experiment. They found that if the title was presented after the passage, performance on a memory test was just as poor as it was if no title had been presented. From this it can be argued that unless the passage is well understood at the time it is encountered, too little information is accessible in memory to enable subsequent reconstruction, even if a title is given afterwards. A rider to these observations should be added: with texts which are less metaphorical, and hence somewhat more intelligible, enough appears to be stored to enable some reconstruction on the basis of a title presented after the passage to take place (e.g. Bransford and Johnson 1973). Nevertheless, advance titles are superior.

Titles are one way of providing thematic cues prior to the body of the text proper; such cues can also be, and usually are, an integral part of the discourse itself. Thus it is customary in discourse to indicate what the broad theme or topic of the discourse will be early on in the discourse itself. A particularly well-studied aspect of this is *story structure*. It has been argued that stories have a fairly conventional form, and that the form derives from what is essential to make a story intelligible. For example, one possible top-level description of a story format is as follows (Thorndyke 1977):

STORY → SETTING + THEME + PLOT + RESOLUTION

In chapter 9, we shall describe story grammars in more detail. For the present purpose, the formulation given above can be read as stating that a story consists of an ordered set of categories. First, there is a *setting*, in which time, place and main characters might be introduced. Then there is a *theme*, which is often some problem which the protagonists in the story are going to try to overcome. The *plot* describes the efforts of protagonists to overcome the problems, and the *resolution* indicates how successful they were, and so on.

In one experiment, Thorndyke (1977) compared the recall of two short stories under various conditions. These conditions involved the reordering of component idea units of stories. For instance, in one case, the *theme* statements were removed from the story completely, but everything else was kept intact and in the correct order. In another case, the theme information was transposed to the end of the story. Recall was best with the theme in the usual place, but very poor with no theme at all, and only slightly better with the theme at the end. Ratings of intelligibility obtained from subjects corresponded directly to these recall patterns. Of course, the theme is a statement of the principal motivation for the events of the stories themselves. The theme could act like a title, providing automatic access to knowledge relevant to what will follow.

In his now classic work, Bartlett introduced the notion of 'schemata' into the study of memory. Bartlett's argument was that both the initial understanding of a piece of discourse, and its subsequent retrieval, rely upon the subject utilizing his general knowledge, stored in the form of schemata. An individual schema can be thought of as a packet of knowledge – a depiction of some situation – in memory. In the case of Bartlett's story, for instance, some subjects seemed to understand it as a standard 'western' story, making use of their general knowledge of that particular kind of story. In fact, much about westerns is very stereotyped indeed. Bartlett's claim is that culturally stereotyped knowledge, embodied in schemata, is used in all kinds of understanding. Aspects of a discourse which cannot be interpreted with respect to a schema will be difficult if not impossible to understand, and will not be durably recorded in memory. In Craik–Lockhart terms, one might say that such aspects of discourse could not receive elaborated processing at a deep level.

In more recent years, experiments which have a bearing upon this aspect of Bartlett's argument have been carried out. For instance, Bransford and Johnson (1973) presented the following passage to subjects, and carried out a subsequent memory test:

Watching a peace march from the 40th floor. The view was breathtaking. From the window one could see the crowd below. Everything looked extremely small from such a distance, but the colorful costumes could still be seen. Everyone seemed to be moving in one direction in an orderly fashion and there seemed to be little children as well as adults. *The landing was gentle, and luckily the atmosphere was such that no special suits had to be worn.* At first there was a great deal of activity. Later, when the speeches started, the crowd quietened down. The man with the television camera took many shots of the setting and the crowd. Everyone was very friendly and seemed glad when the music started.

When subjects came to the critical sentence 'the landing was gentle and luckily...', many were confused. Most could not interpret it at all, but some came up with a rationale for what the sentence might mean. Some thought that perhaps 'the landing' referred to a helicopter on crowd control.

Another group of subjects saw the same passage, but were given a different title, 'A space trip to an inhabited planet'. Under this condition, the critical sentence causes no trouble, presumably because it is easily understood within a 'space-trip' schema. In a subsequent recall test, more subjects in the *space-trip* than in the *peace-march* condition recalled at least one of the ideas in the critical sentence (gentle landing; atmosphere did not require suits). This difference remained even in a cued recall test when subjects had to fill in the following sentence frame:

The landing _____, and luckily the atmosphere _____.

It is clear from experiments of this type that titles which are informative as to setting or theme, or themes in stories, serve to facilitate comprehension by providing a key to the relevant knowledge possessed by the reader or hearer. Intelligibility directly correlates with recall. Furthermore, *what* is recalled depends upon which knowledge was used (as in the Bransford, Barclay and Franks (1972) study); another study of this type will be described shortly.

A second part of Bartlett's conception was that once recall was under way, schemata would once again play a role. For instance, if part of a story could not be accurately recalled, but it was clearly related to a schema, then the information in the schema could be used to supplement what the subject could remember of the story. Sometimes this would give accurate infilling of detail, but sometimes it would introduce errors of commission, where the details 'recalled' were not actually part of the story as stated at all. Subsequent research showed that the tendency to make such errors depends upon the materials themselves. Bartlett's original story was somewhat unusual (and therefore not easy to understand). When less exotic materials are used, recall appears to be less reconstructive, and closer to gist (e.g. Gomulicki 1956; Zangwill 1972; Cofer 1973). Such errors are also more prominent after long delays (e.g. Dooling and Christiaansen 1977). Nevertheless, such errors do occur, and appear to be the result of processes operating at the time of recall rather than simply at the time of encoding.

A rather direct illustration of the role of schemata at both encoding and recall comes from the work of Anderson and Pichert (1978) on so-called 'adopted perspectives'. Imagine that you are reading a passage about two small boys playing in a house, and that in the story there is mention of numerous facets of the house – layout, decoration, positions of doors, open and closed windows, and so on. Anderson and Pichert investigated the effect on memory when subjects read such a story from one of two perspectives: subjects either imagined that they were *burglars*, or *housebuyers*. It is not difficult to appreciate that the details of interest would be different under these two perspectives. Burglars are interested in which windows are open, for instance, while housebuyers are not.

As a preliminary, the ideas in the text were ranked according to judged importance to a burglar or housebuyer perspective. Subjects were then presented with the passage, and told to adopt either a housebuyer or burglar perspective. Later, they recalled as much as possible of the text. The *burglar* group recalled the ideas relevant to the burglar perspective readily, but not the ideas related to the housebuyer perspective. In contrast, the *housebuyer* group recalled information relevant to housebuyers more readily. Thus explicitly adopted schemata influence the information which is most readily recalled.

This design allows a further interesting test to be carried out. It is an obvious question to ask whether any housebuyer information was stored under the burglar perspective (or vice versa). Anderson and Pichert tested this by asking some subjects to switch perspective at recall. If they had read the story with a burglar perspective in mind, they were given housebuyer instructions at recall and told to use that perspective. The results showed pretty clearly that subjects *could* remember information from the other perspective. Anderson and Pichert considered two explanations for this: a *conscious selection* hypothesis, and an accessibility hypothesis. With conscious selection, subjects might have decided not to include detail 'irrelevant' to recall under the initial perspective. With the accessibility hypothesis, it was thought that subjects may have written down all they could *recall*, but that a new perspective provided a means of accessing other information which had been stored but which was inaccessible under the first perspective. Interviews carried out by Anderson and Pichert supported the latter interpretation. Most subjects stated that they had, in fact, recalled all that they possibly could in each condition.

Quite clearly, then, perspectives are operative at recall as well as encoding. Do the results mean that everything of a text goes into memory, but that it can only be *retrieved* with respect to some perspective? This is unlikely. Consider an account in which most of what is stored is the result of schemata-based interpretations during reading. It is not plausible to suppose that a burglar perspective specifies one schema (a burglar schema) which is used for interpreting the whole discourse. Rather, various schemata might come into play, regardless of deliberate perspective. Some schemata might be common to both perspectives, and be used in the service of general comprehension of the passage, although the deliberately adopted perspectives may well cause certain information to be more elaborately coded than other information. Thus, while demonstrating the importance of perspectives at retrieval, the experiment certainly does not rule out its importance at encoding.

It appears, then, that Bartlett's overall view is probably correct. Schemata (or knowledge structures) are used to comprehend discourse. The result is a memory for the discourse which is heavily loaded with schema-based information. At recall, schemata can be used again, either to fill in plausible details, or to assist recall proper. In the next section, the idea that discourse memory is for interpreted material is pursued further.


## 2 Inference and memory performance

Apart from the work on global aspects of recall described above, there have been a number of studies investigating how various specific inferences are made during the course of comprehension, and how such inferences affect memory performance. In many ways, these studies provide some rather vivid illustrations of the general conception outlined above. Let us examine four such studies.

Bransford, Barclay and Franks (1972) had subjects listen to one or other of the following sentences:

(i)   Three turtles rested beside a floating log, and a fish swam beneath them.
(ii)  Three turtles rested on a floating log, and a fish swam beneath them.

After a series of sentences, a recognition memory test was administered, which included the following items pertinent to (i) and (ii) above:

(iii) Three turtles rested beside a floating log, and a fish swam beneath it.
(iv)  Three turtles rested on a floating log, and a fish swam beneath it.

The subjects' task was to decide which test sentence ((iii) and (iv) in this case) had been presented before. (Careful scrutiny will show that neither (iii) nor (iv) had been presented before.) Subjects who had been presented with sentence (i) did realize that neither (iii) nor (iv) had been presented before. However, subjects who heard (ii) realized that (iii) had not been presented before, but tended to think that (iv) *had* been presented. The explanation is that (iv) is a *plausible inference* which could be derived from (ii) but not from (i): if turtles are on a log, then largish things (e.g. fish) passing under them would also pass under the log. In a very unlikely case, of course, one could imagine a fish squeezing under the turtles but going over the log, showing that the inference is not *necessary*. But it is the most likely interpretation, and it is the interpretation which is falsely *recognized* as a text statement in the memory experiment.

A similar example comes from an experiment by Thorndyke (1977). Once again, a recognition memory procedure was used to see whether or not people confuse plausible inferences with what was actually presented in the text. Consider the following example:

(i)   The hamburger chain owner was afraid that his love for french fries would ruin his marriage.

Thorndyke suggested that in order to understand this, one might draw upon one or more of the following inferences:

(ia)   The hamburger chain owner got his french fries free.
(ib)   The hamburger chain owner's wife didn't like french fries.
(ic)   The hamburger chain owner was very fat.

Sometime after sentence (i), the sentence below appeared in some of Thorndyke's texts:

(ii)   The hamburger chain owner decided to join weight-watchers in order to save his marriage.

Thorndyke supposed that if (ii) was to be understood, then plausible inference (ic) would be drawn by the reader, and used as part of the interpretation. Furthermore, he reasoned that in a subsequent recognition memory test, subjects should tend to believe that (ic) had *actually been presented* if it was presented as a recognition test item. This was indeed the case. Using materials like these, embedded in longer passages about various topics, Thorndyke found that when a plausible inference had been reinforced by the need to interpret a later sentence, it was more likely to be falsely recognized as having been presented than was the case if the inference had not been reinforced. Thus, what is recognizable in a memory trace for discourse appears to be the product of comprehension. In part at least, the actual discourse content itself, and the inferences used in understanding the discourse, are not distinguishable.

Two other illustrations lead to a similar conclusion, this time using a cued-recall technique. Anderson et al. (1976) presented subjects with a number of unrelated sentences in which the subject noun-phrase was a *general term*, for instance:

The woman was outstanding in the theatre.

Think about it briefly, and it will become apparent that one might suppose the woman to be an *actress* (which is why woman is a general term). If subjects do interpret the sentence in such a way as to make 'the woman' mean 'actress', then, argued Anderson et al., the term 'actress' should be a better cue for recalling the sentence than the term 'woman', although the latter and not the former was part of the original. Indeed this was the case.

A parallel result was obtained for general *verbs* by Garnham (1979). An example of his materials is the sentence:

The housewife cooked the chips.

How are chips cooked? Most people would infer that they are fried. Using materials of this type, Garnham found that specific recall cues (such as 'fried') led to better recall of the sentence than the general cue 'cooked'.

In both of these cases, it is evident that general knowledge about situations being suggested by sentences enters into interpretation, and hence into memory. It is as though what is stored is a mental model or depiction of situations as a whole. In later chapters we shall explore such situational knowledge in some detail, since it is an important part of memory in its own right, and is central to an appreciation of what it means to understand. For now, we shall return to a consideration of Kintsch's propositional representations in the light of these findings on interpretation and memory errors.

## 3 Propositions, gist and representations

The proposition seems like a reasonably good way of specifying an idea unit. Indeed, it can be argued that other sorts of representations can be expressed as propositions. The problem is what to make the *content* of the propositions. Consider Garnham's finding that 'fried' is a better recall cue than 'cooked' for the sentence 'The housewife cooked the chips'. What would be a psychologically realistic propositional representation of the sentence? Before it is interpreted by a reader, one might say that it is (COOKED, HOUSEWIFE, CHIPS). But there is no reference in this to frying. An alternative is to suppose that the appropriate proposition is (FRIED, HOUSEWIFE, CHIPS). The first is close to the sentence itself, but the second is an interpretation of the sentence. Given the preponderance of inference 'error' in recognition memory, one might very well ask which of the propositions would serve as a description of the text as represented in memory.

In fact, neither would do alone for while *fried* is a better recall cue, what is *recalled* is 'The housewife *cooked* the chips'.

A problem of a similar kind can be illustrated by comparing the following pair of sentences:

(a)   The policeman held up his hand and stopped the traffic.
(b)   The wicket-keeper held up his hand and stopped the ball.

Both of these could be represented by very similar sets of propositions: lists for each of them are given in table 6-1. One must now ask precisely *which* aspects of meaning and significance are captured by these proposition lists. While the sentence forms are closely parallel, they designate rather different kinds of actions. Thus, the policeman's hand does not *physically* stop the traffic; it serves as a signal to the drivers of the cars nearest to the policeman. They stop their cars and this causes other drivers to stop, and so on. In so far as sentence (a) is understood, all of these facts are made accessible. Contrast this with (b): here the wicket-keeper's hand *does* stop the ball by physical contact. The point is

---

**Table 6-1.**

---

*Sentence (a)*

(CAUSE, $\alpha$, $\beta$)

$\alpha$ = ((HELD UP, POLICEMAN, HAND) & (POLICEMAN'S HAND))
$\beta$ = (STOP, POLICEMAN, TRAFFIC)


*Sentence (b)*

(CAUSE, $\alpha$, $\beta$)

$\alpha$ = ((HELD  UP,  WICKET-KEEPER,  HAND)  &  (WICKET-KEEPER'S HAND))
$\beta$ = (STOP, POLICEMAN, TRAFFIC)

---

The two propositional structures are homologous, but the two sentences convey very different things. The question is whether the propositional structures adequately represent the data stored in memory after reading them.

that none of this is captured by the propositions of table 6-1; the distinction is simply not made there. Even worse, it is difficult to see what value a memory representation based on these propositions might be, if in order to use one's understanding of the sentences one must translate them into some other mental form. The point is, then, that if propositions are kept close to the text, they do not really capture meaning.

There are two distinct issues in evaluating proposition-based accounts of memory representation. One is whether propositions are a useful way of representing discourse, and the other is whether the propositions should be kept close to the text itself. In brief, *any* set of relationships can be translated into a propositional format so, in one sense, it may indeed be the case that propositions can be used to represent 'molecular' ideas. However, for any particular realization in psychology (or computer programming), it is necessary to say *what* is going to be represented in this way. In his early work, Kintsch (1974) stuck fairly close to translating text into propositions. The view we wish to present here (cf. Sanford and Garrod 1982) is that this text-proposition mapping is not very useful for sentences which can be reasonably well understood. Rather, Sanford and Garrod (1982) conjecture that text is interpreted as a *message*, and that if one wished to represent a text as propositions, then these must include interpretations in the propositional structure. For instance, 'The housewife cooked the chips' might have to be represented as *both* (COOK, HOUSEWIFE, CHIPS) *and* (FRY, HOUSEWIFE, CHIPS). However, it is easier to represent this idea in slightly different ways and the issue will be discussed at greater length in chapters 8 and 10.

The main question is whether text memory consists of representations which are close to the text, or nearer to an interpretation of the text. Kintsch's view is that representations are kept simple unless it becomes necessary to produce more elaborate representations, perhaps in order to answer questions asked about a text. Others, such as Sanford and Garrod (1981) and Schank and Abelson (1977), argue that more complex representations are involved.

## D Memory for objects and visual events

Just as memory for discourse is a function of mechanisms of interpretation, so too is memory for objects and events. Objects are not merely visual patterns, but visually categorical *objects*. Events in the world are understood by us as causal chains of one sort or another, and such interpretations will be important at the point of encoding events. And just as was the case for discourse memory, it may be difficult or impossible to discriminate between events which actually occurred (what actually happened) and things which may have only been very plausible. This becomes a problem of great social significance when the issue becomes a legal one. For instance, if you are acting as a witness in a court of law, say about a car accident, the very form of the questions asked by a lawyer can lead to genuine errors of commission on your part, or at least raise doubts as to the accuracy of your memory. While the latter state of affairs may sound desirable, errors of commission are obviously not desirable. Part of the problem is the issue of *leading questions*, which are known to be undesirable, but which are not always easily detected.

## 1 Visual memory and the influences of interpretation

One might naturally suppose that memory for visual objects and events is categorically different from that for prose. At one extreme, one might have a theory that memory stores some sort of 'picture' representation of objects and events. Yet such a portrayal is quite inadequate. For instance, on such a simple view, one might suppose that forgetting is rather like degrading the 'picture', which would suggest a somewhat *random pattern* of inaccessibility of aspects of the original stimulus. Even one's own experience will probably suggest the inadequacy of such a viewpoint, and there is considerable evidence to show that what is remembered of pictorial stimuli is a function of interpretation.

One of the earliest demonstrations of the effects of interpretation on memory for visual objects was a study carried out by Carmichael, Hogan and Walter (1932). Their subjects were shown varieties of shapes, which they were expected subsequently to reproduce on paper. For each shape, subjects could either see the shape alone, or the shape with one of two names. An example shape and name is shown in figure 6-3. Two results emerged from this: first, the presence of a verbal label facilitated recall: more items were remembered if they had been presented along with a name. Second, the kinds of errors introduced into the reproduc-

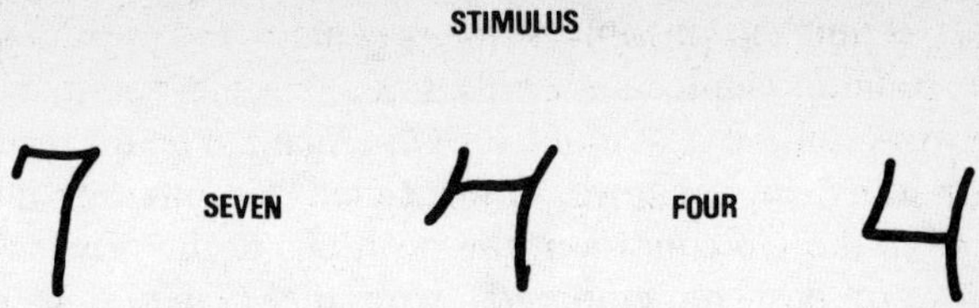

STIMULUS

7   SEVEN   $\sqcap$   FOUR   4

*Figure 6-3.* An example of the kind of figure used by Carmichael, Hogan and Walter (1932), shown in the centre. If presented along with one or other of the labels, systematic distortions appear in the reproductions (outside figures).

tions could in part be attributed to the *labels* presented with the shapes. Thus the detail of the small upper strokes is lost in the 'seven' version, and exaggerated in the 'four' version. Such effects of labelling are not restricted to reproduction, but can also be demonstrated with recognition tests (Daniel 1972).

Both the errors and the superior recall with labels suggest that perhaps *interpreted* shapes are better recalled than uninterpreted ones, but that interpretation brings distortions, just as was the case with verbal stimuli. Even more potent evidence for this claim comes from studies by de Groot (1965; 1966) who investigated the recall of the positions of men on a chessboard, using master chess players. For configurations that came from real games, de Groot established that after only a five-second exposure, master players could reproduce the board. However, this skill seems to depend upon having an interpretable pattern: when the placement of the chessmen was random, performance at reproduction was poor, and did not differ from the performance of novice chess players. Such results show that for more complex scenes, visual memory is a function of attention allocation and the significance of the pattern, rather than being a snapshot.

Other phenomena may be understood in the same way. For instance, Eisenstadt and Kareev (1975) trained subjects to play one of two Japanese board games, *Go* and *Gomuku*. Both games are played by placing 'stones' in appropriate locations on a gridlike board, but the goals are different. In *Gomuku*, the object of each player is to capture as many of his opponent's pieces as possible by surrounding them with his own. In *Go*, the object is to put five pieces in a continuous row. After training on the games, subjects were presented with a board configuration, and told that their task was to determine the next best move for *Gomuku*. After they had done this, they were given a blank board, and were asked to recollect as much as possible of the original board positions. Much later in training, subjects actually saw the same board, but were told to work out the best move for *Go*. Again, a board reconstruction task followed. What was best recalled was different in the two cases. With the *Go* condition, the positions of the pieces relevant to *Go* were best remembered; with the *Gomuku* game, the (different) pieces associated with *that* game were best remembered. Subjects seemed to remember the board in an *interpreted* way, not as a complete picture. One final example is that cited by Norman, Rumelhart and LNR (1975). Students living in particular apartments in San Diego obviously have regular and substantial experience of the shapes of the apartments. Similarly, the outside view of a building visited daily should be well known. Norman and his colleagues had subjects draw these things from memory, and noted considerable errors and distortions of various systematic kinds. Whatever visual memories are, their recalled form does appear to depend upon other general experience.

Despite the obvious similarities between interpretation phenomena in discourse memory and visual memory, one should not be over-zealous in dismissing the possibility that there are two types of long-term memory. There are various lines of evidence to suggest that this may indeed be the case, the most potent of which is that in recognition memory tests, the recognition of visual objects (or pictures) is extremely good. For example, Standing, Conezio and Haber (1970) presented 2,560 pictures at a fairly fast (one per ten sec) rate, in a continuous recognition test, and found recognition scores of 93 per cent! However, the pictures were of fairly complex things (rich in discriminating elements), and were not likely to be confused with each other. Under these circumstances, recognition memory is superior to scores for similar tests using words (e.g. Standing 1973) and sentences (e.g. Shepard 1967). This apparent superiority of picture recognition over the recognition of verbal material has been used in support of the claims that picture memory is separate from and superior to verbal memory, or that memory for pictures can be stored as both images *and* verbal codes (cf. Paivio 1971).

One possible interpretation of the outstanding recognition memory which we have for pictures is that the brain easily stores detailed analogues of the pictures themselves and, because of the detail, recognition scores are good. Recently, Nickerson and Adams (1979) reported a study in which they attack such a point of view. The tasks which they used required subjects to recall what they could about the layout of a US cent (penny). (To get the flavour, try drawing a British new penny.) They found that subjects were remarkably bad at doing this. Each subject's drawing was scored with respect to whether each of eight critical features was present, whether each was located on the correct side of the coin, and whether it was drawn in the correct position. Only four of the twenty subjects got even half of the features right, let alone in the right position.

In another experiment, the authors used a modified recognition paradigm. Subjects were presented with an array of fifteen drawings, only one of which was correct – the others each had one or more things wrong with it. (Note that this is in effect a *fifteen alternative* recognition test.) Subjects then *rated* the alternatives for plausibility. Although the correct drawing was more likely to be judged more plausible than were any of the 'counterfeits', less than half of the subjects actually made that choice. Furthermore, certain of the alternatives were also judged to be very plausible. Nickerson and Adams argue that given a broad choice like this, it is clear that recognition memory is not especially good, and that the previously very high levels of recognition performance obtained by others was due to using a two-choice paradigm. The overall conclusion is that familiar objects are not even *recognized* particularly well, and, consequently, that pictorial memory is not so detailed as may have been believed.

## 2 Eye-witness testimony

Problems associated with eye-witness testimony are those concerning retrieval rather than those concerning encoding. One way to elicit testimony from a witness to an event is to ask for free recall: the witness simply states what he thought he saw. But, of course, there will often be critical elements missing from such recall, and lawyers or police officers will then have to ask questions to try to obtain more appropriate memories from the witness. This is fair enough, but is also where all the trouble starts.

Elizabeth Loftus and her associates have carried out a considerable amount of seminal research in this field. To take one example of their work, Loftus and Palmer (1974) showed a group of subjects a film in which there was a traffic accident. They then asked the subjects questions about what they had seen, asking different groups different questions, for instance:

(a)    How fast were the cars going when they *hit* each other?
(b)    How fast were the cars going when they *smashed into* one another?

The results from this comparison were clearcut. Subjects who were asked question (b) reported speeds which were substantially higher than speeds reported by subjects asked question (a). While 'hit' is neutral with respect to speed, 'smashed into' implies a high-energy collision, which would normally be associated with high speed.

Subjects appeared to have incorporated information contained in the question into their retrieval processes, and this had a direct effect upon what they thought they remembered. The second phase of the experiment demonstrated a subtle and far-reaching consequence of this. A week later, the subjects returned and were asked more questions, including 'Did you see any broken glass?' There had been *no* broken glass in the film. However, some subjects reported that they *did* remember broken glass, and more subjects who were asked the 'smashed into' question the week before behaved in this way. Plainly, the initial question had actually *altered* the memory representation which the subject had, and this had consequences for the way in which subsequent questions would be answered. Loftus and Palmer cite other experiments of a similar type, yielding similar results. For instance, it is possible to suggest the existence of things which were not in the films, by introducing them indirectly into the questions.

From a purely theoretical point of view, experiments such as these indicate how information provided at recall can affect the outcome of retrieval, and can apparently alter the content of memory. However, with the eye-witness research, the most obvious issues are practical ones. One might well ask whether one method of questioning is better than another from the point of view of establishing the 'real truth'. Research into this issue yields a great deal of what might be expected on psychological grounds. For instance, in studies comparing free recall (i.e. the subject says what he saw in his own words) versus question answering, it is generally found that free recall produces a certain proportion of 'correct' details, along with a few false reports. On the other hand, with a question-answering procedure, it is possible to improve the absolute number of correct details report, but only at a cost of an increase in false reports (e.g. Lipton 1977). This clearly resembles the effect of criterion shift in signal detection terms, and one must seriously wonder whether questions actually improve recall efficiency. In any event, on this basis it would appear that an effective interrogator must develop a skill of sorting out correct statements from false ones which the subject perhaps believes to be correct. Research comparing skilled and unskilled questioners indicates that the skilled people can indeed do this, but cannot obtain more 'true' reports (Dent 1978).

## E  Summary

As two samples of 'naturalistic' memory, we have considered text memory and aspects of visual memory. In each case, it was clear that what is recalled is the product of what was understood. Thus a full account of text memory will of necessity involve the study of comprehension itself. Even the most casual look at memory recall protocols indicates the interrelationship. If what is remembered is *ideas*, then we need some notion of an idea unit. Kintsch's 'propositional' theory provided an example of this, and although it is inadequate to deal with many problems, it still provides a useful way of describing a text for many purposes, especially for scoring recall protocols. Nevertheless, it was equally clear that the theory does not say enough about the process of understanding – a topic which will be addressed in a later chapter.

On the practical side, many of the experiments described in this chapter warn us how difficult it is to distinguish between what was read, said or seen, and what was *inferred* as a natural part of understanding. Furthermore, the research on eye-witness testimony offers a clear example of how the conditions of retrieval affect both what is retrieved, and, perhaps, what is remembered at a later date.

Quite apart from its value in the study of text memory, working out ways of representing *ideas* is an important issue in its own right. When we think, make decisions, understand, solve problems, and so on, we would normally say that we were comparing ideas. The use of propositional representations is *generally* useful for this, and we will use them again in chapter 7, along with a graphical version called *semantic networks*. Up to now we have only vaguely introduced notions like background knowledge and schemata, although they have been given a position of some importance in our picture. Chapters 7 and 8 are concerned with some of the aspects of knowledge representation in memory which have been explored by cognitive psychologists and other cognitive scientists.

# 7 Memory 3:
# Semantic memory

One major aspect of memory is the memory as a mental database, which of course includes all knowledge possessed by a human being. Such knowledge is so vast and full of variety that a complete listing would be impossible, and to attempt one would be quite pointless. Broadly speaking, however, much knowledge can be divided into two types: knowing facts about things (declarative knowledge) and knowing how to do things (procedural knowledge). Typical examples of declarative knowledge might be knowing that Paris is the capital of France, or that a dog usually has four legs, or that a dog with three legs is relatively uncommon, and that such a state of affairs would be the result of an accident, and so on. In contrast, typical procedural knowledge would be how to ride a bicycle, drive a car, carry out a parallel ski turn, or stop a bus. Both types are present in human memory.

The field of semantic memory has been largely concerned with the declarative class. The term *semantics* refers to the study of meaning, of course, and at the centre of semantic memory is the question of what certain concepts mean, and how meaning is represented. The meaning of 'meaning' itself is a vexed issue, but for psychologists and many computer scientists, semantic memory has been treated in a relatively straightforward and pragmatic fashion. Consider, for example, what is meant by the generic term *dog*. Statements which can be made about dog divide into three broad types. First, we could say to what superordinate conceptual class the class *dog* belongs: *animal*, say. Second, we could give examples of types of dog: bouvier, great dane, French poodle, and so on. Finally, we could describe *attributes* of dog (generic), such as has four legs, usually has tail, usually smells, considered by some people to be a public nuisance, likes bones, and so on. The idea is that the meaning of nominal concepts can be captured by describing it in terms of other concepts. This means that when one considers what one knows about dogs, it turns out to be intrinsically linked to what one knows about other things. The problem then becomes one of saying what is linked to what in memory, and how it is linked.

In addition to knowing about the meanings of nominal concepts, people also know about actions, which are described by verbs in language. Consider the verb 'eat', for instance. It means something like 'transfer food from somewhere to one's mouth, chew it, and swallow'. Beyond that, what 'eat' means depends upon the context. But even on this intuitive examination, it is clear that *eat* is a concept which is understood in terms of other concepts. It is the relationships which are important.

Knowledge of this type must be represented somehow in human memory, and semantic memory is concerned with how. There has been rather less concern with procedural knowledge, although as we shall see, even declarative knowledge is bound up with procedural knowledge at some level. Until relatively recently, semantic memory has been largely concerned with concepts denoted in language by single words. However, whole situations, such as 'what happens when one visits a hairdresser' can be described as a network of descriptions, and memory representations of such things are, of course, extremely important for many cognitive activities. We shall consider these extensions in chapter 8.

To begin with, we shall step back a little and consider the view that ideas or concepts are connected to one another, or can be reached from one another. This fundamental truth has been conceptualized in a number of ways, but all can be looked at as successive refinements of the rather simple notion of *association*.

## A  Association, random access and connectivity

One of the earliest techniques used in psychology which has relevance to semantic memory is the word-association test. The technique is quite straightforward: the subject is presented with a word, and asked to say the first word which comes to mind as a result. The interest in the technique lies in the fact that the responses given are not random, but usually bear seemingly explicable relationships to the words presented. For instance, when the word *table* is given to a large number of people, the predominant response is *chair*, followed in likelihood by *food*, and

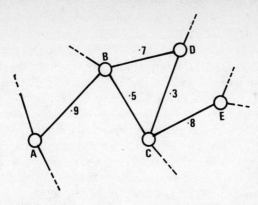

*Figure 7-1.* A fragment of a simple associative network. Letters denote *nodes*, which can be thought of as ideas stored in memory, or word concepts. The numbers denote strengths of connexion. In a word-association task, given B as a start-point, responses are most likely to be A, then D, then C.

then by *eat* (Palermo and Jenkins 1964). Such a pattern is typical, and is consistent with the view that some concepts lead to others in a non-random way. There are, of course, problems with this conclusion. What kind of rules govern the way in which one concept leads to another? For instance, Palermo and Jenkins found that a number of subjects responded with *leg, food, fork* or even *wood* – in fact they quote thirty-six different responses, although the most outstanding in terms of frequency was *chair*. The various responses bear very different relationships to the stimulus word.

Word associations appear to reflect something of the way in which ideas are organized. In fact, one way of thinking about semantic memory is as a large interconnected network of ideas, a fragment of which is shown in figure 7-1. There is something attractively concrete about such a diagram. Although ideas or words are only shown as nodes in a network, they are at least connected, more or less strongly. Indeed, some quite sophisticated theories of semantic memory storage make use of the philosophy suggested by such diagrams: that activity might spread from one node to another, reflecting changing patterns of information being retrieved (see, particularly, Collins and Loftus 1975 and section C below).

One property of such network representations is thus that some nodes are more easily accessed from a given node than others. A rather different type of experiment illustrating this is Meyer and Schvaneveldt's (1971) dual lexical decision task, described in chapter 3. The point of interest is that with associated word-pairs (e.g. NURSE–DOCTOR), the time taken to make the decision is shorter than when the words are unrelated (e.g. BREAD–DOC-TOR). The effect accrues whether the words are presented simultaneously or sequentially, and even holds between the first and last members of sequentially presented triplets (e.g. BREAD–STAR–BUTTER). The results clearly indicate that accessing the recognition procedures for words is not random, but is consistent with a system organized along some sort of associative lines, where activity at one node spreads to adjacent nodes.

Returning to word association tests per se, apart from variety and strength of associations, a second feature emerges from the word association norms, in which many subjects are tested on each word: association is asymmetric. Some of the asymmetry appears to result from word sequences normally used in a language. For instance, *white* is the response to *black* more often than *black* is the response to *white*. The expression 'black and white', of course, occurs more often in the language than the reverse. Such sequentially determined associations are called *syntagmatic*. A somewhat less obvious and more interesting example of asymmetry comes from Miller (1969), who analysed a number of existing norms, and showed that more responses of a superordinate kind (e.g. 'dog', 'animal') occur than of a superordinate kind (e.g. 'animal', 'dog'). Indeed, Miller suggests that people may have information like 'A dog is an animal' stored in memory, rather than information like 'Animals have as an example dog'. A similar sort of relationship was also unearthed by Miller. He showed that whole-to-part responses were more likely (e.g. 'table', 'leg') than were parts-to-wholes (e.g. 'leg', 'table'), which appears to indicate that information like 'A table has legs' may reflect memory organization, but not 'legs are parts of tables'. This seems intuitively reasonable.

The idea of asymmetry means that the representation of an associative network shown in figure 7-1 is potentially inadequate. The links between the nodes in that diagram do not indicate direction at all. In contrast, figure 7-2 shows a network in which such asymmetries are allowed for. The importation of *pointers* captures the ideas of a spread of activity between concepts, but only in the direction of a pointer.

Associative networks of this type are really shorthand ways of expressing the ease of getting from one node to another but it will be clear from figure 7-2 that the *relationships* between concepts are not yet expressed in the diagram. It is the relationships between concepts which bring us closer to representing *meaning* in memory. One solution is to suppose that the relationships are stored – for instance, the pointer from 'dog' to 'animal' would be labelled

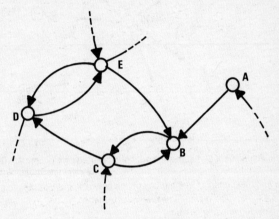

*Figure 7-2.* The nodes in this diagram are connected by unidirectional pointers. Thus, starting with B, it is possible to get directly to C, but not to E. In this network, E can be reached by the sequence B–C–D–E. Pointers are necessary to accommodate directionality effects.

as a class membership relationship, sometimes written as ISA. Such networks are known as *semantic* networks, and an example is shown in figure 7-3. Not only do such networks capture the connectivity of concepts, they also indicate the relation which one concept bears to another. Indeed, in a sense one might say that the concept of 'a dog' is to some extent captured in the network fragment shown.

Of course, figure 7-3 omits any representation of the strength of connexion between nodes. One could argue that strength could be represented by means of a value of some sort, as we did for the simple associative network. Another way in which associative strength can be thought of is in terms of the number of nodes which have to be traversed to get from one node to another.

This introduction was designed to show some of the things which are meant when one speaks of a semantic network, or an association network. Various aspects of these representations recur throughout this chapter.

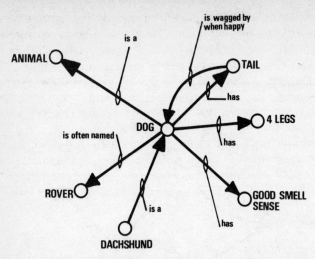

*Figure 7-3.* A fragment of a semantic network, centred on the concept DOG. The nodes are now labelled (upper case), and the pointers are labelled with relationships (lower case). On the basis of this network, it is possible to derive the answer 'DOG' given the query 'What wags its tail when it's happy?', or to decide that 'A dachshund is a dog' is true.

## B  Noun concepts

We shall begin by considering some of the interesting psychological notions which have arisen as a result of work with superficially simple concepts which are normally described by nouns. To start with it is necessary to introduce the notion of the componential analysis of meaning, which is rooted in philosophy and linguistics.

### 1  Componential analysis

The basic idea behind the componential approach is that the meaning of words can be expressed as a series of underlying components. For instance, the word 'boy' might bring to mind the following simple description:

- A boy: is a male, is non-adult, is human ... etc.

This informal description is simply a list of elements which taken together seem to capture the sense of the word 'boy'. Often lists of components like this are expressed in a slightly more formal way, as a set of propositions. (The notation used here is only a variant of that introduced in chapter 6.)

- Boy (x)→Male (x) & Non-Adult (x) & Human (x).

The arrow indicates 'can be re-written as', and (x) designates any particular boy.

The basic method of componential analysis is to compare words with one another in such a way that the contrasts made serve to indicate the presence of components which might distinguish one word from another. For example, comparing *man, woman, boy* and *girl* would yield the components (or 'features') +*Male* and +*Adult*:

| *Man* | *Woman* | *Boy* | *Girl* |
|-------|---------|-------|--------|
| +Male | −Male | +Male | −Male |
| +Adult | +Adult | −Adult | −Adult |

To extend the range of features, one simply adds other new words to the set under consideration. For instance, the inclusion of *father* would reveal a *parent* feature. Indeed, one might represent *father* in the following way:

- Father (x, y)→parent (x, y) & Male (x) & human (x) & Human (y).

Notice that father has two arguments, *x* and *y*; *x* is the person who is the father, and *y* is the child.

The outcome of componential analysis is thus a set of components or features which are appropriate to the adequate description of the word in question. There are many problems and difficulties with the approach, but something like it is quite necessary if one is to examine people's conceptual knowledge. One problem concerns the vast number of words, even nouns, which are used in a language. How could one possibly compare every word with every other? Componential analysts do not. By and large, componential analysis has proceeded in a simpler way, trading upon the way certain groups of words seem to be conceptually related to one another. Examples of such groupings include kinship terms, verbs of motion, verbs of possession, terms for containers, and so on. Such intuitively obvious groupings are termed *semantic fields*, and it is within a semantic field that comparisons between words are made, and even then seldom exhaustively.

Componential analysis reveals certain regularities: for instance, consider the relationship between the words *man* and *father*. *Man* could be written as follows:

- Man (x)→male (x) & human (x) & adult (x)

Notice how the features (male, human, adult) also appear in the representation of *father*. We could therefore rewrite *father* as

- Father (x, y)→parent (x, y) & man (x)

Rewriting components in this way makes it clear that certain words can be thought of as being more highly specified versions of other words. For instance, *father* is a more specific version of the word *parent*. Similar arguments can be made for verbs – for instance, an important component of most verbs of motion is something akin to 'travel' (Miller and Johnson-Laird 1976). Others have suggested 'move' as a basic component, but Miller and Johnson-Laird argue that *move* is more complex than *travel*.

Componential analysis is used by semanticists to explain why certain statements are self-contradictory. For example, 'That man is a girl' is self-contradictory because man entails *male* as one of its features, while *girl* entails female. In the same way, it is possible to explain sentences which are termed 'semantically anomalous', such as 'A table is a father'. Table does not possess an *animacy* feature, while father entails one. Clark and Clark (1977) and Bierswich (1970) discuss this use of semantic components. But our interest is in the psychological implications or uses of componential analysis. Quite obviously, analysis of this type improves our awareness of relationships between words, and of the meanings of words themselves, but what else does it do?

One very important aspect of this type of analysis is that it has the potential to reduce meaning to a set of core concepts – the semantic features themselves. A good analogy is with chemistry: there are thousands upon thousands of chemical compounds, each with its own properties, but they are all compounds of only ninety-two natural elements. Perhaps words themselves are compounds of a number of primitives (although the number is unknown). The analogy goes further. Just as chemical compounds fall into 'families', related in their properties (for instance, metallic halides, simple alcohols), so words appear to fall into semantic fields. Chemical compounds fall into families because the members are made up of atoms with similar properties, structurally compounded into similar patterns. Could this be the case with words in semantic fields, with similar or the same primitive components being configured in similar ways? Possibly. Indeed, something of this sort seems to be necessary if we are to explain, for instance, why a whale is like a fish but is not a fish.

Our brief digression into the theory of semantics has been necessary because, while it may appear only loosely related to psychological matters, it is an important launching pad for what follows. We shall now turn to some research on the structure of semantic memory.

## 2  The structure of semantic memory

One way of tapping knowledge of what we know about things which can be described by words is to ask people to verify statements about them. For example, everyone knows that a dog is an animal, and that a chihuahua is an animal. If asked whether these statements were true, people would answer yes. But what kind of memory representation embodies this type of knowledge? One way of approaching this question is to ask what kind of computational system, or what kind of database, could embody it. Indeed, such an approach has figured greatly in the psychologists' models of semantic memory.

Imagine a number of locations in memory, each of which can hold statements about things. One such statement might be

$$\text{DOG}(x) \rightarrow \text{ANIMAL}(x) \text{ \& 4-LEGS}(x) \text{ \& HAIRY}(x) \dots$$
etc.

roughly following the decomposition idea. The idea is that the definitional information pertaining to dog is stored in the same location, which we shall call DOG. Now what about chihuahua?

One way would be to store the following information at the CHIHUAHUA location:

CHIHUAHUA (x)→DOG (x) & ANIMAL (x) & 4-LEGS (x) & HAIRY (x) & SMALL-SIZE (x) & POINTED SNOUT (x) ... etc.

The first four properties of the rewrite consist of the fact that a chihuahua is a dog, and the definitional information about dogs in general, while the second part consists of properties *peculiar to the Chihuahua*.

Now suppose that instead of chihuahua the dog in question was an Irish wolfhound. We would have something like the following:

IRISH WOLFHOUND (x) →DOG (x) & ANIMAL (x) & 4-LEGS (x) & HAIRY (x) & LONG-HAIRED & TALLEST DOG (x) & ... etc.

Apart from the second part, which specifies distinguishing characteristics of a wolfhound, the rewrite is *exactly* the same as for chihuahua. In fact, it would be exactly the same for any other dog, and there are very many breeds of dog. Each one could be given a description which had a common core, that which is common to all dogs. So we could store the information in a different way:

DOG (x)→ ANIMAL (x) & 4-LEGS (x) & HAIRY (x) ... etc.
CHIHUAHUA (x)→DOG (x) & SMALL-SIZE (x) & POINTED-NOSE (x) ... etc.
WOLFHOUND (x)→ DOG (x) & TALLEST DOG (x) & ... etc.
ANY OTHER DOG (x)→DOG (x) & ... (specific properties) ... etc.

In this case, the information about dogs in general, which is part of the specification of any breed of dog, is summed up by DOG (x). All of this may look like a trivial exercise, but it is not. Consider how one might establish that a wolfhound has four legs from the memory structure above. If all of the information pertinent to dogs in general is stored at location WOLFHOUND, then one simply looks it up there. But if it is *not*, then one would have to go first to location WOLFHOUND, and then to location DOG to get the answer. In the one case the information is stored directly, and the other indirectly with respect to the starting address.

The indirect storage idea relies upon what is termed a *generalization hierarchy*, and is usually illustrated as a semantic network. An example fragment of such a network is shown in figure 7-4(a). At each level there are a number of *nodes*, which are the memory locations of the names of the entities in question. Between each node is a *pointer*, which is labelled ISA, denoting class membership. So a Clydesdale ISA horse; a horse ISA animal; an animal ISA living thing. Figure 7-4(b) shows a small part of the network with properties attached: information general to dogs, for instance, is stored at the DOG node, while information specific to dalmatians is stored at the DALMATIANS node.

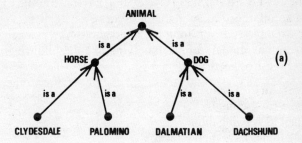

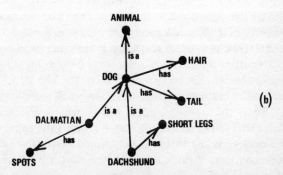

*Figure 7-4.* A fragment of a generalization hierarchy (a), and a portion of it complete with pointers to properties (b). Note that what is stored at the DOG node is true of all dogs, but that what is true of specific dogs is not true of all dogs. This is captured in a generalization hierarchy. *(After Sanford and Garrod 1981.)*

Arguing along these lines, psychologist Alan Collins and computer scientist Ross Quillian set out to examine some of the consequences of such reasoning, and founded psychological studies of semantic memory. Let us consider three points, the first of which is computational. With the generalization hierarchy, information general to dogs, for instance, is stored at only one location: the DOG node. With a full description system, this information would be stored at the node for each and every dog. So, if there are X dogs, it would be stored X times. Accordingly, the generalization hierarchy is more economical of memory – the so-called *cognitive economy* argument. If it were true that storage economy was important in the human brain, then to have memory organized in a generalization hierarchy would be biologically sensible. The second point is quite different. If memory in humans is organized in this way, then while the truth of some assertions could be readily established (e.g. 'A dog has hair'), others would require an inference to be made in order to verify them. A really bizarre example is 'Elton John has a metabolism'. On a generalization hierarchy model, a link something like the following would have to be established:

Elton John IS A human
Human IS A animal
Animal IS A living thing
Living things have metabolisms

This is a rather heavy-handed illustration of the fact that with a cognitive economy principle, certain relationships can only be established by tracing out a route between the relevant nodes. The third point is that generalization hierarchies provide a means of making inference plausible. If I tell you that there is a bird called the lesser-spotted mulberry warbler, you would infer that it had wings because it ISA bird, and BIRDS HAVE WINGS, although you could not possibly have any knowledge of that bird directly. Similarly, a young child who learns a new bird name would infer that it had wings. Obviously, some inferential mechanism is necessary. While this necessity is not a strong argument for cognitive economy, it does establish the need for generalization hierarchies.

Collins and Quillian (1969; 1972) carried out experimental work in an attempt to discover whether people's knowledge of nominal concepts was organized in accordance with the cognitive economy principle. Their reasoning was that if a proposition has to be verified through inference, then it should take longer to verify than one which does not require inference, because of the extra computation. The experimental set-up was simple. The procedure was to present subjects with sentences for verification – they had to make a true/false decision as quickly as possible for each sentence by pressing the appropriate one of two keys. The sentences were of two types: class membership statements and property statements. For example, class membership statements cited by Collins and Quillian include:

| | |
|---|---|
| A maple is a maple | Level 1 |
| A cedar is a tree | Level 2 |
| An elm is a plant | Level 3 |

Examples of property statements include:

| | |
|---|---|
| An oak has acorns | Level 1 |
| A spruce has branches | Level 2 |
| A birch has seeds | Level 3 |

Subjects were asked to verify sentences of these types, and the times taken to carry out the verification were measured. In several studies, Collins and Quillian found that statements which should

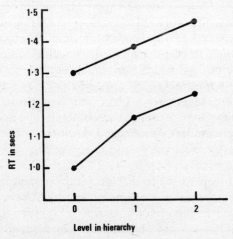

Figure 7-5.  The relationship of mean verification time to level in an assumed generalization hierarchy. *(After Collins and Quillian 1972.)*

require inference to be made did indeed take longer to verify, and an orderly relationship obtained between time and number of assumed steps. An example of their data is shown in figure 7-5. Their claim was that the cognitive economy hypothesis holds, and that semantic networks with generalization hierarchies must be characteristic of human semantic memory.

### 3  Problems with class membership judgements and the feature comparison model

Collins and Quillian's initial work produced a veritable hive of industry in cognitive psychology, with numerous papers appearing which cited the use of similar techniques. A number of problems with the initial formulation quickly emerged, and we shall review some of these in the next few pages. We shall start with problems concerning class membership judgements – that is, situations in which statements of the type 'An X is a Y' are used.

One complication which emerged fairly quickly was that for any given category, judgements that things are members of that category can take systematically different lengths of time. For instance, it takes considerably less time to judge that 'a robin is a bird' than it does to judge that 'an ostrich is a bird'. Eleanor Rosch (1973) argues that conceptual classes, such as 'bird', have typical and atypical members. In one experiment she invited people to rate various examples of a set of categories in terms of how closely they corresponded to the subjects' idea of what constituted a 'typical' example of class, using a 1-7 'typicality' scale. In the bird category, the ratings, which were highly consistent, were 1.1 for *robin*, and 3.8 for *chicken*. *Murder* was rated as a typical crime (1.0), while vagrancy was not (5.3), and so on. Rosch went on to investigate how long it took subjects to decide that typical or atypical class members were indeed members of the appropriate class. The less typical the item, the longer the verification time turned out to be.

Rosch went on to argue that people have concepts of things which are 'prototypes'. For example, they might have a concept of a prototype bird. This is not as strange as it may sound, and the force of the argument may be illustrated by a linguist's technique known as *substitution*. It is an easy matter to compose sentences about birds:

A bird sat on a branch near my window.
A bird sang as the sun went down.
Two birds flew past us as we walked.

Now substitute 'robin' for bird. The sentences are still sensible.
Substitute 'chicken', and the sentences seem less plausible, or even
ludicrous. Rosch (1977) carried out just such a study, and discovered that when less 'typical' members were substituted, the
resulting sentences were indeed rated as less sensible than was the
case when 'typical' members were substituted.

Rosch's view is that the representation of concepts such as 'bird'
in memory consists of a set of semantic features, made up of
*necessary features* (e.g. feathered (x), winged (x), has-beak (x)),
and *characteristic features*, such as a typical body shape (which is
almost impossible to represent as a simple feature!), a typical size,
and so on. This is in straightforward contrast to Collins and
Quillian's earlier point of view. In terms of memory storage,
the node BIRD has only the necessary characteristics of
birds attached to it, according to Collins and Quillian.
According to Rosch, the node BIRD would have necessary *and*
characteristic features associated with it. (In fact, it could be
held that a generalization hierarchy would be invalid given Rosch's
claim.) At the BIRD node we might have *is about 6 in beak-to-
tail*; and at the OSTRICH node, *is 5 ft beak-to-tail*. Since an
ostrich is a bird, the system would then be self-contradictory!
There are ways around this, however, such as adding to the 5 ft
beak-to-tail.

It is a simple matter to see how typicality might originate. If one
sees a number of examples of something, and some of these have a
great deal in common, then that which they have in common may
be seen as the 'typical' features of the class as a whole. Indeed,
Rosch and Mervis (1975) explored the idea that typicality results
from shared features. They asked subjects to list the attributes or
features which they could think of for a number of items from each
of six categories, such as fruits, weapons and clothing. They then
counted the number of features in common to the five most typical
and five least typical members of each of the categories. The
number of features in common was much higher for the more
typical members.

The line of reasoning taken by Rosch and her colleagues is
extremely important, and will be considered in greater detail

shortly but there are other problems for the original Collins and Quillian formulation. In a verification task, it is necessary to include items to which the answer is 'No', for instance 'A canary is a robin'. Consider this particular example carefully. What is notable is that the nodes CANARY and ROBIN should be closely connected in Collins and Quillian's original model, related through the node BIRD. In contrast, the negative statement 'A canary is a tulip' contains elements which should be far more distantly connected. One might suppose, therefore, that any procedure to check each of these statements against the network would take less time to complete in the first (related) case than in the second (unrelated) case. However, the *reverse* is the case. Negative items which contain related elements take *longer* to check (e.g. Rips, Shoben and Smith 1973; Schaeffer and Wallace 1970). On the face of it, this is yet another embarrassment for the original Collins and Quillian theory.

A third problem for the Collins and Quillian formulation is that it has been claimed that the property verification results, the basis of the cognitive economy theory, can be explained in another way. Conrad (1972) argued that certain properties are more typical features of objects than others. For example, 'a salmon is pink' may be a statement of greater typicality than 'a salmon has fins', which in turn may be more typical than a statement like 'a salmon can eat'. In her study, Conrad asked subjects to provide a written description of the things designated by a number of words (e.g. *salmon*). She then ordered the properties for each in accordance with the number of subjects who used each property in providing the descriptions. From these data, several two- and three-level hierarchies were constructed, in which probability of mention was controlled.

She then carried out a verification study using these items, and found that when probability of mention was controlled, no systematic effect of hierarchy was forthcoming, but probability of mention itself was a good predictor of verification time. Her claim is that in Collins and Quillian's experiment, frequency of property was confounded with hierarchical level, and that when this is controlled for, there is no evidence for cognitive economy.

The need for a better formulation of verification procedures and the nature of semantic knowledge storage is clear. We will now review some alternative approaches.

# C  Later accounts of memory structure and processing procedures

## 1  The feature-comparison model

Smith, Shoben and Rips (1974) offer an account of how we might verify statements of the type 'An X is a Y' which differs from the original Collins and Quillian account, and which accommodates many of the problems just listed. They call it a 'feature-comparison model', and make the explicit assumption that every concept is stored as a list of the features which define it, along with typical features of its class, much as Rosch outlined. So, there will be a feature list for a typical *dog* associated with the memory table for *dog*, a feature list for a *collie* associated with the memory table for *collie*, and so on. This is in obvious conflict with the cognitive economy notion discussed earlier.

Following customary philosophic lines, Smith, Shoben and Rips assume that each concept is described by a set of features made up of essential (or *defining*) features and 'accidental' or *characteristic* features. For instance, being a biped, having wings, and having a red breast are essential characteristics of a robin, while being undomesticated and that they perch in trees are really only characteristic.

In their model, they suppose that deciding whether or not 'an X is a Y' occurs through a comparison of the feature lists associated with X and Y. They propose two stages: first, an initial global comparison is made of the feature lists, without regard to whether the features are defining or characteristic. A second (optional) stage occurs if the overlap of features found at the first stage is only small. In this stage, only defining features are compared.

Consider an example like 'A robin is a bird'. The argument is that because a robin is a typical bird, there will be a high degree of feature overlap at stage 1, so that a 'yes' response will be given without further analysis. On the other hand, 'A chicken is a bird' will not yield a high common feature count, and so the evaluation will proceed to stage 2, in which defining features will be compared. So in the first case, the response will be a fast 'yes', in the second, a slow 'yes'.

The model works in exactly the same way with negative statements. If there is little or no feature overlap between the concepts being considered, as in 'A bird is a house', then stage 1 will produce a 'no' response without recourse to stage 2. But if there is sufficient feature overlap, as in 'A bat is a bird', then no decision will be possible at stage 1, and defining features will have to be compared at stage 2. So 'unrelated negatives' will be processed quickly at stage 1, while 'related negatives' will be slower because of the involvement of stage 2. In this way, the model can accommodate the observed data.

The model also has the capacity to account for errors. Subjects do not always answer 'no' to highly related items like 'A bat is a bird' or 'A whale is a fish', but sometimes respond 'yes' under conditions where the emphasis is on speed of response. It is easy to see that if the feature overlap is sufficiently high, it may pass the criterion for a 'yes' response at stage 1.

The fact that subjects are usually aware of having made these errors show that processing does continue to stage 2 eventually, however, but after a 'yes' response has been initiated by stage 1. Finally, error rates are under the control of the subject. If a large proportion of the negative items in an experiment are related negatives, then the stage 1 criterion for 'yes' responses is adjusted so that an extremely high overlap is necessary before a 'yes' is initiated, with a corresponding increase in 'yes' reaction times, since more positive items will go to stage 2. This adjustment of criterion is a special case of varying the criterion in reaction-time tasks as discussed in chapter 2.

The strengths of this account are clear: it explains both typicality effects and relegated-negative effects. Furthermore, a simple extension of typicality arguments enables the model to explain why 'An alsatian is a dog' might be verified faster than 'An alsatian is a living thing'. The feature overlap in the former case is arguably greater. Furthermore, the model does not make the cognitive economy assumption – but it does not provide an explanation of how property relations (An X (has)/(can) Y) are evaluated either. It was not designed to.

## 2  The Collins–Loftus spreading activation model

The Collins and Loftus (1975) paper proposes a very general account of how information in semantic memory might be organized, gives a good all-round discussion of the processes through which it might be organized, and expands enormously upon the earlier reports from Collins and Quillian, which readers may have noted has been described carefully as the 'original' model. In it they examine all of the critical issues described above, and others which we have omitted. At the same time, they point out the need for theories of semantic memory to handle much more than verification tasks.

First of all, it should be stated that feature-comparison theories and the Collins–Quillian network model have been somewhat oddly interpreted in literature in various ways. For instance, there is a tendency to speak of feature theories and networks as though they were mutually exclusive, which they are not. A concept, represented as a bundle of features, can be expressed as a semantic network. So if dog is to be thought of as a bundle of features, these features can be represented as a network in which the features are all connected directly to dog. Whether one writes:

DOG (X) → ANIMAL (X) & 4-LEGGED (X) & HAIRY . . . etc.

or

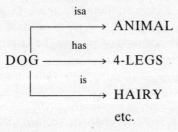

is simply a matter of convention. After all, the representation of all of this in the brain is in terms of neural or chemical activity anyway. What is being represented in the diagrams above is a functional description representing such things as what information can be directly accessed from some starting point, and what cannot; what is stored as a memory, and what can be worked out from what is stored by inference. Except through some particular difficulty in using the different notations, it is not meaningful in terms of these theories to ask whether memory is arranged as features or networks. The real differences between the theories discussed lie in what they assume about what is stored with what, and how it is retrieved or compared.

Collins and Loftus, following Collins and Quillian, view concepts as nodes in a network. Information about concepts is obtained by searches through the network, as in the original model. However, it is emphasized that links between nodes can have different strengths (or 'criterialities') which is a measure of how *important* each link is to the node in question. The criterialities may be different for links in two directions: for instance, TYPEWRITER *ISA* MACHINE may have a high value, while MACHINE *HAS AS AN EXAMPLE* TYPEWRITER may be less so. The notion of cognitive economy is also modified. Rather than assume that cognitive economy *always* holds, the assumption is that when assertions are specifically encountered in what one sees or hears (e.g. an albatross lays eggs), the new information is stored directly, so 'lays eggs' will be stored as a property of ALBATROSS. However, if this assertion had not been made, it would not be stored directly, but would have to be inferred from *a bird lays eggs* and *an albatross is a bird*. To make the illustration more extreme, it is unlikely that *has protons* would be classed as a property of *Richard Nixon*, since *has protons* would be learned with, hence stored with, the concept *atom*. On the other hand, if a subject encountered 'Nixon has protons' in an experiment, then it should be stored directly, because the true assertion would now become part of the subject's direct experience.

This property, which is called 'weak cognitive economy', and is a statement about learning, reflects back on Conrad's (1972) evidence concerning the apparent falsity of cognitive economy. Collins and Loftus point out that, in her experiment, Conrad showed test items on more than one occasion to the same subject, presumably to reduce the standard error of their reaction times, in the best experimental tradition. However, this should have the consequence of facilitating *direct storage* of these assertions, which would be perhaps inferred in a way consistent with the cognitive economy hypothesis before being encountered. In fact, Conrad did find an interaction between levels and practice. Her finding that the higher the frequency of mention of the property during normal collection, the faster the items were verified can be handled in a similar way: the high frequency properties are more likely to be stored directly, on the weak, economy notion.

The weak economy notion may look at first sight like a weak theory as well. But it has the following advantages: it explains existing results, while maintaining that inferences will sometimes *have* to be made. This is surely the case with the evaluation of any novel proposition, for instance 'Nixon has protons'.

It is argued that the links between concepts are not undifferentiated, but must be complex enough to represent any relation between two concepts. Examples include superordinate (or ISA) links, as in A CAT *ISA* ANIMAL and subordinate linking, as in A CAT *HAS* FUR. To this list can be added other types of link, which we will discuss more fully later on, since they include concepts of predication. For instance, 'game' might be related to 'people' through the link *PLAY*. They also suggest that exclusion links may be present – for instance, A ROBIN IS NOT A SPARROW. This is not as arbitrary as it may sound. A child calling a robin a sparrow will learn pretty directly that it is not. This enrichment of link types certainly enables a fuller range of relationships to be stored than was evident in the original model, but it adds complexity to the model, which, although necessary, is difficult to see at a glance.

From these assumptions, various structural properties emerge. For instance, the entire semantic system is organized by *semantic similarity*. This is a straightforward concept, relying upon an obvious corollary of what has gone before: the more properties shared by concepts, *the more links there are between nodes*. Thus the more typical birds, such as robins, sparrows and wrens, will be heavily linked (through size, flying, shape, etc.). *Semantic relatedness is thus specified as the aggregate of links between the concepts*. Consequences of this are easy to work out, even if the overall picture might appear a little baffling at this stage. For instance, *red* things (fire engines, cherries, sunsets) will not be highly related, although they all have one property in common. On the other hand, red, yellow and other colours *will* be richly connected, and thus highly related. An illustration of a part of semantic memory, based on such considerations, is shown in figure 7-6.

Several new features are discernible in this model. It is obviously more complex than the two considered previously, and as a result it is much more flexible although this flexibility is a double-edged weapon. Clearly, the complexity of the network and the properties which emerge seem more psychologically viable than either rigid hierarchies, or exhaustive feature lists, which are replaced by a hybrid. And the proliferation of link types (actually discussed in Quillian's early formulation of 1968) adds greatly to the kind of information which can be directly stored, which in turn

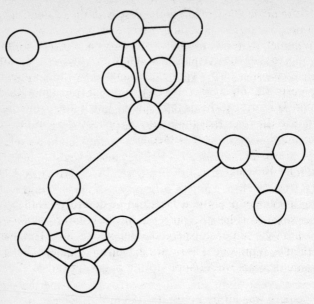

*Figure 7-6.* Part of a semantic net as envisaged by Collins and Loftus (1977). Certain nodes are *highly connected* to one another, others less so; the *distance* between nodes represents the degree of association between nodes.

adds to the power of the theory. However, for the purposes of experimental test, the model has so many degrees of freedom that many psychologists have expressed the view that it may be impossible to test in the way the simpler models could be.

## D  Action concepts

Not only do we have concepts of objects and other things designated by nouns: we also have concepts of states and actions, which are usually designated by verbs. By and large, semantic memory studies of action concepts have been rather different from those described above. This probably results (in part at least) from the fact that on the surface verbs are more complex, and from the verb's somewhat central position in the meaning of sentences. Indeed, verbs can be thought of as organizing the relationships between the nominal concepts in a sentence.

## 1  Verbs and cases

The nominal concepts can play various *roles* depending upon the kind of verb it is, the particular form in which the verb is used, and the characteristics of the entities designated by the noun phrases. One fairly common method which cognitive scientists have adopted to represent this is the network, with the arrows labelled to indicate the roles that the nominal concepts play in the action. For example, consider the sentence:

Felix hit Rosemary.

Accept for the moment that *Felix* can be described as the *agent* in the sentence (it is he who does the hitting), and *Rosemary* is the *recipient* in the sentence (she is the one who is hit). This sentence may then be represented as shown in figure 7-7. Notice that exactly the same diagram would apply to the passive form:

Rosemary was hit by Felix.

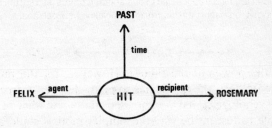

*Figure 7-7.* A graphical representation of 'Felix hit Rosemary'. The verb node has labelled pointers, based on cases, which point to the instantiations 'Felix', 'Rosemary' and 'Past'.

In fact, the underlying roles of agent and recipient are the same in all eight possible syntactic variants of the sentence, as outlined in table 7-1.

The roles of agent and recipient are easy to identify in many sentences, but of course there are many more possible roles than this. Indeed, this form of representation is known as *case representation*, the roles being known by linguists as *cases* (e.g. Fillmore 1968; Anderson 1971). One of the ideas behind linguistic case analysis has been to describe the different roles, or parts of an

Table 7-1.

| Sentence type | Example |
| --- | --- |
| 1 Active | Angela worries Simon. |
| 2 Passive | Simon is worried by Angela. |
| 3 Negative | Angela doesn't worry Simon. |
| 4 Query | Does Angela worry Simon? |
| 5 Negative passive | Simon isn't worried by Angela. |
| 6 Negative query | Doesn't Angela worry Simon? |
| 7 Passive query | Is Simon worried by Angela? |
| 8 Negative passive query | Isn't Simon worried by Angela? |

event, using as few cases as possible. Cognitive psychologists have tended to use cases as ways of describing the relations between verbs and nouns, and they have become central to some ideas about how actions may be represented in memory.[1] As a final, somewhat fuller illustration, an analysis is given in figure 7-8 of the

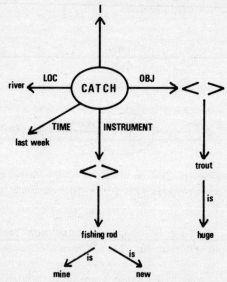

Figure 7-8. Graphical representation of 'Last week, at the river, I caught a huge trout with my new fishing rod'. (From Sanford and Garrod 1981.)

---

[1] The commas used in propositional notations of the type used by Kintsch can now be seen as punctuating different *cases*, with Keith as agent and London as destination. In fact, Kintsch's representation is really equivalent to a case analysis, but not to a schema analysis.

sentence 'Last week, at the river, I caught a huge trout with my new fishing rod'.

The cases used in this diagram, and the linguistic entities which fill the cases, are:

Action – Catch
Agent – I
Object – a huge trout
Location – River
Instrument – My new fishing rod
Time – Last week

## 2 Verb meaning

Now let us think about the representation of action concepts in memory. An action concept serves to organize the roles things play in the action depicted, so the semantic description of a verb should make this explicit. For instance, what does the idea of *breaking something* involve? When something is *broken*, some agent brings about a change in the state of some object, such that although it was whole in the first place, after the action it is not whole. Now this description uses not only the *case* notions of agent and object, as described above, but also introduces particular events which define the peculiarities of the verb itself. While some notion of agent and object is clearly essential, it is not sufficient.

Several cognitive scientists have attempted to describe the meanings of verbs in terms of how they might be represented in memory, including computer scientist Roger Schank (1973), and psychologists Donald Norman and David Rumelhart (Norman, Rumelhart and LNR 1975). Let us take a brief look at the representation of verbs as described by Norman and Rumelhart. They use network representations to express possible memory structures for verbs, referring to the structure as *verb-schemata*, using Barlett's term for a 'packet of knowledge'. An example, the schema for the verb 'to break', is shown in figure 7-9. The diagram can be read in the following way. Break is defined as (IS WHEN) someone (an agent 'X') *causes* a *change* to come about. The *change* is in an object 'Y' (which must be brittle), and is FROM a whole state TO a not-whole state. This is achieved when an agent 'X' DOes something using a method 'M'.

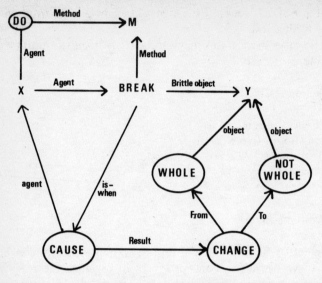

*Figure 7-9.* Verb schema for 'Break', adapted from Rumelhart and Ortony (1977).

X, Y and M are variables – they can take a range of appropriate values. Suppose for a moment that you read the sentence 'John broke the window with a hammer'. To interpret this sentence, according to the schema theory, X, Y and M would be given the values X = John; Y = window; M = hammer. The philosophy behind this approach is reasonably straightforward. Each verb-schema has a structure which is designated to encapsulate the meaning of the verb, and a sentence is understood when the variables (e.g. X, Y, M) are discovered from the sentence itself.

Notice that in the verb-schema outlined above, the network consists of *other schemata*: for instance, whole state and not-whole state are themselves schemata for which a further definition would need to be written. In this way, the representation of verbs raises the same questions of semantic primitives or components as encountered already when dealing with nominal concepts. The idea that a verb-schema can be expressed as an organized system of other schemata leads naturally to the question of whether there are any *basic irreducible* schemata out of which all action concepts are constructed. This is a very obvious parallel to semantic primitives obtained by componential analysis, and, indeed, componential analysis has been applied to certain verbs. Miller (1972), for instance, and Miller and Johnson-Laird (1976) have carried out analyses of this type on verbs of motion. In their analysis, they identify 'travel' as a primitive component which recurs constantly in the description of verbs of motion. Perhaps the concept of travel is indeed an 'ultimate' primitive.

## 3 Decomposition and working representations: back to text memory

If action concepts are represented as schemata in memory, then one might presume that the schemata will be part of the memory representation of a sentence which depicts the action. For instance, the memory representation of 'John broke the window with a hammer' might well be organized around the 'BREAK' schema, with the values of X, Y and M filled in appropriately. The consequences of this are interesting, and have received a good deal of attention. To illustrate with an example: what might the representation in memory be for the following sentence?

- Keith drove to London.

Obviously, the reader *understands* the sentence, and we presented evidence in chapter 6 to show that the memory representation will be the product of understanding. Accordingly, one might guess that the schema for *drive* contains information like:

- DRIVE is when X (an agent) *TRAVELS* from Y (a place) to Z (a place) by means of X (an agent) *controlling* a *car* (a necessary instrument).

If one simply replaces X with *Keith*, and Z with *London*, then one has a candidate for a meaning representation of the sentence. The memory representation is thus a temporarily modified schema.

All well and good, but where does one stop? Does the memory representation include all of the actions of controlling a car? Does it include a definition of car? Does it include a list of types of car? The breakdown of the meaning of a word into component schemata is called *decomposition*. The problem of where to stop when one thinks of representing a sentence, for instance, has been described as the problem of *when to stop decomposing*. It is an important issue, because it is not only a question of what the memory code for a sentence is, but it has consequences for how we think of understanding itself as working.

One point of view, put forward by Kintsch (1974) and others (e.g. Fodor, Fodor and Garrett 1975), is that when a sentence like our example is held in memory, it is coded as something very close to the words themselves – the verb-schemata do not come into play. In the previous chapter we met Kintsch's 'propositional' representation, in which our example sentence would be thought of as stored in the form:

(DROVE, KEITH, LONDON)

Kintsch's predilection for an undecomposed memory representation rests upon the idea that there is no need to decompose to hold the sentence in memory, and that it is impossible to say where decomposition should stop. He also adopted the view that simple structures like that above would be less of a load on memory than a more complex schema-based structure, which seems a fair point if one believes that smaller structures are easier to remember.

An alternative point of view is that a much fuller schema, 'decomposed' to some depth hitherto unknown, will be the memory structure for a sentence. The a priori argument in favour of this view is that memory does seem to be decomposed for the product of comprehension. How could one understand without accessing the meaning structures in semantic memory?

Let us go through some of the experimental work which has been aimed at the decomposition question, beginning with a study of Kintsch's (1974) which he claims points against the theory that sentences are represented in decomposed forms. One piece of evidence which he presented relied upon a study of sentences which combined either simple or complex predicates. For instance:

John is accused of stealing.
versus
John is guilty of stealing.

Kintsch argues that *the first is more complex*, since it could be decomposed into something like:

Someone says that John is guilty of stealing.

The first sentence is more complex, because it appears implicitly to contain the second as part of it. Kintsch argued that the first should be more difficult to remember for this reason, if it was decomposed in memory. However, there were no differences in the memorability of simple and complex sentences, so he concluded that sentences are not represented in memory as decomposed forms. A somewhat different study by Kintsch (1974) was cited as supporting the same conclusion. In this study, the time taken to read sentences of the two types described above were compared. The argument was that if the more complex one was decomposed on being read, then it would take longer to read because the decomposition process would be more complicated. Since reading times for simple and complex sentences of this type were not different, Kintsch argued that they were not processed into a decomposed form. Similar arguments have been made by other researchers, for instance, Carpenter and Just (1977), who obtained the same null effect for reading times of sentences in which verb complexity was systematically manipulated.

Such evidence is not without its problems, however, and a number of other studies not only suggest that some version of the decomposition theory is correct but also offer explanations as to why these results to the contrary had been obtained. Let us first look at some results concerned with sentence memory. Gentner (1981) contrasted what she called 'complexity' theories of decomposition with 'connectedness' theories. The argument she made is that Kintsch assumed a 'complexity' theory: memory for sentences containing complex decompositional structures would be poorer because the structures contain more (propositional) information. This contrasts with an alternative, the 'connectedness' theory: complex structures will be easily retained in memory if the crucial elements within the structure are richly connected. The reader may recognize the fact that connectedness is a way of guaranteeing good retention; think of the additional complexity, but increased *connectedness* which is achieved by using mediators and other mnemonics in memory studies (chapter 5, pp. 101–2).

Gentner carried out a study of memory for sentences containing *simple verbs, complex and poorly connected verbs,* and *complex and well-connected verbs*:

Ida *gave* her tenants a clock (simple).
Ida *mailed* her tenants a clock (complex, poorly connected).
Ida *sold* her tenants a clock (complex, well connected).

*Sold* is more complex than *gave*: *sold* implies two changes of possession (goods and money) whereas *gave* implies only one. Similarly, *mailed* is more complex than *gave*, but this time because not only is there a change in possession, there also must be an associated 'mailing routine' scheme. However, not only are *mailed* and *sold* more complex, but they differ from one another in the degree of 'connectedness' between *Ida* and *her tenants*. According to Gentner, Ida is the principal agent of *mailing* and the tenants are the recipients. However, with *selling*, Ida is not only the principal agent of the whole act, and the one who transfers possession of the clock, but she is also the recipient of money whose transfer is due to the tenants. Thus 'selling' is more 'richly connected'. She presented subjects with various sentences exemplified by these three, and at a later point carried out a cued-recall test, using the head noun ('Ida' in this case) as the recall cue. Subjects were asked to recall the rest of the sentence in each case. According to the complexity theory (Kintsch), if decomposition occurs, then sentences containing simpler verbs should be better recalled than more complex verbs. If decomposition does not occur, then there should be no difference, in line with Kintsch's (1974) report. However, according to the connectivity theory, the predictions are different. Recall is presumed to be dependent upon the number of connexions between different parts of the sentence (e.g. *Ida* and the *tenants*). So if decomposition occurs, the simpler verb should lead to *poorer* cued recall than would be the case with *highly connected* complex verbs. Again, if decomposition does not occur, there should be no difference.

Gentner's results showed a pattern consistent with the prediction of connectivity theory, given that decomposition occurs. It is an easy matter to see how Gentner's analysis would handle Kintsch's original finding of no effect of complexity. Since Kintsch did not control for connectedness, his materials were presumably of a composition which precluded the possibility of detecting evidence for decomposition given that the basis of any effect depends upon connectedness, not mere complexity. Thus the argument from Gentner's analysis is that sentences are represented in memory in a decomposed form. What of the rest of the argument, that if decomposition occurs, reading times for sentences containing complex verbs should be longer than for comparable sentences containing simple verbs? Does not a failure to find such an effect (Kintsch (1974) and Carpenter and Just (1977)) rule out decomposition? The answer depends upon the *process* which one supposes underlies decomposition. Sanford and Garrod (1981) have argued that the time difference would only show up if complex verbs took time to decompose – for instance, if a complex schema takes longer to 'assemble' in working memory. But an alternative view is that verb-schemata do not have to be 'assembled'. When a verb is used, its entire schema is accessed in a roughly fixed time, regardless of complexity. According to this view, verb-schemata can be thought of as *modules* in memory. In this way, there would be no conflict between Gentner's conclusions that decomposition occurs, and the finding that sentences containing more complex verbs take no longer to read.

There is a third way of looking at decomposition, which provides support for Sanford and Garrod's idea. This line of reasoning is related directly to the process of comprehension itself. Consider the simple two-line passage:

Keith drove to London.
The car broke down.

If, on encountering the first sentence, a decomposed representation is set up, then there would be no problem in finding an antecedent for the definite reference 'The car' on subsequently encountering the second sentence. Alternatively, if a decomposed representation is *not* set up, it would be necessary to execute a search through the decomposition *at the point of encountering* the second sentence in order to find out what the reference 'The car' actually referred *to*, since *car* is not explicitly mentioned in the first sentence. Sanford and Garrod (1981) and Garrod and Sanford (1982) attempted a test of the decomposition theory by comparing times taken to read the following types of material:

Keith went by car to London.
The car broke down halfway.
versus
Keith drove to London.
The car broke down halfway.

In the first pair, the initial sentence explicitly mentions *car*. In the second, it does not. In the experiment, subjects were presented with a number of trials on which they saw sentences of these types.

For each material, the subject is presented with the sentences one at a time. The subject paces himself, so every time he is ready for a new sentence, he presses a key. The key variable is the time the subject spends reading the final ('target') sentence. Sanford and Garrod argue that if the first sentence is represented in an undecomposed form, reading times for the target sentences would be longer for the second pair than for the first pair, because no representation of 'car' would be there for the new reference to it to connect to, and on-the-spot decomposition would have to occur after the subject had read the second sentence. In fact, such a reading time difference did not appear, supporting the view that a decomposed form of representation is set up on encountering a sentence.

Both memory studies and reading-time studies thus suggest that the representation of sentences in memory is in a complex form, probably related to the underlying structure of the verbs in the sentences. The Garrod and Sanford (1982) study hints at the potential importance of this for models of how text is understood, a topic which will be discussed in chapters 8 and 10.

## E  Primitives and test-procedures

Before leaving semantic memory, we shall turn briefly to a most important issue – that of primitives. Ultimately, analyses of concepts in terms of primitives or components must come face to face with the fact that verb, noun and other concepts have not merely to be related to one another, but also have to be related to the world of perception and action. No semantic network or schema is much use if it only makes contact with other networks and schemata (although it must do this, of course). The solution to the issue of conceptual primitives is a vexed one, but that does not make it any less real.

It is a simple matter to find commonplace expressions which make the point rather clearly. Consider the meanings of the terms *trudge, saunter* and *march*. These verbs are all highly specified forms of the verb *walk*. One would be fair in assuming that *walk* is a primitive element of these verbs but it is more interesting to simply add *walk* to the initial list, and ask how any of them could be sensibly decomposed. Behind all four of them is a strong non-linguistic factor, some representation of movement patterns, gait, stance, etc. It is a salutary experience to try to write a schema for each of these verbs; one soon discovers that one has to try to describe complex movements in physical space.

One way to approach the problem is to determine which verbs are used to describe which styles of walking, and which *cues* in the movement patterns determine the choice of verb. Johansson (1973; see also Levelt, Schreuder and Hoenkamp 1976) made some headway in this direction by reducing available movement cues to the skeletal joints of people. The technique is straightforward: light-emitting diodes (LEDs) are attached to the limbs of actors at the joints. Films can then be made of the actors performing various movements, in the dark, so that the only information available comes from the LEDs. As an actor 'trudges', for example, the result is a set of complex periodic waveforms traced out by the LEDs. This information was sufficient to enable subjects consistently to choose the same verbs to describe the intended (acted) movement pattern.

While it is possible to describe the waveforms produced in words, this will not be very accurate and will not capture all of the significant discriminations which people can make. In fact, it would be better to describe the waveforms mathematically although even this is difficult and is well beyond most people. The point is that part of the meaning of these verbs is non-verbal, and is rooted in perceptual tests on the visual environment. In addition, of course, there *are* verbal relations between the verbs. Quite clearly, then, it is insufficient to look at semantic memory simply in terms of relations between concepts. In fact, the situation is somewhat more elaborate than is implied by the introduction of perceptual tests. After all, the perceptual tests themselves will have to consist of primitive operations (chapter 3). One can also think about the problem of 'trudging' to order. The actor must interpret 'trudge' as requiring the activation of a set of motor programs to produce the movements. Yet even a child, told to 'stop trudging', can usually do so, by manipulating some discriminable aspect of its movement system. Thus, one might say that the 'meanings' of these verbs consist of three elements (at least):

(a)  A set of relationships to other concepts.
(b)  A set of relationships to *perceptual tests*.
(c)  A set of relationships to motor activity and motor memory.

By and large, studies of semantic memory have been restricted to (a).

Directional terms provide a rich area for the illustration of similar problems. Consider the extremely useful expression '. . . (on the) left'. What does *left* mean? Dictionary definitions are really quite surprising on this question. There are basically three types. The first is something like 'the opposite of right' (no prizes for the definition of right). The second is something like 'that side of the body which is weakest in most people'. The third, the most elaborate, is 'that side of the body which points west when a person is looking north'. Such dictionary definitions epitomize the difficulty associated with simply relating verbal concepts to one another. Yet 'left' is a very simple term to use and understand. Rather than defining it *statively*, it seems better described *procedurally*. For instance, 'look left' means something like scan the visual scene in segment (a), where segment (a) is illustrated in figure 7-10. Perhaps 'left' has such a procedure at its core.

In each of the cases discussed above, purely stative information about word concepts has had to be supplemented with *procedures*. Such an approach is a facet of procedural semantics (cf. Miller and Johnson-Laird 1976), which offers the most valuable approach to understanding an important aspect of primitives – that they are

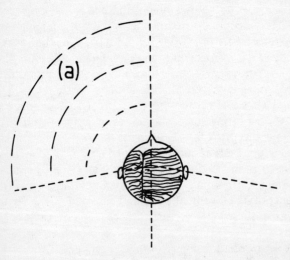

*Figure 7-10.* Could the basic semantics of 'left' be an instruction to scan in segment (a), or to imagine something in segment (a)?

essentially *non-verbal*. One might claim that while this is true of verbs and spatial relations, it is not true of noun concepts, 'table' for instance. But it is. At root, a schema for a table would have to have access to a number of factors which could not easily be represented as a simple list. For instance, one might try to describe a table as a network, with factors like has four legs, has flat top, and so on. But things can be called 'tables' which have one leg (pedestal tables), three legs, no legs (suspended by chains). Even a table with a corrugated top could be called a table. Thus the term 'table' can be used with respect to:

(a) Normal stereotype.
(b) Something which could *function* as a table. For instance, a tree stump when one is having a picnic.
(c) Something which technically resembles a table, but which could not function as one.

These problems of deciding upon the conditions which have to be met in order to call an X an X are well known in philosophy. They certainly indicate that semantic information-processing is very flexible, and that one should look towards tests on objects with respect to the *purpose of description* in order to develop an adequate psychological model.

In this section, we have moved some way from the elements of semantic networks with which we began. There is a danger in thinking of human semantic knowledge as being something like a dictionary. It seems more appropriate to think of it as consisting of programs (procedures) for testing for when it is appropriate to use one term or another, and in procedures for testing perceptual conditions. In turn, this implies that knowledge may be organized in functionally useful packages. It is to this question that we now turn.

# 8 Memory 4: Using knowledge in understanding, and the implications for memory organization

The network models described in chapter 7 illustrate how simple pieces of knowledge might be represented in memory. And yet it would be quite false to believe that all the knowledge we possess can be expressed in these ways without considerable elaboration. In this chapter we will examine some other issues of knowledge organization. Much of what follows is speculative, exemplifying the kinds of issue raised by workers in artificial intelligence and on the theoretical side of psychology. Despite the fact that it is speculative, it is very important, because it is tantamount to theorizing about the kinds of structures which may be abolutely necessary for the mind to function. Furthermore, some aspects of the structures have been investigated experimentally with interesting results.

The essential argument is that the organization of knowledge is likely to be a function of the way in which that knowledge will normally be used. A corollary is that knowledge will be organized in the way in which it is learned, since it should be learned in generally useful packages. We shall use the term 'situation' to describe bundles of events that generally occur together and replace the term with technical alternatives as they arise. The idea that knowledge is organized in a way which makes it useful is partly a function of the fact that the organization of knowledge is a problem which occurs directly when one is trying to develop a system to *use* knowledge. In fact, the most popular ideas on knowledge organization at present come from scientists who have been trying to simulate understanding in computer programs.

This in turn raises the question of what understanding might be. Of course, understanding can occur at shallow or deep levels – a 'full' understanding of something may mean being able to draw out all of the implications of that something. One thing is clear, however. Understanding presupposes having some prior notion of *what makes sense*. Even a small child could understand the following:

- Jane was invited to Jack's birthday party. She wondered if he would like a kite. She went to her room and shook her piggy bank. It made no sound. (Charniak 1972).

This sad little tale is a now classic example of just how much extant knowledge is necessary for simple understanding to occur. We must recognize that an invitation to a birthday party obligates the partygoer to take a present for the host, that the host must like the present, that presents cost money, that piggy banks are a potential source of money, that shaking a piggy bank is a way of checking the contents, and/or getting the money out, and that an absence of sound implies emptiness. Furthermore, to appreciate the *point* of the story, we must appreciate that lack of funds is blocking Jane's unstated, but implied, goal of buying Jack a kite. It is also the case that most people will think of Jane as being a child, although it does not say so.

At once such an analysis presents us with a simple message: no existing knowledge base to which the discourse can be related means no understanding! Unfortunately, the example also serves to indicate the kind of complexity which besets the analysis of knowledge and its utilization. This issue is central to the study of cognition, although until recently it has received rather less attention from the mainstream of cognitive psychology than it deserves. It has received most attention from those computer scientists who are concerned to produce programs capable of understanding discourse, and perhaps hold conversations (Winograd 1972), summarize stories (Schank and Abelson 1977) or carry on 'tutorial sessions' with students on various academic subjects.

Faced with the enormous bulk of human knowledge, computer scientists have attempted various simplifying strategies in the hope of taming the knowledge problem. One strategy is to produce programs which only know about a very limited world like that of blocks and pyramids which can be moved around (Winograd 1972; see also chapter 10). This is sometimes called the 'microworld' strategy. Allied to this is the concept of the 'expert system' – systems which have built into them often very substantial expertise in certain limited subject domains, such as the knowledge-based medical consultation program, MYCIN (for an overview, see Shortliffe 1976). A somewhat different orientation has been taken by others, in particular by Roger Schank (e.g. Schank and Abelson 1977). This approach is to leave the domains of know-ledge to be programmed open-ended, but to develop theories of how knowledge might be organized into convenient 'packets'. In fact, the microworld and 'packaging' approaches have much in common. If a system identifies which packet of knowledge is relevant to a particular situation, then that packet becomes, in effect, a microworld for the duration of its use. Perhaps the main difference is that the 'packaging' approach raises questions about the interrelationships between the packets and how any particular packet of information is identified as appropriate.

In what follows, we shall begin by looking at a particular kind of knowledge packet, called a *script*, and see how a script is supposed to mediate the basic understanding of simple episodes. We shall also look at some psychological evidence which relates to the script concept. The general class of knowledge packets of which scripts are an example are known as *frames* or *schemata*. In a later section we shall discuss some general properties of the frame/schema approach to cognition. Of course, situations will arise where there may be no convenient knowledge packet to assist understanding, and this is also considered later. The utilization of social know-ledge and knowledge of personality traits are also discussed.

## A  Scripts and useful sequences

### 1  Sequence stereotypes

Think about situations which have a conventional ordering of events and actions, such as going to a cinema to see a film, visiting the doctor, catching a bus, or eating in a restaurant. Each of these is a distinct sequence of events which most people would agree upon. Clearly we all have knowledge of situations of this type. They seem so stereotyped that computer scientist Roger Schank and social psychologist Robert Abelson (1977) assume that part of our knowledge might be organized into structures, and they used this idea in producing a computer program which has some simple properties of understanding. They call these knowledge structures *scripts*.

An example of a script is shown in figure 8-1. It consists of a stereotyped order of events (in this case of what is normally entailed in eating out at a restaurant). The basic idea behind the theory is that bits of a simple story will retrieve a script from memory, which can then be used to fill out the details necessary for understanding to have taken place. As an illustration consider the following fragment of discourse.

John was feeling hungry so he went to a restaurant.
The waiter brought him a menu.

This is easy to understand, but not without the reader having to fill in a number of details. Imagine the following simple test of understanding:

Q: Why did the waiter bring the menu?
A: So that John could decide what to order.

The idea that John intends to order, or the implicit idea that it is food that he intends to order, are simply *not given* by the fragment of discourse. They have to come from somewhere, and Schank and Abelson's idea is that the relevant facts come from the script. The processing chain is something like this.

1   Read 'John was feeling hungry, so he went to a restaurant'. Being hungry means wanting food; going to a restaurant is where food can be got. These two facts are sufficient to indicate that John is going to a restaurant to eat. So
2   Activate (get ready to use) the RESTAURANT SCRIPT.
3   Set Customer = John in the restaurant script.

The effect of all of this is to produce a cognitive structure in which John is now playing a role in the script. From this it is easy to answer questions like 'Why did the waiter bring the menu?' even

## Scene 1: Entering

> Customer goes into restaurant
> Customer looks for table
> Customer decides where to sit
> Customer goes to table
> Customer sits

## Scene 2: Ordering

> Customer reads menu *or*
> Waiter brings menu and customer reads it
> Customer decides what to eat
> Customer signals waiter
> Waiter goes to table
> Customer orders

## Scene 3: Eating

> Cook gives food to waiter
> Waiter brings food to customer
> Customer eats food
> Optional repeat on 2

## Scene 4: Exit

> Customer calls waiter
> Waiter brings bill
> Customer pays bill
> Customer leaves tip
> Customer leaves retaurant

*Figure 8-1.* A script-like sequence expressed in natural language based on Schank and Abelson's script concept.

though no waiter has been mentioned, and the answer is not explicit in the text.

According to the script point of view, wherever there is a stereotyped situation which we know about, there is a script for it. At the bottom of script-based understanding is finding the right script in memory. Understanding then proceeds by mapping the things mentioned in the discourse into the script. All of the work of sorting out the inference has already been done, because the connexions are *provided* by the script.

Now consider a different story:

John could not get a waiter to take his soup order. So he contented himself with eating his sweet course.

This is clearly nonsense, or else it requires a considerable amount of explanation! But how does one *know* that it is nonsense? Only by mapping the sequence of events depicted into one's knowledge of the normal sequence of events. For instance, if the waiter has not taken John's soup order, how did he get a sweet course? No-one in our culture eats a sweet course at the start of a meal. By providing a representation of *normal expectation*, a script enables the abnormal to be appreciated as abnormal.

Let us briefly indicate some of the things which a script can achieve:

(a)   They provide a simple way of representing stereotyped event sequences which are difficult to represent in any other way. Try drawing a semantic network containing script information. You end up with a script.

(b)   Given an activation of an appropriate script, it will provide a way of predicting what should happen next.

(c)   If something unexpected happens, it will not fit the script sequence and so will stand out an *unusual*.

(d)   Scripts rid expressions of ambiguities because they provide an unambiguous contextual background. Consider the following:

The waiter talked with John about which wine he wanted. He brought a well-chilled Puligny-Montrachet.

Who is the 'he' in line 2? It is logically ambiguous. Compared with:

Fred talked with John about which wine he wanted. He got out a well-chilled Montrachet.

In the first example, *He* is clearly *the waiter* in line 2. In the second example, the reference remains ambiguous, though for syntactic reasons it is often interpreted as Fred rather than John.

(e)    Scripts enable events to be inferred which may have been omitted from a story:

Mary ordered Steak au Poivre.
She wasn't happy, and left a small tip.

One can infer that Mary probably got her steak, and that it was not to her liking.

Schank and Abelson (1977) propose a wide variety of scripts. First, *situational* scripts (like visiting a cinema, restaurant, etc.) in which the idea is that stylized social interactions may be captured, in which the roles of the participants are clearly known. However, Schank and Abelson also posit the *personal script* as a possible knowledge unit. These are really stereotyped *roles* for individuals, examples including *good samaritan, pickpocket, spy, jilted lover*, etc. The final type of script which they consider is the *instrumental script*. This is simply the name which they apply to stereotyped action sentences: examples might include *boiling an egg, catching a bus*, and *making a chilli con carne*.

Hopefully, it is clear that the script is designed to deal with certain types of stereotyped knowledge: other processes will be necessary for novel situations. It will be equally clear that if human knowledge is organized into script-like packages, then there will be a very large number of them indeed. It is an easy matter to make a very long list of possible situations for which a script might be a plausible representation.

## 2  Some psychological studies related to scripts

Assume that human beings have script-like knowledge structures in memory. If the scripts are to enable different people to understand a description of relevant events in the same way, then two simple conditions must be met. People should be able to produce script-like sequences readily and easily and, secondly, they should be consistent in what they produce for all but personal scripts. Bower, Black and Turner (1979) showed that there was considerable agreement among subjects when they were invited to list the stereotyped events which would characterize, say, *a visit to the dentist*, or *a visit to the doctor*. Subjects tended to include main actions rather than details, but the order of the actions showed a typical stereotyped sequencing. This would seem to be a minimum requirement before scripts could be considered as viable candidates for human memory structures.

Although not intended as a direct test of the script notion, a study by Byrne (1981) produced data which was clearly in concordance with it. First of all, he invited subjects to tell him the list of ingredients necessary for the preparation of two culinary dishes: lemon meringue pie and sherry trifle. After they had produced the lists, he asked them to describe their own recipes for these dishes. He found that there was a close correspondence between the order of mention of the ingredients in the listing task, and the order in which they were introduced in describing the recipes. This led him to suggest that the listing task was accomplished by mentally simulating a run through the recipe. Corroborative evidence came from the comments of subjects, and from an analysis of the pauses between items mentioned in the listing task. For instance, long pauses occurred where new operations in carrying through the recipe would occur – for instance, shifting from making the pastry case to making the filling. The results thus provide good evidence that knowledge about ingredients is accessed through the reading of some sort of instrumental script.

A rather different line of attack on the psychological usefulness of the script concept is centred on the predictions which script theory make about remembering stories woven around stereotyped situations. The predictions are that, first, since script-type knowledge enables a reader to 'fill in' a simple story with stereotyped details which are not actually part of the story as presented, then readers should tend to believe that such details were in fact presented when a recognition memory test is used. For instance, if part of a story consisted of:

... John went in to the *Shalimar* for a curry.
He only left a small tip.

then a typical confusion might be to accept 'John ate a curry' as having been presented. In part of their paper, Bower, Black and Turner (1979) describe an experiment in which subjects were presented with simple multi-episode stories, the understanding of which, if the script theory were correct, would be based on a series of episode-related scripts. Subjects did indeed make such confusions. Another prediction is that relatively unusual events described in stories – that is, events which would not be part of a script – should be very well remembered. The reasoning (taken from Schank and Abelson) is that if an event is important to the central sequence depicted in a script, but is some unpredictable variant on it, then it will be especially remembered, possibly because of the additional (deeper) processing which would have to be applied to understand it. For instance, in a restaurant script, the *waiter* is expected to take an order and deliver the food to the table. If in a story one reads that 'the waiter ignored the customer's efforts to catch his attention', this both violates the expectation of a waiter's behaviour pattern (as defined by the script), and prevents the smooth flow of actions depicted in the script. Bower, Black and Turner confirmed that such unusual events are indeed well remembered.

Finally, script theory makes a prediction about *gist* remembering. A script can be thought of as a series of main actions (called MAINCONS by Schank and Abelson), together with subsidiary actions which enable the main actions to be carried out. In a sense, the main goal of visiting a restaurant is to eat – the rest of the script defines the actions necessary and the conditions which have to be met to enable this to happen. Obviously events depicted in a story which block the realization of this main goal will be important, and so are well-remembered, as in the example given above. In fact they fit one's intuitions of what *gist* is. However, events or states which are not important to the main goal constitute mere *details*. For example, *the colour of a waitress's hair* would be a detail. Bower, Black and Turner found that subjects recalled 54 per cent of interruptions to their scripts but only 32 per cent of the details.

The studies cited in this section are quite consistent with the script notion, but of course they neither prove nor disprove any contention that people have script-like modules, or packets of knowledge, in their heads.

What the reader must bear in mind is that cognitive scientists are still coming to grips with how understanding might be modelled. On one hand, explorations by theorists and programmers are unravelling *the kind of procedures and knowledge structures* which seem to be necessary to explain our understanding of even the meanest of descriptions. On the other hand, the experimentally oriented cognitive psychologist has the task of relating the various theories to the empirical facts. Eventually the gap might be bridged, and result in a satisfactory theory of comprehension. It is hardly surprising that the problem of comprehension has been central in the development of a multidisciplinary cognitive science.

## B  General schema theory

A script is a particular kind of knowledge structure, organizing events, actions, people and props into a connected structure. As the name implies, the script is particularly useful for the description of sequential, program-like activity. Various other concepts are closely related to the script, and are used to build models of understanding in a similar way. The oldest name for this group of structures is the *schema*, as introduced in our discussion of Bartlett's work on remembering, and subsequently used to describe verb networks in chapter 7. We shall refer to the entire set of hypothetical structures as *schema theories*, but there are names besides script and schema for the same kind of thing. The most important of these is the term *Frame* (Minsky 1975). Of course, since these various names are used by different investigators, they can be given slightly different interpretations. Nevertheless, they all have some important aspects in common.

### 1  Understanding and interpretation as mapping

The most important single feature is that these schema-theory structures are supposedly used by people for understanding. Consider the verb-schemata discussed earlier. They are assumed, within many theories, to be central to the understanding of sentences. For instance, the BREAK schema indicates the roles which agent (X), method (M), and object (Y) play in the break action. The idea is that when the word *break* is used in a sentence, it retrieves the BREAK schema from memory, and the variables X, M, and Y are temporarily assigned the values of the relevant parts of the sentence. If it is 'John broke the window with a stone' then X = John, Y = window, M = stone. In other words, understanding essentially proceeds along the same lines as described for scripts.

In Minsky's terminology, a verb-schema is a kind of frame. A script is another kind of frame, depicting stereotypic action sequences. Minsky (1975) discusses other kinds of frame, like *narrative frames*. When we come to discuss the understanding of stories, the proposition that a story is put together according to a rule-defined structure, depicting normal sequences of setting, plot, etc., will be described. It has been suggested that we may well have 'story-schemata' which are memory structures embodying this information (e.g. Rumelhart 1975; Thorndyke 1975; cf. chapter 6), and which are used to enable us to *understand* stories. Minsky calls this general class of structures narrative frames; he also describes *object* and *scene frames*. This makes the scope and generality of the frame notion unmistakable. From Minsky's point of view, perception is a matter of mapping perceptual input on to object and scene frames. Suppose, for instance, one enters a room. In perceiving a room, one matches one's sensory input to a room frame, according to Minsky. It is worth sketching out some of the elements of a room frame:

Room has (normally four) (normally at right angles to each other) (normally straight) walls
  has (normally at least one) (normally in walls) windows
  has floor
  has ceiling

This description contains only a little of our normal expectations of a room, but contains various important elements. Without looking at what is in the brackets, one finds ROOM has *walls, window(s), floor, ceiling*. Take away any one of these, and one would scarcely call the result a room. Within the brackets are less essential aspects. Suppose that you enter a circular room. Minsky argues that perceiving it is equivalent to finding in the sensory input features like *wall, ceiling, floor*. The room frame is called from memory by this data, and the rest of the tests are applied. For instance, if *wall* is *circular*, then this breaks default expectations and, because of this, the frame enables *noticing* to take place: one might well consciously note the fact that the room is circular. This is exactly parallel to the script providing a facility to spot unusual events in stereotyped situations.

The final example of a frame which we shall consider is the *scientific paradigm*. In science, certain consistent and longlasting ways of looking at things, which are powerful in the sense of being able to handle many phenomena, develop. Newtonian physics is a good example of this since, within it, all of the phenomena of classical physics could be interpreted. Eventually, phenomena were discovered which simply did not make any sense within the Newtonian paradigm. It was with immense difficulty that new paradigms, such as relativistic physics, were developed, and classical physics was interpreted into it. Minsky sees the whole interpretative machinery of a scientific paradigm as a frame.

The general family of schema theories reflects the recognition of two important but simple principles:

1  Understanding (and perception) rely on mapping data such as sensory information, the perception of events, fragments of discourse, and so on, on to appropriate information in memory. The 'appropriate information' acts as an interpreter of the input.
2  The 'appropriate information' seems to be a whole conglomerate of information which is useful and readily and rapidly accessed. By assuming that information is organized in appropriate bundles, with the relationships between the elements of the bundles made readily accessible, the mapping process seems to be much easier to understand. The bundles are variously known as scripts, frames and schemata.

## 2  Aspects of schemata and frames

Let us now turn to some other general aspects of schemata and frames. We shall consider two general issues – first, the *consequences* of the idea, and secondly, the internal *architecture* of the data structures.

The consequence of the idea is very powerful indeed. Not only is it a specific hypothesis regarding interpretation, but it has built into it the capacity to handle *point of view* in several different senses. Consider first the experiment by Anderson and Pichert (1978) on memory for a story about a house after reading from the point of view of a burglar or from the point of view of a homebuyer (chapter 6). On a schema-theory account, the assumption is that the reader, in adopting the point of view of a burglar, brings in a 'burglar schema' which is his knowledge of the kinds of things which might interest a burglar when looking over a house. Within such a schema, means of entry (like open windows) are variables waiting to be filled by data. So, if the reader encounters a statement to the effect that *a window is open*, this will be interpreted directly by the schema, and stored. In contrast, the colour of the paintwork will not. By the same argument, when operating with a 'housebuyer' schema, colour of paint will be important, and an open window will not. The memory results, it will be recalled, showed a strong effect of reader perspective.

A further example is a perceptual one: that of literal, physical angle of view. A cube frame consists of information including the fact that cubes have six faces, but, of course, at any time, it is possible to see only three of these. As angle of view changes, it becomes possible to see a new face, and one of the old faces is no longer visible. Knowledge that the extra faces are there, and 'expecting' them, can be handled by a cube frame.

The consequence of a schema account of understanding is that point of view is built into data structures. The roles played by a window in the following situations are markedly different:

1  Installing a window (glazier script).
2  Recognizing a window (room and window frames).
3  An open window from a burglar's point of view (burglar script).
4  An open window in a stuffy room.

The point is that it seems ridiculous to try to capture all of this in a simple (if richly connected) unitary associative network. In situation 4, a property such as 'useful for entry' is inappropriate. In 3, it is quite appropriate. The importance of various states and aspects of windows is dependent on the situation. The frame and schema solution to this question is to have data structures which depend upon how the word is normally used.

## C  Experimental studies relating to modular knowledge structures

It is difficult to test theories of the schema variety experimentally. Nevertheless, there are experimental studies which relate to the idea that understanding depends upon the retrieval of complex mental structures. Consider the arguments on whether sentences in sentence-memory experiments are stored in the memory as propositions closely related to the sentences themselves, or whether they are stored in some sort of 'decomposed' form. The results which were outlined earlier suggested that some sort of decomposed form was near the mark. One of the studies cited in favour of the more complex representation (Garrod and Sanford 1982) was based upon the apparent availability of representations which were only implied by a verb, and not explicitly stated. Thus, whether a prior sentence was 'Keith *drove* to London' or 'Keith *went by car* to London' made no difference to the time it took subjects to read a subsequent sentence 'His car broke down halfway'. Garrod and Sanford interpreted this result as meaning that the verb *drove* activated a schema in memory which represents *drive* as something like *travel by car*, in which case, on encountering a reference to *His car*, there is no problem in determining the reference in memory.

The reading-time method can be used to test a much broader range of questions than this, and Sanford and Garrod have attempted to use it to establish some of the characteristics of the comprehension process. To take one example, suppose that a subject is reading a passage entitled 'A trial in court'. If such a title singles out a script-like memory structure, with the aid of which interpretation of the subsequent story takes place, then it might be argued that various key characters and props would be represented within this structure, and so part of the information should be easily available to subjects. In turn, this should be reflected in reading times.

Table 8-1 shows a pair of passages used by Garrod and Sanford (1983) to test this idea. The two passages are similar, except that the titles are different. The target sentences – those of particular interest – are identical. The first sentence in each passage has two variants – in one case a character (the *lawyer*) is introduced; in the other, no such character is mentioned. The idea is that whether or not *lawyer* is mentioned in the *Court case* passage should have little effect on the working memory structure of the subject, since *lawyer* is a representation which should be triggered by the title alone. On the other hand, in the *Telling a lie* title, a *lawyer* will only be part of the representation when it is explicitly mentioned.

The two passage types (called '*appropriate*' and '*inappropriate*' *titles*, because the titles either suggest a lawyer or do not) and the two *antecedent* conditions (stated antecedent – e.g. *lawyer* mentioned, or 'unstated antecedent' – e.g. lawyer *not* mentioned) give

Table 8-1. Example materials from the *Garrod and Sanford (1982)* study

*Passage 1   Title appropriate to the target*

In court

Fred was being questioned (*by a lawyer*).
He had been accused of murder.
The lawyer was trying to prove his innocence. (Target.)

*Passage 2   Title inappropriate to the target*

Telling a lie

Fred was being questioned (*by a lawyer*).
He couldn't tell the truth.
The lawyer was trying to prove his innocence. (Target.)

---

a total of four conditions. Subjects read a number of passages under each condition, using the self-paced reading method. Reading times for the target sentences in each of the four conditions are shown in figure 8-2. It is clear that the only condition where the target sentence is any problem is in the unstated antecedent condition with an inappropriate title. Garrod and Sanford concluded that some representation of *lawyer* is made available simply by reading about being 'in court' even though the lawyer was not in fact mentioned, and so a reference to the lawyer can be understood very rapidly. In the case of 'telling a lie', the reader has no representation of *lawyer* available (unless one is explicitly introduced), and so has to carry out additional processing to accommodate the fact that a lawyer has unexpectedly turned up in the story. This takes extra time.

It might be argued that this effect is due to little more than associative priming: *lawyer* would after all be associated with *court*. However, while some sort of priming may well underlie the effect, it does not really constitute an alternative explanation. Indeed, one might say that rather than being an explanation, the association of two ideas is something which itself has to be explained. Sanford and Garrod (1981) believe that the basic memory structures being tapped in this experiment are prototypes of situations, much in the way that a script is a prototype of a

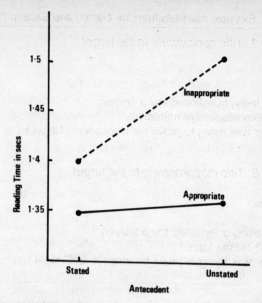

Figure 8-2. The influence of 'appropriateness' of title, and status of antecedent on reading time in the Garrod and Sanford (1983) study. (From Sanford and Garrod 1981.)

situation. Such an explanation seems to be supported by two other experimental studies.

Consider the following example, taken from Sanford and Garrod (1981):

- John was on his way to school.
  He was very worried about the maths lesson.

What could you say about John? Most people make presuppositions about who he might be. Because of these, they often feel a little surprised when the following sentence is added to the two above:

- Last week he was unable to control the class.

The point is that most people apparently interpret the first sentences as conveying *John is a schoolboy*. When it becomes obvious from the third sentence that he is not, they are surprised.

But such changes can be made over and over again in a carefully contructed passage. The following contains three such shifts:

- John was on his way to school.
  He was worried about the maths lesson.
  (John = schoolboy)
  Last week he had been unable to control the class.
  (John = teacher)
  It wasn't fair that the teacher left him in charge.
  (John = schoolboy)
  After all, it isn't a normal part of a janitor's duties.
  (John = janitor)

In order to establish that such interpretations are indeed made as people encounter each part of the text, the reading-time technique may be employed again. The idea is that if a target sentence requires a shift in the assumed role of a person, then it should take longer to understand than one in which no shift is required. Typical materials for these two conditions are shown in table 8-2. Reading times for targets do indeed reflect this.

Table 8-2. Materials and target reading-time results from the role-shift study

|  | Reading time (sec) |
|---|---|
| Condition 1 – No role change | |
| John was not looking forward to teaching maths. The bus trundled slowly along the road. He hoped he could control the class today. (TARGET.) | 1723 |
| Condition 2 – Role change on target | |
| John was on his way to school. The bus trundled slowly along the road. He hoped he could control the class today. (TARGET.) | 1893 |

From Sanford and Garrod (1981).

Sanford and Garrod (1981) suggest that *John* in this particular example is classed as a schoolboy because a stereotyped memory structure for 'being on the way to school' has a default slot for 'schoolchild', and *John* is interpreted into this slot. So comprehension once again seems to rest on a situation-specific memory structure. Since the scripts of Schank and Abelson have very particular structures, these experiments cannot really be said to support the involvement of scripts in understanding. However, they do seem to implicate situation-specific memory structures. Sanford and Garrod (1981) refer to the structures of *scenarios* to make it clear that they are not necessarily scripts.

A final example from the work of Sanford and Garrod is somewhat more complicated. Many stereotyped episodes have boundaries of time and space. For example, for a person to spend three hours at a cinema is within the normal stereotyped time range for that activity. However, to spend twelve hours is very unusual, and to spend two days is simply ridiculous. That we can recognize these facts so quickly and easily implies that some representation of the normal time period over which an episode can be expected to run is stored along with other characteristic features of the situation.

Anderson, Garrod and Sanford (1983) used the possibility of temporal information in scenarios to investigate various aspects of text comprehension. The aspect which is of particular interest here is that which lends support to the notion of the scenario itself. Subjects read passages in the self-paced reading setting: a sample passage, showing the experimental variants, is shown in table 8-3.

Table 8-3. Example of materials used in the *Anderson, Garrod and Sanford (1983)* study

---

At the cinema

Jenny found the film rather boring.
The projectionist had to keep changing reels.
It was supposed to be a silent classic.
Ten minutes ⎫
Seven hours ⎭ later the film was forgotten.          (Time reference.)

He  ⎫
She ⎭ was fast asleep.                                 (Target.)

---

The first sentence is simply the orienting title. The second sentence introduces a main character (*Jenny*), and the third a scenario-bound character (*the projectionist*). Following this is a time-shift sentence, which moves the narrative present forward by an account either *within* the scenario time boundary or *beyond* it. The idea behind the experiment is that a time-shift *beyond* the scenario boundary should signal to the processor that the current scenario is no longer relevant, and should be dropped as a mechanism for text interpretation. A consequence of this should be that representations *depending upon* the current scenario should become less available in memory. Thus, in the present example, representations of *the projectionist* should be less available. One type of target sentence in the materials contained a reference to the scenario-dependent character, and the prediction was that reading time for such targets should be longer following a *beyond* time shift than a *within* time shift.

The second type of target sentence serves as a control: *She was fast asleep.* In this case, *she* refers to the main character, which is not scenario dependent. Thus, accessibility, and hence reading time for the main-character target, should be unaffected by the kind of time reference the sentence used. After all, a main character should pass from episode to episode in a simple story. The main/scenario-dependent distinction is, in fact, quite difficult to specify fully; at this point we must rely upon intuition to understand the distinction.

The results of three different aspects of the experiment are shown in figure 8-3. First, look at the reading times for the target sentence in figure 8-3(a). The data are in the right direction: scenario-bound characters are less 'available' after the shift, though main characters are certainly not less available. However, the effect was not statistically sound (Anderson, Garrod and Sanford (1983) discuss reasons for this). But as part of the materials, *questions* were included at the end of each passage which referred to either the main or the scenario-dependent characters. Analysis of the times to answer these questions indicate quite clearly that while scenario-dependent characters became less accessible as a result of large time shifts, nothing of the kind happened with main characters (figure 8-3(b)). This and other evidence cited by these authors supports the view that the manipulation was successful.

The final graph, figure 8-3(c), shows the time which people spent on reading the sentence in which the time shift itself occurred. If the shift was beyond the scenario limit, the time spent on the sentence was reliably longer.

The explanation put forward was as follows: text is matched

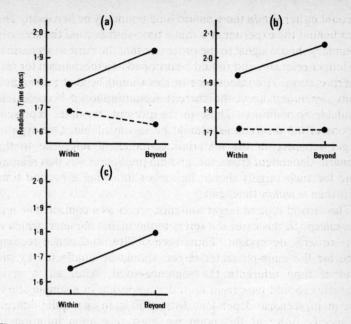

*Figure 8-3.* Measures of (a) target sentence (reading time), (b) question-answering, (c) reading time for time-shift sentence. 'Within' and 'beyond' refer to the time shift in relation to expected scenario durations. Dotted lines indicate the main character references and solid lines the scenario-dependent character references. *(Data from Anderson, Garrod and Sanford (1983) and figures modified after Sanford and Garrod 1981.)*

against a scenario. In the case of a time shift which exceeds the scenario limit, a mismatch is found. This mismatch serves as a cue that the scenario is no longer going to be appropriate for interpretation. The result is that the scenario, along with all of the things that depended on it (including representations of scenario-dependent characters), is removed from active working memory. Thus the text is controlling the availability of scenarios in a rather direct way.

Sanford and Garrod (1981) considered the time-shift experiment important for their general theory of text comprehension (chapter 11). Let us concentrate on the apparent increase in difficulty of reference to the scenario-dependent characters in the beyond-episode time condition. In particular, think of this from the point of view of a simple association explanation of those effects which have been ascribed here to scenario structure. One might argue that 'waiter' is somehow primed by the word 'restaurant': this could explain why it is easy to resolve a definite reference to a waiter, given a story scene about a restaurant, even if a waiter was not explicitly mentioned beforehand. But it is difficult to see how such an explanation would predict a drop-off in the priming effect when temporal information like that used in the present study indicates the end of a restaurant episode. Are we to suppose that the representation of 'a waiter' has temporal information associated with it? Not at all: after all, a waiter getting a haircut would have a time range of up to an hour, say; a waiter 'on holiday' has a time range maximum of three weeks, say. It is *the restaurant setting* which has the time range associated with it, and in the present case, the time range is applicable to the main characters. It seems necessary to suppose that memory representations of stereotyped situations are real, and that the scenario concept is worth pursuing. Relevant knowledge about 'waiters' depends upon the setting in which they are placed.

## D   Understanding less stereotyped situations

In artificial intelligence, a distinction is made between *routine* problem-solving and *creative* problem-solving. Routine problem-solving is the application of some pre-formed set of procedures to a problem for which the procedures are appropriate. In contrast, *creative* problem-solving requires building up a set of procedures for producing the solution which is required. This distinction will be treated in more detail when we examine problem-solving per se (chapter 11). For the moment, note that an application of a script to aid interpretation is a routine problem-solving method, in that many of the problems of interpreting events can be solved simply by selecting the right script. However, for the interpretation of events or descriptions for which there is *no* script, or similar schema structure, other methods would have to be employed. To illustrate this, consider the following description of an episode. How is it understood?

- At the puberty rite, little Kamathi's mother dropped her shoga.
  The crowd drew back in horror.

Computer scientist Yorick Wilks (1976) used this example to

show that understanding can occur without recourse to scripts. His argument is that most people would not have a 'script' (or any other substantial knowledge structure) for a puberty rite, and yet understanding occurs. He suggests that the description is understandable because people possess general *rules of inference*. For the present example, he suggests the following:

| (Humans show horrified reaction.) | ⇒ | (Other humans did something wrong.) |
|---|---|---|

For a rule of inference to work, some machinery is obviously needed so that the description of the situation retrieves the appropriate rule. The sentence 'The crowd drew back in horror' would obviously map on to the left-hand side of the inference rule given above.

Wilks's point is that we do not need to posit large script-like structures in order to understand. Indeed, this is true. Beyond that, a system of 'general rules of inference' would have its own organizational problems. Take just the left-hand half of the rule:

(Humans show horrified reaction.)

There are clearly many things which could be put on the right-hand side (all the things that lead to a horrified reaction). The net result would be a complex memory structure, built around the left-hand side.

## 1  Plan-based understanding

Schank and Abelson (1977) recognize that it is ludicrous to postulate a script for every conceivable situation, and devote considerable discussion to ways in which understanding without scripts might occur. One of their examples is this:

John knew that his wife's operation would be very expensive.
    There was always Uncle Harry. . . .
    He reached for the suburban phone book.

It would be absurd to posit a 'paying for an operation' script, since there are many methods of paying for an operation: indeed, there are many methods for paying for lots of things. As Schank and Abelson point out, what connects the second and third sentences of their example to the first sentence is that John is operating under a general goal state, which Schank and Abelson call the goal of 'raising a lot of money for a legitimate expense'. What the understander has to do in order to make sense of the example is to appreciate that this *is* the goal, and that the activities which ensue are carried out in pursuance of it. Such understanding is called *plan-based understanding*, and is necessary when no stereotyped script knowledge is available, and on occasion can be necessary even with script-based understanding.

A script can be thought of as a prepacked stereotyped goal and plan structure. For instance, the basic goal in the restaurant script is to eat a meal. In order to achieve this goal, certain procedures have to be followed, like getting a table, ordering, being able to pay, and so on. All the processes involved in getting through these requirements could be viewed as problems to be solved, with plans being involved to solve them. However, eating a meal at a restaurant is a routine problem-solving process – we simply use an acquired stereotyped behaviour pattern. If we wanted to perform some relatively novel activity, however, we would have to be creative about the methods we employed to achieve the goals associated with the activity. Indeed, if the activity were sufficiently novel, it might be carried out in a purely plan-based way. In between the purely script-based activities and the purely plan-based will be a set of activities which are a mixture of the two: some parts of a behaviour sequence in pursuance of a goal may be based on novel plans, and some parts may be routinely handled by scripts.

These principles are important for a proper appreciation of the work of Schank and Abelson. Many summaries of their work deal with the script aspect alone, but they are really talking about continua of predictability, from the most stereotyped to the most novel of situations.

According to script theory, and to schema theories in general, the process of understanding consists of mapping descriptions on to structures in memory. In the case of scripts this is fairly straightforward to imagine, but what happens in the case of plan-based descriptions? Schank and Abelson argue that the process of understanding follows a similar pattern. With plan-based understanding, they argue that the steps that the understander goes through include discovering the main goal. Some-times, what the main goal might be is made fairly explicit, for instance, if a description begins 'John wanted some beer for a party', the main goal is established directly if we assume (reason-ably) that to *want something* is to have the goal of obtaining it. At other times, the goal could be inferred from stated descriptions, such as 'John was feeling very hungry'. Feeling hungry would have to be represented as a state implying the goal of obtaining food, and so on. Of course, under some circumstances, things may be considerably more complex, and a goal may have to be inferred from a number of aspects of a description.

The second aspect of plan-based understanding is the establish-ment of the particular set of ways which a specific character is using to satisfy the main goal. These subgoals and associated plans are termed 'deltacts'. Abelson (1975), and Schank and Abelson, argue that many situations can be understood on the basis of a handful of deltacts. One example which they use serves to illustrate what a deltact is:

- John was lost.
   He pulled his car up to a farmer who was sitting by the road.

Their claim is that the first sentence enables a goal to be identified: 'John wants to find out where he is'. This means that John requires knowledge, and requiring knowledge is a D-goal (the goal part of a deltact), specifically it is D-KNOW, their term for the goal of getting knowledge. D-KNOW is one of the handful of D-goals which we will describe later.

Schank and Abelson theorize that associated with D-KNOW are a number of plans which might be implemented to satisfy the goal: asking people and consulting books are examples of such plans, and the details of these plans are called *plan-boxes* by Schank and Abelson. The *third* stage of plan-based understanding is supposed to be the identification of which plan-box is being used by a character in a description. For instance, in the example, given above, the plan-box is called ASK, one of the standard ways of achieving the D-KNOW goal.

D-goals form an intermediate step in plan formation when no stereotyped or scriptal sequence can be used. If a main goal is EAT, for example, then using a restaurant, cooking, or buying sandwiches are standard scriptal sequences which can realize the EAT goal. However, situations depicted in descriptions may sometimes preclude the direct application of a script, even if there is a script available. For instance, if John is out in the country camping, and decides that he wants to go to the cinema, he will have an intermediate D-goal of getting to a place (town) where a cinema might be found. Such situations are easy to think of, and of very great variety.

## 2  D-goals: simplifying through goal primitives

A general way of conceptualizing goal-based behaviour is that the goal-state, X, in which a person finds himself is equivalent to the difference between desired-state and current-state. Thus, if John is at point P and wishes to be at point Q, then a *plan* will be a tentative or usable procedure to enable him to get from P to Q. (In fact, it is because goals lead to state-difference reduction procedures that they are prefixed by D- or delta- for 'difference' in the Schank–Abelson work.) Now consider the following simple story:

John was camping some miles out of town.
He decided that he wanted to go to a cinema.
He thought that he should try to get a bus.
However, he didn't know where or when to catch one.
He went to the nearest farm to ask.

In Schank–Abelson terms, to realize the main goal, two other goals have to be realized. First, operating directly in the service of the main goal, is to get from country to town. This is a D-goal, called D-PROX. Associated with D-PROX are a number of methods (plans): walk, get bus, etc. John elects the get bus method. This appears solved, but a crucial pre-condition is revealed as missing: he does not know where or when to catch a bus. In general terms, then, this generates *another* (different) D-goal, which Schank and Abelson call D-KNOW. Associated with D-KNOW are methods (plans) for realizing it: read book, consult map, etc. are some possible ways, but ASK is a more general and frequently used procedure and this is what he intends to do. Obviously, one could make the story more and more complex, involving frustration of the realization of goals, setting up new D-goals, and so on.

Up to now we have introduced two D-goals. Is it possible to define a small and powerful set of D-goals, or are there so many possibilities that a list would fill a sizeable book? This is similar to the question of semantic primitives described in earlier chapters. Does the vast variety of human goals reduce to a small set of primitives, to which one must only add specific bits of information peculiar to the situation at hand.

Abelson, the social psychologist of the Schank–Abelson team, has been concerned with just such questions (cf. Abelson 1975). In fact, Schank and Abelson (1977) tacitly claim that only *five* D-goals enable a huge number of goals to be accommodated. These, together with their significance, are indicated in table 8-4.

They are offered as *general goals* used in planning when specific stereotyped goal realizations are not available. For instance, the goal of SEE FILM could presumably be handled by a cinema

Table 8-4.  Five delta-goals. *(After Schank and Abelson 1977.)*

| Name | Significance |
| --- | --- |
| 1 D-KNOW | Goal is to obtain knowledge.<br>ASK<br>CONSULT BOOK |
| 2 D-PROX | Goal is to get to a particular location (in the physical sense). Examples of plan-boxes are RIDE ANIMAL; USE VEHICLE; USE PUBLIC TRANSPORT, and USE SELF (e.g. walk). |
| 3 D-CONT | Goal is to gain control of a physical object. Plan-boxes include:<br>BUY<br>STEAL<br>OVERPOWER. |
| 4 D-SOCCONT | Goal is to obtain social control, or power and authority to do something. Plan-boxes include:<br>PERSUADE<br>USURP<br>GO OVERHEAD. |
| 5 D-AGENCY | Getting someone else to pursue a goal on your behalf. Plan-boxes include:<br>PERSUADE. |

script if the protagonist in a description was at a cinema. Similarly, the goal MAKE OMELETTE could be handled by an omelette-making script.

## E  The role of personality and social interaction

The analysis of understanding discussed in this chapter is almost totally concerned with understanding the actions of people. Even the very simple situations considered up to now invoke a vast amount of 'mundane knowledge' about situations which are determined by routine social interactions. But many of the ways in which people interact, and our understanding of those inter-actions, are determined by the belief systems of people, and what we assume about those belief systems. This has been a long-time research interest of Abelson, among other cognitive social psycho-logists, and is an important part of the Schank–Abelson analysis.

People have goals and plans, but where do they come from? Obviously, goals and plans are not arbitrary, but are structured. Hunger is a basic biological drive, common to all humans, and so to say that 'John felt hungry' is to assert a common and easily understood state of affairs. But to say 'He thought he'd start with *Boeuf Bourguignon* followed by *mangetout* peas, washed down with a Château-Lafite Rothschild' is to indicate something special about satisfying his goal. It is clearly different from eating a hamburger! It may well be saying something about his lifestyle. Similarly, different roles have different expectations associated with them. For example, a policeman might be assumed to be always vigilant for crime, a doctor always ready to save a life, and so on. This is easily demonstrated:

- John was a physician of some standing.
    When he was on holiday, someone was injured by a malibu surfboard. John shouted for help, and then went back to his villa for dinner.

Schank and Abelson argue that many goals and plans are organized by even higher level structures, which they term *themes* (cf. also Abelson 1972). They identify three useful types of theme: role theme (like that above), interpersonal theme, and life theme. Let us consider each in turn.

The following interaction from Schank and Abelson (1977) is clearly strange:

Jake:    Sheriff, my cattle were stolen this morning.
Sheriff: It's been fine weather, Jake. How's your kid with the mumps?

The strangeness resides in the way that the sheriff is acting in a way which is not part of his *expected role*. In fact, as Schank and Abelson point out, it is as though the sheriff is taking a roundabout route to saying that he is not interested in Jake's problem. The whole interaction is, in fact, interpreted in terms of the sheriff's normal modus operandi. Next consider the following, again from Schank and Abelson:

Jake told the sheriff, 'My cattle are gone!' The sheriff went to the saloon to find Slim, Ernie, Baldy and Pete.

One makes the strong inference that the sheriff acts in order to round up a posse (or perhaps to check out potential culpability), both of which are consistent with interpretation of the actions within the expectations of a sheriff's normal modus operandi.

All of this suggests that the explanation of action (i.e. the inference of goal and plan patterns) can be made in terms of what Schank and Abelson call *role themes*. The influence of role themes on interpretation is fairly obvious in the case of the following contrasts:

- Tom, the baker, asked his sidekick to bring the dough.
  versus
- Babyface, the gangster, asked his sidekick to bring the dough.

The interpretation of 'dough' depends upon the role themes associated with baker and gangsters respectively!

Role themes are construed as bundles of knowledge associated with a role name; the knowledge consists of representations enabling recognition that the role is to be played, and goals, plans and scripts which enable the role to be played. For instance, the use of the word 'sheriff', along with a description of a situation in which the law has been broken, should instigate a sheriff role theme. Given this, the role theme is defined in terms of goals. (The top goal, for example, might be 'maintain law and order'. This might point to instrumental scripts, such as 'routine investigation procedures for sheriffs', and to specific plans for identifying the criminals, getting control over them, etc.) In short, role themes serve as knowledge-organization packets.

Schank and Abelson postulate two other 'themes' which work in much the same way. These are *interpersonal themes* and *life themes*. Interpersonal themes define social relationships, such as the set of general goals and plans associated with *love*. The knowledge that 'John loves Mary' is equivalent to having a set of predictions about how John will act towards Mary. Again, only a superficial indication of the argument is possible here. Schank and Abelson assume that each interpretation theme label (e.g. 'LOVE', 'ENEMY', 'FATHER/SON') is connected to a representation of particular goal conditions, which are in turn connected to plans or scripts. These structures amount to expectancy rules, enabling predictions to be made regarding behaviour, and enabling the unusual to be spotted. For instance, Schank and Abelson suggest that one of the expectancy rules for 'LOVE' might be 'If two people are positively emotionally related then the recognition of a *potential* negative change in one person's state will cause the other person to develop the goal of *preventing* the negative change in the first person's state'.

The third (and final) set of themes postulated are the 'life themes', which represent the general position or aim that a person wants in life. Examples given include 'LUXURY LIVING' and 'GOOD PROFESSOR'. Life themes are fairly obvious packages of goals, plans and scripts. For instance, under a 'LUXURY LIVING' mode of life, the theme can be recognized in a person through cues such as 'hobnobbing with the jet-set', 'owing a yacht', and so on. The *general goals* include owning desirable objects, having lots of money, having servants, etc. Instrumental goals are to make money, get a rich spouse, etc.

Our discussion of these three themes has taken us far from where we started, with the questions of how knowledge might be organized. It has also taken us far from the well-trodden paths of experimental cognitive pychology. However, it is pretty clear that we do use knowledge of rules, social expectations, and life themes in our understanding of the world. And it is equally clear that there is much that is *stereotyped* about these themes. What Schank and Abelson are suggesting is that themes serve as nuclei around which goals, plans and scripts are organized. Their speculations make for some interesting points of contact between computational considerations and social psychology and personality dimensions. In fact, what they are suggesting is that if a computer program is to be able to understand the significance of social interactions, or to understand why a person acts the way he does, then theme information is essential. It is therefore of equal importance for human understanding. Probably the most important aspect of the Schank–Abelson work, and for that matter the work of Minsky, is that they map out the field of what is entailed in understanding in some detail. The expanded horizons produced in this way may serve as a stimulus for more empirically founded research by mainstream experimental psychologists.

## F  Overview and final remarks

In this chapter we have considered some problems of memory (knowledge) from a new perspective, concentrating on its utilization in the understanding of everyday events and episodes. For the most part, understanding is an automatic non-conscious process. Somehow, when an adult reads a simple story, or sees some event in the world, or engages in some social interaction, the superstructure of inferences which support interpretation go unnoticed. While this degree of automation is very convenient from an everyday viewpoint, it makes it difficult for investigators to unravel just what is the full range of inferences being made, and just what sorts of knowledge are being used at any particular time. Philosophers have studied aspects of the inference problem (such as presupposition and entailment) for some time, and to these studies computer scientists have added ones of their own. Indeed, the illustrations taken from Charniak, Minsky, Schank and Abelson, Wilks, etc. show some of the complexities which are currently being studied. While even simple narratives are complex enough (especially when the motivations of characters are involved), analyses of this sort have been applied to even more tricky situations, such as conversation, lying, and so on (see chapter 10).

One problem is obviously how to discover the *range* of knowledge required for the comprehension of various situations. In many ways studies such as those of Schank and Abelson (1977),

Abelson (1975), Norman, Rumelhart and LNR (1975) and Sanford and Garrod (1981) are *natural history* explorations of inferential mechanisms and of ranges and types of inference. Natural history can be distinguished from biology in that while biology is based on a sound (if recent) theoretical superstructure, natural history consists more of observation and taxonomizing, looking and seeing. We believe that this is a very important phase in cognitive science, and currently characterizes a great deal of it.

One or two things are clear from our explorations up to this point, however. First, *many and varied* types of knowledge are drawn upon in understanding. Second, these types of knowledge can be retrieved very rapidly and automatically. This leads to the very serious question of how a processor accesses the right knowledge at the right time, and with such speed and facility. One solution to the problem is to have knowledge organized into useful packets (schemata), so that the main task becomes one of finding the right packet for the situation at hand. Once the packet is found, most of the work will have been done. Scripts exemplify such knowledge packets. By retrieving an appropriate script, many useful inferences are already made and do not have to be carried out on the spot, and relevant props, characters, and relationships between things are readily accessible. On a somewhat different scale, the same is true of verb-schemata. In fact, what schema theories highlight is the importance of a trade-off between the richness and variety of knowledge packets, and the need to indulge in complex plan-based comprehension. Suppose that we did not have a script for what to do at the cinema. Rather than rapidly access a simple structure, it would be necessary to build up a plan-based interpretation every time it was needed and this would be time-consuming. While schema theories assume the existence of many pre-formed plan structures (e.g. scripts, or situational schemata), it has to be acknowledged that there will be no such structures for novel situations, of course. Such theories are difficult to test empirically, and at present cognitive scientists are still working out what the alternative accounts may be like. Psychological work, like that of Sanford and Garrod, for example, hardly provides an acid test of schema, or any other, theory.

Background knowledge is not only used in the comprehension of stories. In fact, the little stories used in this chapter are merely convenient 'natural laboratories' for the investigation of comprehension. Bringing in the right knowledge is equally important for visual perception (chapter 3), and for thinking and problem-solving (chapters 11, 12 and 13). Indeed, when one considers problem-solving, the role of stereotyped knowledge becomes very striking indeed. People often have difficulty with problem-solving because they invoke some standard knowledge package which *seems* appropriate but turns out not to be. Schema theories are very well designed to explain such phenomena.

# 9 Language 1 : Language and grammar

Language is ubiquitous among humans. Most language is spoken, and through the spoken word we can learn things by proxy, test our plans and ideas on others without having to enact them, and indicate our intentions. Written language is secondary: there are many spoken languages which do not have corresponding written systems. Yet if spoken language enables thought to be demonstrated without enactment, then written language greatly augments the range of possibilities. It is through written language that we learn the ideas of people remote from us in space and time. It is through written language that we know that language itself was studied at the time of classical Greece: records of those ideas exist in ancient Greek and in Sanskrit (Lyons 1968). Given the ubiquity and value of language, it is scarcely surprising that it has been a central topic of study for centuries, and that its study plays a major role in cognitive science. People study language for different reasons. Linguists are interested in language as a phenomenon: how words change their meanings, how one language relates to another, and how grammars work are part of their interests. To the developmental psychologist, the astonishing capacity a child has to acquire language poses a fascinating problem. To information-processing psychologists, how ideas are translated into utterances, and how utterances are understood, are key problems which involve practically every mechanism we have discussed so far. To computer scientists, there is the problem of how to design programs which can either understand 'natural' language input, or produce natural language output. Needless to say, each of these groups of interested researchers has much to contribute to the disciplines of the others.

We have already seen the importance of background knowledge to the interpretation of simple stories. We have seen something of the role that semantics plays in understanding. Some of the details of these points will be discussed in chapter 10. In this chapter, we will discuss another major aspect of language: the role of *syntax*. Syntax is concerned with the order of words which is admissible in a particular language. From a processing point of view, this is extremely important. One illustration of its importance was tacitly given in the chapter on semantic memory: the assignment of noun phrases to slots in a verb-schema (subject, object, instrument, etc.) requires a good deal of syntactic analysis. After outlining some of the issues associated with syntactic analysis, we will discuss the process by which a sentence may be broken down into its constituent parts, a process known as *parsing*, and relate this to how people may carry out the same operation. The discussion will include illustration of a computer program which 'understands' natural language instructions.

In this way, the present chapter is focused towards language as *made up of sentences*. Of course, this is a rather narrow view. Some attempt to redress the balance is given in chapter 10, which treats language as *discourse* – that is, as connected structures conveying messages for some purpose. Many interesting topics are omitted from the introductory treatment of these two chapters, but some guidelines for further reading are provided in the comments at the end of chapter 10.

## A  Syntax and word order

### 1  Parts of speech and grammars

It is intuitively obvious that the ordering of words to make up admissible sentences in any language is restricted in some way, or governed by rules, even if we cannot say for certain what those rules might be. Thus, in English, 'John burnt his boats' is an acceptable sentence, while 'Burnt his John boats' is not. An important aspect of syntax is the study of just what constitutes admissible word orders within a particular language. The description of rules for admissible word order is of course a problem in *linguistics*, but it is also important for psychology, because people must have some set of procedures by which they produce only strings which are admissible, on the whole. So if we are to develop an information-processing account of language production, or of understanding, then the account must handle the linguistic facts.

The same argument applies to the production and understanding of language by a manmade computational device.

How can one specify which word orders are admissible and which are not? One way would be to write down every admissible sentence, and simply assert that as the answer. However, this is quite impossible and misses the point. Words and word groupings seem to fall into categories intuitively, and there would appear to be only certain ways in which examples of these categories could be ordered. A theory which defines these categories, and indicates how they can be ordered, would be *a descriptive theory of syntax*. Let us begin with some rather direct methods which were developed in recent times to track down the precise way in which words fall into categories, and how they can be combined.

Consider the following simple sentence:

John loves Mary.

These three words can be thought of as three symbols, which we can call $X'$, $Y'$, $Z'$. The problem is to ascertain to which general classes $X'$, $Y'$ and $Z'$ belong. One standard linguistic procedure is to see what happens when some word, say $X'$, is put into another position within a sentence. In the present case, we see that John and Mary seem to be interchangeable, so 'Mary loves John' is an admissible string within the language (although it means something different, of course). In contrast, $X'$ cannot take the position of $Y'$, since 'loves John Mary' is not admissible. Clearly, words which can be interchanged have something in common, and this commonality is the grammatical class to which they belong. Rather obviously, Mary and John are both examples of proper nouns. This method works extremely well for the groupings of many words, and leads to the identification of nouns, adjectives, adverbs, and so on. (There is, however, a 'class' of words which do not readily conform to simple rules of transposition; these are termed 'particles'.)

The method of substitution reveals certain interesting properties of natural languages. For instance, 'John' is a noun, but is interchangeable with 'The old man' which is clearly more than a noun – it is a complete *phrase*. This and other similar phenomena demonstrate that whole structures can play the same syntactic role as single words.

The linguist Harris (1951) used the expressions 'noun-phrase' to indicate those complex structures which can stand as nouns, and 'verb-phrase' for those structures which can stand as verbs. Breaking up sentences into units of this type is called the *immediate constituent structure approach*, and as a result, the structure of a sentence can be represented as a simple tree, as shown in figure 9-1.

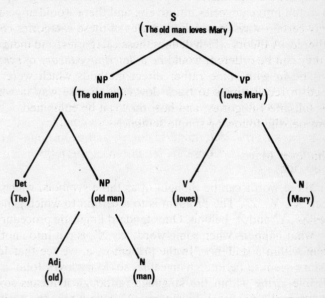

*Figure 9-1.* Tree diagram illustrating the constituent structure of 'The old man loves Mary'.

The tree shows how distributional units break down into subsets, starting with the whole sentence, then into noun-phrase + verb-phrase, and so on, down to individual words. Notice that on the left, there is a unit (a noun-phrase) 'The old man', which breaks into two constituents, a determiner (The) and *another* noun-phrase (old man). *Old man* is considered to be a constituent structure because it stands as a *unit*, and can be substituted where other units such as nouns go.

From this approach to breaking down the constituents of sentences, it becomes possible to express the structures of various kinds of trees as *rules*. These are rules for combining the individual constituents to give the class of grammatical sentences in the language in question. Here are three such rules, known as rewrite rules, since the arrow means that the left-hand expression is to be rewritten as the right-hand expression:

Rule 1   S   $\rightarrow$ NP + VP
Rule 2   VP $\rightarrow$ V + NP
Rule 3   NP $\rightarrow$ Det + N

With this set of rules, numerous grammatical sentences can be produced, including 'The boy hit the girl', 'The man rode a horse' and so on, provided we specify what a noun, a verb and a determiner are.

A set of rules of this type, when complete, is called a *phrase-structure grammar*. Of course, analysis has shown that the rules for English would have to be considerably more complex, admitting adjectives, adverbs, determiners, nouns, and even noun-phrases on an *optional* basis. Consider, for instance, the following set of revised rules:

Rule 1′   S   $\rightarrow$ NP + VP
Rule 2′   VP $\rightarrow$ V + NP*
Rule 3′   NP $\rightarrow$ Det* + Adj* + N
(The asterisks denote *optional* entries.)

With these three rules, some rather different sentences, such as 'The boy hit the small girl', 'The boy jumped', and 'The car struck Harry', can be constructed.

Now that we have illustrated how one might begin to describe a language in terms of a phrase-structure grammar, let us reflect upon the linguist's purpose in pursuing such an exercise. First of all, it is an attempt to capture the syntax of a language, to describe it. But what does *that* mean? Ultimately, a grammar must identify *all* grammatical sentences in a language, but *only* grammatical sentences. A set of rules which allows 'Two down top me go' would not meet this criterion.

Linguists are still working on phrase structures and it is clear that the task of meeting the 'all and only' identification criterion is a tough one. No-one has yet succeeded in doing it fully. Furthermore, there are serious theoretical reasons why it might be impossible or, if it were possible, inadequate in certain respects. We shall continue by examining first of all why it might be considered inadequate.

One illustration comes from a comparison of *passive* and *active* forms of sentence. Compare the following sentences:

The lecturer upset the student.
The student was upset by the lecturer.

Although these sentences are different on the surface, it is clear that they are related. One way in which they are related is the way in which *the student* and *the lecturer* play the same roles in the two sentences. Thus, *the student* is the agent in each sentence, and *the lecturer* is the patient. Yet on a straightforward analysis of the type discussed up to now, this commonality would not be captured. The linguist Chomsky (1957) considered this to be a fault in phrase-structure grammars. He argued that the passive sentence was related to the active sentence by a rule which should be part of a grammatical description of a language. A rule which relates passives to actives is called a *transformation rule*, and looks like this:

$$NP1 + V + NP2 \Rightarrow NP2 + was + V + by + NP1$$

Note that the positions of NP1 and NP2 are changed by the transformation, although they are still identified as the same noun-phrase. Chomsky argues that all sentences are generated from a string called a *deep structure* by the application of transformation rules. The observed sentences so generated are called *surface-structure* strings. The active surface-structure form is assumed to be a close approximation of deep structure for most purposes.

Transformations can be described for the relationship between active sentences and passives, negatives, interrogatives, and so on, as discussed under *cases* in chapter 7. In fact, case grammars are the result of attempts to describe the role of noun-phrases regardless of the surface sentence form. The analysis derives directly from the deep-structure concept (see Fillmore 1968).

Notice that the transformation rule described above is quite different from the other rules described up to now. The left-hand side of the rule is a complete *string*, as is the right. Phrase-structure grammars do not describe transforming complete strings into other complete strings. This is discussed in more detail in the next section.

## 2  The power of grammars

Grammars of the phrase-structure and transformational type differ in certain extremely important ways. The problem is to ascertain exactly what class of grammar is appropriate for the description of human languages. Looked at in a more abstract way, the first problem is to specify the types of rules necessary for generating all the strings which are possible in a language, and only these. The first pertinent fact is that an infinite number of sentences could occur, in theory, in a given language. Consider the following sentence:

The woman is at the station.

The sentence can now be extended by *embedding* it into the middle of another:

The man who said (the woman is at the station) is at the bus stop.

This embedded structure is clearly acceptable and would be judged as grammatical by native English speakers. The point made by Chomsky is that there is no limit to this process. If the sentence above is grammatical, then so too would be:

The taxi driver who noticed (the man who said (the woman is at the station) who is at the bus stop) is in his cab.

Although speakers rarely use such long expressions because they are so difficult to understand, they exist as a possibility, and infinite expansion of this type does not appear to be ruled out by any intuitive grammatical rule. Thus Chomsky concluded that English cannot be a finite state language. How can a finite set of rules generate structures of this type? The trick is to construct the rules in such a way that rules are embedded *recursively*, and the idea can be illustrated by means of a simple artificial language. Suppose that a language has only two admissible classes of symbol (say A and B) – they can be thought of as corresponding loosely to, say, noun-phrases and verb-phrases but, of course, with an artificial language, they could just as easily be merely As and Bs.

Now suppose that the following exemplify possible sentences in the language:

(i)  AB
(ii)  AABB
(iii)  AAABBB etc.

This is the same kind of embedding as we discussed for the English example above. This is clear if parentheses are put in, for example:

A (A(AB)B)B

The rules necessary for generating this class of sequence are:

Rule 1   S→ ASB
Rule 2   S→ AB

Rule 1 simply indicates that between the elements generated by rule 2, another sentence (S) can be inserted. A system with at least this degree of flexibility is necessary to allow for the embedding found in English. Rule 1 is *recursive* in that the left-hand side S rewrites into an expression which also contains S.

A phrase-structure grammar with a recursive rule allows for embedding of this type, but there are sentences in English and other languages which cannot be handled by rules of this type. Chomsky pointed this out with respect to right-branching sentences exemplified by the following expansions:

The boy went to the park.
The boy and the girl went to the park and the cinema (respectively).
Father, the boy, and the girl went to the park, the cinema, and the theatre (respectively).

The notable aspect of this sort of example is that the order of terms in the second part of the sentence depends upon the order of terms in the first part of the sentence. Using another example from an artificial language, this ordering principle could be represented as the following admissible strings:

AA
BB
ABAB
BABA
AAA
BBB
ABABAB
BABABA

(And so on – there is no limit to this, just as there is no grammatical limit to the examples given above in English.)

The problem now is what sort of rules can capture *this* structure. Chomsky argues that a phrase-structure grammar cannot. One might begin with the following rules:

Rule 1   S→ AS
Rule 2   S→ BS
Rule 3   S→ T

Rules 1 and 2 will generate a first string of As or Bs. Rule 3 will end the generation of the first string when it is called into use. What is then required is a further set of rules that enables the generation of the same sequence again, repeating the first string. One way of doing this is to introduce a set of *context-sensitive* rules indicating interpretations of T given various prior contexts. For instance:

Rule 4   T→ A *in the context* A . . .
Rule 5   T→ B *in the context* B . . .
Rule 6   T→ AB *in the context* AB . . .
Rule 7   T→ ABAB *in the context* ABAB . . .

and so on, for any length of context string.

These context-sensitive rules certainly allow the right sort of strings to be produced, but introduce a new problem. Because there is no limit to the length of a context string, there will be no limit to the number of rewrite rules in the grammar. Chomsky's solution is to introduce a new type of rule, called the *transformation*. A transformation rule effectively has two parts to it: the *conditions of application* and the *transformation to be applied*. In the present case, one could have the following:

(a)  Given the structure XT, where X represents *any string*.
(b)  Transform 1 2 $\Rightarrow$ 1 1, where 1 and 2 denotes a first string followed by a second string.

Given this rule, the string ABAB can be produced by starting with ABT (rules 1, 2 and 3 above), and then applying the transformation described above to this – AB being the first string, and T being the second, to get ABAB. The transformation can of course be applied over and over again.

The difference between transformational and simple rewriting rules is straightforward. Transformations work on *whole strings*, not just on elements. The idea of deep structure, discussed in the earlier section, is dependent upon such a principle, since Chomsky argues that it is from a deep-structure *string* that surface variants on that deep structure are generated and, he argues, operating on strings requires rules of the transformational type. The argument he makes is that English cannot be described adequately by a context-free phrase-structure grammar, but that rules as powerful as transformations are required to explain many English constructions, including the branching construction given in this section.

A more detailed discussion of the types of grammars is inappropriate for this introduction; guides to further reading are provided at the end of the chapter. However, even this limited discussion raises several points of interest. First, linguists aim to be able to describe grammars which are sufficient to capture the various types of sentences which are possible within languages, but only these sentences. Chomsky has shown that these grammars must contain rules which are of greater power than simple rewrite rules. This issue of *types of rule* is extremely important when one turns to the issue of what kind of automaton (computer program) would be necessary to understand natural language. The point is that the automaton must be able to accept and parse strings which are generated by a process as complex as one which requires transformational rules for its description. In the next section, we shall look at how this might be done.

# B  Parsing

Up to now, we have seen a little of how grammars are constructed and a few of the considerations of what kinds of rules grammatical rules might be. Parsing is the process of taking a complete sentence, and breaking it down into its constituents. The *method* for doing this defines a *parser*, and the output of a parser corresponds to a grammar. If people make use of syntactic information in the understanding process, then one can speak of the 'psychological parsing mechanism'. Tracking down how such a mechanism might work in people is a thorny problem, and we shall concentrate on just one possible way.

Our basic assumption will be that parsing takes place in a 'left-right' way in English: that is, from the start of a sentence through to the end, in that order. It is possible to devise parsers which do not do this (Winograd 1983). The problem is, then, to build a device which considers the components of sentences until it has assigned the words to their appropriate grammatical categories.

## 1 Transition networks

Suppose that we wished to parse all sentences with the structure NP + VP + NP such as 'The woman hit the boy'. To recognize sentences of this type, the parser must first check for an NP, then for a VP, then for an NP. If it finds each of these in sequence, then it has found an *acceptable sentence*. Such a series of tests would depend upon the parser having a dictionary which specified what was a noun, a verb, an article, etc., so that the particular *words* of a sentence could be tested appropriately. As a result of applying the tests, it would be possible to list the articles and nouns and verbs of any given sentence.

This would be no problem at all if all sentences could be described in terms of such a simple grammar, but it is not so simple. The kinds of test sequences required become a little awkward to write down, and it is useful to express the possibilities in terms of *transition networks*, which represent the tests and paths between tests as a diagram. Consider the example shown in figure 9-2.

The diagram begins with a *state*, designated $S_0$. This is the start state prior to doing any parsing. To get to state $S_1$, an *arc* must be traversed; to traverse it, the condition that the current phrase is an NP must be met. If an NP is identified, then state $S_1$ is reached. After $S_1$, a VERB is tested for in the next arc. If one is found, then state $S_2$ is reached. At this point, two things could happen. Either another NP would lead to state $S_3$ (the end state), or nothing (JUMP) would do it. This option handles *transitive* verbs (John hit Mary) and *intransitive* verbs (John coughed). The option is necessary.

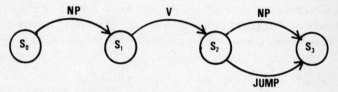

*Figure 9-2.* A transition network for some simple sentences. If, and only if, the conditions on each successive state are met does a transition to the next state occur. After $S_2$, two options are open: another NP (if the verb is transitive), or a JUMP if the verb is intransitive. $S_2$ is the final state.

Having introduced transition networks, they can be used to illustrate parsing of a somewhat more realistic range of sentence types. The transition network is an embodiment of a grammar, so the problem is to find a network which is suitable for the grammar of English – that is, which will capture all sentences of English, but not ungrammatical ones. Let us begin with the idea of noun-phrases. Sometimes they have articles or determiners, sometimes not ('Jane', 'man'), sometimes adjectives, and so on. The network shown in figure 9-3 will handle cases with or without determiners, and with or without adjectives. At stage NP, any number of adjective tests return to NP.

When we described the problem of the power of grammars, the

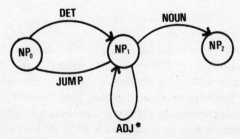

*Figure 9-3.* An NP subnetwork, with a facility for handling NPs with no determiners, and with any number of adjectives (denoted by the asterisk).

need for *recursive* rules was noted. For an adequate treatment of NPs, the transition network itself must embody a recursive principle. This is well illustrated by the problem of *prepositional phrases*, as in 'The little boy *with the balloon*'. Although this is an NP, it has another NP as part of it. Figure 9-4 shows a network with a facility for handling an NP with prepositional phrases (PPs), and a subnetwork for a PP. In the NP net at $NP_2$ any number of PPs can be added. But notice that the PP subnetwork itself has an NP test to bring about the transition from $PP_1$ to $PP_2$. Such a

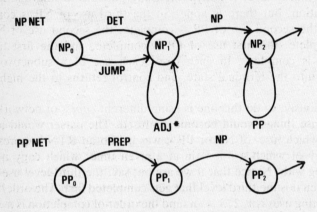

*Figure 9-4.* An NP subnetwork with a facility for a preposition phrase (PP). The PP subnetwork is indicated below: it tests first for a preposition (PREP), and then for an NP. Arcs following the final states denote delivery of incomplete PPs or NPs.

property makes the transition network recursive (it is known as an RTN, where R denotes recursive). To illustrate what this means for parsing, consider this NP:

The little boy with the balloon on a string.

To begin with, the parser will use an S network, which in our examples gives a call to an NP subnetwork. The subnetwork accepts 'The little boy' yielding The = determiner, little = adjective, boy = noun. At this point, either the NP net could be exited (turning to the main S network), or there could be a PP. To test for a PP, the PP subnetwork is invoked, and to get to $PP_1$ in this net, a preposition must be found. 'With' passes this test, so the PP network must now test for an NP. So we have:

First use of NP   ●   Has found 'The + little + boy',
and is still waiting to be completed.

First use of PP   ●   Has found 'with', and is at $S_1$. It
calls NP:

Second use of NP   ●   Now tests and classifies 'the
balloon', and calls:

Second use of PP   ●   finds 'on', and calls:

Third use of NP   ●   this finds 'a string'.

At this third stage, it is hypothetically possible to find another preposition, but there is none. So the third use of NP is complete, the second use of PP is complete, the second use of NP is complete, the first use of PP is complete, and the first use of NP is complete. In each case, each use of a subnetwork passes into the terminal state, and control returns to the higher level.

Obviously, to do this one is using different *copies* of networks, otherwise things would become confused. The parser would not know which 'use' of NP or PP it was in! So an RTN requires a *memory* of which *use* it is in at a given time: which copy it is working with. Notice that if we are on, say, the third-level use of NP, then it is the third level that gets completed first. The order of generating uses is 1, 2, 3 . . . n, and the order of completion is n . . . 3, 2, 1. This particular memory input and output order is called a 'pushdown stack' and works on a last-in first-out basis. With three uses of an NP, it is that most deeply embedded which is resolved first, then the next deepest, and so on. Its relationship to grammar is that English grammar must be powerful enough to allow the insertion of a string in the middle of the elements of another string of the same type. To do this, a parser must keep track of which string it is currently dealing with. A recursive transition network (RTN) can represent a recursive phrase-structure grammar, and because an RTN can be treated as a parsing scheme (as has been illustrated), it can parse sentences which are acceptable to a recursive phase-structure grammar.

Unfortunately, RTNs are not sufficient to parse English for various reasons. First of all, they cannot handle many of the structures which led Chomsky to say that a context-free phrase-structure grammar could not be a sufficient description of English – they cannot, for instance, accommodate the relationship between actives and passives. If we compare:

Mary hit the little girl.
and
The little girl was hit by Mary.

At the surface level, in the first sentence 'Mary' is the subject, and is $NP_1$, and in the second, 'The little girl' is the subject, and is $NP_1$. Yet on a case analysis, representing the deep structure of the sentences, 'Mary' is the *agent* in both cases, and 'the little girl' the patient. The passive transformation accommodates this fact, but how is a parser to accommodate it? One way is to *augment* the RTN in various ways (it is then called an augmented transition network, or ATN).

To illustrate an ATN in action, we will consider the sentence network shown in figure 9-5, which has a simple provision for handling passives. Beneath the diagram is a list of the arcs, together with special conditions that must be tested for as the arc is traversed, and the actions which a parser takes as a result. To illustrate how it works, let us put 'The baby was hit by Mary' through the network. $S_1$ is reached and 'The baby' is assigned the role ACTOR. 'Was' puts the state up to $S_2$, but is a form of BE, so 'The baby', assigned the role ACTOR, is noted as being OBJECT. Arc 4 finds the verb 'hit', and this is labelled ACTION. Arc 5 finds 'by', and 'The baby' has the ACTOR label dropped, leaving only the OBJECT label. Arc 6 finds 'Mary', who is labelled ACTOR. Thus 'Mary' ends up ACTOR, and 'The baby' ends up OBJECT.

The process is simple enough, relying upon the syntax of passive structures, but it also relies on keeping track of which labels have been assigned, and relabelling later on.

## 2  Human parsing

One of the assumptions made above is that parsing takes place on a word-by-word basis, from the start to the end of sentences. This seems to fit some of the data on how humans understand sentences. Check quickly, for instance, which of the following sentences are grammatical:

- Mary jumped through the gap in the fence.
  The steel ships are transporting is expensive.
  The cups the person heavy.
  The old man the boats.
  Mary likes George.

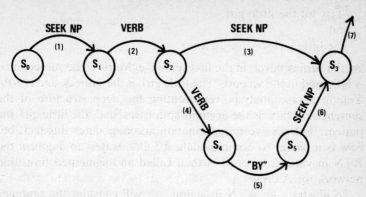

*Figure 9-5.* An S network which can handle passives, via arcs (4), (5) and (6). Each arc has various conditions and actions to be followed in an ATN. In the present case, these are:

| Arc | Condition | Action |
|---|---|---|
| 1 | — | Assign label ACTOR to current phrase |
| 2 | Current word matches ACTOR in number | Assign ACTION to current word |
| 3 | — | Assign OBJECT to current phrase |
| 4 | ACTION = BY; current word is past participle | Assign ACTION to current word; assign OBJECT to current ACTOR |
| 5 | — | — |
| 6 | — | Assign ACTOR to current phrase |
| 7 | — | Deliver current parse as SENTENCE |

It is likely that you faltered on 'The old man the boats', an elliptical sentence which could be expanded into 'The old (persons) man the boats'. You may also have had a little difficulty with 'The steel ships are transporting is expensive'. These sentences are examples of *garden-path sentences*, so called because the initial parse of them leads to inappropriate results. Suppose that an ATN device were applied to 'The old man the boats'. It should identify 'The old man' as an NP, and then look for a verb. But the next word is a determiner, so it does not fit a sentence ATN. It is only by backing-up through the parse that 'The old (something)' becomes the NP, and 'man' the verb. Similar arguments apply to the second sentence in the list.

It is possible to uncover the point at which difficulties arise on an experimental basis. For instance, Kramer and Stevens (cited by Rumelhart 1977) required subjects to read written sentences out loud, and then they investigated the points at which pauses occurred. In the case of example two in the list above, for instance, many subjects paused between 'transporting' and 'is expensive'. Similarly, with 'The old man the boats', pauses tended to occur between 'man' and 'the boats'. These and similar studies (e.g. Wanner and Maratsos 1974) appear to be consistent with the general principle of left-right word-by-word processing, and conform to plausible ATN structures.

Within the ATN framework, it is possible to evaluate the difficulties which people have with various types of sentence structure. For instance, compare the ease of understanding the following sentences:

The dog that chases the cat chases sheep.
and
The dog that the cat chases chases mice.

The second is certainly more difficult. Wanner and Maratsos (1974) suggest that the difference in degree of difficulty results from different demands made on the memory stack. In each case, 'the dog' is identified as the first NP, and the word 'that' indicates that a *relative clause* is coming up, so the NP is saved on the stack. In the case of the first sentence, finding a verb, 'chases', indicates that what follows belongs to the first NP, so it comes back off the stack. In the second case, this does not happen until the second 'chases' is encountered and so the first NP has to be held for a longer time in the second case. This, claim Wanner and Maratsos, is the source of the difficulty. Readers should follow up ATNs through references given already, or by consulting Rumelhart (1977). The framework certainly makes a number of common difficulties intelligible. At this point, however, we shall leave ATNs and look at some other features of the human parser.

First of all, our entire discussion up to now has been focused on *syntax*: using information about word order where words are treated entirely as grammatical classes. Thus where we have written NOUN in an ATN, *any* noun will do. Meaning (semantics) has not been taken into account at all. The network in figure 9-5 will accept, for instance, 'A woollen stone thought cryptic cars' as an English sentence. Note that although this sentence is *grammatical*, it is not *meaningful*, and since humans use language to convey meaning, it would be strange if we had parsing mechanisms which did not make use of meaning. In fact, it is possible to show that meaning does play a role in the parsing process in human beings. Compare the following sentences:

The steel ships are transporting # is expensive.
versus
The granite carpets are covering up # is ugly.

Kramer and Stevens (Rumelhart 1977), using a task in which subjects had to speak such sentences, found that the delays due to backtracking (indicated by #) were less likely to occur in the second case. Presumably, this is because 'granite carpets' is semantically anomalous, and the human parser is not prepared to accept it has a noun-phrase, while it is prepared to accept 'steel ships'. Thus semantic analysis is used in parsing. Granite does not combine with carpets to form a unit, while steel does combine with ships.

A more dramatic example comes from Schlesinger (1968), using embedded sentences. He found that comprehension is greatly facilitated if semantic cues can be used to assist syntactic processing. For instance, subjects found the first of these examples easier to understand than the second:

This is the hole that the rat which our cat whom the dog bit made caught.
versus
This is the boy that the man whom the lady whom our friend saw knows hit.

The argument is that the first one is somewhat easier to understand because of one's knowledge of what behaviour typifies rats, cats and dogs. But there is a trick. In the first sentence, the semantic cues are actually *incongruous*:

- This is the hole that the rat (which our cat (whom the dog bit) made) caught.

The brackets show that the rat *caught* the hole, and the hole was made by the cat. Obviously semantic cues can override syntax-driven parsing in these difficult examples.

Many sentences are syntactically ambiguous, yet we do not get the wrong reading because of the broader, pragmatic context in which they occur. Terry Winograd (1972) provides a beautiful example which he encountered during the design of a highly successful computer-dialogue system. His program consists of three separate subprograms: syntax, semantics and problem-solving. It operates on a world of simple blocks, pyramids and boxes, which it can move around. To 'speak' to the operator, the program puts messages on a visual display unit. To speak to the program, the operator types messages on the keyboard. All messages are in natural English, the only restriction being that the dialogue has to be about the block world. Let us trace through the processes involved in the program's acting on the instruction 'put the pyramid on the block in the box'.

It will be clear that this is ambiguous. It could mean:

put (the pyramid on the block)      in (the box)
$\qquad\qquad$ NP$_1$ $\qquad\qquad\qquad\qquad$ NP$_2$

or:

put (the pyramid)      on (the block in the box)
$\qquad\qquad$ NP$_1$ $\qquad\qquad\qquad\qquad$ NP$_2$

Which parse is correct? Well, which parse is *relevant* depends upon the state of the block world, as shown in figure 9-6. Winograd's parser operates in a left-right fashion, rather like the way in which we used ATNs to introduce this section. It uses a rather different grammar from those discussed here (Halliday's *systemic grammar* 1967), but this is not important for our purposes. The first word is a verb (put), and is in a form and position which indicates a *command*. Syntax expects a noun-phrase next. But which structure is NP$_1$? Sequential checks for determiner first and then a noun find *the pyramid*. At this point, parsing stops. A definite article (the) is generally used to front a noun-phrase which refers to something *unique* which has been singled out. Because of this, the problem-solver searches for a unique pyramid in the block world. If the block world is like (a) in the figure, then the search will fail, because there are *two* pyramids. In this case, control returns to the parser, which effectively looks for a clear specifi-

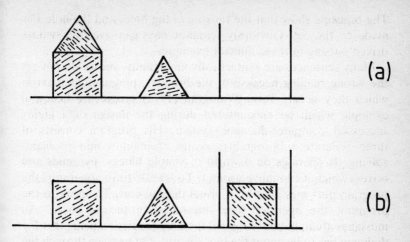

*Figure 9-6.* Two possible states of the block world which may be used to select the appropriate parse of 'Put the pyramid on the block in the box'.

cation of the unique referent which was indicated. This amounts to staying in an NP net. 'On' is then identified as the start of a PP, which should have an NP next. It does – 'the block'. So now we have an NP: 'the pyramid on the block'. Control returns to problem-solving, which *does* find a unique referent. The parser accepts this string as $NP_1$. Commands of the sort being discussed here have the general structure 'Put $NP_1$ (on, in, etc.) $NP_2$'. The parser expects a locative (on, in, etc.) next, followed by $NP_2$. It finds these, and can then execute the command.

In the case of (b) in the diagram, things are different. When the parser has 'the pyramid' as a potential $NP_1$, it will find a unique pyramid in block world. So the parser will *now* expect a locative, which it will find – 'on'. So 'the pyramid' is $NP_1$, and $NP_2$ should come next. By the same process, there are two blocks, so the only uniquely referring $NP_2$ is 'the block on the box'. Thus the two situations yield different parses of the same surface structure. This comes about because problem-solving takes over from parsing at expediently chosen points.

While it is unlikely that human parsing is quite as simple as this, it *is* likely that parsing does not go on independently of semantic and pragmatic considerations. As an example, let us consider some recent work by Crain and Steedman (1981) who were concerned with the general problem of garden-path sentences.

Their claim is that there is *no such thing* as an intrinsically garden-path sentence, because prior context serves to control how parsing takes place. As an example, consider the following:

> A psychologist was counselling two married couples. One of the couples was fighting with him, but the other was nice to him.
> *The psychologist told the wife that he was having trouble with to leave her husband.*

The first two sentences comprise a context which introduces two married couples. The italicized sentences (a *target* sentence) picks out the wife of one of the couples, *the wife that he was having trouble with*. Crain and Steedman showed that this target was judged grammatical by most of the subjects. But compare this with the alternative target sentence:

> *The psychologist told the wife that he was having trouble with her husband.*

Such a sentence was judged *ungrammatical* by over half of the subjects. Of course, as a sentence it is quite grammatical, but it does not make much sense in the context because it is not clear to which wife reference is being made. Given the context, the argument is that the parser should identify as an NP *the wife that he was having trouble with*, which leads to the expectation of a verb next, but a verb does not follow. So the sentence appears ungrammatical (like 'the old man the boats'). Crain and Steedman argue that whether or not garden-path parsing takes place is dependent upon prior context, and that the parser is sensitive to what are the referential possibilities based on prior context, in the manner suggested by Winograd.

## C  Summary and discussion: parsing and the problem of interpretation

Parsing is an important issue in language understanding, because syntax is important in interpretation, but syntax (rules for combining classes of symbols) is only part of the problem. As we have seen, within our examples and most accounts of syntax, most natural language sentences are syntactically ambiguous, and interpretation has to rely upon semantics and pragmatics. There is strong evidence that these two sources of information are used, along with syntax, during sentence processing. Furthermore, syntax and other sources seem to be quite microscopically inter-related in the processing activities of human beings. To unravel the information-processing mechanisms under conditions of such extreme interaction is very difficult. Yet not only is this necessary for psychological theory; it is also likely that artificial natural language understanding systems will have to have a similar level of interaction, so the problem is a technological one as well.

The programs of Winograd and Schank, and the experiments of Crain and Steedman, among others, indicate the degree to which many syntactic issues can be resolved by taking into account prior context, or the 'domain of reference'. Domain of reference is, broadly, those things which are being distinguished and talked about at any given time. If the processing system has access to *this* information, then by checking on the state of domain, it is often possible to decide what kind of objects, or which specific objects, are likely to be referred to. This in turn can serve to guide parsing.

At this point it is useful to remind ourselves that language is produced for some *purpose*. If a speaker says something like 'Put the X on the Y', then the way in which X and Y are described will depend upon what is in the reference domain (Olson 1970). Imagine two cubes, one red and one green, and a box. A speaker would have to say one of the following, or something very similar to one of them:

Put *a* / *any* / *one of the* / cube(s) in the box.
or
Put the red / green / cube in the box.

The choice depends upon what the speaker wants and the choice of expression one is likely to encounter depends upon the *joint domain of reference* in which both speaker/writer and listener/reader operate. It should hardly be surprising that domain of reference is important in parsing. However, should anyone think syntax unimportant, he should notice the big difference between 'Mary loves John' and 'John loves Mary'. Furthermore, syntax is just as important in production as it is in comprehension!

We are now at a fork in the path. Either a fuller treatment of recent work on the processing details of how sources of information interact could be given, or the broader aspects of discourse research could be discussed. It is perhaps more appropriate to choose the latter. The reason is straightforward. The evidence we have presented up to now suggests that it is misguided to think about language understanding without taking into account the whole *point* of language, which is communication. In normal conversational discourse, many of the sentences uttered are not strictly grammatical, or are incomplete. Yet this usually goes unnoticed. Try listening to a colleague talking, and this will quickly become obvious, unless he or she is a natural orator! The lack of difficulty indicates that messages can be conveyed because both participants are simply looking for signals which modify a pre-established domain of discourse. Language expressions used for communication are called *discourse*, and this is the approach taken in chapter 10. Both syntactic interpretation and interpretation of meaning depend upon the receiver having an appropriate model of the discourse at any given point, so the ordering of material in discourse production is of the utmost importance. Furthermore, given the constraints of short-term memory, there is a strong temporal localization of what can be the *embodiment* of a working discourse model. These are technical problems for process models of discourse although underlying the whole argument is a theme which is by now familiar. Interpretation would appear to be founded on the use of models of the world and of the discourse domain to guide processes at all levels.

# 10 Language 2: Discourse

Up to now we have not really considered language in terms of communication but, of course, communication is the *raison d'être* of language. Speakers speak so that listeners can understand what they say, and writers try to express their messages in such a way that readers will find them intelligible. When we come to look at language as communication, it is in some ways artificial to separate investigations of the producer from investigations of the recipient. Although the processes of production and reception will undoubtedly differ in various respects, the common ground between the two is the message itself.

When language is used to communicate, it is called *discourse*, and discourse consists of language *utterances* which cohere, or hang together, to produce an integrated whole. The linguistic study of discourse concerns itself with the way in which the structures available in a language are used to produce this coherence, and how they can be used to signify different meanings at different times. The psycholinguistic study of discourse has similar aims, but is of course equally concerned with the psychological basis of choice of utterance, and the consequences a particular choice of utterance has on the receiver. In this chapter we shall concentrate on these issues.

Most of the discourse produced by human beings is spoken – it is conversation. Written discourse constitutes a very much smaller subset. Yet there has been very much more work carried out on written discourse, particularly of the receivers' (readers') activities. It is not difficult to imagine why: in a culture where the written word is a primary means of learning, being able to read efficiently is of major importance, so there are many many studies of reading and reading comprehension. While in no way decrying such studies, from a more theoretical stance the imbalance is too great. There are really very few studies of writing behaviour, for instance, and yet there is not a book in the library which has not been *written*. Some books are difficult not because the readers are not good readers, but because the writers have not produced a flow of ideas which is suited to readers, or because the writers' choice of words and text structure is simply difficult to process. This argument suggests that production and comprehension are processes which must be matched if communication is to be effective.

In conversation, the problems are similar. The speaker must make sure that the listener recognizes the ideas being communicated, and must choose sequences of words to enable this to come about. There are, however, great differences between spoken and written communication. In dialogue, a listener can interrupt a speaker and demand clarification. A reader cannot do this. Writing is seldom spontaneous: what one reads is usually the product of careful planning and revision, all designed to guarantee intelligibility. On the other hand, speech is usually spontaneous and relatively unplanned: speakers frequently revise their utterances as they are producing them.

## A  Discourse production and discourse structure

One property of the machinery of human language is so obvious that it is likely to go unnoticed at first sight: the end product must be *sequential*. A discourse utterance consists of a sequence of sounds or squiggles on the page – it will be heard as sequence, or read as a sequence. Yet the ideas to be expressed may not be like that at all: if one is describing something, for example, one may wish to include many elements in that description, and one has the problem of how to order the elements in the description. This problem, temporally organizing potentially co-existing ideas into a linear sequence, is one of the key problems in discourse production. It is known as the 'linearization problem'.

A second major problem concerns what a writer or speaker can assume a listener to know. Obviously, it is pointless to keep referring to things or situations of which the recipient has no knowledge. Effectively, a producer has to have a model of the recipient's knowledge state in mind, and use this in forming an appropriate choice of expressions and topics. This is sometimes referred to as the 'background-knowledge' problem, and is complex, because knowledge can come from so many sources:

1   Events or objects in the world surrounding the participants.
2   Stated or inferred goals of the participants.
3   General knowledge possessed by the participants, including factual knowledge and 'social-convention' knowledge, and past experiences which they have in common.

The background-knowledge problem does not stand independently of the linearization problem. A producer can introduce new knowledge to a receiver, and then assume that this is now knowledge which the receiver has. Order of presentation of information is thus of crucial importance.

Apart from these two general problems, there is a more plainly psychological one. As a discourse unfolds, the receiver will be paying attention to certain aspects of it, usually the more recent aspects. This follows from the general properties of human memory, but has implications for the structure of discourse itself. For instance, events and objects mentioned early in a discourse may not be in the receiver's focus of attention later on. If the producer wishes to refer to these earlier things, he will have to use some appropriate form of words to reintroduce the old ideas. The problems associated with this are very closely linked to choice of syntactic form, and are sometimes known as problems of *focus*, *foregrounding* and *anaphora*.

Of course, all three problems emerge at various levels. Sequencing problems, for instance, emerge when a writer is trying to work out an effective way of ordering information for an entire book, and also when one tries to answer the question 'What is a Polo mint?'. In this latter case, speakers will sometimes correct themselves thus: 'Well, it's got a hole .... It's a mint with a hole ....' Linearization and choice of word order are unavoidably related. In presenting a discussion of the three topics described above, we shall adopt the strategy of looking at global (large-scale) aspects of discourse structure initially.

## 1 Ordering of utterances and global discourse structures

Imagine someone narrating a simple story to you as part of a conversation which you are having. Suppose she says:

John vowed never to return. He called the waiter and politely asked to see the manager. But the waiter snatched his pâté away, and denied everything. He had ordered a pâté which sounded delicious. John came in very angry last night. He'd been at a local restaurant. When he started to eat his meal, he found a pin inside.

With two or three readings, it is possible to get the gist of this snippet of discourse, but it exemplifies poor (infelicitous) discourse. The ordering of the ideas is all wrong, and it appears to be completely disjointed. Compare it with a more natural ordering:

John came in very angry last night. He'd been at a local restaurant, and had ordered a pâté which sounded delicious. When he started to eat it, he found a pin inside. He called the waiter and politely asked to see the manager. But the waiter snatched his pâté away, and denied everything.

The two versions of the passage differ mainly in the ordering of the facts. In terms of independent propositions, assertions about the world in general, and John in particular, the two passages are more or less identical. But there are considerable differences in intelligibility. The disjointed passage poses problems of several kinds, because it does not conform to the kinds of constraints discussed at the start of this section.

Consider the statement 'John vowed never to return'. Unless one knows *to where* or *to what* he vowed never to return, it seems to be impossible to integrate this statement with anything else. On the other hand, if one has already been told that 'John went to a restaurant' in some way, then integration is possible. By saying 'John vowed never to return', the producer of the discourse is presupposing that the receiver already knows what the place is. The place is stated explicitly before this sentence occurs in the acceptable passage, but not in the unacceptable version. Similar considerations apply to the rest of the text. With the sentence 'John came home very angry last night', the question which we seem to ask ourselves given this statement is *why*? or *what happened*? In the acceptable version, the remaining narrative serves the function of answering this question, while in the unacceptable version, the statement appears as a *reaction* to events which have not been properly explained, but have been partially explained. Furthermore, in a conversation, it is perfectly reasonable to assume that a good starting point is something which happened to a mutual friend. To introduce this part of the way through provides neither a *reason* for the story, nor a description of an outcome of events.

Two primary features of felicitous orderings of statements thus appear to be:

(a)  A naturally ordered unfolding of events, and
(b)  The narrator makes reasonable assumptions about what the receiver may already know as a result of what has been said.

In the psychology literature, these two features have been explored indirectly through studies of story structure and paragraph structure, largely with an interest in what makes certain orderings more intelligible and more memorable.

Let us first turn to stories. Several linguists and anthropologists have noted that ways of telling stories in various cultures seem to be describable in terms of formulae (e.g. Colby 1972; Lakoff 1972; Propp 1968). Stories appear to have certain fixed elements, and certain fixed orderings, almost like the syntax of a sentence. In fact, it has now become common psychological currency to speak of 'story grammars' – sets of rewrite rules which define the internal architectures of the idea of a story. These were briefly alluded to in chapter 6. Rumelhart (1975) has offered a set of phrase-structure rules which try to capture this. One such set is illustrated in table 10-1.

The starting point is the following rewrite rule:

Story → Setting + Theme + Plot + Resolution

To see how the rules apply, consider the following 'story':

Fred was in the cinema watching a Western.   (Setting)
He was thirsty and wanted a drink.   (Theme)
He went to the kiosk, but found he had no money, so he persuaded a total stranger to give him 50p.   (Plot)
He got his drink, and went back.   (Resolution)

Although this is not a very interesting story, it does indicate the

Table 10-1. A set of grammar rules for simple stories.
*(From Thorndyke 1977.)*

| Rule number | Rule |
|---|---|
| 1 Story | → Setting + Theme + Plot + Resolution |
| 2 Setting | → Characters + Location + Time |
| 3 Theme | → (Event)* + Goal |
| 4 Plot | → Episode* |
| 5 Episode | → Subgoal + Attempts* + Outcome |
| 6 Attempts | → { Event* / Episode |
| 7 Outcome | → { Event* / State |
| 8 Resolution | → { Event / State |
| 9 Subgoal / Goal / Characters | } → Desired state |
| 10 Location / Time | } → Statives |

| | |
|---|---|
| → | Can be rewritten as. |
| ( ) | Content optional rather than necessary. |
| * | Could be more than one of these. |
| } | Alternatives. |

principal elements in the story-grammar account. The *theme* sets up the *main goal* (get a drink). In fact, one of the story grammar rules is:

Theme → (Event)* + Goal

meaning that one or more optional events leads to a main goal. The *plot* consists of one or more *episodes*.

An episode is in turn defined in the grammar as a number of attempts to realize a goal, leading to an outcome:

Episode → Subgoal + Attempts* + Outcome

Note that our 'plot' contains two episodes. First, Fred went to the kiosk with the subgoal of getting a drink. His attempt at purchase was thwarted by the outcome 'no money', which generated a new (unstated) subgoal of 'get some money'. This led to a new attempt, 'ask a stranger', with a positive outcome, satisfying the subgoal, enabling purchase, which led to the final *resolution* of the goal defining the theme.

In more complex stories, one could devise a longer and more imaginative series of subgoals which are thwarted by various means. In fact, on this conception of a story, a plot consists of embedded goal structures which may reach any degree of complexity.

Thorndyke (1977) demonstrated that if a story was presented in a way which did not match the order defined by his adaptation of Rumelhart's story grammar, then both rated intelligibility and memory for the story suffered. A typical manipulation was to remove the *theme* section from the start of the story, and either put it in at the end or remove it altogether. Remember, this experiment was discussed in chapter 6 in support of the view that what is remembered depends upon how the material was understood. In fact this manipulation of theme is pretty crude, but it does make the point that it is hard to remember and understand the plot of a story if one does not know *why* the actions depicted were being carried out.

The exact role which a person's knowledge about story structures (story 'schemata', or 'narrative frames') plays in comprehension is somewhat contentious. What studies of story grammars *do* illustrate is that it is quite possible to discern structures in many stories. However, it may be the case that rather than define story grammars in great detail, three basic statements might sum up what is useful about them:

(i)   Stories are usually anchored in space and time, and anchored to key characters (SETTING).
(ii)  Main goals are usually stated early on (THEME).
(iii) Episodes consist of various attempts to satisfy the main goal (STORIES HAVE A GOAL STRUCTURE).

It has been argued that many stories do not fit the story-grammar format, and that things which are not really stories can fit it, so that story grammars cannot be proper grammars (cf. Johnson-Laird 1983). However, they do represent interesting attempts to capture some of the structure which we can recognize in stories.

Among the interesting aspects of story grammars is the principle of introducing a setting, followed by a theme or main goal. This is interesting because it appears to reflect an important aspect of the normal course of human thinking. One starts with a problem of some sort, which presupposes knowledge of the general situation from which the problem emerged, which is of course the setting. One can view the setting as providing a wide range of important information, in part comprising:

(i)   Introduction of characters having general capabilities for solving problems.
(ii)  Introduction of time and place, which will constrain the *facilities* which are likely to be useful in solving the problem.
(iii) Introduction of time and place in which it is possible for certain classes of problems to emerge.

A problem stated in such a context will be more intelligible than one presented out of the blue. So a naturally intelligible ordering would be *setting* then *problem*. It is obvious that activities associated with solving a problem should follow the problem statement.

While stories as a whole constitute one level of looking at the sequencing problem, there are other levels which have much greater generality. At a somewhat lower level, there is the problem of *paragraph structure*. Most written texts are arranged in paragraphs which are clusters of sentences that somehow relate to one another. When most of us write, paragraphing tends to be an intuitive affair. But what determines a paragraph as a module, and are there any things which we can say about their structure?

A number of workers have attempted to classify different types of paragraph according to structure. For instance, Bissex (see Gilliland 1975) put forward an analysis based on three basic forms, which he termed *inductive*, *deductive*, or *balanced*. The inductive type he sees as starting with a *point*, to which further points are then added, and finishing with a 'conclusion, moral, or generalization'. The *deductive* type begins with a generalization, which is then illustrated with points. Finally, the balanced type begins with a series of points, introduces a generalization based on them, and then goes on to list points which either *contrast* or continue. The problem with this scheme, like others, is that many paragraphs are either too short to fit the classification, or seem to be mixtures of his different types. However, one can discern a principle of some importance: what the analysis does is to contrast points of detail or support with major themes, and indicates that there is more than one way in which these might be ordered. Since one presumes that writers, either consciously or unconsciously, order the details and major themes for a purpose, it is clearly of interest to psychologists to ascertain what *effects* various types of orderings have.

Investigations of such effects as yet are relatively primitive but promising. A study of direct relevance was carried out by Kieras (1978), who termed the theme-first paragraph *top-down* and the theme-at-the-end paragraph *bottom-up*. Using rather artificial paragraphs of seven sentences, he established that recall was best for a top-down format, and poorest for a bottom-up, which is the same sort of result as Thorndyke found for stories, only on a smaller scale.

One way of understanding the general superiority of theme-first presentation has been touched upon in chapters 6 and 8. A theme provides a mental framework into which new material can be readily incorporated and, hence, understood and recalled. The principle is similar to the schema-based theory of understanding. According to this view, then, the *writer* should elicit just those knowledge structures which he wants the *reader* to use in order to understand the text. Of course, this means that a writer can *control* the understanding of a reader through the order in which the ideas in the text are presented, giving an opportunity to persuade, to cause a reader to concentrate on one thing and not on another, and so on. This *rhetorical* aspect of discourse construction has not received the attention it deserves from psychologists, given its obvious importance in political propaganda and persuasion in general.

The internal architecture of the paragraph is one thing, but what of the choice of topics to put together to form a paragraph? Where do paragraph boundaries come from? It sounds like a truism to say that new paragraphs are used when a new idea is introduced. Ideas are made up of subideas, and so on, so this is not very useful. However, a start has been made on determining what makes people choose to use a new paragraph. Anne Anderson (1982) in her unpublished doctoral work used a technique of presenting people with passages which were not arranged in paragraphs at all, but rather as a complete block. Subjects were then invited to indicate where paragraphs should go. She discovered that with the narrative passage, new paragraphs tended to be started at points where there was an explicit shift in the *narrative present*. The narrative present is the 'now' of the main character in the story. Examples of text devices which shift this included statements of the *passage of time*, e.g., 'Two days later', 'At the end of May', and so on), and new temporal reference points which were associated with time having passed (e.g. 'On 18 June', 'On 31 January 1982', and so on). For narrative types of discourse, the progression of events seems to be an important organizational feature. Hopefully, broader use of this interesting technique should indicate conceptual boundaries determined by different devices in various types of discourse. For instance, what are the preferred rules of paragraphing in such expository discourse as explaining a scientific theory?

## 2  Local aspects of discourse: the control of memory and attention

In discussing the global aspect of discourse production, the essential problem was ensuring that the receiver had the right information in mind so that the discourse would be intelligible. This is easy to construe in very global terms: a protagonist's goals in a story need to be known if his actions are to be sensibly understood; a scientific experiment will only be understood if the reasons why it was undertaken are made clear. In all cases, the circumstances must be described so that it is reasonably clear what kinds of things or actions might be expected. Much of chapter 8, in which scripts and schemata were introduced, dwelt upon such matters. But it is important to know how the microstructure of discourse works, how choice of words and expressions sets the state of mind of the receiver.

In the chapters on memory, a distinction was drawn between short-term and long-term retention, and the idea of working memory was introduced. Although the issues surrounding the distinctions were shown to be complex, we can see how they might be related to the understanding of discourse. Eliciting background knowledge can be thought of as a process of bringing about retrieval from long-term storage; of course, it is the expressions which make up a discourse which do this, so one function of discourse is as a set of instructions to the receiver to retrieve particular (hopefully relevant) information. A second function is to provide new information to interpret with respect to the background knowledge which is made available. This is the commonplace function, and presumably draws upon working memory as an area in which interpretation takes place. There is a third function. The discourse has to be so structured that interpretation is *possible*. Incoming expressions must interact with the relevant knowledge so that the product constitutes the appropriate message. This is tantamount to the message controlling what it is that the receiver attends to. Finally, as the discourse unfolds, the three functions must combine to produce a memory trace which is recorded in long-term memory. All of this has to be triggered by the discourse itself, and is of course a dynamic affair. What is pertinent or important at one moment may not be at the next, and the discourse controls pertinence in a direct way.

There are many ways of describing local aspects of discourse structure, and a wealth of phenomena to be described. Our approach will be a relatively psychological one, and we shall concentrate on only a handful of issues. Nevertheless, in looking into these issues, questions which are applicable to the wider range of phenomena will be raised.

One obvious characteristic of any discourse is that it will contain references to people, objects, locations, times, events, etc., or some set of such things. They have to be introduced, and frequently they are referred to on more than one occasion. The producer's problem is to select an expression (a description) which produces the appropriate representation in the mind of the receiver. Let us take as an example the problem of introducing some object of interest, say a football:

Little Charles was kicking a football along the road.

In this case, the choice of description is an indefinite noun-phase (*A* + noun). Such expressions are commonly used to introduce new things into a discourse, that is, things which are not already in the mind of the receiver. It is convenient to think of the effect of encountering 'a football' in the sentence above as setting up some sort of token for 'football' in the mind of the receiver. Suppose we now wish to mention it again:

Little Charles was kicking a football along the road. He kicked a bit too hard, and *the ball* went into someone's garden.

In this second usage, a definite noun-phrase has been used. Typically, definite noun-phrases are used when the receiver can be assumed to have a token for it in mind. It is a simple matter to demonstrate the strange effect of using an indefinite expression to refer back to something for which there is already a token:

Johnny kicked a ball in the street.
A ball broke a window.

Although most people would take this to mean that it was the first-mentioned ball which broke a window, the second sentence 'sounds' as though the ball is an altogether new one. These illustrations show the way in which definite and indefinite expressions cause people to set up quite different kinds of processes: by and large, indefinite expressions seem to cause new tokens to be set up, while definite expressions seek out existing representations. This is an oversimplification, in fact, but serves to illustrate the general tenor of our argument.

It is not only definite noun-phrases which can be used to signal a reference back to something already introduced. Indeed, one of the most frequently used descriptions for this purpose is the *pronoun*. Compare the following pairs of sentences.

A lorry came hurtling down our street.
The lorry almost struck a parked car.
versus
A lorry came hurtling down our street.
It almost struck a parked car.

Although in the first pair the expression 'The lorry' clearly refers to the same lorry that was introduced in the first sentence, the second pair seems more natural, because of the use of the pronoun 'It'. Pronouns seem particularly well suited to signalling a reference back to a recently introduced entity, person, or event, and are often used in preference to full definite noun-phrases. One problem of discourse analysis is to discover the conditions under which one expression is used in preference to another. The psychological counterpart is to explain how this happens in terms of information-processing.

Expressions which refer back to something already mentioned are generally called *anaphoric expressions*, or anaphors; the phenomena are termed *anaphora*. Not all anaphors have to be pronouns or definite noun-phrases with repeat nouns. For instance, in an article about Mrs Thatcher, one might find her referred to as 'The Prime Minister', 'Maggie', 'She', 'The Iron Lady', and so on. Obviously, producers will select descriptions to obtain particular effects. The question then becomes one of how the effects come about from processing. It is also important to establish the mechanisms through which a processor establishes that all of the expressions refer to the same individual. They must map on to a common memory representation, otherwise the discourse would seem like a series of disconnected statements about different individuals.

Simple noun-phrases are not only the only ways of introducing or referring to things. In chapter 9 we saw that noun-phrases can be quite complex. Consider the following familiar expression:

- The pyramid on the block.

Such an expression, as we saw, is well suited to singling out which one of several possible blocks in a world is the block of interest. By the same token, if you only had several blocks *described* to you in a discourse, then this expression would be suitable for identifying the right one *in memory*. The same applies to adjectival qualifications: imagine a red ball and a yellow ball. The yellow ball is bigger than the red. To express this, it was necessary to identify which ball was the one that was larger, by including the adjective. More complex descriptions are sometimes needed in order to enable the right member of a set to be established.

Our discussion indicates a little more of what it means to say that expressions act directly to produce memory structures in the mind of readers. We have identified two necessary processes: the establishment of token representations of things newly introduced, and the establishment of reference to particular representations already established. The major part of the discussion has been about anaphora, rather than how new tokens are introduced, but note that there are many expressions which would cause identifiably different token structures to be set up: for instance, 'some people', 'few people', 'most people', 'three/five/two hundred people', 'elephants'. Each of these expressions, and many more, can be used to introduce discourse entities for subsequent references. It is beyond our aims to go into the details, although a discussion of the term 'some' is entered into in chapter 13.

Apart from the structure of descriptions themselves, we have to consider the way in which they are introduced into a discourse. When active and passive constructions were introduced in earlier chapters, it was suggested that the roles of agent and patient stayed constant under active and passive surface forms, thus 'the girl' and 'the cat' are in the same roles in both of the following:

The cat is being petted by the girl.
The girl is petting the cat.

Syntactically, they may be assumed to come from the same deep structure. But when they are looked at as *discourse*, one has to ask when a producer would choose one form over the other. The fact is, they are *not* identical from the point of view of function in discourse. One way of seeing this is to ask what *question* might be answered by each of the sentences. For the passive form, the question could be 'What is happening to the cat?', while for the active form, it could be 'What is the girl doing?'

This contrast between active and passive is just one instance of a general idea about sentences: that expressions at the start of a sentence are what the sentence is *about*, while what follows is a comment of some sort. In the case above, the first sentence is about the *cat*, and in the second it is about the *girl*. In terms of the effect of discourse on the human processor, one might suppose that if there is a sentence about $X$, to which new information is to be appended in memory, then the first task would be to find out what $X$ is. Indeed, Hornby (1972) presented some evidence supporting this view, using sentences like the passive/active pair shown above. He showed subjects one of the sentences, and asked them to choose which of a *pair of pictures* the sentence 'was about'. A typical picture pair might be a girl petting a dog, or a boy petting a cat. With *the girl* in the first noun-phrase position, subjects almost always selected the picture of *the girl petting the dog*. With *the cat* in the first position, they selected the picture of *the boy petting the cat*. In short, there is some psychological and linguistic evidence that initial noun-phrases are the major point of reference in sentences. For this reason, they are commonly referred to as the *topic* of sentences (Lyons 1968).

There are many illustrations of the priority assigned to the initial parts of sentences. For instance, Broadbent (1973) illustrated the role that topicalization plays in pronoun assignment. The sentence he used for this purpose was one from engineering:

- The feedpipe lubricates the chain, and *it* should be adjusted to leave a gap of half an inch between itself and the sprocket.

Broadbent asked people to indicate to what they thought *it* referred. Most people thought that the referent was *the feedpipe*, although, logically, it could be either the feedpipe or *the chain*.

This demonstrates once again that the opening part of a sentence is taken to be what the sentence is *about*, and goes hand-in-hand with the view that pronouns are essentially devices for referring to things which are in the attentional focus of the receiver of the discourse.

Terms like 'what a sentence is about' and 'attentional focus' are rather vague expressions, of course. It is much better to look at the effects of sentence structure on processing mechanisms. While it must be recognized that we are speaking of a very subtle and complex area, it is nonetheless appropriate to indicate how such things can be construed in processing terms. Thus Broadbent (1973) and others (e.g. Haviland and Clark 1974) have offered an explanation of topic effects in terms of the memory-search operations necessary for discourse comprehension. The suggestion is that the early part of a sentence conveys a reference point (usually a *connexion* to an earlier part of the discourse). The later part (called the comment) is information to be *attached* to the reference point. In many ways this is reminiscent of the general problem of ordering information in discourse with which we began.

Intelligibility demands that an early reference point is found. In this respect, sentence structure seems to obey the same kind of principle as does the sort of global structure found in paragraphs or stories.

## B Processing and discourse

Having introduced just a few of the properties of discourse, they now have to be put into the context of processing. In chapter 9, we got as far as seeing parsing as a left–right process which took in words successively and partitioned them into groups which correspond to some grammar. At the other extreme, discourse is seen as a stimulus which acts on the processor to produce an interpreted message as a result. Many of the studies of discourse processing have been concerned with filling the gap between these two extremes. In this section we shall be concerned almost exclusively with the interpretation of discourse in contrast to its production.

## 1 A psychological framework based on search and control

Sanford and Garrod (1981) attempted to integrate various facets of the problem at hand within a general framework. Essentially, they argue that discourse triggers various search and control processes within a particular memory architecture. The aims were to posit a psychologically viable memory architecture which could be related directly to the effects of various devices in discourse, and perhaps explain some of the linguistic facts about discourse devices. The use of the term framework was deliberate, since within it various particular problems could have a number of solutions. It is being used here to illustrate how various facets of discourse structure and psychological processing might be tied together.

The memory structure is assumed to be based on two apparently inescapable requirements. First, the mental representation of a discourse must consist in more than that which is explicit in the discourse itself. It is considered by Sanford and Garrod as being a structure of mappings between discourse fragments and underlying schemata which support the interpretation of the discourse fragments. Evidence in favour of this 'extended' representation was given in earlier chapters, where its psychological reality was argued for. However, it is also argued that 'explicit' information from the discourse itself, and information from memory to which it becomes attached (termed 'implicit information' for convenience), are not confused during processing. Sanford and Garrod's terms for the memory stores underlying this are *explicit* and *implicit* focus. The justification for this will come shortly. The second inescapable requirement is that the memory system be *dynamic*. Thus, when one reads a lengthy text, one does not keep all of the detail of all of the text continuously in mind. Rather, as a text unfolds, so the reader seems to attend to different things, usually things which have been mentioned recently, or which are currently being mentioned. This requirement explains the use of the term 'focus' in implicit and explicit focus. Memory representations are assumed to be partitioned either into current focus, or out of focus. Two unfocused partitions of memory are posited: general long-term memory, and memory for the text itself. This split really reflects little more than the fact that in LTM, memory for the *particular* discourse in question is marked as a separable representation. Thus the four partitions assumed are:

(a)   Explicit focus.
(b)   Implicit focus.
(c)   General LTM.
(d)   Memory for the text in question.

Each of these partitions is assumed to have special properties. Thus explicit focus consists of tokens for things and events

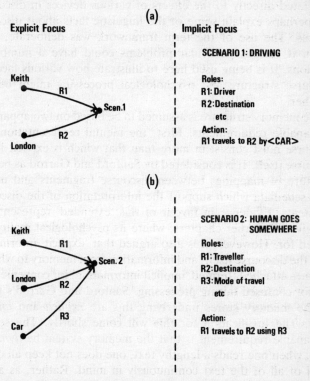

*Figure 10-1.* Focus representations of (a) 'Keith drove to London', and (b) 'Keith travelled by car to London'. Explicit focus contains tokens of entities mapped via role-pointers (R) to a scenario token. Implicit focus consists of the appropriate scenario by which explicit focus was and can be interpreted.

mentioned in the text, and can be represented as a network. Figure 10-1 shows explicit focus representations for two similar sentences: 'Keith drove to London' and 'Keith travelled by car to London'. Note that there are tokens (or nodes) for various things mentioned in these sentences, and that the things mentioned play *roles* in the actions. The figure also shows hypothetical structures in implicit focus. These are really just schemata for 'travel' and 'drive'. So, explicit focus consists of a structure based on the text, while implicit focus consists of underlying knowledge which is relevant to the text.

To understand the figure more, it is necessary to introduce the first processing assumption: *memory searches are initiated by any incoming discourse fragment*. In the case of 'Keith drove to London', Sanford and Garrod assume the process to develop like this: the parser identifies *Keith* as an NP, and searches memory for a unique individual fitting the description Keith. Most readers will have none, so it is a *new entity*. A token for Keith is put into explicit focus. Next 'drove to London' is encountered. At this point, several things happen. A search for 'drove' is initiated, and it too is a new entity: however, it is a main verb, and so its schema is identified in LTM. *This schema then becomes current focus*, and a token showing where it can be found is put in explicit focus. Keith is assigned to the agent role, and London the destination role, both in accordance with syntactic analysis.

While this illustrates why figure 10-1 looks as it does, it does not explain why there are two memory partitions. Why not just one partition, with the filled-in schema in it? First of all, subjects can discriminate between what is in a text and what is inferred, up to a point. Recall the fact that while 'fried' is a good retrieval cue for the sentence 'The housewife cooked the chips', it is still the original sentence that they remember. Secondly, through an analysis of forms of anaphoric reference, it seems that while definite noun-phrases can be used to refer to things which are only implicit, pronouns cannot. Compare the following:

Keith drove to London.
It broke down halfway.
versus
Keith drove to London.
The car broke down halfway.

The first sounds strange, because 'it' refers back to something (the car) which was only implicit. Sanford, Garrod, Lucas and Henderson (1983) present evidence supporting the view that pronouns are used most often to refer to explicitly mentioned entities. This and other evidence forces a distinction to be made between explicit and implicit focus.

Sanford and Garrod ascribe the properties of a short-term, working buffer to explicit focus: they assume that only a certain number of tokens are effectively displaced by new ones. In contrast, implicit focus is assumed to be only a currently privileged data structure in LTM, which is currently being used for interpretation.

To illustrate the system a little more fully, consider the interpretation of some discourse. To start with, there will be no entry in explicit focus. When the first sentence is parsed, it is assumed that some structure in LTM is isolated (which becomes current implicit focus), the tokens for entities mentioned are put into explicit focus, and mappings between the two are established, as in figure 10-1. As the text continues to be parsed, two things can happen. Either the descriptions found will map into what is in focus, or they will not. If they do, all that happens is that the structure in explicit focus is enlarged until the point is reached that certain (usually earlier) parts of the representation are lost. It is assumed that the longer structures reside in explicit focus, the stronger will be their trace in LTM.

Of course, in a fuller discourse, the important background knowledge will not stay constant. For instance, even the following simple narrative signals a number of changes of scene:

> Mary was dressing the baby. (dressing a child)
> When she had finished, they went to the shops.
> (taking a baby to shops)
> She felt thirsty, so she sat down in a cafe. (cafe scene)

Scene changes are assumed to be supported by the identification of appropriate information in long-term memory. A scene change can be triggered by an expression like 'When she had finished . . .', in which case the processor is assumed to drop the current implicit focus, and expect a new knowledge structure (scenario) to be singled out by what comes next in the text. In the present example, it is assumed that '. . . they went to the shops' is a sufficient description to identify a new scenario in memory. Apart from the need for a change in implicit focus being triggered by specific expressions like 'When she had finished', it can also be triggered by sufficient expressions which do not map into the current scenario. So, in the case of 'She felt thirsty, so she sat down in a cafe', being thirsty cannot be interpreted in terms of being at the shops, and neither can the action of sitting down in a cafe. Attempts to search the focus for an interpretation will fail, and so search continues into long-term memory, in which another new scenario is isolated. This then becomes the *new* implicit focus. The sort of structure which Sanford and Garrod assume to be produced is shown in figure 10-2.

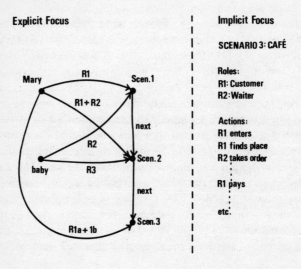

*Figure 10-2.* After two scenario shifts, explicit focus contains several tokens, including ones for earlier scenarios. But only scenario 3, the current scenario, constitutes implicit focus.

Our discussion serves to show what is meant when one says that discourse can be considered as instructions to search and control memory. Now we can turn to a brief look at some discourse phenomena within this framework. Let us begin with types of anaphoric expressions. The assumption is that these serve to trigger searches. Pronouns trigger searches in explicit focus, since they are almost always used for referring to explicitly mentioned things. Definite noun-phrases, on the other hand, trigger searches in both *implicit* and explicit focus:

Fred had trouble cutting his hair.
*The scissors* were too blunt.   (implicit reference)
and
John dropped the ball as he ran past the touch line.
*The ball* was too muddy to grip.   (explicit reference)

Pronouns are thus thought of as triggering search in a more *restricted* part of memory than definite noun-phrases, within the Sanford–Garrod (1981) memory partitions.

It is inappropriate to go too far into the details of the theory here. However, it should be clear that the account is essentially schema-based. Schema-like structures are assumed to be searched for as early as possible during processing ('scenario' is the term Sanford and Garrod use for these structures). Interpretation proceeds on the basis of the current scenario through attempts to match new text input to scenario content or to explicit focus. This kind of processing is termed *primary processing* by Sanford and Garrod, because the procedures behind it are assumed to be tried continuously by the processor. However, primary processing can break down if no match between an input and current focus can be found, or even if only a partial match can be found. When the match fails, Sanford and Garrod assume that *secondary processing* occurs, based on an attempt to find new ways of producing mappings between discourse and memory. For instance, an initial goal will be to see whether *some* sort of interpretation based on extensions of current focus is possible. An illustration of this is:

Harry went into the cinema to see a new Western.
The cashier wouldn't give him a ticket.

References to *cashier* and *ticket* will map very well into the cinema scenario, but the whole event does not. Of course, it is just this sort of mismatch which is important in a story. The fact that some mapping is possible gives the message an anchor, making it essentially intelligible. But a failure to be given a ticket breaks normal expectations, so the processor is assumed to be set to the goal of 'seek a reason why Harry didn't get a ticket'. Such wait-and-see processing is termed *secondary processing*. It is seldom the case that *no* mapping can be made between current focus and a new description – there is usually some continuity of people or event but there may not be enough to generate a proper goal. It is in such cases that the processor is assumed to search for a *new* scenario.

The structure of discourse is thus construed as a balance between inputs demanding primary and secondary processing. Primary processing provides a smooth interpretation of material which is uninformative; secondary processing entails more complex processing of material which conveys the novel aspects of a message.

## 2  A processing issue: when is significance established?

Sanford and Garrod, like many other theorists, have made the assumption that expressions are interpreted *as early as possible* during processing (see also Marslen-Wilson and Tyler 1981). This follows because it is assumed that references are resolved as soon as possible, appropriate background knowledge is retrieved as soon as possible, and so on. However, little evidence has been reported to offer direct support for such a contention, although it is obviously an important issue in relation to how we think of discourse processing as being carried out. In fact, not all theorists would support the view that such immediate significance determination takes place. For instance, Kintsch and van Dijk (1978) argue that significance is only determined *when it needs to be*. Clearly, there is no limit to what the significance of something might be – it is like the problem of decomposition – yet it seems unreasonable to suppose that some of the significance of a message is not ascertained as early as possible, since the whole point of a message is to convey significance in some way.

The problem is a general one of how quickly a processor checks new linguistic input against background knowledge. Does it do it on a phrase-by-phrase basis? Remember that in Winograd's work, described in chapter 9, his program was arranged to do just that, only in his case it checked definite noun-phrases against the block world. Crain and Steedman's study of garden-path sentences suggested that noun-phrases were checked against existing text models by readers in a similar way.

In a recent experiment, Garrod and Sanford (in preparation) attempted a direct test of the immediacy-of-interpretation idea. Subjects were presented with passages, one sentence at a time. Each passage introduced a general setting, and two characters, a main character referred to by name, and a secondary character referred to by a role description. A sample passage is:

> Elizabeth was a very inexperienced swimmer, and wouldn't have gone into the pool if the lifeguard hadn't been nearby. But as soon as she was out of her depth she started to panic and wave her hands about in a frenzy. Within seconds Elizabeth/the lifeguard jumped/sank in the pool . . . .

The passage continues, but the snippet given here is enough for our arguments. In the last line, there are two optional character references which could be made: either to *Elizabeth* or to *the lifeguard*. Suppose it is to *Elizabeth*. Reading one, one finds a choice of verbs: *jumped* or *sank*. Obviously, the verb *sank* is predictable for Elizabeth, while *jumped* is not, because of Elizabeth's circumstances. The opposite is true of the lifeguard, of course. Now if this predictability were used *at the moment of encountering the verb*, it would mean that the term 'Elizabeth' had been mapped into the memory structure already, because the processor would have established something like 'Elizabeth is the person who is in the water, and can't swim, and is afraid of sinking' etc.

By the same logic, if the processor finds 'jumped' the predictable verb for the lifeguard, then the processor would have had to have established something like 'The lifeguard is the person who sits on the side of the pool (an assumption), and who has to jump in to save people in distress'. The trick is to determine whether there are any influences of the character on the processing of the verb.

Garrod and Sanford used four versions of each passage, in which the two compatible character-action pairings occurred, and in which the two incompatible ones appeared. Each verb was modified slightly, so that it was *misspelled*. The subjects' task was to read each passage, and press a button as soon as they detected a spelling error. (Half of the materials in the experiment had spelling errors in various different places.) The prediction was that *if* the character reference was mapped into memory as soon as it was encountered, then this should influence the predictability of the verbs. In particular, work on word recognition demonstrates that predictability makes it easier to recognize words (cf. chapter 3), so one would expect error-detection latencies to be shorter for the predictable verbs if the significance of the characters was established *as soon as their descriptions were encountered*. This pattern emerged quite clearly, supporting the claim that the processor establishes significance as soon as possible.

In another experiment, a similar but slightly more complex pattern emerged when he/she pronouns were used instead of noun-phrases. Obviously, in the example given above, *she* could be substituted for Elizabeth. The results show evidence that *she* is interpreted as soon as it is encountered by the processor.

At the present stage, the important thing is to establish the conditions under which immediate interpretation does and does not occur, and whether there are some expressions which cannot be immediately interpreted. The pronoun 'it' is a good problem case, and a very complex one. We can only illustrate some of the difficulty here. In some circumstances, there seems to be no reason to suppose that significance is not established immediately:

John dropped the ball. It$_1$ bounced into the gutter.

This looks like a *prima facie* case where a processor executing a search back from point 1 would have to correctly identify 'the ball' as the antecedent. The problem is, if the reference is resolved at point 1, without further examination of the sentence, then what would happen in the following cases?

John dropped the ball. It$_1$ was just not his day$_2$.
John dropped the ball. It$_1$ felt like the right thing to do$_2$.

With this example, it is clearly necessary to process the rest of the sentence, perhaps as far as point 2, before making an assignment. Thus although significance may be ascertained as early as possible for noun-phrases and he/she pronouns, this procedure may not apply to 'it', which is a very general-purpose pronoun indeed. It can be used to refer to almost anything. There seems to be evidence to suggest that significance is established immediately in some circumstances in which 'it' is used (e.g. Carpenter and Just 1977; Sanford, Garrod, Lucas and Henderson 1983) and not in others (e.g. Sanford 1984).

It is clear from this discussion that a major aspect of how a discourse processor might work depends upon on how quickly significance is established. There is evidence to support the view that significance is established as soon as possible. Such a view means that the processor *commits* itself to a particular interpretation, of course. One might well argue that such commitment is necessary if the processor is to operate in a substantially top-down mode.

In the next section, we look at some other issues which indicate yet another class of factors which are important for determining the significance of utterances.

## C  Issues raised by the study of dialogue

In the preceding section of this chapter, most of the discussion tacitly centred upon understanding written language, to the neglect of conversation. In this brief section, we shall redress the balance somewhat, considering problems which are made evident when one studies conversation. In fact, many of these issues are directly applicable to the understanding of reading comprehension too although they have tended to be raised with respect to dialogue.

### 1  Dialogue as a contract

Dialogue is probably the communication situation with which we are most familiar in our daily lives. In a dialogue, two protagonists take turns in producing utterances with a view to communicating about some issue which is usually of common concern to both of them. It will be recalled that understanding written language is dependent upon the writer enabling the reader to access the right knowledge at the right time and without this the entire act of understanding can falter. The same argument applies to conversation, but it can be illustrated there par excellence.

First of all, the study of dialogue makes it clear that protagonists operate under conditions that resemble an unspoken *contract*. There appear to be conditions which speakers themselves normally fulfil, and which they expect their partners to fulfil also. Grice (1975) suggests that there are four 'maxims' to be met in efficient conversational interaction:

### (a)  Maxim of quantity
Contributions should be as informative as possible, but not

over-informative. Clark and Clark (1977) provide the following example of a failure to abide by this maxim:

Steven:  Wilfred is meeting a woman for dinner tonight.
Susan:   Does his wife know about it?
Steven:  Of course she does. The woman he is meeting is his wife.

### (b) Maxim of quality
Contributions should convey propositions which the speaker believes to be true. To do otherwise is obviously to mislead.

### (c) Maxim of relation
The contribution should be relevant to the aims of the conversation.

Suppose, for instance, that an obviously impoverished person stops someone in the street, and says: 'Can you tell me where I can get a good meal?'

It will be obvious that the following reply breaks maxim (c): 'They serve a first-rate smoked salmon at Luigis.'

### (d) Maxim of manner
Contributions should avoid obscurity and ambiguity.

The few examples given above at least serve to illustrate that conversation, to be effective for both participants, must be carried out according to certain unspoken rules. But these maxims have a very special feature – they depend upon each protagonist having an idea of what is relevant and appropriate *from the point of view of his partner in dialogue*, as well as having his own objectives. Each protagonist must have some idea of the goals and plans under which the other protagonist is operating.

This point can be illustrated with the interesting case of *indirect speech acts*. For instance, suppose that William and Mary have just moved in to a new house. At some point the following interaction occurs:

William:  'We seem to have run out of milk.'
Mary:     'There's a shop around the corner.'

Superficially, we have two *statements* here. William's is being taken by Mary as meaning something like 'We don't have any milk, and may need some, so what can we do?' Mary's reply, which required that she interpret William's utterance as described above, will be interpreted by William as something like 'Mary thinks that the shop probably sells milk, and that she thinks that there is a reasonable chance that the shop will be open'.

This analysis, in which William is seen as *indirectly* requesting help (hence 'indirect speech act'), and Mary is seen as providing relevant information, fits naturally into the view that humans usually have a goal in mind when they make an utterance, and that a key part of understanding is recognizing that goal. The consequences of not co-operating in this way can be unpleasant. Suppose that Mary thought that the shop would be closed. She should have said: 'Well, there's a shop around the corner, but I think it may be closed.' If she did not, she would be breaking the maxims of quantity, relation and manner. William would be justified in supposing that Mary was being very unpleasant. It is interesting to note that in the *Kama Sutra*, the Sanskrit treatise of love, systematically 'misunderstanding' one's lover in ways like this is a recommended method for terminating the relationship.

There are many examples of indirect speech acts which are met routinely during life. Suppose that you are in the living room, and someone walks in and leaves the door open. You might say:

- Would you mind closing the door?
- Can you close the door?
- Could you close the door please?
- I wonder, could you close the door?

and so on.

In each case, you mean to ask the person to close the door, but in no case is the utterance literally asking for this. You could do it by a direct speech act (a command) 'close the door'. Quite obviously, the various ways of asking someone to do something differ in politeness, which is an interesting question in its own right. But from a processing point of view, we must ask how interrogative constructions are interpreted as commands, how statives are interpreted as requests for comments, and so on. This problem is sometimes referred to as the issue of *illocutionary force*. Thus we may say that, on some occasions, the illocutionary force of an interrogative is a command. Quite obviously, the basis of interpretation is in terms of the listener's idea of what the speaker is trying to achieve by making an utterance. These ideas must enter into the processes which so automatically and easily guide utterance selection in conversation.

To summarize up to this point: it is clear that protagonists in conversations have certain expectations of each other's conduct with respect to what is being said. These are summarized in a general way by Grice's postulates. It is also apparent that conversation is very elliptical: two statements, one by each protagonist, can be a useful interaction, provided each protagonist is justified in believing that the other is acting under the kinds of rules suggested by Grice. But equally clearly this means being able to infer the intention of the speaker, which generally means establishing what plan the speaker is operating under. Among the better-known specific problems which can be handled within such a framework is that of interpreting the illocutionary force of indirect speech acts.

## 2 Mutual knowledge

Everything we have discussed in section C1 points to the obvious importance of what each speaker knows or can plausibly assume about his partner. Such knowledge is often termed *mutual knowledge* (e.g. Clark and Marshall 1981). The role of *background* knowledge is obviously important to the process of understanding, and unless two protagonists in a dialogue have some background knowledge in common, they will not be able to communicate. This 'common ground' of background knowledge can be termed *shared knowledge*, in the sense that both protagonists will have to have it, but this is not the same as mutual knowledge. Suppose we have two football fans, and they both happen to know that Italy won the World Cup in 1982. This could be written as:

A knows that Italy won the World Cup in 1982.
and
B knows that Italy won the World Cup in 1982.

Now suppose that A wishes to communicate about this to B. He must first *establish that B knows this fact* before he can go on to give his opinions about it. In other words, a condition is needed in which:

A knows that B knows that Italy won the World Cup in 1982.

This knowledge, or assumption, of what another person knows is the start of mutual knowledge. The idea has been rather fully explored in an accessible form by Clark and Marshall, and we shall follow part of their argument. They make use of an example problem in communication. One must imagine a scenario in which there is a film festival on at the Roxy cinema, and that it is dedicated to a short season of Marx Brothers' films. Their first case is the following:

On Wednesday morning, Ann reads the early edition of the newspaper, which says that *Monkey Business* is playing that night. Later she sees Bob and asks, 'Have you ever seen the film playing at the Roxy tonight?'

The interest lies in Ann's question. What are the appropriate conditions for saying 'the film playing at the Roxy tonight', rather than describing it in some other way. Obviously, if Bob did not know what the film was, and Ann asked this question, then he would be forced to ask what the film was before he could answer the question. Since Ann would not choose this form of expression if she thought he did not know what the film was, we can say that the following must be the case:

(i)   Ann knows that (the film at the Roxy is *Monkey Business*). and
(ii)  Ann knows that Bob knows (X) (where X is the expression in brackets above).

There are many ways in which (i) and (ii) could be met. For instance, they may both have read the paper together that morning, and discussed what films were on that day. Conditions (i) and (ii) would then be met. The problem is that one can show that (i) and (ii) are not sufficient. Suppose that something happened so that *Bob* thought that *Ann* had the wrong film in mind. Clark and Marshall offer the following scenario:

On Wednesday morning Ann and Bob read the early edition of the newspaper, and they discuss the fact that *A Day at the Races* is showing that night at the Roxy. When the late edition arrives, Bob reads the movie section, and notices that the film has been corrected to *Monkey Business*, and he circles it with his red pen.

Later, Ann picks up the late edition, notes the correction, and recognizes Bob's circle around it. She also realizes that Bob has no way of knowing that she has seen the late edition. Later that day, Ann sees Bob and asks, 'Have you seen the movie showing at the Roxy tonight?'

Ann's question is infelicitous, because the following condition has not been met:

(iii)   Ann knows that Bob knows that Ann knows (X).

So in order to use the expression *the movie showing at the Roxy tonight*, conditions (i), (ii) *and* (iii) should be met. Unfortunately, more and more complex scenarios can be drawn up, showing that the set of conditions is never-ending. For instance, Clark and Marshall demonstrate the conditions up to 'Ann knows that Bob knows that Ann knows that Bob knows that Ann knows that (X)'!

The point is this: when we make a speech act, we wish it to be felicitous. In order to make it felicitous, we have to be sure that an infinite number of conditions have been met, on the present scheme of representing mutual knowledge. (More complete philosophical treatments are given by Lewis (1969), Schiffer (1972), Harman (1977) and Cohen (1978).) But, quite obviously, it is unreasonable to suppose that people ever check an infinity of conditions. Clark and Marshall suggest that people use heuristics (principles that *usually* work) through which they can assume the infinity of conditions to have been met. These they term *co-presence heuristics*.

The simplest example arises from a situation where the two protagonists are together in the presence of an information source – say Ann and Bob both read the cinema section of the paper together. In this situation *Ann and Bob have reason to believe that each of them will see the information*. On the basis of this, it is possible for Ann to infer the infinity of conditions, though rather than check through them, she will simply assume that they have been met. While later events may alter her beliefs about what Bob knows, or what Bob thinks she knows, it is no longer necessary to attempt an impossible check on an infinite number of conditions at every stage.

Physical copresence of the two participants and the critical information is one direct way of bringing about a state of mutual knowledge. Another way is from prior conversation. For instance, by saying 'I bought a Black Forest gateau yesterday', to Bob, Ann can once again assume mutual knowledge of that statement to exist. Another extremely important case is termed *community comembership* by Clark and Marshall. The idea here is that two protagonists may very well overlap in terms of their experience – they belong to a common community. For instance, they might both be psycholinguists. Having established this fact, they may then (in principle!) assume mutual knowledge of a particular set of issues. Thus one protagonist may be able to ask straight off 'What do you think are the weakest aspects of Winograd's program SHRDLU?'. Without an assumption of mutual knowledge, this would be an infelicitous utterance.

It is important to realize that while people normally strive to make their utterances in a conversation felicitous, it is quite easy for people to misinterpret each other if the mutual knowledge condition is not met. The following example comes from Shadbolt (1983). Generally speaking, the fans of the two well-known Glasgow football teams, Rangers and Celtic, consider their own teams to be the best in all respects. In the light of this, consider the following:

Celtic fan:      'That is the best team in the league out there.'
Rangers' fan:   'Yes, it is.'

One can imagine many ways in which this dialogue can be understood. Suppose that neither knows which team the other supports, but each makes an unwarranted community copresence assumption (i.e. the Celtic fan assumes the other is a Celtic fan too, and so on). Then the Rangers' fan will think that it is Rangers which is being referred to. More subtle variations could come about if the Rangers' fan knew that the Celtic fan was indeed a Celtic fan, but that he also knew that the Celtic fan did not know that he himself was indeed a Rangers' fan. Under these circumstances, the Celtic fan would be referring to Celtic, and would believe that the Rangers' fan accepted this reference. On the other hand, the Rangers' fan would be practising deception, because he would allow the Celtic fan to believe that he too was a Celtic fan, but would secretly think that what was being attributed to Celtic was in fact true of Rangers.

Deceptions can take place at any level in the infinity of

conditions that make up mutual knowledge, and when they are practised by one or more protagonists, the conversation will no longer be co-operative in the Gricean sense. This may be for good reason. For instance, the Rangers' fan may not wish to reveal his allegiances. After all, the initiator of a conversation will be seeking a reply, but the second protagonist may be an unwilling one.

In deception, mutual-knowledge assumptions are systematically and knowingly violated by one or other protagonists. But misunderstandings can arise if unwarranted mutual-knowledge assumptions are made, albeit unwittingly. This does not mean that they cannot be repaired at some later point in the conversation, however. In real conversation, some misunderstandings may go unnoticed, and others may be detected in the normal flow of interaction. Thus part of the conversation itself may lead to the establishment of mutual-knowledge conditions:

| Barchester United fan: | 'That's the best team in the league out there.' |
| Brick City fan: | 'Yes it is. . . . They did very well last week. (Barchester United did poorly.) |
| Barchester United fan: | 'Are you trying to be funny?' |

At this point, mutual knowledge of the possibility that they are fans of opposing teams begins to dawn.

It is clear from this that the interactive nature of conversation *enables* mutual-knowledge conditions to be met with respect to some aspect of the world (in this case, fanhood). The example also makes clear a very real distinction between *mutual* knowledge, and *shared* knowledge about the world. Thus both fans may well have the same knowledge of football, they may even have been to the same matches, but unless they have mutual knowledge, communication will falter. The interactive nature of conversation enables misunderstandings to be detected by participants, however, and they can try to establish proper background and mutual-knowledge conditions if they wish.

## D  Summary: discourse and cognition

In this chapter we began by pursuing two aspects of discourse form, which we termed problems of *linearization* and *background knowledge*. It was claimed that much of the structure of discourse can be accounted for in terms of the order in which information is presented. The basic problem at the global level was portrayed as one in which producers have to ensure that receivers have the appropriate background knowledge available at any given time to interpret what follows. The argument rested on schema-theory accounts of understanding. At a more microscopic level, the very form of words, particularly *descriptions*, revealed the same sort of problems. An indication was given of how various expressions seem to require particular events to have preceded their use.

In the most psychological section, it was shown how one might put together a process model to handle some of these phenomena. A sample of detailed problems one meets when trying to do this was also given.

In the third section, the discussion was broadened to show the range of processes entering into conversation. This meant something of a departure from discussion of conventional experiments, but showed various necessary conditions for effective communicative acts. As yet, there are no psychologically testable process models of conversation. Yet the development of such models is an important issue, not merely for theoretical reasons, but for practical ones too. With the interest in 'fifth-generation' computers, it is desirable to be able to communicate with programs by using natural language. While programs such as Winograd's are reasonably successful, they are, on the whole, limited. A successful program, given a query of some sort, would have to be able to work out what is an appropriate answer. This entails most of the processes described above. To get the feel for the problem, consider how you might answer the question 'Where do you live?'. You might say:

Glasgow
or
Scotland
or
Cathcart
or
Bridge Street
or
Number 15

depending upon the circumstances. The top one might be appropriate in reply to a stranger at a foreign conference, the bottom one to a neighbour. The right answer and the appropriate answer are two rather different things!

The study of discourse is a most exciting facet of cognitive science. Man is a very verbal creature – *the* verbal creature – and to explore discourse is to explore one of man's unique cognitive skills. The relationship of language skill to man's cognitive capacities as a whole is not well understood but doubtless verbal facility is intertwined with his capacity for thinking, which is extremely sophisticated by phylogenetic standards. The necessary conditions for conversation, the most ubiquitous form of discourse, provides a key to some of the flexibility and complexity of mental organization. Not only is the interpretation of utterances dependent upon rapid access to a vast range of background knowledge – call it KNOWLEDGE 1 – but participants in dialogue must have reasonable knowledge of what they can take *each other* to know, or shared knowledge – call it KNOWLEDGE 2. Furthermore, for dialogue to be felicitous, they must also have mutual knowledge – KNOWLEDGE 3. All three types of knowledge are used constantly and flexibly in conversational exchanges. When a listener cannot interpret an utterance, a complete range of problem-solving methods become available, usually quite regularly.

The interplay of all of these knowledge types and problem-solving procedures is a very rapid, usually unconscious, process. Part of the attraction of trying to develop process models of discourse understanding and production is that the *requirements* for discourse are now getting to be understood, and so one can ask questions about what kind of structure a device would have to have to handle this enormous flexibility. What kind of working-memory system would be suitable? What kind of long-term memory retrieval procedures would back up such rapid and appropriate processing? There is a feeling on the part of some cognitive scientists (e.g. Newell 1972) that only by fully exploring a substantial domain of competence (like discourse) will appropriate answers to questions of mental architecture be found. To this the present author would like to add that the domains should be *natural*: after all, man's brain must be designed to cope with language. Although discourse studies have enjoyed a vogue status in recent years in psychology, the canvas is still very sketchy. As was the case with the analysis of knowledge representations, much of the research is still at the natural history stage.

## Chapters 9 and 10: Chapter notes

We have covered a number of technical issues in these two chapters, but have omitted a number of very important things. The whole issue of speech perception and production has not been discussed at all. Many introductory books contain excellent discussions of these issues. George Miller (1981), *Language and Speech*, W.H. Freeman, San Francisco, is an excellent introduction, and more substantial discussions are given in H. Clark and E. Clark (1977), *Psychology and Language*, Harcourt Brace Jovanovich, New York. The latter book offers a discussion of many interesting aspects of language, though its slant is somewhat different from the one presented here.

The linguistics of grammar and semantics is a very technical subject, but is central to the cognitive science of language. A good new textbook on grammar is T. Winograd (1983), *Cognitive Processes in Language Understanding*, Vol. 1, Addison-Wesley. The linguistics of discourse may appear at first sight to be even more remote from psychology, but J.E. Grimes (1975), *The Thread of Discourse*, Mouton, Janua Liguarum, The Hague, is interesting in its own right, and should be a valuable stimulus for psychologists. A.J. Sanford and S.C. Garrod (1981), *Understanding Written Language*, Wiley, offers a more psychologically oriented account.

# 11 Thinking 1: Problem-solving

We now turn to one of the central issues in cognitive science: the nature of thinking. We are not abruptly entering a totally new field. Throughout this book, we have gradually moved more and more towards an understanding of thinking. The next three chapters deal with three different aspects of the topic: this chapter is about problem-solving, chapter 12 is about some aspects of judgement, and chapter 13 is about logical reasoning. These aspects are not exclusive categories, of course; the decision to present the material in this way is instead determined by two factors. First, problem-solving as a *theoretical matter* forms the basis of judgement and deductive reasoning, and so some appreciation of the theory of problem-solving is essential. Secondly, the work described comes from three rather different traditions. There is a long tradition in psychology of observing the behaviour of subjects working on well-defined problems, the solutions of which may require some thought to reach, but which have solutions that are not difficult to understand. It was with such well-structured problems that the theory of problem-solving, including computer modelling, began. The aspects of judgement tackled in the chapter which follows have their origins in studies of how effectively human beings function as intuitive judges, intuitive statisticians – judging the frequency of events, the likelihood of events, and so on. But, of course, when one poses a question of judgement, one is requiring problem-solving to take place. Logical reasoning, the third topic, has a history which derives from logic itself. When the first ideas about logic were forthcoming, the problem was to determine the form (rules) of valid reasoning. With the development of formal logic, it has now become possible to tackle the question of how people reason in comparison with the prescriptive models of formal logic. One kind of question which has been asked by psychologists working in this field is whether people are logical or not. This is a difficult question, and it may not even be a sensible one in any non-trivial sense. Our approach will be to treat logical reasoning as the application of problem-solving procedures.

The three areas offer quite different perspectives on goal-directed thinking processes, despite having common underlying elements. To begin with we shall treat matters which have commonly been referred to as problem-solving. Two preliminary distinctions must be made. The first is between *routine* and *creative* solving. The characteristic of routine problem-solving is that although some problem occurs which must be solved, the subject (or rather, some processor) can recognize it and apply a stereotyped procedure which leads to a solution. For instance, in discourse, anaphor resolution can be considered a problem, but a problem which appears to be (usually) solved by *routine* procedures.

In contrast, creative problem-solving occurs when there is no readily available procedure leading to a solution. Under such conditions, a route through the problem has to be constructed. Of course, much problem-solving on real-life tasks will be a mixture of these two sorts of problem-solving methods. The more one knows about a problem domain, the more 'routine' procedures one will possess.

The second distinction is slightly more tricky. Problems can be classed as well-defined or ill-defined. On one view, a well-defined problem is one in which all of the relevant information is essentially available in the problem statement, and where a solution is possible. For instance, many problems in algebra and logic, crossword puzzles and Christmas parlour puzzles are well-defined, while trying to decide how to lead a meaningful life is poorly defined. However, one can take two perspectives on this. One is that of an investigator who is familiar with the problem. A problem will be termed 'well-defined' by him if he knows all the relevant information and knows the solution path. But from the point of view of a *subject*, the problem may be ill-defined simply because he does not have in *his* mind a representation which is appropriate.

## A  Some problems and a classification

In this section some problems are introduced – mostly ones which are often used to illustrate various important phenomena. The problems are varied, ranging from picture puzzles, through ana-grams, analogies, and more complex problems. In the face of such variety, it is useful to group the problems in some way. To this end, we shall use a classification devised by the psychologist Greeno (1978). Although not meant to be a completely watertight classificatory scheme, it is useful in that it does capture some important distinctions. The three types of problem which he identifies he calls problems of *arrangement*, of *inducing structure*, and of *transformation*. Let us consider each in turn, noting both their general character, and some phenomena associated with each type.

## 1 Problems of arrangement

In this type of problem, some entities are presented to a subject and the task is to rearrange them to meet some criterion. Anagrams are a most obvious example of this: thus S,S,S,I,T, T,A,I,C,T can be rearranged to form a word – STATISTICS. The following features are characteristic of anagrams:

(a)   The solution is always a word (or words).
(b)   There are a large number of arrangements possible of the component elements (e.g. SSSTTIAICT; CAIISTSSTT; etc.).
(c)   Although it would take a very long time to write down all of the conceivable arrangements, many can be ruled out by general knowledge about words. For instance, no English word will have three Ss, or five consonants together; certain letter strings are more likely than others, and so on.

In fact, Greeno suggests that for anagrams (and other arrange-ment problems), the necessary skills include: first, fluency at generating possibilities; secondly, knowledge of principles to constrain search (as in (c) above), and, thirdly, fluency in retriev-ing solution patterns. In the case of anagrams, solution patterns are words. Suppose that as part of your attempt to solve S,S,S,I,T, T,A,I,C,T you began a new string STAT. . . . This may call to mind STATISTICS. By testing the remaining letters against ISTICS you could then conclude that you had the answer. Ease of retrieving words on the basis of minimal evidence clearly aids anagram solution.

While anagrams exemplify arrangement problems, there are plenty of other types. In one classic experiment, Duncker (1945) tested subjects in a room which contained three candles, three drawing pins, and three small boxes. Otherwise, the room was empty. They were instructed to fasten the candles to the door of the room in any way they could devise. The solution was to attach the boxes to the door with the drawing pins, and then place an upright candle in each box. All subjects discovered the solution quite quickly. However, with another group of subjects, a minor change was introduced. This time, the boxes contained matches. This small change resulted in less than half of the subjects solving the problem. This is an interesting result, and has been replicated (e.g. Adamson 1952). The suggestion is that if subjects perceive the boxes as *containers*, they will tend not to perceive them as platforms.

This result is known as *functional fixedness*. There are other illustrations of the same phenomenon, one of the best known of which is a problem devised half a century ago by Maier (1931). In the experimental room, two strings hang from the ceiling, but are too far apart to enable a person to hold one string and walk to the other. On the floor are various objects, including a pair of pliers. The problem is to decide how the strings could be tied together. The solution is to tie the pliers to the end of the string, thus making a pendulum. By swinging the pendulum, it is possible to catch the second string on its way up, while at the same time holding on to the first. Maier reported that only 39 per cent of his subjects found the solution within ten minutes. Once again, the argument is one of functional fixedness. Most of the subjects saw the pliers as a tool, and so, it is argued, ruled out novel uses – such as being a weight for a pendulum – for them.

More recent experiments on fixedness have demonstrated an importance of labelling. Glucksberg and Weisberg (1966) studied the candle problem, and in one condition had labels attached to the objects (*box, tacks, candle, matches*), or had no labels. With the labels, the average solution time for subjects was only 0.61 minutes, but without the labels, it was nearly nine minutes. Glucksberg and Weisberg argued that the labels encouraged people to see the objects *in isolation*, rather than as related to each other, or even to their typical uses, thus facilitating a solution. Indeed, people who succeeded on the problem tended to talk about *the box*, while those who failed tended to talk about *the box of matches*. Functional fixedness can be viewed as a constraint on possible ways of rearranging objects, but rather than being a *useful* constraint, it actually precludes the solution from being discovered, or makes it take very much longer to be discovered. These experiments clearly illustrate the importance of the initial *conception* of problems, a point to which we shall return.

## 2  Problems requiring the induction of structure

Greeno's second class of problems requires the *discovery* of a relation between objects. One example of this is an *analogy* problem, for instance:

Listen is to hear as look is to?

Here the problem is to find the relation which exists between listen and hear which can be replicated on the basis of *look*. Another example is series extrapolation: given this series, what is the next number?

9 1 2 8 3 4?

We shall consider some of the characteristics of extrapolating from series in a later chapter, and shall briefly describe work on analogy later on. For the moment, simply note that while rearrangement means generating new relations among things, induction means discovering an existing relation.

## 3  Transformation problems

Greeno's third class of problem has been very widely studied in recent years. In a transformation problem, the subject is given a goal state, and an initial state, and often sequences of admissible operations which would enable a solution to be reached if they are applied properly. One puzzle of this type is as follows. You have a cat, a hen, and a bag of grain on one side of a river. You want to get yourself and these possessions to the other side, and find a small boat which will just take *one* of your possessions, and yourself, to the other side on a trip. You cannot leave the cat alone with the hen, or the cat will kill it, and you cannot leave the hen alone with the grain, or the hen will eat it. The problem is how to get everything to the other bank intact. (Try it before moving on.)

In this problem, the goal state is clearly specified, as is the start state, and the admissible moves. In fact it is a relatively easy problem, the solution being:

1  Self and hen to other side. Leave hen.
2  Return alone.
3  Self and grain to other side. Leave grain.
4  Return with hen. Leave hen.
5  Self and cat to other side. Leave cat (with the grain.)
6  Return alone.
7  Self and hen to other bank. DONE.

There are a number of varieties of this type of problem, the most common of which are *hobbits and orcs, cannibals and missionaries*, and *jealous husbands*. For instance, the cannibals and missionaries problem requires that cannibals never outnumber missionaries. There are five of each, and a boat which carries only three people. The difficulty of the problem is exemplified by the fact that although it can be solved in eleven moves, people typically require more than twice this number to reach a solution.

These are rather picturesque examples of transformation problems. Others do not have the friendly ring of the Christmastime puzzle, but include proof problems in logic and mathematics. If one is told that A implies B, and invited to prove that not-A implies not-B, using principles of logic, then one is being invited to solve a transformation problem. Similarly, in mathematics, an invitation to prove some relation is a transformation problem.

Transformation problems rely upon a complex skill of comparing the current state of a problem with the desired state, and finding some series of operations which will transform the current state into the goal state. Often this will involve many intermediate stages, each of which can be looked upon as a new and simplified transformation problem. Just how this is done has been the subject of considerable enquiry by both psychologists and computer scientists. Indeed, the very earliest problem-solving program (Logic theorist; Ernst and Newell 1969) was written to prove logic theorems from the *Principia Mathematica* of Whitehead and Russell (1910). This choice of problem is not as curious or esoteric as it may sound. With logic, the rules which can be applied are well-defined, and the proofs themselves, as worked out by human problem-solvers, were readily available. Little or no 'world knowledge' beyond the logical rules themselves was required. Given the complexity and sheer bulk of world knowledge needed for understanding more mundane, everyday problems (see chapter 8), the choice of logic theorem proving for the early computer problem-solvers is obviously sensible.

In the next section, we shall examine transformation problems in more detail, for it is with this sort of problem that the clearest advances in problem analysis have taken place.

## B Chains of events in problem-solving

As with any other psychological process, the object of developing a process model of problem-solving is to specify the chain of events which occurs between the presentation of a problem and the point at which it is solved, or it is concluded that no solution is possible. With transformation problems, this entails representing the current state in some way, representing the goal state, and selecting admissible operations to turn the current state into the goal state. The kind of thing which is wanted can be seen in figure 11-1. The problem is to move the disks from peg A to peg C under the conditions stated. Now this is a very simple problem – so simple that it is doubtful whether its solution requires creative problem-solving at all. The sequence of operations required is:

1  Small disk to B.
2  Large disk to C.
3  Small disk to C.

Despite its simplicity, and the fact that our everyday experience with stacking objects on tables and so on may make this task a routine one, it can be used to illustrate a few simple points which are applicable to much more complex situations.

As presented, the problem consists of a start-state and a goal-state, and a set of admissible operations which can be performed. The set of admissible operations are all of the following type: (MOVE, DISK (X), FROM CURRENT LOCATION TO ANOTHER). In applying these operations (the

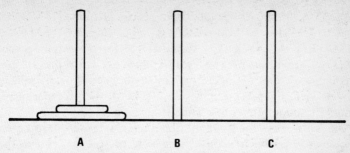

*Figure 11-1.* The two-disk Tower of Hanoi problem. The object is to stack the two disks currently on pole A on to pole C in as few moves as possible. The rules are that only one disk may be moved at a time, and that the large disk must never be put on the smaller one. When five or more disks are used, the problem becomes extremely difficult.

procedures themselves are usually called *operators*) the problem will leave its initial state. Furthermore, depending upon which specific operators are applied, a surprisingly large number of possibilities arise for such a simple problem.

## 1  Representations for thinking about problem-solving

Figure 11-2 shows a network in which the various possible transitions from one problem-state to another are mapped out.

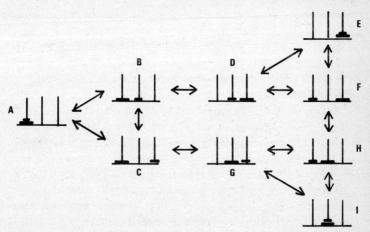

*Figure 11-2.* Possible legal states of the problem. The arrows denote legal transitions. The optimal path is, of course, A–B–D–E. A is the start-state, E the goal-state.

Thus, at the start, two operators can be legally applied: (MOVE, SMALL-DISK, FROM A-TO-B) and (MOVE, SMALL-DISK, FROM A-TO-C), resulting in two new states. Once again, two operators may be legally applied to each of these states, plus the inverse of the operators already applied. For the sake of convenience, figure 11-2 shows each state of the problem represented by the letters A to I, nine states in all.

The network depicts *all* of the possible routes of progress through the problem. Considering how easy it is to solve this problem, the network is surprisingly complicated. The problem as stated demands finding the optimal route through this network, such that A and E are connected in the smallest number of steps. Let us begin by considering what would happen if one attempted this problem on a one-step-at-a-time basis, but did not backtrack to the state one had achieved immediately before. One might trace a path like A–B–D–E, which would be optimal. Or one might trace a path like A–C–G–I–H–F–E, which would do, but which would be *suboptimal*. Finally, one might trace a path which led back to a previously encountered non-goal-state, like this: A–C–G–I–H–G. Provided we recognize that we have been to G before, we would not repeat the path again from that point, and thus avoiding getting into a cycle. Each of these paths of exploration start at the initial state, and either become dead ends (like the last example), or lead to the goal-state.

We can represent the possible trial and error routes formed in this way as a *tree diagram*, where the tree branches if more than one operator may be legally applied at a particular state. Such diagrams can be surprisingly complex: figure 11-3 depicts the one which results from exploring the network for the two-disk problem.

Now that we have a complete plan of the possible states of the problem, let us reconsider the ease with which adult human beings can solve it. In no way do we try to imagine our way through possible routes at random. Let us consider the ways in which this might be done, however, because it puts a proper perspective on the nature of this problem. Generating a new state and seeing what it turns out to be is a *search* of the possible problem states. Suppose that all possible moves at level 1 were generated first, and then all possible moves at level 2, and then all possible moves at level 3. At level 3, the goal-state would be among the set generated, and this is in fact the solution. Such a procedure with

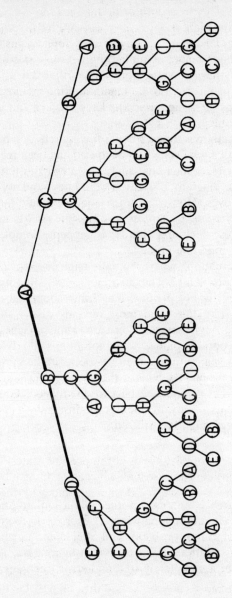

*Figure 11-3.*  Tree diagram showing all possible legal-move sequences that can be generated by the network in figure 11-2. Reading from the top down, if on a particular track a previously encountered state is encountered again, the track terminates. The diagram illustrates a very large number of suboptimal paths. The question is one of how to isolate the optimal path, shown in bold lines.

this particular problem leads to the discovery of the *best* solution, because all other solutions will be at lower levels, and hence require *more steps*. The procedure of finding new problem-states exhaustively from the highest to lower levels is called *breadth-first* search. In the present example, seven operator-applications would have had to have been made, assuming the left-most states to be discovered first. If the goal-state were any further down, many other applications would have to be made, and the memory load would be enormous: it is necessary to keep track of all of the branches in the problem.

An alternative method is to use a *depth*-first search – keep going down one track until a goal-state or a dead-end had been reached. By convention, on tree diagrams, search is down the left-most branch first. On our diagram, a solution would be found at level 3 after only three moves. However, notice that we would have no way of knowing whether a solution was possible in less moves, because other routes which may (but, as it happens, do not) have solutions at level 2 might be possible.

Are there *any* situations where humans might use such blind searches to solve problems? The answer is yes. Any situation where direct routes are not obvious may bring about the use of search procedures like this. The most obvious case would be finding one's way through a maze. There are simply no clues as to which might be an optimal path, and exploration is clearly called for. Trial-and-error search may sometimes occur in the middle of more sophisticated problem-solving if there are no clues or good ways of guessing what it might be best to do. Indeed, Greeno's category of problems of arrangement contains many examples where such a strategy might be utilized.

## 2 Heuristics and search control: GPS

Trial-and-error search is not usually the 'intelligent' solution to anything. A good (if rather long-winded) exercise is to try the three-disk Tower of Hanoi problem, and after doing it, plot out a tree graph of possibilities similar to that in figure 11-3. Adults simply do not adopt a completely trial-and-error tree-generation procedure.

Exhaustive search is a brute-force-and-ignorance technique, which relies upon computational speed and large working memories. Thus a machine could discover a solution to the two-disk problem, or even larger problems, provided it was fast enough and had enough memory. But such a mode of processing is not even remotely intelligent. Furthermore, in many problem-solving situations, it would not even be plausible in principle. Winston (1977) points out the absurdity of the idea for discovering winning sequences in chess by blind searching. He calculates that with an estimated depth of one hundred or more in chess, and an average branching of thirty-five, the tree of all possible moves would be about $2.5 \times 10^{154}$. Even if a new path could be generated every nano-second, it would still take $10^{138}$ years to do the calculation! The solution is to adopt *search-restriction methods*, the discovery of which is tantamount to discovering *techniques of artificial (and natural) intelligence*.

Rather than continue with a discussion of the search-tree aspect, we shall now consider mechanisms which give a device some control over what it is doing. Of course, these are simply ways of controlling movements in the problem tree.

An early and successful attempt to control search is the program known as the General Problem Solver, or GPS (Ernst and Newell 1969; see also Newell and Simon 1972). GPS relies upon the heuristic device of *means-ends analysis* for controlling search in the problem-space. In means-ends analysis, search is guided by attempting to *reduce the difference* between the start-state of a problem and the goal-state, selecting from a set of available means.

The basic principle can be illustrated by considering a very straightforward difference-reduction problem, such as travelling from one place to another. Suppose that you live in Plymouth and want to visit your aunt in Thurso, in the north of Scotland. The problem is to reduce the distance between you and your aunt (say 600 miles for the sake of argument) to zero. Now suppose that your own personal rules about getting from A to B are as follows:

If distance is less than 1 mile, then walk.
If distance is between 1 mile and 5, then take a bus.
If distance is between 5 miles and 100, then drive.
If distance is between 100 miles and 600, then take a train.

Now these 'rules' are the admissible operators for your journey.

The rules also exemplify procedures, called in GPS an operator-difference table. For instance, the first rule could be rewritten as:

IF DIFFERENCE LESS THAN 1 MILE, THEN APPLY 'WALK' TO REDUCE DIFFERENCE

and so on. For any particular problem, GPS begins with just this sort of information.

In evaluating the problem, a GPS-like procedure would begin by trying to reduce 600 miles to zero. The appropriate operator, *take train*, is within this range, so we have the following goal:

GET TO THURSO USING TAKE TRAIN

The other sorts of knowledge needed to tackle this kind of problem are the *enabling conditions* for an action. Thus to *take train*, you have to *be at station*; to *take bus*, you have to *be at bus-stop*, and so on. And one needs to know what current states are – for instance, let us assume:

1    You live 200 yards from the bus-stop.
     and
2    There is a bus-stop 100 yards from the station.

When a GPS-like routine tries to TAKE TRAIN, the enabling conditions are not met, so the subgoal GET TO STATION is set up. Looked at as a subproblem in its own right, the appropriate operator is TAKE BUS. But once again, the enabling conditions will not be met (you are not at the bus-stop). So a new subproblem has emerged. In the operator-difference table, the appropriate procedure is WALK. There are no problems here, so each goal can actually be realized as the sequence:

1    WALK TO BUS STOP
2    TAKE BUS TO STATION
3    TAKE TRAIN TO THURSO

The sequence realizes the bottom subgoal first, enabling the next subgoal to be realized, and so on.

At this point in the problem, you are at Thurso station (a new subproblem). What happens next depends upon where your aunt lives in relation to the station. If it is, say, 4 miles, then a simple sequence of goals can easily be built up. But if it is 10 miles, what should be done? Your car will be at Plymouth! There would be no point in going back for it(!), and GPS has rules built into it to prevent such a goal from being set up. It is so constructed that it rejects movements to adjacent states more distant than the current state is from the goal. GPS tries the next-best operator – in this case take a bus.

Of course, this example is an extremely simple one, but essentially the same processes have enabled GPS to solve a whole variety of problems, including multi-disk Tower of Hanoi problems. Since this was the problem with which we started, it is worth reconsidering our own absurdly simple problem with two disks.

A GPS-like program would attempt to reduce the difference between the start-state and the goal-state. The major difference is that the big disk is at the bottom of the wrong pole. There is only one operator, MOVE DISK X from A to B, and a set of preconditions for its application. The main goal is:

MOVE LARGE DISK TO RIGHT-HAND POLE

This is not possible, since the small disk is on top. So the next goal is:

MOVE SMALL DISK TO MIDDLE POLE

(If it were moved to the right-hand pole, it would violate a precondition of the main goal.)

This is possible, so this sequence is done:

MOVE SMALL DISK TO MIDDLE POLE
MOVE LARGE DISK TO RIGHT-HAND POLE

The remaining difference is that the small disk is on the wrong pole, but the goal of rectifying this is not blocked, and MOVE SMALL DISK TO RIGHT-HAND POLE can be executed, and the problem is done.

### 3 Means-ends analysis and human performance

Clearly, GPS captures some important aspects of problem-solving, and has been shown to work on a wide range of problems. Perhaps its most important function has been to set the ball rolling in the direction of a better understanding of problem-solving. Furthermore, for some sorts of problems, human beings seem to behave in much the same way as GPS, breaking down a problem into subproblems, and applying means-ends analysis. For example, Newell and Simon (1972) took detailed 'speak out loud' protocols of subjects working on elementary logic proofs. The choices of procedures used, and the order in which they were introduced, parallels GPS in many respects.

However, GPS and human beings do not always behave in the same way. One way in which they differ results from limitations in the working memory of humans. In the two-disk example of the Tower of Hanoi problem, the number of subgoals to be maintained in working memory at the same time is only *one*, and so planning the sequence is reasonably easy. With a *three-disk* Tower of Hanoi problem, it is necessary to remember *three* subgoals. Even with the three-disk problem, people will typically behave in a GPS-like way, but will sometimes lose track of (forget) how the subgoals relate to one another, thus producing errors, so that necessary backtracking will occur in the move sequence. With more disks, the problem gets worse, of course. GPS will have no such problems if subgoal depth can proceed to some very deep level. Thus while means-ends analysis cuts down the enormous memory load which would result from exhaustive search procedures, when people employ means-ends methods, there are still severe working-memory restrictions in dealing with subgoals. This will be generally true of problems in which subgoal depths are large (i.e. there are many nested subgoals).

With some problems, then, people seem to behave rather like GPS in that they adopt a means-ends evaluation of movement within the problem-space. However, this is not always the case. One example where other strategies are adopted is in the missionaries and cannibals' problem:

> There are five missionaries and five cannibals on one bank of a river, along with a canoe capable of holding three people. So long as cannibals never outnumber missionaries, they are not dangerous, but if they become the majority, then they will eat the missionaries. The group of ten people wish to cross to the other side. How shall they do it?

Simon and Reed (1976) have investigated performance on this problem in some detail, and the problem-space which they worked out for it is shown in figure 11-4. With a means-ends strategy, the rules the subjects operate under should be:

(i) Move as many people as possible across the river; and

(ii) Bring back as few people as possible.

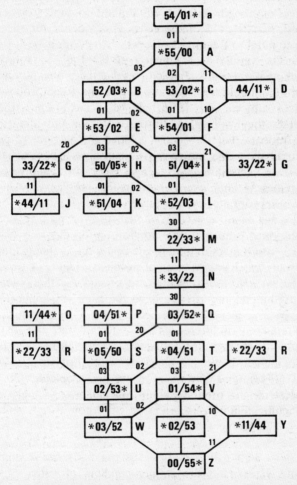

Figure 11-4. The problem-space of the missionaries and cannibals' problem (Simon and Reed 1976). Letters designate states of the problem. The numbers in the boxes, such as 54/01*, show how many missionaries are on each bank (five on the left, none on the right), how many cannibals (four on the left, one on the right), and where the boat is (on the right). The number pairs on the lines (e.g. 01) show how many missionaries (none) and cannibals (one) are moved to reach an adjacent problem state. A is the start-state, Z is the goal.

One need only consider the opening position and the first move to see whether subjects conform to this: they should move to state B (three cannibals across); yet the preferred move was to state D (one cannibal and one missionary across). This and other data suggested that subjects are not guided purely by a means-ends strategy; rather, they use what Simon and Reed call a *balance strategy*, attempting to keep an equal number of missionaries and cannibals on each side of the river. As evidence for this, it is possible to point to stages G and J, which are both balanced states that subjects may reach, but which are blind alleys, from which backtracking is necessary. In fact, to solve the problem, a means-ends strategy should be used, and Simon and Reed propose that the sooner subjects shift from balance to means-ends, the less blind alleys they will enter. Furthermore, by providing a hint (telling students that they must achieve the subgoal of getting three cannibals across the river by themselves without the boat (state L)), subjects shifted strategies sooner, presumably because it exemplifies an *unbalanced state*. In this problem, means-ends analysis is appropriate, but people do not use it initially.

Means-ends analysis is only a *heuristic* for problem-solving. What this means is that the application of the rule will not necessarily result in a solution, or the best solution, being found. It is simply *useful* for many types of problem. (Heuristic principles contrast with *algorithms*, which are procedures that guarantee outcomes, but do not usually have the range of application of heuristics.) The mean-ends heuristic is based on a principle of gradual reduction of differences between start-state and goal-state in a problem, but certain problems are not well handled by the heuristic, including one of a classic series of problems devised by Luchins (1942), and known as water-jug problems. We shall briefly describe this problem, show how means-ends analysis runs into difficulties with it, and then describe how people solve the problem. The problem is this:

You have an 8-gallon pail, a 5-gallon pail, and a supply of running water. How do you get 2 gallons of water measured out? TRY IT.

To obtain the simplest solution to this problem, a steady reduction in the smallest amount of water you have is not possible. The step-by-step solution is this:

(i)   Fill the 5-gallon pail.
(ii)  Pour into the 8-gallon pail.
(iii) Refill the 5-gallon pail.
(iv)  Pour the contents of the 5-gallon pail into the partially full
      8-gallon pail carefully. You will have 2 gallons left in the
      5-gallon pail. (Because there was room for 3 gallons in the
      8-gallon pail.)

It is obvious that such a set of procedures does not continuously minimize the difference between the 2 gallons of the goal-state and the smallest measured amount of water possessed (see Reed 1982, for a fuller discussion). Atwood and Polson (1976) investigated the performance of human subjects on problems of this type, although rather more complex. They specifically set out to investigate whether subjects attempted to use means-ends procedures in tackling the problems, and concluded that they did. The basic idea was that a version of the task which fitted the means-ends heuristic should be easier to solve than one that did not, and that the difficulty with the latter example should result from attempts by the subjects to stay within a means-ends framework.

All of the problems used involved three jugs of varying size. In every case, the largest jug was full at the outset, and in each case the problem was to distribute the water in the large jug evenly between the large jug and the middle-sized jug. The problems were:

(a)  A  Large jug (full)  = 24 pints    (The problem is how to
     B  Medium jug        = 21 pints    get 12 pints into A
     C  Small jug         =  3 pints    and 12 pints into B.)
(b)  A  Large jug (full)  =  8 pints    (The problem is to get
     B  Medium jug        =  5 pints    4 pints into A and
     C  Small jug         =  3 pints    4 pints into B.)

(It is advisable to try these problems before proceeding.) In example (a), a means-ends analysis will solve the problem in thirteen moves – a steady progression towards the end-state without any moves away from it. On the other hand, while problem (b) can also be solved in thirteen moves, six moves away from steady minimization are required. Atwood and Polson found that subjects took more than twice as many moves to solve (b) than to solve (a), and in a detailed analysis of performance on the task, they showed that this resulted, in part, from adopting a means-ends strategy with a fairly minimal look-ahead. The account which they give of how subjects proceed states that if subjects can use means-ends analysis, then they will. Subjects thus evaluate a number of possible moves from a given position with a view to reducing the difference between the current-state and the goal-state. However, Atwood and Polson estimate that the maximum number of alternatives which people attempt to evaluate is only three, which they quite plausibly ascribe to a working-memory limitation. Thus some problems of performance result from subjects not actually checking an optimum path. Another important aspect of their results was the finding that subjects are very good (90 per cent correct) in recognizing an *old* state (i.e. one which they had been to before). Because the number of old states increases steadily, such information must be stored in long-term memory.

## C  Discovery, learning and understanding in problem-solving

The studies described above exemplify the way in which problem-solving can only be understood when the problem-space and the application of various strategies are *both* taken into account. The best strategy for one type of problem may very well not be applicable to another type of problem. In fact, there are now a number of very detailed studies of how people operate within carefully researched problem-spaces – perhaps the best known of these being the monumental study *Human Problem Solving* by Newell and Simon (1972). It must be appreciated that we have only touched the surface of the analysis of problem-solving strategies in our prior discussion. However, rather than concentrate on strategies used within a specified space, as we have done up to now, we shall turn to the issue of the problem-space itself.

Really, the problem-space as discussed above is just an abstraction: the examples given show every legal move and what the consequences are, along with a description of legal operators and the conditions of legality. Doubtless you are aware that for noughts and crosses (tic-tac-toe), a similar complete space could be written, but it is unlikely that you would ever use the whole space. Indeed, the whole point of heuristic or algorithmic search procedures is to prevent you from ever having to know the whole space. On the other hand, we have seen how knowledge of a problem-space may help in ruling out a suboptimal strategy (e.g. the water-jug problem).

There are a number of ways in which the characteristics of problem-spaces become known to people and, in one way or another, they all rely upon experience and exploration. First, there is expertise: someone who is an expert in symbolic logic or mathematics will have had experience of a very large number of problems, and given a new problem will be better than a novice at spotting some of the characteristics of a search-space, and will know some useful heuristics. Secondly, for a non-expert, there is much to be gained from working on a problem for a period, because the problem-space characteristics will be learned by exploration. Thus the use of relatively unsophisticated strategies at the outset can result in the discovery of aspects of a problem which allow other, possibly more sophisticated, strategies to be used.

An important point which relates to these rather obvious observations is that a person's knowledge of a problem grows with experience of it. It is therefore important to know what a person's knowledge *is* at various points as they work on a problem. Throughout these chapters on thinking, we shall develop the notion of a mental model introduced earlier: the argument is that when people work on problems, they do so by forming mental models of the problems and working upon them. In relation to the problem-solving activities described in the previous section, mental models will include those parts of the problem-space which the subject has in working and long-term memory, and which are *accessible to him* from his memory.

In this section, we begin by looking at a way of capturing a subject's expanding view of problems. We then move on to the issue of *initial representations* of problems.

## 1 Tracking behaviour on problems

As subjects work on problems, they both explore the theoretical problem-space, and utilize strategies in their attempts to do this and to solve the problem. This gradual unfolding of the problem from the subject's point of view represents a change in the potential resources which a subject has potentially available, rather as the gradual unfolding of a discourse increases the receiver's knowledge of the message. Of course, much of the process of working on a problem is not directly accessible, in that it goes on inside the head of the subject. To get around this, some researchers have made use of speak-aloud protocols, in which subjects attempt to verbalize what they are trying to do as they work on problems, usually in the presence of an experimenter. Although this sounds difficult, subjects come to be able to do it with a little practice. Newell and Simon (1972) have made extensive use of this method in studying human performance on a wide range of problems, and have introduced some useful techniques for the analysis of how subjects proceed through them. By taking each part of a subject's narrative bit by bit, they produce what is referred to as a problem-behaviour graph (PBG). One of the most widely quoted examples of PBG determination is with the cryptarithmetic problem below:

$$\begin{array}{ll} \text{DONALD} & \text{D} = 5 \\ + \underline{\text{GERALD}} \\ \text{ROBERT} \end{array}$$

Each letter represents a digit $(0, 1 \ldots 9)$, and $\text{D} = 5$. What digits can be substituted for the letters, such that the sum is satisfied?

As Newell and Simon's subjects worked on this problem, they verbalized their thoughts to the best of their abilities. The protocols are converted into PBGs. Suppose that the subject begins with:

... each D is 5; therefore T is zero ...

The subject's knowledge-state about the problem has changed by the application of an operator (broadly termed 'process column 1' or PC1 by Newell and Simon). This gives the first step in constructing the PBG, as in figure 11-5(a). Box 2 represents a new knowledge-state that has been added to the old one. Suppose that the subject now indicates that he is seeking other Ds ($=5$) or other Ts ($=0$). The former will succeed, producing another knowledge-state. Another box is added to the PBG, connected through the operator *get new column* (GN), as depicted in figure 11-5(b).

Next the subject tries another new column – column 2, noting that $\text{L} + \text{L} = \text{R}$. At this point, he can conclude that R is odd,

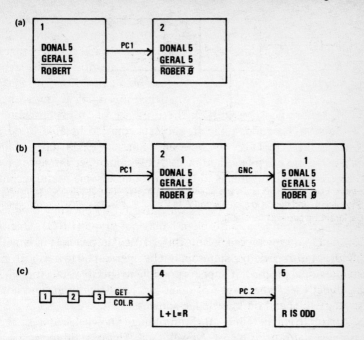

*Figure 11-5.* Growing a problem-behaviour graph (PBG). (a) shows the first two problem-states, and the operator applied to get to the second from the first; (b) and (c) show a continuation of this process. In (c), the first three states have been represented as small boxes for convenience only. The diagrams are based on those devised by Newell and Simon (1972).

because (a) adding two identical numbers produces an even number, and (b) from knowledge-state 2, there is a carry to be added to the even number, so R is odd. The resulting new knowledge-state is added to the PBG as in figure 11-5(c).

Suppose that at the next point, the subject does not follow up the idea that R is odd, but rather goes back to knowledge-state 4, reasoning that '... any two numbers added together has to be even and R can be 1 or 3, not 5, 7 or 9'. The PBG grows as shown in figure 11-6. Notice the level of detail in the PBG – because the subject reported going back to 'any two numbers added together ...' his new analysis is a new branch of knowledge-state 4.

The problem-behaviour graph thus shows the changes in knowledge-state which subjects have as they explore (and solve) a problem. Time on task flows left to right and downward, and changes to a new level after the right-most point on a line has been

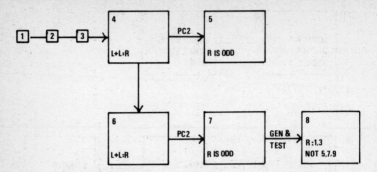

*Figure 11-6.* The PBG is a more advanced state, showing backtracking from state 5 to state 4, and hence to states 6 and 7. In PBGs, time flows *right* and *down* when backtracking causes branching.

reached. A typical graph for this particular problem contains hundreds of knowledge-states linked by operators. However, from an individual protocol it appears possible to specify what strategies a subject uses, what range of operators are being used, and how strategies depend on knowledge-states.

Apart from detailing the unfolding knowledge-states and strategy patterns, one of Newell and Simon's subjects spent twenty-five minutes on a cryptarithmetic task, apparently considering various problem-space conceptions. The subject saw himself as looking for a way to approach the problem. Newell and Simon identified no less than seven possible spaces which he considered, and which they term as follows:

*(i) Basic problem-space*
This is seeing the problem as a set of letter-digit assignments. (Within such a space, problem-solving could proceed by random substitutions – people are always smarter than this!)

*(ii) Augmented problem-space*
As above, but including standard arithmetical operations.

*(iii) Number problem-space*
Each word is seen as a number, one for each word of the problem. (Although this is not much use for the problem given above, it is useful for $AA + BB = CBC$.)

*(iv) Algebra problem-space*
The problem is seen as a set of equations.

*(v) Word-meaning problem-space*
The *words* in the problem are seen as a potential source of information. Newell and Simon cite the example:

BILL
*WAS*
KING

Reasoning within this space might then go:

BILL   WILLIAM   WILLIAM the Conqueror   1066.·.
B = 1, I = 0, L = 6

*(vi) Cryptogram problem-space*
The problem is seen as a rule-governed mapping between letters and numbers (e.g. A 1, B 2, etc.).

*(vii) Typographical problem-space*
The problem is seen as having a correspondence between some surface feature of the letters and the digits. For instance 'E looks like 3', '2 looks like S'.

This list should at least serve to illustrate the number of potentially different problem-spaces which could be associated with such a simple problem. Typically, subjects on the problem given above work within spaces (i) and (ii). Although some of the spaces considered appear to be bizarre, many puzzles are puzzles simply because they *are* bizarre.

Problem-solving can thus be seen as applying operations within a problem-space, and discovering problem-spaces to work within. We now turn to a fuller discussion of the initial conception of a problem.

## 2  The importance of the initial interpretation

Consider the problems depicted in table 11-1, simple algebra word problems, devised by Silver (1981). Of the three, which problems are most closely related? From a narrative point of view, problems 1 and 3 are obviously closely related. From a mathematical point of view, problems 1 and 2 are most closely related. The issue is which similarity one opts for when the problem is to answer the questions. These examples are straightforward for most adults

Table 11-1.

| | |
|---|---|
| 1 | A farmer is counting the hens and rabbits in his barnyard. He counts a total of 50 heads and 140 feet. How many hens and how many rabbits does the farmer have? |
| 2 | Bill has a collection of twenty coins that consists entirely of dimes and quarters. If the collection is worth $4.10, how many of each kind of coin are in the collection? |
| 3 | A farmer is counting the hens and rabbits in his barnyard. He counts six coops with four hens in each, two coops with three hens in each, five cages with six rabbits in each, and three cages with four rabbits in each. How many hens and how many rabbits does the farmer have? |

*(From E.A. Silver 1981.)*

who have a smattering of mathematics, but they are not so straightforward for seventh-grade schoolchildren. What Silver showed was that while good problem-solvers could readily recognize the mathematical isomorphs (*1 and 2*), poorer problem-solvers did not, but rather thought that problems *1 and 3* (close to narrative isomorphs) were more closely related. The initial classification made implies that the problems were either represented in narrative mode or mathematical mode by the children. Such a representation means that a mapping would be made either on to the narrative domain, or on to a mathematical domain, and this makes predictions for memory. If primarily mathematical schemata were used, then the young subjects should recall information pertinent to the mathematical structure. In contrast, poor problem-solvers who used narrative structure should not recall much about the mathematical structure, but rather should remember 'story' details. Silver found that this was indeed the case.

The results regarding classification are not especially surprising, but are very important. Not only do they indicate that perception of a problem relates to performance ability, but also that forming an appropriate mental model by extracting the appropriate elements may determine subsequent performance. Spotting the *form* of a problem can be understood as interpreting elements of a problem by forming a mapping between some memory structure and certain essential elements of a problem: what results is a *mental model*. Hinsley, Hayes and Simon (1977) were of the opinion that seasoned problem-solvers in mathematics would pick out an appropriate interpretative structure on the minimum of evidence. They asked high-school and college students to classify problems taken from a high-school algebra test by problem-types, where 'classify' was left vague. Students were able to do this consistently. The next step indicated that the subjects actually *use* these classifications to assist in problem-solving itself. The experiment differed from the first in that problems were presented to students a little at a time, and they were on a continuous invitation to guess at a class. Half of the subjects were able to classify the problems correctly after hearing less than one-fifth of each problem. The subjects could thus classify a problem before they had enough data to formulate a solution.

Together, their results suggest that knowing the class of a problem enables search of a problem to be restricted. This is tidy if unsurprising. For instance, GPS needs to know the essential *dimensions* to be minimized in order to solve a problem by a means-ends procedure. Classifying a problem in our terms means selecting a mental model which provides the dimensions. If the dimensions are wrong, problem-solving will falter.

A very good illustration of how the initial model influences problem-solving comes from Carroll, Thomas and Malhotra (1980). Their technique was to present subjects with two problem isomorphs, which were dressed up in very different descriptive formats. They allowed subjects to make use of notes and diagrams during their attempts at solutions. The problem isomorphs were complex. In one condition, the *temporal isomorph*, subjects were given a hypothetical manufacturing process, consisting of seven stages of processing. The task was to order the manufacturing stages in such a way as to satisfy no less than nineteen constraints. Example constraints included statements to the effect that one particular process was of higher priority than another, one particular stage should follow another, and two particular stages use different resources, and so on. The other problem was the spatial isomorph. The task here was to assign seven employees a corridor, and the nineteen constraints were differences in prestige of employees, differences in the extent to which various employees used various resources, and differences in compatibility. Thus, both problems were *order* problems, with analogous constraints on the possible or best orderings: one was simply sequential, and the other was spatial.

The subjects in the spatial task performed much better than did the subjects in the temporal task both in terms of the number of constraints which their solutions satisfied, and in terms of the length of time over which they worked on the problem. This of course is despite the fact that the problems were isomorphic. Carroll, Thomas and Malhotra also observed that nearly all of the subjects in the spatial version of the task used a graphic representation to aid their design. What the graphic representation seemed to do was to make the search-space of the problem more explicit, enabling better configurations to be recognized more readily. Presumably, because the problem was a spatial one, physically representing adjacency possibilities was a procedure which was found in long-term memory without any difficulty. Temporal progressions are not normally represented in such ways by most people.

Finally, Carroll, Thomas and Malhotra showed how the problem representation facilitated performance. By taking two other groups of people, and instructing them to use a diagrammatic method of representation, they found that they could produce *no differences* in performance on the two problems.

In one way or another, these studies demonstrate the importance of the initial mental model which is set up as a subject attempts to solve a problem. Aids to mental models, such as using notes or diagrams or equations, can be viewed as symbolic physical extensions of mental models, and are of obvious assistance given the limited capacity of human working memory. Over the course of the remainder of this section on thinking, the importance of initial mental models will crop up from time to time in a variety of different contexts. The reason why the initial model is important is because it provides the starting point for mental experimentation with its elements. If it is inappropriate or over-constrained, then it is fairly obvious that there will be trouble in reaching a solution.

### 3  A powerful constraint on the initial model: presupposition

Presupposition is ubiquitous in the interpretation of verbal descriptions, including statements of problems. While many mental models are built up by selecting various aspects of the problem as stated, presuppositions are constraints on mental models which are imported from general knowledge usually without our being aware of them. Presupposition puzzles capitalize on this, and the whole point of an amusing puzzle can be to discover what looks like an astonishingly simple presupposition. Two reasonably well-known examples are the following:

> Cleopatra walks into a room to find the following scene: Antony is lying dead on the floor, surrounded by water and bits of broken glass. The window is open. Asking only Yes/No questions, how can you explain what happened?

> A man and his son were away for a trip. They were driving down the motorway when they had a terrible accident. The man was killed outright but his son was alive, although badly injured. The son was rushed to hospital and was to have an emergency operation. On entering the operating theatre, the surgeon looked at the boy, and said, 'I can't do this operation. This boy is my son.' How can this be?

TRY THE PROBLEMS NOW.

The first example stacks the odds in a rather unfair way. The solution is that Antony is a goldfish. The bowl was knocked over and broken by a cat which came in through the open window. Antony and Cleopatra are strong memory-search cues – well-known figures from Roman history and from plays. The problem-solver 'presupposes' that they will be people in this problem, too.

The second problem has a rather more elegant structure. The presupposition here is that surgeons are males. In this case, the surgeon is the boy's mother. Consistently, in classroom demonstrations, students who think they 'may have a solution' offer explanations like 'One of the *men* was only his step-father'!

One of the things which makes presupposition problems so difficult is that holding presupposition is normally desirable, even essential, for communication. Breaking gender presupposition in discourse produces some rather startling effects:

> Miss Smith asked her secretary to take a letter. His pencil kept breaking.
> When a computer scientist writes a program, first of all she makes a rough plan.

Reading-time experiments, like those described in earlier chapters, have shown that when target sentences contain a pronominal reference which breaks a presupposition of gender, then those sentences consistently take longer to read (Sanford, MacDougall and Simons 1984). The explanation favoured by Sanford, MacDougall and Simons is that pragmatic expectations of gender are built into the roles defined by scenarios.

The *necessity* of some presuppositions of a slightly more complex type is clear from the analysis of speech acts (chapter 10). The following example illustrates this:

> Mrs Brown: 'Can you close the door, Fred?'
> Fred Brown CLOSES THE DOOR.
> Mrs Brown: 'No! I just wanted to know whether you *could* do it!'

Many presuppositions are peculiarly difficult to spot, and appear to show little transfer once they are spotted. One of my colleagues reported to me about a tutorial in which the surgeon example was discussed with a set of first-year students. Among the issues discussed was whether attitudes towards women's liberation might influence the ease with which such problems are solved (the answer is 'probably not' (Sanford, MacDougall and Simons 1984)). Some minutes afterwards, he could not remember the Christian name of a psychologist with the surname *Conrad*. Relieved at a sign of a teacher's incompetence, the tutorial group called out numerous random Christian names. Turning the tables, my colleague pointed out that they were all names of men!

Our understanding of presupposition is really quite limited. All we can really say is that although presuppositions are useful for comprehension, they normally go unnoticed and so are difficult to spot when we attempt to solve problems.

## 4  The interpretation of problems by analogy

Analogy represents an important way of understanding, and is an important source of problem-solving strategies. Analogies have the general form *x is to y as a is to?*. In using analogy in problem-solving, a subject spots similarities or isomorphisms between the current problem and one which has been tackled before (between x and a in the paradigm quoted above), and then, knowing that a particular method was useful in the old problem, proceeds to try a similar method with the new problem (y determines ? in the above paradigm).

A simple example is provided by a study carried out by Rumelhart and Norman (1981) of students learning to use a computer text editor by working through a manual and trying out each instruction as they come to it. One instance of interest is the sequence of learning to type out particular lines of text, and then how to delete lines. Students are instructed that the third line of the buffer can be read by typing keys *3P* and *RETURN*. Having done this, students are instructed to print the *fifth* line of the buffer. Rumelhart and Norman argue that this little problem is solved by analogy, where the command is interpreted as:

Print-text-S is like 'print-text-3' with 5 for 3.

Yielding *5P* and *RETURN*. It is further assumed that by analogy the following generalization can be made:

Print-text is like 'print-text-3' with x for 3.

Although this is an extremely simple example, it is an important one, because much learning (cumulative problem-solving) takes place in this way. Furthermore, it is possible to be in error. To illustrate this point, Rumelhart and Norman describe an episode which occurred later when students were learning to delete a line of text, again by the problem-solving method of trying it. The authors supposed that, reasoning by analogy, a student would interpret 'delete' as:

delete-text is like 'print-text' with *d* for *p* and 'delete' for 'print'.

When a student tried the delete instruction, he typed 4d, the right thing to do, but he expected the line to vanish (by analogy with printing a line) which it did not (this was evident from the student's comments). In fact, it should not disappear given the particular editor system in question. The subject simply did not have enough knowledge at that point to make an appropriate analogy.

## 5  Mental models and intuition

We have argued that when a subject initially encounters a problem, the normal process of understanding begins with a mapping being made between the problem-statement and scenarios or schemata which the subject has in long-term memory. Analogy is a good illustration of the use of such a mechanism. Let us term this *primary-level understanding*, since current theory suggests that it is basic to the more elaborate processes, and that it is automatic, as illustrated by the results of discourse-comprehension studies, and presupposition phenomena. Once this mapping has been achieved, further problem-solving activity can proceed. Elsewhere, Sanford (1983) has argued that the mapping process is one interpretation of what it means to have an *intuition* about a problem: an 'intuitive' solution is one that is spotted quickly and easily. In a recent study, Sanford (1983) and his colleagues (Sanford and Leiser in preparation) studied the primary-level understanding of a problem in probability which many people find remarkably difficult to solve. It is introduced here as an example of how intuitive understanding can be misleading.

The problem is called 'the three cups'. (It will make things clearer if the reader simulates the tasks with real cups.) Imagine that you have three cups placed upside down in front of you. While you look away, the experimenter slips a coin under one of the cups, so that you do not know which cup it is under. Now you are invited to guess which cup the coin is under. After you have made your choice, instead of being told whether you are right or wrong, the experimenter removes *one* of the cups. He *never* removes the cup that you picked out, and he *never* removes the cup that the coin is under (if it is different). So you are now faced with two cups, and are invited again to make a choice. The question is, should you change your choice, or does it not matter, or should you stick? Of twenty-five people asked to give an answer, twenty-three (wrongly) said that it did not matter. (To prove their conviction, most people said they would stick.) The correct answer is that you are more likely to get the coin if you shift. Let us begin by considering why most people might believe the chances to be even. We can imagine subjects using a memory-schema something like this in their interpretation:

Random selection. If there are n elements to choose from, one of which is special, THEN the chance of selecting the special one at random is 1/N.

Mapping the problem on to this schema alone should result in two separate aspects of the problem, which could be summarized as:

When there were three cups, the chance of being correct is $\frac{1}{3}$; when there are only two, the chance of being correct is $\frac{1}{2}$.

One subject, verbalizing his thoughts about the problem, said the following (Sanford 1983):

... Two independent situations. The first situation gives a likelihood of being correct of one third. The second is independent of the first, and is a 50:50 situation. So it doesn't matter whether you change your choice.

Such comments are so typical as to virtually force one to conclude that the mapping account is the correct one. But there are other consequences of such a mapping, which match up to our general discussion of schema theory. One part of the problem-statement details the procedure by which the removed cup is selected (which is certainly not random). Subjects typically *forget* this part of the instructions, even to the extent of suggesting that the presenter of the problem *omitted to mention it*. It is entirely consistent with schema theory that elements of a description which neither find a match in the schema, nor clash with it, are forgotten.

We shall not enter into a discussion of how subjects come to appreciate a different (correct) solution, but simply note that the initial mental model achieved by the subjects made it extremely difficult for them to see it in any other way.

## D An overview

Practically everything which requires thought – thinking in the usual sense of the word – can be construed as problem-solving. Small surprise, then, that problem-solving has been at the heart of much of the original work in artificial intelligence. All we have achieved in this chapter is a very superficial tour of some of the first-rate work which has been carried out in the field. Because of its enormity, there is a danger that a rather sketchy and biased picture has been presented, and it is therefore appropriate to step back a little way and take an overview.

First, there is an immense variety of problem-types ranging from anagrams, through presupposition puzzles, through obvious transformation puzzles, to problems in geometry, algebra, logic and so on. One goal of problem-solving research has been to look for generally useful heuristics – like means-ends analysis, and breaking a problem into subgoals. But one thing has been made particularly clear by forty years of intensive research: the problem itself determines the strategies which are best, and restricts that which it is possible to do. Problem-solving research is as much concerned with the problem itself as with the problem-solver.

Secondly, because of the variety of problems, researchers naturally search for *groupings* of problems: consideration of what it is that could possibly relate subgroups of problems to one another had led to attempted taxonomies (like that of Greeno, in the introduction), and to considerations of how people might solve problems by analogy. Ultimately, whether two problems are treated as similar by a subject will depend upon having mental representations of the problem which are similar. As one might suppose, if two problems seem to use much the same sort of wording, a naïve subject may very well see them as similar, even if this is counterproductive. It is probable that the only way in which the important relationships between problems come to be recognized is by intensive learning about problems in specific fields – i.e. the development of expertise.

The third major point in this chapter is that for a problem to be worked on, the problem-statement has to be *interpreted*, and it was suggested that this process might resemble the processes of interpretation in discourse understanding. Apart from isomorphy and analogy, presupposition problems are pertinent to this part of the story. Indeed, with presupposition problems, half the fun can be in just discovering what problem-space the problem-setter has in mind (viz. the Antony and Cleopatra problem). In artificial intelligence, heuristic operations within a space were tackled first; setting up initial models and using analogy is a rather later development. In psychology, the development was reversed: the Gestalt psychologists were more concerned with problems involving few steps, but reconfigurations of 'perceptions' – we can take perceptions to mean 'models' in the present context. However, it is only in the last few years that real progress has been made.

In the face of these points, we shall round off with two other perspectives: the first task is to provide a summary account of the issues; the second is to discuss what various views of problem-solving say about man's mental facilities.

## 1  An integration of some points

*What follows represents the author's analysis, and is an attempt at indicating how various aspects of problem-solving relate to one another.*

1   When a problem is initially understood, it is assumed that the problem-statement isolates relevant schemata or scenarios in LTM. What is formed is a mapping between the explicit problem-statement and the knowledge structures in LTM, constituting an initial model of the problem.

2   The resultant structure can be manipulated in WM; operators may be applied, but the success of such manipulations will depend upon not overtaxing working memory, and making use of *chunking* through rich mappings into LTM. In this way, problem-solving can begin.

3.   As problem-solving progresses, various states already gone through will be stored in LTM. If states discovered in WM match a structure in LTM, then this will result in a new structure in LTM. Hence there is a two-way traffic between WM and LTM.

4   Attempts to solve problems are attempts to reach new knowledge-states. It could well be that in a complex problem, another look at the problem from a new angle would provide information that suddenly became important. In much problem-solving, new data may be obtained from outside sources. The solver may *ask someone* about a specific part of the problem – either for a clue or for more information, or may consult books or other information sources.

If there is any value to such a summary, it is that it points to the involvement of many familiar processes and elements. It also points to the centrality of the process which maps what is in WM on to structures in LTM. More evidence showing the importance of this mapping will be encountered in chapter 13.

## 2  The limitations imposed by WM

The summary account above makes the strong assumption that when one works on a problem, one does so within the constraints of working memory. Indeed, this conclusion is forced by much of the literature. It is also the case that most views of problem-solving make similar assumptions – for instance, Newell and Simon (1972). Such an argument implies a severe constraint on how easily and how quickly people can solve problems, and how easily and quickly they can explore and develop problem-spaces, thus gaining insights. This view of problems unfolding through working-memory operation is, however, rather recent.

An alternative view, given more attention in earlier work on thinking (e.g. McKellar 1957; Wallas 1926), is that much problem-solving goes on unconsciously. For example, one might work on a problem for a while, stop for a long period, and then come back to it, to 'discover' that one has a new way of looking at the problem – possibly a way which leads to a solution. There are many anecdotes of great discoveries related to periods in which the discoverer was not consciously working on the problem. For instance, the organic chemist Kekule, discoverer of the benzene ring, apparently fell asleep after working for a long period on the structure of benzene. The solution (a ring rather than a simple linear structure) came to him during a dreamlike state, in which he saw snakes in his mind's eye, one of which started to swallow its own tail. On waking, he realized that a ring structure was the solution to his problem. There are many more examples of this type.

Does this then mean that the approach to problem-solving discussed above missed an important element of the process? At present, it would appear that there is no important point being missed. Classically, creative problem-solving of any difficulty has been seen as involving four stages (e.g. Wallas 1926):

(i)   Preparation: determining the nature of the problem, gathering information which may be relevant to generally understanding the problem-space.

(ii)  Incubation: one does not think about the problem in any goal-directed sense, but unconscious mechanisms continue to work on it.

(iii) Illumination: incubation puts forth a putative solution.

(iv)  Verification: consciously checking the putative solution against the known facts, and refining it.

The mathematician Poincaré (1913; 1946) reports cases of

outstanding discoveries, discussed against such a framework. From his anecdotes, it would appear that the end-point of a period of incubation is not a complete solution, but rather *raw material* for a plan which has to be consciously worked out. Such a suggestion would be quite consistent with the analysis of problem-solving which we described earlier. For instance, Simon (1966) suggests that in working memory the effectiveness of incubation may lie in some straightforward memory phenomena. When people work on problems initially, they form an initial representation which may not be appropriate. As they move on, they gather more and more relevant information. If they stop in the middle, argues Simon, they tend to forget the initial representation, while they retain more recent aspects. On starting up again, they have to form a new plan, based on more useful information than was the case for the now-forgotten initial plan. Thus the new plan (after the pause) should be better than the old.

This view of Simon's is shared by others (e.g. Posner 1973; Sanford 1983): obviously, whether or not incubation effects occur in any given situation will depend upon retrievability. Indeed, Sanford (1983) conjectures that the persistent 'intuitiveness' of the wrong solution to the three-cups problem is because of the ease of retrieving the wrong schemata while a new one is being built up. It is thus scarcely surprising that experimental studies of incubation effects have not been uniformly successful. Thus Silviera (1971) showed that subjects given a 'break' in the middle of problem-solving performed better than controls who were given no break. However, other workers have found little or no effects of this type (e.g. Dominowksi and Jenrick 1972; Murray and Denny 1969). In general, the role of unconscious processes in problem-solving may be arguably restricted to selective memory function. Nevertheless, it should be stated that far more serious study has gone into the investigation of conscious goal-directed problem-solving than into studies of unconscious mechanisms, so the issue is far from decided.

# 12 Thinking 2: Aspects of reasoning and intuitive judgement

The psychology of intuitive judgement is traditionally concerned with how people make decisions in the face of uncertainty, usually without the formal models of probability and decision theory to help them. It is, of course, true that people do reason about and make judgements of the probabilities of future events, and can assign numbers and confidence ratings to their decisions. It is also true that people may combine probabilities and values in coming to a decision, and these are the fundamental classes of variable in decision theory. But they do not appear to conform to the prescription of mathematical models of probability and decision theory in either a conscious or an automatic way. Intuitive judgement, then, refers to the way in which people normally make decisions, and not what an expert does when he applies a formal theory. It is notable that many 'expert' decisions, such as choosing the appropriate number of subjects for a psychology experiment, very often suffer from the same arbitrary and inadequate consideration of relevant variables as do more everyday decisions, such as choosing a motor car (Tversky and Kahneman 1971).

Over the course of study of intuitive judgement, a research strategy has been adopted in which the judgements of people were compared with the judgements which *should* be made according to an appropriate formal model. Such models are referred to as *normative*, and by comparing people's performance with the models' predictions, it is possible to obtain an idea of what kind of biases occur in intuition. More recently, a more cognitive approach has been taken, and happily there is now a proliferation of studies concerned with what people actually *do* to produce judgements.

In the first section, we shall consider a major effort in this direction, initiated by the efforts of Daniel Kahneman and Amos Tversky. These two researchers believe that they have isolated some major heuristics, or guiding procedures, which people apply when trying to make judgements. Recently developments along this line of enquiry have led to some extremely interesting observations on how the problems come to be represented. Although there is, as yet, no process model to describe intuitive judgement, the present author supposes that it will not be long before one is attempted and some possibilities are discussed.

We shall also consider the general issue of confidence, and how good a reflection confidence is of performance. Here too some pervasive and interesting biases are to be found. Finally, we shall consider the possibility of explaining some of these biases as resulting from mechanisms which may be expressed as process models.

## A  Heuristics and biases in intuitive judgement

Over the past decade or so, a number of apparent biases in intuitive judgements have been isolated by Tversky and Kahneman (e.g. 1974) and by people working within their theoretical framework. These biases have been discussed in terms of a set of decision-making heuristics which people are assumed to employ. Although under many circumstances the use of these heuristics might be well-founded, their blind application can lead to sub-optimal performance. Let us begin by examining each of them in turn.

### 1  The availability heuristic

The first heuristic, availability, is a procedure of estimating the likelihood of an event by assessing how readily instances of it come to mind. For instance, one might assess divorce rate by recalling divorces among one's friends, family and colleagues. A similar strategy might be used if one is buying a new vacuum cleaner – how readily do reports of a particular model breaking down come to mind? Obviously the heuristic is potentially applicable to a large number of life's routine decisions.

Tversky and Kahneman (1973) argue that the availability of relevant information is assessed without exhaustively checking through memory for relevant instances. Instead, an estimate of availability could be made by seeing how readily any instance comes to mind. The use of such a procedure is dependent upon likely instances being easier to think of than unlikely instances, and by instances of large classes being more readily thought of than instances of small ones. Tversky and Kahneman claim that lifelong experience teaches us that this is generally the case.

The availability heuristic can be used in situations where instances of some class have to be retrieved from memory in order to assess availability. Tversky and Kahneman have shown that subjects' *estimates* of the number of examples of a category (e.g. flowers, Russian novelists) they can think of in two minutes is very highly correlated with the number that they *can produce*. Similarly, the heuristic can be used in situations where alternatives have to be imagined (e.g. number of words in the letter sets XUZONLCJM or TAPCERHOB). Again, estimates can be highly correlated with the number of items a person can actually produce over a short time.

While this heuristic will sometimes produce reasonable estimates, there are clearly potential biases in its use. For instance, if an estimate of the frequency of something depends upon how readily it comes to mind, then any factor which influences this readiness will influence the outcome of the availability heuristic. If a recent road accident is readily remembered, for instance, it may bias one's estimate of the safety of travelling by car. Similarly, things which are readily imaginable could produce biases in estimates of the frequency of such things, even if things which are hard to imagine are in fact more frequent. Let us consider two experiments carried out by Tversky and Kahneman (1973) to illustrate this point.

The first study relies on searches of memory as a way of assessing availability. Subjects were presented with recorded lists of names of known personalities of both sexes. It was established that the more famous names were most readily recalled, and conjectured that availability is a function of fame (familiarity). Separate groups of subjects then heard lists of personalities: in one group the females listed were more famous than the males, and in the other the males were more famous than the females. For the 'female famous' group there were nineteen females, and twenty males. The opposite was the case for the 'male famous' group. Subjects were given the task of judging whether the list they had just heard had more men or women in it. Of ninety-nine subjects, eighty erroneously judged the more famous class as being the most frequent. Obviously, availability underlies the erroneous conclusion.

The second study was designed to investigate the ease with which situations could be *imagined* as a foundation for the application of the availability heuristic. The argument is that if mental models of one situation are easier to construct, more quickly constructed, or in greater variety then that situation should be judged as actually being more numerous. The study provides a neat illustration of the impact of the heuristic:

- Consider a group of ten people who form committees of k members (k was specified within the range $2 \leqslant k < 8$). How many different committees of k members can be formed?

The correct answer is given by the binomial coefficient, (10/k). An important feature is that the function reaches a maximum of 252 committees for k = 5, and that it is symmetrical for k and (10 − k). This is easy to understand if it is appreciated that any group of k members defines a unique group of (10 − k) non-members.

Tversky and Kahneman argue that if mathematically naïve subjects attempt this task, then they may try to see how readily committees of k members come to mind. It is further argued that when k is small, the task is easier. For instance, it is easy to imagine five disjoint committees for k = 2, but even two disjoint committees cannot be generated if k = 8. Thus, by using availability as a heuristic, estimates of the number of committees which could be formed will be greatest for the smallest values of k. This was borne out by the data. The suggestion is that with complex combinational tasks of this type, subjects construct models of a few combinations, and extrapolate a final value on the basis of how easy it seems to be to construct mental models. Because model construction is easiest with only two tokens to manipulate, this gives the greatest numerical estimate.

## 2 Representativeness

Suppose that you are told some characteristics of a person, and invited to decide on the basis of the information provided whether they are more likely to be a scientist or a master of ceremonies at a social club. The most obvious way open to you is to compare the similarity of the features of the character sketch to your stereotypic model of scientists and MCs. For instance, they might differ in anticipated extroversion, intellectual skill, and so on. Such a procedure exemplifies the use of the representativeness heuristic in determining what is likely.

More subtle examples arise when one considers processes. Suppose that the Round-the-World Airline has a generally higher accident rate than does Global Wings. Given a report of a new air accident, is it more likely to be Round-the-World or Global Wings which was involved? Clearly, an air accident is more representative of the processes by which Round-the-World's track record was produced.

Formally, Tversky and Kahneman (1982) describe representativeness as a relation between a process or a model M, and some instance or event X, associated with that model. A sample (X) is more or less representative of a model (M). The domains in which representativeness has been explored are for the most part related to the intuition of likelihood, and often of likelihoods in explicitly statistical situations.

As with the availability heuristic, representativeness is interesting from the information-processing point of view because it seems to embody a fundamental way in which people actually *do* problems, and probably the way in which they do them in everyday life. From a normative point of view, the heuristic often leads to entirely appropriate conclusions. However, it can also yield intuitions which depart markedly from the normative solution under some circumstances. Such departures can result either from having an inappropriate model in the first place, or through the heuristic diverting a person's attention away from other critical aspects of the situation.

A dramatic (and now classical) illustration of a failure of statistical intuition arose during the intensive bombing of London during the Second World War. It was believed that the bombing of London could not be random, because certain parts of the city were not hit at all, while other areas suffered repeated strikes.

However, professional statistical analysis revealed that the distribution fitted random expectation remarkably well (Feller 1968). Indeed, the statistical concept of randomness is very difficult to grasp, and a considerable amount of experimentation has shown that people's models of it deviate from true randomness in a number of significant ways. For instance, Baddeley (1966) and Tune (1964) have shown that when people are asked to simulate a random process, such as the outcomes of tossing a fair coin, they produce sequences which have far too many short runs of one of the alternatives (see also Wagenaar 1970 for a fuller review). Furthermore, they tend to regard truly random sequences, with the correct distribution of run lengths, as unlikely to have been produced by a random process. The general conclusion from this type of observation is that people generally expect samples to conform in structure to a very large, or parent, population, no matter how small the samples are.

A simple example of this principle at work is demonstrated by expectations regarding birth order:

All families of six children in a city were surveyed. In *seventy-two* families, the *exact order* of births of boys and girls was GBGBBG.
What is your estimate of the number of families surveyed in which the *exact order* was BGBBBB?

These two orders are in fact about equally likely, but in an experiment using this problem, Kahneman and Tversky (1972) found that of ninety-two subjects tested, seventy-five claimed that the second sequence was less likely. The same sort of result was reported earlier by Cohen and Hansel (1956). It would appear that knowing that a child born has a roughly equal likelihood of being a boy or girl, or that the populations of boys and girls is about equal, then this equality should apply even in the case of very small samples, but it does not.

In this instance, use of the representativeness heuristic has the effect of causing people to ignore sample size, producing results which deviate markedly from the normative prediction. Similar examples of sample size occur with problems of judging the likelihood of distributions. The following problem, which is similar to ones studied by Kahneman and Tversky (1972), comes from Jones and Harris (1982):

Imagine a box divided into two sections. Balls dropped from above are equally likely to fall into either section. Person A drops ten balls; person B drops one hundred balls; person C drops one thousand balls. Which person is most likely to end up with 60 per cent of his balls in one section and 40 per cent in the other: A? B? C? Equally likely?

Overwhelmingly in tasks of this exact type, more subjects assume the proportion to be independent of sample size than assume anything else, although the larger a sample, the more likely it will be representative of the parent population. A little later we shall examine other proportion-related effects which have been attributed to the operation of representativeness. For a moment we shall turn to a rather different issue.

A very interesting test prediction for the representativeness heuristic arises with what is known as the conjunction rule. The best way to illustrate the theoretical interest in and nature of conjunction is to try the following problem:

- Bill is thirty-four years old. He is intelligent, but unimaginative, compulsive, and generally lifeless. In school, he was strong in mathematics, but weak in social studies and humanities.
  Please rank order the following statements by their probability, using one for *most* probable, and eight for the least probable.
  (a) Bill is a physician who plays snooker for a hobby.
  (b) Bill is an architect.
  (c) Bill is an accountant.
  (d) Bill plays jazz for a hobby.
  (e) Bill surfs for a hobby.
  (f) Bill is a reporter.
  (g) Bill is an accountant who plays jazz for a hobby.
  (h) Bill climbs mountains for a hobby.

In an experiment, Tversky and Kahneman (1982) found that (c) was given the highest rank, which is hardly surprising given the closeness of the character sketch to people's stereotypic expectations regarding the kind of personalities attracted to various professions. Outcome (d) was considered very unlikely – it does not fit the stereotype. The interesting thing, however, is that (g) was given a ranking between (c) and (d).

Logically, of course, Bill cannot be more likely to be *an X who does Y* than someone who *does Y*, because Xs who do Y are *included* in the set of people who do Y. The conjunction rule is just this: for any joint probability, P(A & B), the value has to be less than or equal to the smaller of P(A) and P(B). Thus if the probability that Bill plays jazz is 0.1, and the probability that he is an accountant is 1.0 (unity), then the probability that he is both is $0.1 \times 1.0 = 0.1$. If the probability that he is an accountant is less than unity, then the value will, of course, be less than 0.1.

Results similar to the one described above have been obtained in other similar experiments. The argument from representativeness is fairly straightforward: the character description is representative of the mental-model stereotype of an accountant, and of the model of an accountant who happens to play jazz (though this is less likely). The description has more *features* in common with the stereotype of someone who is an accountant regardless of the rogue feature of playing jazz than it does with the stereotype of someone who plays jazz. Thus the overlap of features in the three mental models with those specified in the description predicts the ordering of likelihoods which subjects tend to produce.

## 3  Adjusting from an anchor: a third heuristic

Adjustment from an anchor is a procedure in which some starting value of an estimate is taken, and then the value is adjusted up or down in the light of new evidence. Tversky and Kahneman (1974) report a demonstration of anchoring effects in which subjects were asked to estimate various quantities, such as the percentage of African countries in the United Nations. A wheel of fortune was spun in front of each subject, yielding a random number between 0 and 100, and they were asked to indicate whether the proportion was higher or lower than whatever was the value of the number. Then they were asked to provide a numerical estimate of their own. The results showed that for low starting numbers, the numerical estimates were low, and for high starting numbers, they were high – for instance, given a start point of 10, subjects' estimates were *25*, in contrast to a start point of 65 giving an estimate of *60*. This suggests that subjects used the numbers as some sort of anchor, even though subjects were free to give *any* number they wished. It is as though any initial value put into the head of the judge, regardless of it being accidental, influences his judgement when there is little other evidence to go on.

The treatment of anchor effects by Tversky and Kahneman is not as extensive as that of the other two heuristics, but such effects are well known in the fields of psychological scaling and psychophysics. For instance, Poulton (e.g. 1968) discusses a number of anchoring and related effects and claims that many results in psychophysics which are taken as being characteristics of the human perceptual systems in fact result from anchors, adjustment, and similar biases called 'range-effects'.

## B  Adjusting probability estimates

Under many circumstances, people not only have to estimate the likelihood of things, but have to revise these estimates in the light of new evidence. For instance, suppose that two countries engage in armed conflict, and each accuses the other as being the instigator. If you know that news bulletins from one of the countries are generally less reliable than from the other, then your initial reaction may be to suppose that it is (marginally) more likely that the country with unreliable news' sources started the conflict. In the period which follows, news reporters from other countries who were there at the outbreak start to get fresh evidence through, which, although not definitive, seems to support the view that it is the *other* country which started the conflict. It is highly likely that you will revise your opinion of the relative likelihood of a particular country having started the war in the light of the new evidence, and it is reasonable to do so. In general, the more evidence favouring one particular alternative, the greater should be the subjective probability, or confidence, that that alternative is the correct one.

Situations calling for adjustment can sometimes be explicit, where people state confidence before the new evidence arrives, restate confidence when it does arrive, and carry on iteratively, until no more evidence comes in. Continuously predicting future market trends on the basis of new evidence is of this type, for instance. In other situations, we may simply have two facts, each giving rise to subjective confidence estimates which have to be combined. In fact, the psychological mechanisms operating in the explicit case and the implicit cases produce rather different judgements, as we shall see. However, before we begin to look at experiments, we have to consider the technical background to the problem of probability revision.

## 1 Bayes's theorem

In probability theory, conditional probability is defined as:

$$p(i/j) = \frac{p(i \cap j)}{p(j)} \qquad \text{(equation 1)}$$

where:
$p(i/j)$ is read as 'the probability of i given j'; and
$p(i \cap j)$ is read as 'the probability of i and j'.

This can be understood if we consider a sample space, S, containing, say, two event spaces $E_i$ and $E_j$, as in figure 12-1.

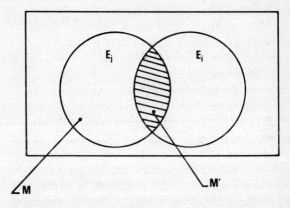

*Figure 12-1.* A diagrammatic representation for the derivation of Bayes's theorem. The circles denote two event spaces, $E_i$ and $E_j$. Assume that there are m equally likely outcomes in $E_i$. $E_i$ partly overlaps with $E_j$, in the shaded portion, and this region is designated $E_i \cap E_j$. Let there be m' equally likely outcomes in this region.

Let M = the number of equally likely outcomes in $E_j$ and M' = the number of equally likely outcomes common to $E_i$ and $E_j$; i.e. the number in $E_i \cap E_j$. Then, by definition:

$$P(i/j) = \frac{M'}{M} = \frac{(M'/S)}{(M/S)} = \frac{P(i \cap j)}{P(j)}$$

Now, $p(i/j) = p(j/i)$, so from equation 1:

$$p(i/j)p(j) = p(j/i)p(i)$$
or

$$p(i/j) = \frac{p(j/i)p(i)}{p(j)}$$    (equation 2)

This is known as *Bayes's theorem*.

Instead of using *i* and *j*, the formula can be expressed in terms of *hypotheses*, *H*, and evidence, *e*, which gives the following:

$$p(H/e) = \frac{p(e/H) \times p(H)}{p(e)}$$

where
- $p(H/e)$ is the probability of a hypothesis being right given a certain piece of evidence;
- $p(e/H)$ is the probability of obtaining that evidence if the hypothesis is correct;
- $p(H)$ is the *prior* probability of the hypothesis being the correct one; and
- $p(e)$ is the probability that the evidence will occur.

What the formula does, then, is to show how the prior probability of a hypothesis combines with the impact of evidence to determine a new probability of the hypothesis (the *posterior* probability).

An example is appropriate at this point. Suppose that there are ten boxes in front of you. *Two* of the boxes are type-A, *eight* of the boxes are type-B. The boxes contain the following proportions of balls of different colours:

Type-A: 80 per cent white balls, 20 per cent red balls.
Type-B: 40 per cent white balls, 60 per cent red balls.

Suppose now that one of the ten boxes was chosen at random, and four balls were removed, randomly with replacement. *They were all white.* Our intuitions would be to the effect that the box from which we sampled was a type-A box (predominantly white). On the other hand, there are only *two* type-A boxes, that is, our prior probability of selecting a type-A box was 0.2.

Bayes's theorem enables a calculation of the exact probability of the hypothesis that the balls came from a type-A box.

- First, note that $p(H_1) = 0.2$ (the prior probability that $H_1$ is correct, where $H_1$ is that we have a type-A box). Also note $p(H_2) = 0.8$ ($H_2$ – we have a type-B box).
- Second, from basic probability theory, the probability of getting four whites one after the other from a box with 80 per cent white balls is:

$$p(e/H_1) = 0.8 \times 0.8 \times 0.8 \times 0.8 = 0.8^4$$

while the probability of getting four whites from a box with 40 per cent white balls is:

$$p(e/H_2) = 0.4 \times 0.4 \times 0.4 \times 0.4 = 0.4^4$$

- Third, from these data we can work out $p(e)$. By definition,
$p(e) = p(e/H_1)p(H_1) + p(e/H_2)p(H_2)$,
thus

$$p(e) = (0.8^4 \times 0.2) + (0.4^4 \times 0.8) = 0.1$$
- Finally, substituting in Bayes's rule:

$$p(H_1/e) = \frac{0.8^4 \times 0.2}{0.1} \simeq 0.8$$

So the a posteriori probability that the sequence came from a type-A box is 0.8, although the prior probability pointed to a type-B box.

Bayes's theorem may be reapplied over and over again in the light of new evidence. Thus, if the above experiment were continued by drawing *another* ball, the original posterior probability would become the *new prior* probability.

Ward Edwards (1968) carried out a considerable series of studies, some of which were of the type described above. He found that *subjects* underestimate the effect of new evidence, an underestimation which was reflected by their estimates of posterior probabilities being lower than that predicted by Bayes's theorem. Edwards termed this behaviour *conservative*. Kahneman and

Tversky have offered an explanation of conservatism based upon the representativeness heuristic. Consider the following sets of possible results from a balls-in-the-boxes experiment:

In a sample of six we get         five white      one black
In a sample of twelve we get      eight white     four black
In a sample of thirty-six we get  twenty white    sixteen black

Now ask yourself, what is the probability in each case that the balls were drawn from predominantly white boxes? Most people believe this probability to get less and less as they move through the list, because they consider the *ratio* of white to black as the important element on which to make a judgement. In fact, the answer is that the true probabilities are *identical*, with an actual value of 0.17! This is so counterintuitive that it is worth proving, and the reader is referred to Appendix 2 on page 345.

Conservatism is an underestimation of the impact of new evidence on old prior probabilities. Edwards (1968) has reported an extensive series of studies showing this trend, all of which are explicit *revision* tasks.

*(1a) Note on Bayes's theorem*
Sometimes Bayes's theorem is expressed in a more convenient form, called the *odds formulation*. Thus we can let:

$$\Omega_0 = \text{prior odds on } H_1 = \frac{p(H_1)}{p(H_2)}$$

and

$$\Omega_1 = \text{posterior odds on } H_1 \text{ (after 'the evidence')} = \frac{p(H_1/e)}{p(H_2/e)}$$

and finally

$$\Lambda = \text{the likelihood ratio} = \frac{p(e/H_1)}{p(e/H_2)}$$

Hence:

$$\frac{p(H_1/e)}{p(H_2/e)} = \frac{p(e/H_1)}{p(e/H_2)} \times \frac{p(H_1)}{p(H_2)}$$

or
$$\Omega_1 = \Lambda . \Omega_0$$

(i.e. 'posterior odds = likelihood ratio × prior odds').

This formulation is readily applicable to situations in which there are two and only two alternative hypotheses, and where it may be impossible to specify p(e). In the examples which follow, the odds formulation is used.

## 2 Radical 'revision'

In the experiments described above, the tasks were largely ones of explicit probability revision. In these situations people generally turn out to be 'conservative' with respect to the Bayesian norm. However, the conservatism relies upon an adjustment from the base rate (or prior odds) which in turn relies upon recognizing that base rate has an effect. That base rate will have an effect seems trivially obvious in the above examples – these are all the data a subject has to start off with. However, subjects can sometimes neglect base rate completely in some situations. Tversky and Kahneman (1980) presented the following problem to a large number of people:

A taxi-cab was involved in a hit-and-run accident one night. Two cab companies, the Green and the Blue, operate in the city. You are given the following data:
>    (i) 85 per cent of the cabs in the city are Green, and 15 per cent are Blue.
>    (ii) In court, a witness identified the cab as a *Blue* cab.
> The court tested his ability to identify cabs under appropriate visibility conditions. When presented with a series of cabs, half of which were Blue and half of which were Green, the witness made correct identifications in 80 per cent of the cases, and was wrong in 20 per cent.
>    What was the probability that the cab involved in the accident was Blue rather than Green? _____ per cent.

Try it before moving on.
With this judgement, Tversky and Kahneman found the median response to be 80 per cent. That is to say, subjects restricted their

analysis to the reliability of the witness. Of course, the normative value is given by Bayes's theorem, with the prior odds being 85:15 in favour of the cab being *Green*, since 85 per cent of the cabs in the city *are* Green. Thus the normative expectation of the cab in the accident being Blue is as follows, using the odds formulation of Bayes's theorem:

$$\frac{15}{85} \times \frac{80}{20} = \frac{12}{17}$$

(or $\frac{12}{12 + 17} = 0.41$ as a probability, which is 41 per cent as a percentage).

Quite clearly, ignoring base rate leads to a radical overestimate of the posterior probability.

Another example of radical overestimation was obtained in a study carried out by Hammerton (1973). It is particularly understandable in an intuitive way. Suppose that 1 in 10,000 people contract a particular kind of cancer. The test for this cancer results in a positive test 95 per cent of the time; on the other hand, the false positive rate is only 5 per cent. Now suppose that you take a test for the cancer as a routine medical check and your result is positive. What is the probability that you have the disease?

Apparently, most people believe it to be 95 per cent (which ignores base rate). In fact, base rate should be taken into account, as determined by Bayes's theorem, and the answer turns out to be 0.0019!

What is striking about these examples is that the failure to take base rate into account is *not difficult to understand*, in an intuitive sense. Furthermore, a small change in the format of the problems can induce the majority of subjects to take base rate into account. In one such manipulation, Tversky and Kahneman (1980) changed item (i) of their cab example to:

- Although the two companies are roughly equal in size, 85 per cent of cab accidents in the city involve Green cabs, and 15 per cent involve Blue cabs.

Under these circumstances, the investigators found that base rate was no longer ignored, and the median answer was 60 per cent. What is to explain the difference? It appears to lie in the fact that there is a clear *causal* relation between accident record and likelihood of being involved in an accident. On the other hand, there is no causal relationship with a population difference like that in the first version of the problem. Indeed, as Tversky and Kahneman point out, there is a correlation between cab colour and the likelihood that a cab will be involved in an accident in the causal situation, but no correlation in the case of the proportion situation. They argue that subjects may spot the correlation where it exists, reasoning that there will be some concrete, imaginable reason why the difference in base accident rate should come about, such as poorer vehicle maintenance, or less careful selection of drivers in the case of the Green cabs.

The precise conditions under which base rate is ignored are not clear, notwithstanding the findings on causal schemata being important. Bar-Hillel (cited by Tversky and Kahneman 1982) manipulated the nature of the evidence presented in the original taxi-cab problem, by replacing the witness information with a statement that the hit-and-run cab was known to have an intercom, and that intercoms are installed in 80 per cent of Green cabs and 20 per cent of Blue cabs. Responses indicated that base rate was taken into account, the median value being 48 per cent. On this basis it has been argued that *specificity* may be an important variable in the way that evidence is utilized: the intercom data is not about the specific cab which was involved in the accident, it is about Blue and Green cabs in general. In general, base-rate data appear to be combined with other evidence when the former have a causal interpretation, or when the nature of the other evidence is no more specific than the base-rate data.

## 3 Summary

People do not conform to the Bayesian norm for the revision of probabilities. Given a clear revision task (e.g. Edwards) the overall tendency is not to give sufficient weight to the new evidence, thus displaying conservatism. When the task is not clearly one of revision, but rather one of combining information from different sources which are technically prior odds and likelihood ratio, a number of things happen. Subjects can ignore base-rate information if they do not causally relate the information to the new evidence. However, if they can relate it causally, or if the new evidence is not given in a more specific form than the base-rate data, then adjustments to base rate do occur. All in all, there is no evidence whatsoever that people operate in accordance with Bayes's theorem: they do not produce results consistent with the use of the rule even when both base rate and new evidence are taken into account.

## C Faith in predictability and judgement

When difficult choices are made, a person may be more or less confident that the choice made is the correct one. For instance, in arguing about popular music one might assert that, 'I think *Cars* recorded "The girl of my best friend".'[1] Hedge expressions like 'I think ...' or 'I believe ...' or 'I'm fairly sure that ...' are all indicators of a degree of uncertainty in what are presumably subjective best bets. Statements of confidence are of course extremely important in how one reacts to the assertions of another, or in how one behaves on the basis of one's own thoughts. Furthermore, in many walks of life, it is essential that experts are accurate in their confidence assessment of likelihoods, for instance, in judging risk in military strategy, in the stockmarket, in medical diagnosis, and so on.

### 1 Calibration and overconfidence

How well a person's estimate of the probability of something being the case matches its objective likelihood has been referred to variously as *realism of confidence* (Adams and Adams 1961), *external validity* (Brown and Shufford 1973) and *calibration* (Lichtenstein, Fischhoff and Phillips 1982). We shall use this last term. While it is gratifying to learn that the weather expert's calibration is very good, there appear to be a number of biases outside of expert domains which seem to produce rather poor calibration characteristics. Let us examine these through the medium of a recently used laboratory procedure.

---

[1] Recorded by Elvis Presley. The group Cars recorded 'My best friend's girl'.

Consider the following pair of statements, and pick one as true (one *is* true), and estimate your confidence with the range 0.5 (guess) to 1 (*know* the answer).

(a) Aladdin is Persian.
(b) Aladdin is Chinese.

By asking people to make a large number of binary choices of this type, which rely on general knowledge and produce a range of uncertainty, numerous investigators have found that subjects typically display *overconfidence*. That is, for groups of questions producing 50 per cent correct answers, subjects may say they are 60 per cent (0.6) sure; for questions producing 70 per cent correct answers, they may say they are 80 per cent sure, and so on.

The extent of overconfidence in tasks relying upon general-knowledge retrieval of this type is widely pervasive and most marked. For instance, Fischhoff, Slovic and Lichtenstein (1977) using a variety of situations found that even when subjects were asserting absolute confidence ($p = 1.0$), they were still wrong about 20 per cent of the time. Furthermore, their subjects were willing to bet money on these 'uncertainties'.

Calibration curves for fairly difficult tests show a monotonic relationship between subjective probability and objective frequency, so subjects do monitor the success of their responses with some success. However, the deviations are systematic and ubiquitous, and lead to the question of *why* overconfidence should occur. Koriat, Lichtenstein and Fischhoff (1980) carried out some interesting studies to determine the cause of the phenomenon.

In one experiment, they required subjects to write down reasons for each of their choices (if they could think of any). One group wrote down reasons *supporting* their choices, another reasons *against* their choice, and a third reasons *for and against*. The group listing reasons *against* their choices showed less of a tendency towards overconfidence than did either of the other two groups, and showed less overconfidence than did a control group who did not write down reasons for choosing. The group giving reasons for their choices did not differ significantly in overconfidence from a control group.

The experimenters concluded that overconfidence derives from a tendency to neglect evidence which might contradict the conclusion. Supplementary evidence for this point of view comes from a number of additional observations. For instance, subjects gave more reasons *for* than reasons *against*. Also, in another experiment of the same type, subjects were required to rate the *strength* (importance) of reasons on a seven-point scale. The mean rating of importance was slightly but reliably higher in the case of reasons for. Furthermore, correlational analysis showed that whatever measure was used (the number of reasons produced, the strength of the first reason, or the sum of the strengths of all the reasons), the final expression of confidence as a probability was heavily based upon the evidence supporting the answer chosen. It was not based on evidence supporting the rejected answer.

Koriat, Lichtenstein and Fischhoff put forward a two-stage explanation of how subjects behave in this task. They claim that in the first stage, the subject searches his knowledge for relevant information about the target propositions. In the second stage, the evidence is reviewed and confidence in the chosen alternative is assessed. At the first stage, they suggest that somehow *reasons for* rather than *reasons against* are retrieved, and they suggest a parallel of some (unspecified) sort with the failure to accept relevant negative evidence in logical inference tasks (Johnson-Laird and Wason 1977; and see also chapter 13). At the second stage, they suggest that a bias operates causing evidence which contradicts the chosen answer to be disregarded. The primary evidence for this line of reasoning is, of course, that while writing supporting reasons did not influence calibration, writing contradicting reasons did. On this basis it can be argued that subjects were already thinking of supporting reasons, a point supported by the observation that subjects found it more difficult to produce contradicting reasons.

Finally, although not definitively indicated by their experiment, Koriat, Lichtenstein and Fischhoff suggest a possible mental procedure through which the observed results could emerge. First the subjects start an unbiased search for anything which they know might help them to choose. The outcome of this process is to produce reasoning which is consistent with one of the possibilities. The continuing search is guided by the new information retrieved, and is directed to amassing more evidence in favour of the now-preferred alternative. Such a view is, of course, consistent with the mechanics of search discussed earlier in the sections on language and understanding.

Lichtenstein, Fischhoff and Phillips (1982) offer a thorough review of calibration problems, ranging from the simple laboratory type discussed above to professional problems such as weather forecasting and estimates of changes in the stockmarket. Indeed, the calibration problem is now recognized as being important in many areas of 'serious' decision-making, so much so that there are 'calibration experts' who are aware of the common calibration errors made by predictors, and advise on overcoming them.

## 2  Biases of hindsight

A special case of overconfidence which is particularly interesting to theoreticians is the hindsight bias. In popular everyday conversation, hindsight biases would seem to be at the root of a number of everyday expressions, such as 'I knew it all along' (even if you did not really), or 'I told you so' (even if your advice had in fact been ambiguous).

Hindsight judgements are those made after the fact. For instance, an experiment may have been designed to determine which of (say) two possible outcomes occurs under a particular set of circumstances. At the stage before running it, any expectations of obtaining a particular outcome constitute an a priori judgement, of the type considered up to now. Suppose the experiment is duly carried out, and one of the two outcomes is realized. You tell a colleague, and the colleague judges whether he *would have expected* that outcome. This is a post-hoc judgement, made under conditions of hindsight. The colleague's confidence in his judgement with hindsight reflects his subjective degree of surprise at the outcome.

A number of studies by Fischhoff and his colleagues (e.g. 1977; Slovic and Fischhoff 1977) have been aimed at determining the degree to which hindsight probability assessments match prior judgements. Experimental subjects in these tasks have to put themselves into the position of supposing that they do not know the outcome in judgement situations and make judgements of outcome likelihoods, although in fact they do know the outcome.

In one study, subjects were presented with binary-choice general-knowledge questions of the type discussed earlier. The subjects were then divided into three groups. *A memory group* were shown some of the previously presented items, *but with the correct item* indicated, and asked to indicate their previous answer. *A reliability group* carried out the same task as the memory group, but the correct item was *not* indicated. Finally, a *'hypothetical' group* saw *new* questions with the correct answer indicated, but they had to respond 'as they would if they had not learned the correct answer'. This group corresponds to the everyday hindsight situation.

In terms of recall of previous responses, the memory group performed rather more poorly than the reliability group. That is, information about which response would have been correct actually influenced memory performance. (Note how this result parallels our discussion in chapter 6 of the influence of questions on eye-witness testimony.) Secondly, when subjects in the memory group erroneously thought they had guessed the correct alternative first time, they assigned a higher confidence value to their guess than they had first time around. Subjects in the hypothetical group (the pure hindsight condition) were more confident that they would have made the correct choice than the other groups were in their actual choices. This is, of course, the classic hindsight effect.

A corollary of the classical hindsight effect is that people will be generally less surprised by a reported outcome than they should be. That is, there should be a tendency to see outcomes as being 'obvious', although before the fact they may be essentially undecidable. Slovic and Fischhoff (1977) demonstrated this to be the case. Given a description of an experiment and a statement of a particular outcome, confidence that one would have guessed that to *be* the outcome on an a priori basis was higher than it was in the genuine a priori situation.

## D   Intuitive reasoning and process models

In the examples discussed above, people generally give answers which are *intuitive* rather than *analytical*. Although in some cases confidence might be low, in many, as we have seen, it is far too high. Many intuitions have the property of being both faulty and of high confidence. This is psychologically important, both in terms of theory and for everyday life. It stands in need of explanation.

One possible starting point was hinted at in chapter 11. There, it was suggested that, as with discourse understanding, understanding a *problem* relies upon making a mapping between the problem-statement and the relevant background knowledge. The degree or richness of the mapping may well be a determiner of the feeling of familiarity with the problem. Such an argument, discussed at length in Sanford (1983), depends upon the demonstration that background knowledge, including much presupposition, is necessary for any kinds of understanding. But the problem is that once a particular *model* has been established (i.e. a statement-to-knowledge mapping), it is very difficult to construct another. It is much easier to slot into place new knowledge which *fits* the existing model than it is to handle new knowledge which cannot fit. This schema-theory approach predicts numerous difficulties which 'disruptive' information may encounter.

First of all, there is memory, both working memory and long-term memory. We have seen how information which does not fit schemata tends to be omitted from recall. Yet we noted that things which do not fit command attention for a while – for instance, 'odd' things in Schank's account are put on a 'weird list' in the hope of later interpretation. One would imagine that disruptive information would take up more working-memory capacity than non-disruptive information. but that unless it could be fitted into some sort of interpretative schema, it would soon be forgotten. It is as though disruptive information needs continual rehearsal to be maintained in memory. So while it may be prominent in the short term, it will not be well remembered. In contrast, information which fits may be incompletely analysed, but will be remembered well. This could easily give rise to a phenomenon which we must all have encountered: explaining our understanding of something to someone, giving them the reasons for our account, suddenly to find that we do not really understand in full what some of those reasons are!

A consequence of these arguments is that once an interpretation of something has been made, it is very difficult to form a new one. Furthermore, every time we try to form a new interpretation, sweeping the old one aside, we are up against the fact that the old one will be the most 'available' in memory, and will keep creeping in.

Not being able to form alternative models is a huge problem when one turns to *logical* reasoning. In logic, part of the issue is to establish what is *necessary* rather than what is merely *possible*. To do this, it is necessary to establish that whatever assertion is being tested for necessity is the case in *all possible worlds*. Translated into psychological processes, all possible worlds tend to be downgraded to all *imaginable* worlds. And, of course, the problem is then one of imagining all imaginable worlds. This is not as strange as it may seem, and is one of the central issues in chapter 13.

## Chapter 12: Chapter notes

Choice, decision-making and judgement together constitute a vast and important area. This chapter reports only a narrow part of the field, and is intended to be integral with our treatment of thinking rather than to offer a broad survey. Models of choice behaviour are many, and are, in general, concerned with the way in which the probability of success given a course of action interacts with the value associated with that course of action. Good reviews of behavioural decision theory may be found in the sequence of reviews written over the years in the *Annual Review of Psychology* (published by the American Psychological Association, and readily available in academic libraries). Other sources include:

W. Edwards and A. Tversky (1967), *Decision-Making*, Penguin.

E. Raiffa (1968), *Decision Analysis: Introductory Lectures on Choices under Uncertainty*, Addison-Wesley, Reading, Mass.

F. Warner (1981), *The Assessment and Perception of Risk*, The Royal Society.

Recently, the compilation of papers by D. Kahneman, P. Slovic, and A. Tversky (1982) presents the reader with a good sample of topics, ranging from the logic of choice, through to risk perception, and includes many very practical case studies.

## Appendices

The three appendices which follow serve two different functions. The first is a straightforward demonstration of why differences and not ratios of elements in samples from a binomial population are important in assessing likelihoods. The second and third are addenda which relate back to chapter 2 in which signal detection theory and choice reaction time were discussed. Given Bayes's theorem, particularly in the odds form, it is possible to obtain a somewhat deeper understanding of the ideas of criterion, evidence accumulation, and speed-accuracy trade-off. This material is presented as an appendix because although it is related to chapter 12, it is really only marginally related.

## Appendix 1    An illustration of how differences and not ratios are important for sampling tasks

Suppose you know that there are two bags:

BAG 1 consists of 70 red and 30 green chips.
BAG 2 consists of 30 red and 70 green chips.

Suppose that twelve chips are drawn, comprising eight red and four green. The likelihood ratio (L) favours the bag chosen as having been bag 1 to the following extent:

$$L = \frac{0.7^8 = 0.3^4}{0.3^8 \times 0.7^4} = \frac{0.7^4}{0.3^4} = 29.6$$

Thus the odds are 29.6:1 in favour of bag 1.

Compare this with drawing thirty chips, and getting seventeen red and thirteen green. Here the ratio of red to green chips is much lower, and people seem to believe that the odds favouring bag 1 are thus lower. But the odds are the same:

$$L = \frac{0.7^{17} \times 0.3^{13}}{0.3^{17} \times 0.7^{13}} = \frac{0.7^4}{0.3^4} = 29.6$$

Given bigger bags, the same arguments hold for drawing 400 red and 396 green chips. The odds are still 29.6:1 in favour of bag 1.

In Kahneman and Tversky's view, people are more guided by the ratio of red to green than by the difference, because the ratio seems more representative of the population in a given sample.

For constant differences, the likelihood ratio goes up. Obviously, as the difference increases, so the likelihood ratio goes up. It is straightforward to see what the relationship is.

Suppose that there are a number of occasions, G, on which green chips are drawn from a bag containing mostly green chips, and a number of occasions, R, on red chips drawn from the same bag. Thus the sample difference is G-R. Let the probability of drawing a green chip be Pg, and the probability of drawing a red one be Pr. The arithmetic illustrations given above come from the equation:

$$L = \left(\frac{Pg}{Pr}\right)^{G-R}$$

where L is the likelihood ratio. The relationship can be shown to give a linear one between log L and G-R:

$$\log L = (G - R) \log \left(\frac{Pg}{Pr}\right).$$

## Appendix 2  *Application to speed-accuracy trade-off*

In chapter 2, the speed-accuracy trade-off was described in terms of the accumulation of evidence favouring one alternative or another. This can be construed as a change in likelihood ratio towards the correct response rather than towards an error response as information is accumulated. Expressed as a likelihood ratio, (Pc/Pe) goes up with longer sampling times (i.e. longer RTs). The relationship is roughly $\log (Pc/Pe) = k.RT$ (Pew 1969). This is consistent with the idea that the difference in information favouring the correct alternative against the others is accumulated linearly over time.

## Appendix 3  *The explanation of signal detection $\beta$ in terms of*
### *Bayes's theorem*

$\beta$ is the index of bias towards saying 'signal' or 'no signal' given a certain level of evidence. It is sensitive to cost/payoff and to a priori probability.

Consider a level of evidence, x, on the abscissa of the TSD distribution curves for S and N. The level x will have a likelihood ratio associated with it: it may come from S, or from N:

$$L(x) = \frac{p(x|S)}{p(x|N)}$$

where $p(x|S)$ is the probability of getting a value as great as x in the signal distribution, and $p(x|N)$ is the probability of getting a value as great as x in the N distribution.

Associated with each answer a subject may give ('Yes, there's a signal'; 'No, there's no signal') is an expected value. Expected value as defined as:

$$EV = pV$$

where p is the probability of the action leading to a reward, and V is the value of the reward.

Thus if an action has a 0.5 probability of earning you 20p, the EV is 10p; if an action has a 0.4 probability of earning you 50p, then the EV is 20p. In signal detection, the problem is to establish the EV of saying YES or NO, given a particular level of sensory evidence, a set of payoff conditions, and a knowledge of a priori signal probability. Using the EV equation and Bayes's theorem, it is possible to specify what the optimal value of $\beta$ will be, and this can then be compared with $\beta$ values chosen by subjects. That is, a normative comparison can be made.

The equation for the expected value of saying 'YES' given an observation of magnitude x is:

$$E(Y|x) = V(Y|s)p(s|x) - V(V|n)p(n|x)$$

where

$E(Y|x)$ = expected value of saying *YES* given an evidence level $x$ from the senses;

$V(Y|s)$ = value of reward associated with saying YES given a signal;

$P(s|x)$ = probability that level x results from a signal;

$V(Y|n)$ = value of reward associated with saying YES given a non-signal; and

$P(n|x)$ = probability that level x results from a non-signal.

Similarly, one can write an analogous equation for the expected value of saying NO given an observation of magnitude x:

$$E(N|x) = V(N|n)p(n|x) - V(N|s)p(s|x)$$

In a signal detection task, the problem is to maximize the expected value of a decision. Thus, one could say YES if:

$$E(Y|x) \geqslant E(N|x)$$

otherwise NO.

Substituting from our expressions for expected value in the above expression, it becomes:

$$V(Y|s)p(S|x) - V(Y|n)p(n|x) \geqslant V(N|n)p(n|x) - V(N|s)p(s|x)$$

Hence:

$$\frac{P(S|x)}{P(n|x)} \geq \frac{V(N|n) + V(Y|n)}{V(Y|x) + V(N|s)} \qquad 1.$$

Now Bayes's theorem says:

$$\frac{P(s|x)}{P(n|x)} = \frac{P(x|s)}{P(x|n)} \cdot \frac{P(s)}{P(n)} \qquad 2.$$

Substituting (2) into (1) gives

$$\frac{P(S|x)}{P(n|x)} \geq \frac{P(S)}{P(n)} \cdot \frac{V(N|n) + V(Y|n)}{V(Y|s) + V(N|s)}$$

The RIGHT-HAND side of this equation is designated B, the criterion point. The left-hand side is L(x), the likelihood ratio. Thus the rule is:

$$L(x) \geq \beta$$

That is, respond YES if $L(x) \geq \beta$.

In this way, the influence of costs and payoffs (through V) and a priori signal probability, $P(s)/P(n)$, can be combined under the decision rule to specify and optimal $\beta$. Given this formulation, it is possible to compare the $\beta$ value adopted by subjects with the optimal value, that is, to make a normative comparison. When this is done, people are generally conservative with respect to the optimal (Green and Swets 1966).

# 13 Thinking 3: Some aspects of reasoning in logic and discovery

We have now discussed some issues in problem-solving, in which a particular and definite solution is possible, and some issues of making judgements under uncertainty, in which the answers may vary considerably in confidence. Judgements under uncertainty, decisions about probability, and degrees of confidence, all tend to be made *intuitively*, partly because of most people's lack of knowledge of suitable formal ways to handle the problems. The formal methods in these cases are almost always taken from probability theory and statistics. Furthermore, even if people know about such things, they do not always apply the methods, either because they do not class the problem as a probability problem, or because it would take too long to do so.

In this chapter we turn to some problems looked at from the standpoint of *logic*. Here the issue is much the same. The appropriate logically valid arguments or deductions may be well understood from the viewpoint of formal logic, but the majority of human problem-solvers will know nothing of such treatments. The surprising thing is that even the simplest and apparently most self-evident of rules of inference can be *extremely* difficult to apply and understand. In the first part of this chapter, we shall see evidence of such difficulties, and similar difficulties with other relatively simple logical problems. In fact, the term 'logical problems' sums things up quite nicely, since when one steps beyond the very simplest of ideas, checking on the validity of inference becomes a problem-solving activity no different from those discussed in chapter 11. Recent work on the psychology of syllogistic reasoning, for example, emphasizes the way in which testing for the validity of conclusions based on inferences is dependent upon the manipulation of mental models. Once one adopts this point of view, the question of whether people conform to the rules of logical reasoning, or fall into error, becomes a question of the efficacy of people's mental models. And, of course, the construction and manipulation of mental models is constrained by various things such as the capacity limitations on working memory.

This description is a very psychological way of discussing what is logical. Logic as a *discipline* is concerned with the identification of rules of valid inference. One example of such a rule is very simply expressed: if it is the case that some proposition p implies proposition q, then if p is assumed to be the case, q will also be the case. This is a very straightforward rule called *modus ponens*, and if a person behaves logically, then we would expect that person to apply the rule where appropriate. This way of thinking about what 'being logical' means assumes that the rules of formal logic offer normative prescriptions for correct thinking. In a way, it is parallel to the idea that probability theory offers a normative prescription of how to reason under uncertainty. However, just as it is unreasonable to expect people to 'know' probability theory intuitively, so it is unreasonable to expect them to 'know' logic. Logic as a discipline dates back to pre-Aristotelian times, and was developed considerably by Aristotle. Over the centuries, it has more or less become a branch of mathematics, and many proofs in logic are as difficult as proofs in advanced algebra. The point of saying all of this is to dispel any belief which the reader might have that rules of logic are intuitively known. It has taken mankind centuries to develop detailed and powerful ways of investigating the properties of rules of inference, and the effect of what is presupposed by or allowed within formal systems on their general properties. Of course, the fact that intelligent people can understand formal logic, given enough work, does not mean that logic is 'in the brain' except in a trivial sense. Rather, it reinforces the view that logic may not figure very much in normal reasoning.

You may find this disagreeable. You might argue that much of what you say and do is logical. This raises another issue, which can be looked at quite nicely in terms of mental models. Suppose that you have a particular conception of a task, that you are in a particular knowledge-state exemplified by a mental model. You may apply certain rules to that model, and suppose that the outcome is logically valid. It will not be (or will be for the wrong reasons) if the model does not conform to all that logicians have demonstrated. Since logicians are still discovering many things about the idea of logic itself, even this criterion is a risky one. The *doctrine of mental logic* (i.e. having logic rules in the mind) is arguably fallacious because, formally, there are even different types of logic (Johnson-Laird 1983). We shall restrict ourselves to the question of information-processing models for handling simple logical problems.

## A  Deductive reasoning

Within logic, a distinction is made between two sorts of reasoning – deductive and inductive. Deductive reasoning may lead to logically necessary conclusions, in which the conclusions must be certain if the premises are true. For example, consider the statements:

(a)  If it's Tuesday in Chicago, then it's raining in New York.
(b)  It is the case that it is Tuesday in Chicago.

*If* (a) is true and (b) is true, then it must follow that:

(c)  It is raining in New York is also true.

The conclusion is the outcome of deduction, and is absolutely certain: (c) is a *valid* deduction.

By contrast, inductive reasoning leads only to *plausible* conclusions, and not to absolutely certain ones. For instance, suppose you know the following facts about John: he sees Mary as often as possible; he sends Mary flowers often; and he keeps asking Mary for dates.

One might plausibly conclude that John is attracted to Mary. There is nothing logically necessary about this conclusion, it is merely *probable*. Many inferences which we make are of this type. From a strictly logical point of view, it is not necessary that next time you put a kettle of cold water on a hot gas it will boil. It is simply taken as completely predictable because it has always happened in the past. There is no way to prove that it is true that it will happen in the future.

## 1 Conditional statements

A considerable amount of psychological research has been aimed at elucidating the degree to which people draw conclusions in a way which is consistent with the most general of these principles of logic. One classic rule of inference – a rule which enables deductions to be made from premises – is that of *modus ponens*. In an abstract form, it looks like this:

| | | | | |
|---|---|---|---|---|
| (a) | If A then B | | $A \longrightarrow B$ | |
| (b) | A | or | A | |
| (c) | $\therefore$ B | | $\therefore$ B | |

(where $\longrightarrow$ denotes undirectional implication, and A and B denote propositions of any sort).

A related rule is called *modus tollens*, and can be expressed in an analogous fashion:

| | |
|---|---|
| If A then B | $A \longrightarrow B$ |
| Not B | $\sim B$ |
| $\therefore$ Not-A | $\therefore$ $\sim A$ |

(where $\sim$ denotes 'not').

Although both of these well-explored rules of inference seem quite obvious, people have a great deal of difficulty applying them. The trouble comes from failures to behave in a way which matches the correct interpretation of the rules, and from a tendency to draw conclusions which are not warranted. Let us begin by summarizing four states of affairs which include our two rules and two other possibilities:

| (a) | (b) | (c) | (d) |
|---|---|---|---|
| $A \longrightarrow B$ | $A \longrightarrow B$ | $A \longrightarrow B$ | $A \longrightarrow B$ |
| A | $\sim A$ | B | $\sim B$ |
| $\therefore$ B | | | $\therefore$ $\sim A$ |
| *Modus ponens* | (No valid conclusion) | (No valid conclusion) | *Modus tollens* |

One potential source of difficulty in reasoning comes from drawing false conclusions based on (b) and (c). An illustration of the problem with case (b) can be seen in the example: 'If Fred committed murder, he would to go to gaol. He does not commit murder.' This does not mean that he will not go to gaol. He might commit robbery, and go to gaol. In fact there is no certain conclusion at all. Now consider an example of (c): 'If a man commits murder, then he will go to gaol. He goes to gaol.' Of course this doesn't mean that he commits murder! Once again, perhaps his going to gaol was the result of some *other* illegal activity.

Experimental work using hypothetical examples of a similar type has been carried out by Rips and Marcus (1977). They asked undergraduate college students to evaluate statements in just the format described above, such as:

If the ball rolls left, the green lamp comes on.
The green lamp comes on.
Therefore the ball rolled left.

Rips and Marcus presented all of the possible combinations of premises and conclusions. In the case of *modus ponens* (type (a)) statements, all subjects selected the correct conclusions. However, with statements of other types, a varying proportion of subjects made errors. For instance, with $A \rightarrow B$, $\sim A$, $\therefore \sim B$, one cannot say that it is *never* true, since it is undecidable. In fact, *never* was the answer given in 16 per cent of the responses. This particular error is descriptively termed 'denying the antecedent'. A further example is with the form $P \rightarrow Q$, $Q$, $\therefore P$, which again is not a valid deduction. One cannot say it is *always* true, although it may be true sometimes. Nevertheless, *always* accounted for 23 per cent of the responses. This error is known as 'affirming the consequent'. Finally, with *modus tollens*, having the form $P \rightarrow Q$, $\sim Q$, $\therefore \sim P$, errors were made also. The conclusion $\sim P$ is *always true*, but only 57 per cent of responses were of this type. In fact, 39 per cent of the responses were 'sometimes'.

By now, most readers will probably have begun to appreciate that it is possible to make errors with this type of statement. Why should errors be made? One likely source of error hinges upon the interpretation of the conditional statement itself. Thus $P \rightarrow Q$ means *only* that if P is the case, then Q is the case. It does not mean that if Q is the case, then P is the case. Recall that 'If John committed murder then John goes to gaol' does *not* mean that 'If John goes to gaol then John committed murder'. This unidirectional character of $Q$ following from $P$, but not vice versa, can best be captured by the 'arrow' notation $P \rightarrow Q$. This is totally different from what is known as the *biconditional*, $P \longleftrightarrow Q$. Such a relationship can only be captured in English by the rather inelegant expression 'If and only if . . .', as in 'John goes to gaol *if and only if* John committed murder'. In this case, if John goes to gaol, then he committed murder, and if John committed murder, then he goes to gaol.

Why should a subject treat $P \rightarrow Q$ as though it were $P \longleftrightarrow Q$? The answer to this is by no means decided, but one distinct possibility rests upon the way in which the problem is construed by the subject. Suppose that you are presented with a relatively meaningless statement like 'If the ball rolls left then the red light comes on'. The statement sounds very much as though I am telling you about a bidirectional relationship. I certainly have not *mentioned* any other condition which could put the red light on, although it is *logically* possible. The problem is that it is up to you to think of this possibility. But what is there to help you think of the possibility? As stated, there is only a ball and a red light to imagine, and nothing is being done to signal these other possibilities. The difficulty is that evaluating conclusions based upon conditional statements requires the consideration of possibility although possibility is seldom made clear in the problem-statement.

## 2  More difficulties with modus tollens

A fascinating series of experiments initiated by Wason (1961) and extensively explored since reveals another kind of difficulty – a failure to *apply modus tollens* in a situation where it would be sensible to do so. The tasks are generally known as four-card problems, and an early example is shown in figure 13-1. Subjects

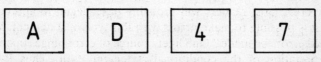

*Figure 13-1.* The Wason selection task. On the other side of a card bearing a number is a letter; on the other side of a card bearing a letter is a number. Which cards is it best to turn in order to evaluate the rule?

see four cards, as depicted in the figure, and are told that each card has a letter on one side and a number on the other. They are then set the task of determining which cards they should turn over in order to establish the truth or falsity of the following rule:

- If a card has a vowel on one side, then it has an even number on the other.

Try the task before reading the optimal solution:

It is optimal to turn over A and 7

The interesting thing about the behaviour of the majority of Wason's subjects was that they chose A and 4 in the first instance, and yet there is no way that such a combination serves to evaluate the rule. Suppose that they found an even number on the flipside of A, then this would be *consistent* with the rule. And if they found a vowel on the flipside of 4, then this too would be consistent. However, to make any logical deduction from this would be fallacious; it is the classical fallacy of *affirming the antecedent*. From a strategic point of view, it is a wasted choice. Very few subjects elected to turn over 7, which is extremely informative. For from *modus tollens*, if the flipside of 7 is a vowel, then the rule is falsified. In brief, the optimal procedure is to turn over A and 7, both of which are critical tests of the general rule. If you found this difficult, and even find the explanation difficult, then you appreciate that reasoning with these simple rules is indeed a problem.

Wason's experiment has been replicated many times, with much the same outcome. Even making it quite clear to the subjects that the biconditional interpretation is not the right one does not change the obtained pattern. In fact performance seems to be impervious to directed exhortations to work within the framework of logic (Johnson-Laird and Wason 1970). What subjects are exhibiting is a *confirmation bias*; they choose their cards in order to confirm hypotheses rather than test the possibility of rejecting them. This is an extremely important finding, and one of some generality, to which we shall return when we discuss inductive reasoning.

A related point which has been discovered through research with this task is that the apparent utilization of *modus tollens* depends upon features of the task which are irrelevant from a purely logical point of view. Consider a version of the task devised by Johnson-Laird, Legrenzi and Sonino-Legrenzi (1972). The four stimuli are shown in figure 13-2.

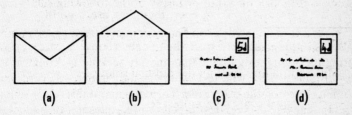

Figure 13-2.   A 'concrete' version of the selection task. To which envelopes is it best to turn in order to evaluate the rule 'If an envelope is sealed, it has a five-pence stamp on it'? *(After Johnson-Laird, Legrenzi and Sonino-Legrenzi 1972.)*

Subjects were invited to imagine that they were postal workers sorting letters on a conveyor belt. They had to test the following rule:

- If a letter is sealed, then it has a five-pence stamp on it.

Given this version of the task, many more subjects adopted the correct strategy, choosing (a) and (d). This suggests that a 'concrete' version of the selection task is somehow easier to understand, and so enables subjects to adopt the correct strategy. However, it is unclear just what 'concrete' means when used in this way, since it could mean at least two rather different things. First, it could mean that if real entities are being talked about in the problem, then in some way this facilitates performance on the task. Alternatively, it could mean that with real-life *situations*, the correct methods for testing rules relating to those situations come to mind more easily. Indeed, there is experimental work favouring the latter interpretation.

Manktelow and Evans (1979) used the following 'concrete' rule:

- If I eat beef, then I drink gin.

This version produced results no different from the original abstract version. Clearly, using familiar words rather than artificial symbols cannot explain the results with the letters and stamps.

However, note that the rule above is itself meaningless and arbitrary. On the other hand, the following rule, examined by Cox and Griggs (1982), is far from arbitrary:

- If a person is drinking beer, then they are over 18.

With *this* rule, subjects overwhelmingly choose a strategy of testing the hypothesis rather than merely seeking to 'confirm' it. For instance, they will test whether the 'under 18' card has 'drinking beer' on the other side. The point about this rule is that it is a familiar one – it relates directly to the question of underage drinking. It is quite possible that everyone who has knowledge of the underage drinking problem will have it stored in memory as a rule of this type:

- IF there are people under X years who are drinking alcohol, THEN they should stop OR sanctions may be applied.

A rule of this type embodies a procedure of *testing* for underage drinking. Now if subjects understand the Cox and Griggs problem by mapping it on to a memory rule like the one suggested above, then the consequence will be a tendency to test for the possibility of underage drinkers. This is the same thing as testing for counterexamples to the rule. If this explanation is correct, then the 'logical' behaviour of the subjects in certain concrete versions of the Wason task may follow from simple social prescription.

An elegant manipulation of the rule was used in another of Cox and Grigg's conditions, and offers some support for the argument. There is no reason to suppose that the underage drinking scenario would be invoked by the following version of the problem:

- If a person is under 18 then they are drinking coke.

Indeed, with this rule (the contrapositive of the other), subjects do not adopt a check for disconfirming instances, but behave in a similar way to those who encountered the 'abstract' version.

The upshot of this selection of studies seems to point to two important principles. First, subjects do not behave in accordance with the logical principle of seeking to falsify rules except under particular circumstances. Second, these circumstances are ones in which a normal interpretation is achieved by mapping the problem on to situation description (e.g. schema or scenario) in memory which effectively *embodies* an appropriate test procedure. Just as problem-solving procedures are determined by the initial representation of the problem, and judgement procedures are determined in the same way, so it appears to be with this particular test of logical reasoning. This will be generalized at various points in this chapter.

*Modus ponens* and *modus tollens* hold whatever p and q might be. Yet we now have substantial evidence that people do not work like a logic system. Not only does the exact form of the problem determine the strategies which subjects use, but having given a 'correct' answer to a suitable concrete problem, subjects seldom do the same thing when they later try an abstract version. In short, they do not even appear to have *learned* to transfer their knowledge of the concrete situation to a structurally identical abstract situation (Johnson-Laird, Legrenzi and Sonino-Legrenzi 1972).

## 3 Categorical syllogisms

Another type of logic task which has received attention from psychologists is the categorical two-premise syllogism. Once again, people make systematic errors which are understandable in processing terms.

A syllogism consists of two premises and a conclusion, an example being:

All As are Bs    (premise 1)
All Bs are Cs    (premise 2)
∴ All As are Cs    (conclusion).

Syllogisms dominated logic from the time of Aristotle, who extensively explored them, until the final quarter of the nineteenth century, when they were superseded by modern symbolic logic. Although they are no longer of any real importance in logic, they have generated a good deal of interest among psychologists, and still do. One might ask why. First of all, it can be argued that a good deal of reasoning has elements which are syllogistic in nature. For instance, Johnson-Laird (1983) pointed out that whenever one argues from a general to a particular, one is employing a syllogistic form:

All As are Bs
X is an A
∴  X is a B.

A second reason is that although of minor interest to the modern logician, people can have a great deal of difficulty reasoning with syllogisms. Is the following syllogism, for instance, valid?

Some Bs are As
No Cs are Bs
Some As are not Cs.

Presumably the greater difficulty associated with this syllogism results from an increase in the number of mental operations which have to be carried out, and/or the complexity of the operations. This is indeed the case, and an analysis of errors and times taken to deal with different syllogisms is illuminating from the point of view of psychological process models.

Syllogisms are also reasonably small in number. This results from the fact that only four quantificational forms are used, namely *All As are Bs*; *No As are Bs*; *Some As are Bs*; and *Some As are not Bs*. The quantifiers are the terms, *all, no, some* and *not*. Other quantifiers would be *most, few, many, nearly all*, etc. These are more complex and are not used. Each premise can take one of these forms. The two premises can be combined in a number of ways to yield *four figures*, in which the order of the terms (A and B in the present example) are assembled:

| A——B | A——B | B——A | B——A |
| B——C | C——B | B——C | C——B |

The net outcome of these combinational possibilities is a total of 256 syllogisms, which is the number usually quoted in logic books. However, as Johnson-Laird has pointed out, from the point of view of syllogisms as *stimuli to be processed*, there are exactly twice this number. For while logically the following are equivalent, from a processing point of view they need not be:

| A——B | B——C |
| B——C | A——B |

The psychological total is therefore 512 meaningful premise-combinations. Of these, only *54* yield valid conclusions; the remainder are undecidable. Psychologists have therefore used syllogisms as a defined and logically well-understood domain in which to investigate deductive reasoning. Much of the interest stems from two types of problem facing the person doing the reasoning:

(a)  The representation of simple quantified statements.
(b)  The problems inherent in combining premises.

In the terms we have been using up to now, (a) corresponds to setting up a mental model of each of the premises, while (b) corresponds to forming *integrated* mental models. As we shall see, each pose their own special difficulties.

Dealing with quantification is one of the major difficulties which people have with syllogisms, and one way to illustrate this is through Euler's diagrammatic method. Figure 13-3 shows Euler's diagrams for each of four possible statements of the form A–B. For instance, the statement 'All As are Bs' can be represented as all As falling within the set of Bs, but the set of Bs being larger, or as the set of As and Bs as being identical. For 'No As are Bs', there is only one possibility. For 'Some As are Bs', there are no less than four possibilities!

It will be obvious at once that the logical interpretation of quantifiers includes everything that they could *possibly* denote. For instance, the interpretation of 'Some As are Bs' includes the possibility that 'All As are Bs'. Thus one possible source of error in reasoning about syllogisms might lie in the failure to think of all the representational possibilities associated with quantified statements.

What mental representations might be set up when a person encounters the premise 'Some As are Bs'? Johnson-Laird (1983) has argued that people might well set up mental tokens for 'some As', an arbitrary number, in some mental workspace, and attach some of these to an arbitrary number of Bs. An illustration, using his notation, is shown below:

```
(A)
(A)
A————————B
A————————B
A————————B
A————————B
           (B)
           (B)
```

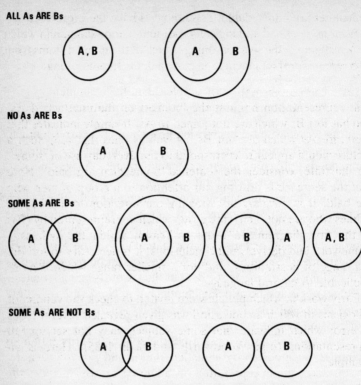

**ALL As ARE Bs**

**NO As ARE Bs**

**SOME As ARE Bs**

**SOME As ARE NOT Bs**

*Figure 13-3.* Euler's circle diagrams showing the possible relations between As and Bs for four premise types. There are no less than four (logical) possibilities for some As are Bs!

This representation indicates three things:

(a)   A number of As which are Bs.
(b)   A number of As ... (A) ... which are *not* Bs. The brackets denote the *possibility* of these.
(c)   A number of Bs which are *not* As.

The symbols denote the tokens in working memory, and this first figure indicates *all* of the possibilities associated with 'Some As are Bs'. It depicts the *mental model* of a subject who appreciates the full range of possibility associated with 'some'. Suppose a subject was not well-versed in the logical use of 'some'. What kind of representation might this yield? Using the same notation, something like this might occur:

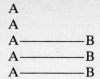

```
A
A
A———————B
A———————B
A———————B
```

This representation has lost the brackets on the unattached As, and has lost Bs which are not joined to As. It simply indicates that there are As which are not Bs, as well as ones that are. Such a picture would appear to correspond to our everyday use of 'some'. To illustrate, consider the sentence 'Some men are bald'. Note that the sentence is drawing our attention to a group of men who are bald. It is *certainly* not drawing our attention to a group of baldies who are not men – the group which are represented by (B)s in the first diagram. In order to reason within the syllogistic framework and derive valid conclusions, it is necessary to use the full range of possibilities, and not a smaller range which is more applicable to natural language.

Early work in which people were invited to check the validity of syllogisms in which a conclusion was given revealed several types of error which indicate that some subjects may not set up full representations (e.g. Woodworth and Sells 1935). Here is an example:

Some As are Bs
Some Bs are Cs
──────────────
∴    Some As are Cs

This is invalid, and yet occurs as a not infrequent error. It can be understood if subjects have a mental representation which is of a restricted type.

Premise 1 yields:
```
    A
    A
    A———————B
    A———————B
    A———————B
```
Premise 2 yields:
```
    B
    B———————C
    B———————C
```

Combining both premises could yield:

```
A
A
A————————B
A————————B————————C
A————————B————————C
```

From this mental model, it is indeed the case that 'Some As are Cs'.

How would a fuller representation yield the conclusion that the conclusion is *not* valid? In precisely the same mechanical way.

Premise 1 yields:

```
(A)
(A)
A————————B
A————————B
A————————B
         (B)
         (B)
         (B)
```

Premise 2 yields:

```
(B)
(B)
B————————C
B————————C
B————————C
B————————C
         (C)
         (C)
```

These can be combined in a variety of ways, *one* of which is:

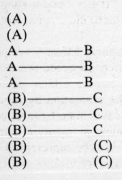

```
(A)
(A)
A————————B
A————————B
A————————B
(B)——————C
(B)——————C
(B)——————C
(B)      (C)
(B)      (C)
```

In this model, a situation is depicted in which 'Some As are Cs' is false. Because this falsity is *possible*, the conclusion cannot be validly deduced.

Let us take stock. First of all, we have introduced a notational format, Johnson-Laird's, in which premises are represented as simple strings between tokens. Secondly, we have shown how an everyday interpretation of 'some' can produce erroneous conclusions with a relatively simple syllogism. Let us call this the 'linguistic' explanation, because it is based on how language is normally used (Sanford 1983).

In the work of Woodworth and Sells (1935), the error made above was called an 'atmosphere effect'. The argument made was that the terms *some, all*, and *no* created an 'atmosphere' which somehow predisposed subjects to accept a conclusion using the same terms. The general argument runs as follows: If premise 1 contains *All* and 2 contains *All*, it predisposes an *All* conclusion. For instance:

All As are Bs
All Cs are Bs
_____

∴    All As are Cs          (false)

Some subjects make the error of accepting this. A similar argument applies to a quantification giving premise 1 = some, premise 2 = some, yielding the error discussed earlier. Things are slightly more complex when the expressions are mixed. For instance, Woodworth and Sells argue that a negative conclusion is preferred if negative and positive premises are mixed, and that they would prefer a particular conclusion (some) when a particular premise is mixed with a general (all) premise. In fact, what subjects appear to display is 'caution'. It has been argued that accepting a particular conclusion is less 'extreme' than accepting a general conclusion.

A full-blown discussion of the Atmosphere Effect is not necessary for this brief introduction, and readers are recommended the original Woodworth and Sells (1935) paper, a later paper by Chapman and Chapman (1959), and the evaluation by Johnson-Laird (1983). Let us simply note one or two main features of the atmosphere explanation. First, it is somewhat vague in that it is not particularly clear how 'atmosphere' is to be represented. This is in contrast to the linguistic explanation which is clear about what the representations might be, and can explain the origins of the errors which it predicts. Secondly, the atmosphere effect simply does not explain how subjects come to be able to reason validly. For instance, fewer subjects will accept the following invalid syllogism than accept the valid one:

| | |
|---|---|
| All As are Bs | Some As are Bs |
| Some Bs are Cs | All Bs are Cs |
| ∴   Some As are Cs | ∴   Some As are Cs |
|      (invalid) |      (valid) |

As Johnson-Laird (1983) points out, according to the atmosphere explanation, there should not really be any difference in acceptability. The fact that there is a difference highlights the fact that the atmosphere explanation cannot differentiate valid from invalid performance. Neither the linguistic nor the atmosphere explanation can explain this difference. What is needed is a fuller theory which is at once capable of capturing valid reasoning, as well as pinpointing the processes which might yield errors. We shall now turn to one such theory, due to Johnson-Laird and Steedman (1978; Johnson-Laird 1983).

In their theory, the main aspect upon which the authors concentrated was the difficulty of combining representations of premises. As we have noted already, if the premises are adequately represented, it is still possible to draw false conclusions by combining premises in a limited way. What is required is a means of combining fully represented premises in a way which distinguishes what is *necessary* in the representation from what is merely possible. A conclusion is deductively valid only if it is necessary. In terms of the representations which we have been using (due entirely to Johnson-Laird and Steedman), the two premise representations have to be reconfigured over and over until *either* exhaustion of possibilities occurs or until a particular conclusion is discovered as not necessary. Johnson-Laird and Steedman concentrated on the difficulties of doing this. The basic points are that some premise-pairs allow more configurations than others, while some premise-pairs are inherently difficult to combine. Both factors lead to various premise-pairs varying in difficulty, and hence to a range of performance across syllogisms. The details of the combinational difficulties lead to errors of predictable kinds creeping in if subjects do not complete an exhaustive combination. To investigate these phenomena, Johnson-Laird and Steedman required subjects to say what valid conclusions, if any, followed from a large set of premise-pairs. Johnson-Laird (1983) describes the various configurations as *mental models*, and we shall use this terminology too.

Consider the following illustration and analysis, described by Johnson-Laird (1975), based on the syllogism:

Some As are Bs
All Cs are Bs
_____

The question is, what valid conclusion, if any, can be drawn. Some As are Bs has a full representation like this:

A————————B
A————————B
(A)          (B)
(A)          (B)

Suppose a person sets up this mental model. What is next required is to map the second premise on to this structure. Suppose the following mapping were made:

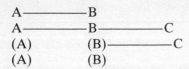

A————————B
A————————B————————C
(A)          (B)————————C
(A)          (B)

This conforms to the pattern of the premises, but because the mappings proceed in different directions, subjects using such a representation would be divided in concluding *Some As are Cs* and *Some Cs are As*. Both of these are, in fact, invalid. The step for testing validity consists of trying to form a model in which new mappings of the second premise are made so that the tokens are no longer linked to tokens of the first premise which are involved in the extant mapping. This is possible:

A————————B
A————————B
(A)          (B)————————C
(A)          (B)————————C

Because the critical link has been broken, the previous conclusion is not a *necessary* one, and so inductively *invalid*. The correct conclusion is, therefore, *No conclusion follows*. In an experiment, Johnson-Laird obtained the following results from twenty subjects given this problem:

| | |
|---|---|
| Some As are Cs | 5/20 |
| Some Cs are As | 5/20 |
| No conclusion follows | 9/20 |

Now compare this with the syllogism:

Some As are Bs
All Bs are Cs

In this case, there is no problem in forming the following model:

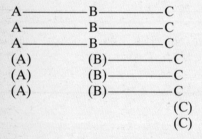

However the model is played with, it is possible to read off the conclusion *Some As are Cs*, which is valid. However, notice that it is *equally* valid to conclude *Some Cs are As*. While Johnson-Laird's subjects rightly conclude the former, none of them concludes the latter.

It is this kind of asymmetry which is at the heart of Johnson-Laird's model. Representations are assumed to be *read in the order in which they enter working memory*. Thus if the input order was A–B, B–C, then the conclusion will take the form A–C. If the input order was A–B, C–B, then the conclusion will be divided between A–C and C–A.

There are many other features in Johnson-Laird and Steedman's (1978) account, and the basic strategy was to consider the amount of model manipulation necessary to reach a conclusion with each type of syllogism. By going through model manipulations systematically, it was possible to specify (a) The *order* of terms in the conclusions; (b) The kinds of errors made if subjects stop manipulating models at various points; and (c) The difficulty encountered and the time taken in manipulating the models. By and large, the predictions of the model fitted the data quite well. Johnson-Laird (1983) compares this particular account with various others – for instance, that people might manipulate 'Euler circles' in their heads. The following very simple three-premise syllogism illustrates the inadequacy of this plausible alternative:

    Some As are Bs
    All Bs are Cs
    All Cs are Ds

As Johnson-Laird (1975) points out, this would involve $4 \times 2 \times 2 = 16$ different combinations of diagram, which would be computationally very complex, while the list-of-tokens structure is:

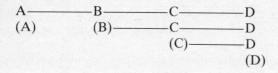

This is computationally simpler. While the Euler manipulation theory would predict great difficulty, Johnson-Laird's, correctly, does not.

Johnson-Laird's theory, and the discussions using his list notation before it, exemplify the idea of mental-model manipulation. Thinking about logic problems, like any other kind of problem-solving, can be understood as the manipulation of mental models. In the present case, the formation of a logical conclusion depends upon testing all of the possibilities associated with the combination of a premise-pair. If this is not done exhaustively, the result is unlikely to fit the rules of logic. If it is, the results *do* fit the rules of logic. Although the manipulations conform to psychological and computational 'rules', there is really no difference in *kind* between manipulations which result in a conclusion being 'the logical one', and a conclusion being illogical.

Work with the syllogism thus focuses on the adequacy of

representation of the quantifications in the premises and on the adequacy of subsequent combination. At both points, it is possible to use inadequate representations. Yet whether subjects answer correctly or incorrectly, the underlying mechanisms are assumed to be the same. To be logical, subjects must *know* how quantifiers are used in logic, and must apply an exhaustive manipulation principle. But even if subjects know that they should do this, limitations on working memory may prevent them from recognizing cases where they have not achieved this goal.

## B Relevant domains, mental models and interpretation

In section A, we reviewed a range of experiments and situations which relate to circumstances defining the likelihood of making valid and invalid inferences in simple logic problems. To some extent, this is a reasonable yardstick against which to evaluate the efficacy of people's thinking. There is no doubt that if people draw conclusions that do not conform to what has been discovered in logic as a discipline, then their conclusions will catch up with them. In particular, the careful analysis of arguments and implications which people make and suggest is extremely important in understanding the world at large.

The analysis above identified two different sorts of problems which might occur in dealing with logic puzzles:

  (i)   The initial representation of the problem. If this is inappropriate relative to the formal logical meaning of the problem, then the conclusions drawn will almost certainly not conform to the logically valid conclusion.

  (ii)  The manipulation of the mental model which is the subject's representation of the problem. For instance, with syllogisms, if the model is not exhaustively tested, then there is a possibility of drawing or accepting an invalid conclusion. However, a person may *be aware of this*, which is tantamount to knowing the logical principle to apply, but still fall short by losing track of whether every possibility has in fact been checked.

         Furthermore, if the problem is put in such a way that alternatives are not obvious, then this will, of course, reduce the chances of spotting an alternative.

Up to now, most of the experiments described have used university undergraduates as subjects. In general, such students at least realize that the logic problems which they are asked to solve are hypothetical, and that they should concentrate on what is in the problem itself and not relate it to 'irrelevant' outside experience. But less well-educated people do not do this, and even well-educated subjects can be caught out in the same way. The main point is that whether one sees an argument as logical or not depends crucially upon one's conception of the problem, and the mental model thus formed.

Some years ago, the Vai people of Liberia entered into an extensive programme of national education. Psychologists and anthropologists were obviously attracted by the possibility of seeing what happened to people's ways of thinking under the educational regime. Scribner (1977) reported on a number of such studies. In one case, uneducated Vai farmers were asked the following:

- All people who own houses pay house tax.
  Boima does not pay house tax.
  Does Boima own a house?

In answering 'Yes' (incorrect, of course), one subject reasoned that Boima was exempt from paying house tax because he was appointed to collect it! The point is that the subject was thinking *outside* of the hypothetical world specified in the question, and drawing on his own experience. Another subject answered 'No' (correct), but reasoned that he could not own a house if he did not pay house tax *as demanded by the Liberian government*. His correct answer was based on evidence from beyond the problem again.

A final example makes a similar point more dramatically:

- All Kpelle men are rice farmers.
  Mr Smith is not a rice farmer.
  Is he a Kpelle man?

One subject, despite exhortation, claimed that it was undecidable because he did not know Mr Smith personally.

Such importation of the seemingly irrelevant is by no means restricted to Vai and Kpelle peoples. Some years back the author was carrying out research on decision-making in the elderly, and used this as a problem:

- Mr Jones mends television sets. When a set comes in broken, the fault can lie in three different parts of the set: tuner, tube or amplifier. Over the years, Mr Jones noticed that the parts differed in reliability, so that faults occurred in tuners 10 per cent of the time, amplifiers 60 per cent of the time and tubes 30 per cent of the time. If a set breaks down, which part should Mr Jones spend time checking first?

Although many of my elderly subjects straight away recommended that the amplifier be checked first, which is the optimal choice, few did not do so initially. One subject volunteered, 'He should get Mr MacKay. I always do when my set goes wrong'. This was not a joke, neither was the subject demented; in fact, when pushed just to solve the problem she got it right with no difficulty.

These illustrations from home and abroad show problem-solving which does not fit the logic of the problem. The solutions are wrong, given the premises, or are irrelevant. But that is not to say that the subjects are not behaving rationally. Thus Scribner points out with her Vai and Kpelle examples that subjects seem to import extra premises, and make *valid deductions* based on these. The process of education serves to reduce the tendency to import knowledge into the problem, and to focus the subjects, whoever they are, on the content of the problem as stated.

The point is a simple one. As it stands, there is no evidence that primitive cultures are made up of people who do not think logically, if by logic we mean draw valid conclusions in simple situations. Rather, the fact that such people do not conform to the 'rules of the game' simply means that the mental model which they use in relation to the task is not the one tacitly required by those rules. In many ways, the situation is the same as that of a naïve student starting logic, who fails to realize that the rules of the game demand no less than four possible interpretations of the word 'some'. However, to maintain such a view, it appears necessary to assume that when people attempt a problem, the first thing they do is to identify a memory structure. In earlier chapters, a considerable amount of evidence has been presented for such a point of view. In the case of logic problems like those discussed in this chapter, the principal necessary memory structures are (i) knowing that in logic problems, the expressions used in syllogisms are hypothetical, and (usually) have no real-world referents; (ii) knowing how quantifiers are treated, and that natural-language interpretations are not adequate; and (iii) knowing how to distinguish possibility from necessity.

As a coda, contrast this requirement with what has to happen when the following piece of discourse is understood:

- The Southern General Hospital treats all of the head injuries in the West of Scotland. Mary was admitted at 5.00 a.m.

It is obvious that no-one would say such a thing unless they meant that Mary had a head injury. Yet deductively, of course, such a conclusion is unwarranted. It should scarcely surprise us if language descriptions engender normal-language interpretations rather than strictly logical evaluations.

## C  Hypotheses and investigations

Science, and other forms of carefully controlled observation, comprise a class of methods which have shown great dividends in the development of mankind. One important method in science is that of inductive reasoning. Observations made on nature are scrutinized for orderliness, for some sort of rule, and such rules are then formulated as hypotheses. Our interest here is in how such hypotheses are tested.

Relationships between observables are of prime importance in everyday life, as well as in science, and in section 2, we shall look at the procedures which statistically naïve subjects employ in drawing inferences from observables. As elsewhere, much of the analysis will be in terms of mental models.

### 1  The logic of hypotheses and rationality

Inductive problems form an extremely important problem-type. Inductive reasoning occurs whenever one spots a rule or commonality between a number of things. An example is the kind of puzzle in which one guesses which number comes next in a series, e.g. 1, 3, 5, 7 . . . ? (Wason 1960). Of course, the answer *need not* be 9, but it is reasonable to suppose that it is.

Scientific and quasi-scientific enquiry constitutes another good example. In many cases, given a set of observations, or a set of data, an *explanation* of them will be given in terms of a *hypothesis*, which will be based upon some observed regularities in the data. Part of the hypothesis will be some sort of description of these regularities. The uncertain nature of induction can be easily illustrated in this way: the hypothesis is based on n observations, or pieces of data, say. If the hypothesis is useful, one would expect that observation n + 1 would conform to the rule. If it does not, either the rule is wrong, or the observation includes some additional variable which might explain the mismatch. These alternatives are, of course, a major source of difficulty in science.

In science, hypotheses are developed on the basis of data, and are then tested in novel situations. What strategies are available for doing this? The logical structure of a hypothesis is usually considered in the now familiar form IF p THEN q, i.e. IF hypothesis H is correct, THEN it will predict q under a new set of circumstances. What is notable about this is that we already know that q might result from mechanisms other than those embodied in H. Take a simple group 2, 4, 6, and ask yourself how you might set about discovering the rule which generated this set. You might guess at 'ascending consecutive even numbers'. How would you now *test* this hypothesis. One way is called the *confirmatory strategy*: generate a new sequence which fits your theory, and see if the sequence is indeed a member of the set. For instance, you may produce 4, 6, 8, and I will say 'yes', confirming your theory. The flaw in this should be obvious. Suppose you were wrong in your hypothesis, and the set was generated by the rule 'any ascending series of numbers'. The way to test a hypothesis is to seek *counterexamples*. Such a strategy is rational for a number of reasons. First, disconfirmatory instances are informative in a way which confirmatory instances are not. For example, the sequence 1, 3, 5, if produced, would generate a 'yes' also. This would immediately eliminate any explanation based upon even numbers. Similarly, a test with 4, 6, 10 would immediately eliminate any explanation based on consecutive evenness. Confirming instances simply fit the established rule.

Peter Wason (1960; 1968) and his associates have in fact carried out a number of studies using the simple sequence 2, 4, 6. Subjects were invited to test their hypotheses by generating sequences, and were told whether they were not consonant with the rule. When they felt sufficiently confident, they were to announce the rule which they had. His results showed an overwhelming tendency for subjects to use a confirmation strategy. He established this by starting in the subject's protocol at an announced rule, and looking back over the series which they generated, checking whether each series fitted or did not fit the rule. The use of the confirmation strategy was plainly indicated.

Similar results have been found in other studies, cited by Wason (1977). For instance, Penrose (1962) used a form of inverted 'Twenty Questions' as a task. One person thought of a logical class (e.g. *living things*) and gave an initial example (e.g. *a Siamese cat*). The person guessing had to produce instances of things, and were told either that they were or were not members of the logical class. Seven of the ten subjects who took part announced one or more incorrect class, and 87 per cent of the instances which they produced confirmed their hypotheses. The remaining three announced the correct class without announcing any incorrect ones, producing 47 per cent confirming instances. All of the instances generated by successful subjects, which did not fit a hypothesis, led to a change in hypothesis.

From a global point of view, such behaviour is suboptimal, breaking a simple rational rule of enquiry. It is precisely the same problem as that observed with the four-card task discussed earlier. And, as with the four-card task, it is quite possible to get subjects to change strategies as a result of changes in the form of the problem. Thus Thompson (1962) used the series 7, 5, 3 with instructions to discover what relation must exist for a test series *not* to conform to the rule. Wetherick (1962) presented the series 4, 2, 6, and invited his subjects to discover what the rule was. In both cases, there was a slight trend towards adopting a strategy of disconfirmation. In Wetherick's case, using 4, 2, 6 would alert subjects to the possibility of order being relevant, and it is perhaps unsurprising that subjects tended to begin with negative series. In a far more complex simulated scientific task Mynatt, Doherty and Tweney (1977) also observed strong confirmatory behaviour, although they did note that subjects could understand the *logic* of falsification.

Why should people adopt a confirmatory strategy? It is difficult to say with such very simple situations as these. Wason draws a parallel with the 'set' phenomena of problem-solving, such as functional fixedness, but this hardly qualifies as an explanation in cognitive science. It could be argued that the strategy transfers from more complex real-life situations. The first step in understanding is to form a mental model, and essentially this consists of putting together bits and pieces of information into a related whole. According to this point of view, it is impossible to think about something without such a model, but getting one together is equivalent to searching for information which fits, rather than information which does not, in the first instance. While in one sense confirmatory instances are not informative, they do at least provide additional explicit mappings between generated sequences and the model which is computationally capable of generating them. Sanford (1983; also chapter 12) has suggested an account which purports to explain such phenomena; confirming instances enrich the explicit representations, and these are supposed (on this account) to dominate working memory, reducing the chance of thinking of alternatives, and leading to a positive feedback cycle which reinforces the current explanation.

The development of theories in science will of course entail the assembly of even more complex arrays of information. The *consistency* and specificity of scientific theories is arguably as important as *testing* them at this level. Consider what might happen with a theory which was not sufficiently developed to make exact predictions. Regardless of outcome, many experiments could be viewed as 'broadly consistent' with the theory. The difficulty is nicely illustrated in a study carried out by Mitroff and Mason (1974). Prior to the Apollo moon-mission series, selections were made among NASA scientists of who should receive samples of moonrock for scientific purposes. The scientists were questioned about various matters, including how the scientists believed the results of moonrock analysis could change their theories. Later, when the moonrock studies were over, they were questioned about how their views *had* changed. Changes were very minor, compared to prior assessments, and the more eminent the scientist, or more fundamental the problem, the smaller the change! Of course, science is a sociological as well as an individually based phenomenon. Although individual scientists may hold on to their carefully developed hypotheses, alternatives will be represented too. In the social group, many hypotheses may be held and presented.

## 2 Hypotheses, data and magic

We now turn to a number of questions which are related to the confirmation bias. Consider the question of the relations between a symptom and a disease. Smedslund (1963) presented a number of Swedish nurses with a pack of a hundred cards supposedly representing excerpts from the medical files of a hundred patients. Each card indicated the presence or absence of a disease and the presence or absence of a symptom. The totals, cast as a contingency table, are shown in table 13-1.

Table 13-1.  The number of cases associated with the presence/absence of symptoms and disease. Subjects tend to take cell (a) into account above all else when assessing correlations.

|  |  | Disease | |
|  |  | Present | Absent |
| Symptoms | Present | (a) 37 | (b) 33 |
|  | Absent | (c) 17 | (d) 13 |

*(From Smedslund 1963)*

Eighty-five per cent of the nurses claimed that there was a relationship between disease and symptom, the predominant justification being that cell *a* was 'the largest or was large'. Of course, the nurses were naïve about statistics, but it indicates the high confidence that is placed in the results from cell *a*.

In a similar study, Ward and Jenkins (1965) presented similar contingency information about the relationship between cloud-seeding and rainfall. The predominant judgement was based upon a confirmatory strategy, using the number of seed-rain days *and* the number of no seed-no rain days, ignoring the other two cells of the contingency table. This result was particularly marked if the information was presented serially, when only 17 per cent of the students showed correlational thinking. Little improvement was achieved by presenting the full contingency table at the end. However, by *just* presenting the full table, most of the students did show correlational thinking. Thus people can think correlationally, if they have been trained, but normally do not do so. Of course, in everyday life, contingency evidence usually comes to us on a piecemeal basis.

The picture painted by these data is now familiar. People attend to supporting evidence for some theory, rather than evidence which denies it. This tendency appears to prevent correlational thinking, although to readers of this book, correlational thinking should appear to be a natural way of looking at things. But beware. Correlation requires considering all four cells of the matrix.

One is tempted to seek an explanation based on the requirements of mental-model construction. In order to make a judgement, one must have a mental model. The simplest model for a correlation notion begins with the relationship between A and B, say. If one notices many beautiful people who also are clever, then one might wish to test this relationship. Simple enumeration of examples fitting is logically insufficient to serve as data, but as argued above, simple enumeration can provide a very coherent model. Suppose now that one realizes that disconfirmation might be important. The most obvious disconfirmatory evidence is As that are not Bs, following the simple principle discussed above, in which As are what the thinking is *about*, and Bs are some *property* of A. Non-Bs that are not As is the most unlikely combination to be considered on this theory, the arguments being the same as those presented for thinking about syllogisms. In short, setting up a relational model in which the alternative structures are exhaustively explored is as necessary for adopting the right strategy in correlation as it is in the adopting the right strategy for solving syllogisms.

According to the general point of view developed in the last few chapters, in thinking about a relationship, the first thing which is done is to form a simple mapping between the elements being thought about. Forming such a mapping requires some means of bringing the two elements together. Simple connecting assertions can often be made plausible by elaboration. The notion of elaboration is of course bound up with notions of causation. Johnson-Laird and Wason (1977) suggest the following sequence describes most people's reasoning, most of the time:

- *A* resembles *B*
  *A* tends to be associated with *B*

This claim can be justified on an number of grounds. The work of Kahneman and Tversky on representativeness is just one illustration; in general, such a relationship could accrue from a system attempting to make mappings. For instance, in schema theory, if a description $A$ resembles a *part* of schema $B$, then A will be associated with $B$.

The second part of Johnson-Laird and Wason's reasoning chain is this:

- If $A$ tends to be associated with $B$
  and $A$ occurs before $B$
  then $A$ causes $B$.

It has been argued that through such an inference chain, *magical* beliefs come about. Indeed, Johnson-Laird argues that the same mechanism will explain how a variety of magical beliefs come about, including some in modern society like the belief that penicillin is good for curing throat infections.

Unfortunately, we do not have the space to pursue this line further, but it is the case that investigations of how we interpret and misinterpret everyday events in the world are growing in number, and becoming a very important aspect of the study of thinking. The reader is recommended the very important collection of articles in Kahneman, Slovic and Tversky (1982).

## D  Summary and comments

In the present chapter we considered first of all how people solve simple problems involving logical reasoning. It is undeniable that logic problems are just as much problem-solving as any other sort of puzzle. We showed how success by the criterion of the rules of formal logic depends upon having the right model of each of the elements of the problem, and exhaustively checking the ways of forming alternative models. Such manipulations have to take place within the known constraints of memory and search, and there are ample opportunities for failure. Even if we know what we should do (e.g. if one understands the mental-model argument), doing it can be very difficult indeed.

The same arguments apply to gathering evidence, and the strategies used in gathering evidence. While it may be logical to seek alternatives, in practice people tend to try to prove the truth of what they have. This is wrong, but is arguably understandable. Even in cases where people do adopt disconfirmation procedures, these can often be attributed to the kind of knowledge which they use in understanding a problem, rather than because they map the problem on to a form-free logical procedure.

The idea that education changes the way in which people think about problems, including logic problems, seems to be justified experimentally. There is no good evidence that 'primitive cultures' produce magical, pre-logical minds which differ in the procedures available for thinking, only that without experience of problem domains, the rules of the game themselves will not be known (see Johnson-Laird and Wason (1977)) for a full discussion of the role of culture on thinking, and also Cole (1975).

Logic as a discipline does have results which are applicable to the everyday world, and knowing the results of such studies can, of course, help in the conduct of one's life, the validity of one's arguments, and so on. But the mere fact that what seem like the simplest of these results have to be continuously reasserted, shows that they are not an automatic way of thinking. In thinking, it is perhaps better to speak of 'applying logical principles' rather than 'thinking logically', since the former clearly implies the act of constraining the manipulation of mental models to stay within the demands of some logical system, while the latter implies some sort of 'mental logic'. For more discussion of this issue, along with a very full account of many of the problems described in this chapter, see Johnson-Laird (1983).

# 14 Thinking 4 : Visual imagination and imagery

## A  Representations, computation and models

Up to this point, we have concentrated in the main upon what we might term 'abstract' representations. The symbolic structures of propositions, schemata, scripts, etc., are a convenient means of describing theories of memory and knowledge organization. Of course, if we look into the brain, no matter how powerful our microscope, we will not see propositions or schemata in the forms in which we have described them. Memory will be coded bio-chemically and neurally. This is not to say that the representation-al formats described up to now are *wrong* in principle. They are simply means of saying what the *organization* of memory might be like, and what kind of necessary information must be present in memory. As is often the case, a computational analogy is useful.

## 1  Descriptive devices and processing representations

At one level – the level of electronics – everything that happens in a digital computer can be described in terms of the physical states of the components which can either be in *one* single state, or another *single* state. The two states are concerned with the electromagnetic condition of the component. Because it can be in two states, we can symbolically represent the states by assigning to them the symbols 0 and 1. Computer programs can be written at that level. Each time a 0 or a 1 is entered into a computer when progamming in this way (called 'binary programming'), the keys for 0s and 1s send electrical signals to the appropriate units in the computer, and 'set' the values of the units to the appropriate physical state. This is, of course, a gross oversimplification, but the

point is that there *are* no 0s and 1s in the machine, only states
which we *call* 0s and 1s for convenience.

Programming machines in this way is terribly inconvenient. One
has to first translate the problem one is trying to solve by computer
into the primitive logical operations possible within the binary
framework (called 'Boolean Operations'). One convenient step is
to treat the long strings of 0s and 1s as *groups*, and arrange for the
machine to interpret these groups. Groups of three are convenient, because each possible pattern of three binary digits can be
assigned a number from 0 to 7, viz:

$$000 = 0 \quad 100 = 4$$
$$001 = 1 \quad 101 = 5$$
$$010 = 2 \quad 110 = 6$$
$$011 = 3 \quad 111 = 7$$

Programming in *this* format, called 'octal programming' is very
much easier: one might enter 1674 instead of 001110111100! But
of course, just as the computer does not contain 0s and 1s, so it
does not contain the octal digits 0–7. Really, it only contains
electrical activity.

By the same logic, octal digits are inconvenient to think with.
The step taken to get around this is called 'symbolic' programming
(though using numbers is of course symbolic in a sense). Symbolic
programming allows words, expressions and numbers to be used in
programs. The following is a sample of BASIC:

```
10      X = 3
20      Y = 4
30      Z = X + Y
40      PRINT 'THE ANSWER IS' Z
```

Unsurprisingly, this program prints THE ANSWER IS 7. All
that has happened here is that the symbols X, Y, 3, 4, Z, =, +,
PRINT, ', etc. put in from the keyboard have been translated into
the primitive physical states within the machine. In fact, this is a
technically complex process, but is not a mystery. Remember that
when you press a key on the keyboard with 'X' on it, all that
happens is that a particular *electronic* signal enters the machine,
'X' does not enter it.

Readers who are familiar with all of this will perhaps excuse the digression. It is important because it can be used to make some straightforward arguments about representation in human beings. When we say a person has a 'verb'-schema stored in memory, and illustrate it as a network, of course we are not saying that the typographical format shown in our figures is stored in the brain. What are 'stored' in the brain are electrochemical states and interconnected neurones, not words, arrows and the like. A schema representation (and propositions, frames, etc.) serves a very different scientific function.

Suppose that you are writing a program in some simple symbolic computer language, and say that the program is designed to do calculations on the data which you are putting in, and store the results. Suppose that when you write the program, you allocate enough memory space for the job of storing twenty three-digit answers. At the end of the program run, the machine reads off these three-digit numbers from the memory. Everything is fine unless you have data which require storage of *forty* three-digit answers. At this point, you would have to reconsider your program, and either arrange for a printout in the middle, or rewrite it to allocate more memory space.

This is a trivially simple example, but can be used to make a point about schemata. We could *represent* the twenty value space as a schema, as shown in figure 14-1.

Of course this schema does not exist in this form in the machine.

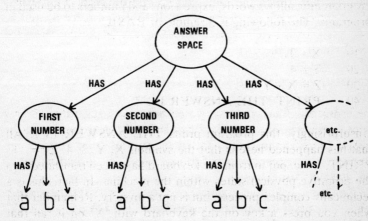

*Figure 14-1.* Part of a schema for an ordered answer space of twenty three-digit numbers, showing only basic relationships. a, b, c are variables that can take digit values.

Rather, the schema indicates an aspect of the *organization* that has been imposed on computer memory by you as a programmer. The schema is entirely symbolic. The same argument holds for schemata, propositions, scripts and the like. They only *represent* the purported organization of information in the brain. In fact, the analogy is quite complete. Notice that 'answer table', 'slot N', and 'digit slot N' are all written in circles. We assume that there is some primitive level within the machine at which these 'subschemata' have an electronic embodiment.

The representations discussed in earlier chapters only indicate a putative organization of data structures, but as has been extensively argued, such organizational questions are central to an understanding of what processes happen easily and quickly, and which are slow or difficult, they are central to an understanding of which processes *have* to go together with other processes, and they are a central aspect of how memory itself is put together – what kind of things go with what.

## 2  Propositions as descriptions of non-linguistic representations

The discussion above illustrates the way in which a schema is an abstraction – it is a way of saying which process or data in memory go with what, and how the different data and processes relate to one another. Much the same can be said of 'proposition'-based theories of sentence representation. If Kintsch asserts, as well he might, that it is psychologically meaningful to represent 'John the dustman drove the cart' as

(DUSTMAN, JOHN) & (DRIVE, JOHN, CART)

he is asserting that we have two *memory units*, regardless of how these units are represented in the hardware (or 'wetware') of the brain. Propositions, claim Kintsch and various other workers, are convenient representations for expressing the organization of mental data structures.

As used in cognitive psychology, propositions have the appearance of natural language expressions. (LOVES, MARY, JOHN) is not all that different from 'Mary loves John'. Indeed, when we look at how language expressions might be broken up into units which we understand, propositions seem to be a good way of representing things. But what of other objects of interest to psychologists, such as the representation of a square, or a face, or a visual scene? At first sight, it seems unlikely that propositions will be very much use there. Yet such a representation has been posited as useful for the description of shapes and scenes (Baylor 1971; Winston 1970; Palmer 1975).

Consider the exercise of describing a square propositionally. A square can be defined as four points in space, arranged in a certain way. Each point is described by co-ordinate values in cartesian space, and then lines can be described in terms of connexions between these points. All of the part-whole relations in the cube can be described in the same way.

There are various aspects of this argument to which the reader's attention should be drawn. First of all, using this sort of representation, it is a straightforward matter to specify operations by which objects can be *rotated*, so that it is possible to say what they would look like from various angles. Indeed, if we use such a representation, and change the values of the co-ordinate of the key *points* of the display incrementally, so that they match the desired direction of rotation, then it is possible to display representations of objects moving about in space. There are many demonstrations of this to be seen in television adverts and in television science programmes. Computer rotations of objects are invariably achieved by operating upon essentially discrete descriptions which are used by the machine in the specification of those illuminated parts of a screen which depict an object. A simple illustration of this is simulating the movement of an object – say a filled-in square – across the screen of a computer. The square, at its starting position, could be described as n illuminated points on the screen, each with a specified position. To move horizontally, all one has to do is increment the x value of every point defining the square successively along the x axis value, until one reaches the other side. If point p is at Loc (5, 10), then it can be moved to Loc (5, 11), and so on.

It would appear as though we can *describe* visual structures, and movements, in propositional terms, or as changes in the values of arguments of propositions. In this way, propositions are not to be equated with descriptions of just verbal phenomena, but are a rather more general format for representing information of any kind. In fact, propositions are not the 'format' of representations in the head, rather, they are a *general way of describing* things which we might wish to treat as separable information units in memory. This leads to the argument that to say 'propositions' are the uniform representation of information within the psychological theories is only *trivially* true. What is more important is how information is packaged so as to be useful for mental functioning. It is merely convenient if propositions are a good *language* for expressing component pieces of information which a theorist may wish to group together. In fact, it is possible to argue that any computationally representable process can be described in terms of propositions (e.g. Johnson-Laird 1981).

We now turn to the main substance of this chapter, which can be looked at as further aspects of the organization of mental processing and representations. Specifically, we shall be concerned with the idea of visual imagery. At first sight, it might appear that visual imagery, and the associated phenomenon of memory for visual things, cannot possibly be described in the terms which we have been using for the more 'linguistic' things discussed so far. Indeed, there has been considerable argument in which people have taken various stances, such as:

1 Visual memory and imagery are quite *different* from a 'more abstract' propositional memory. Humans have both (e.g. Paivio 1971).
2 Visual memory and imagery are not useful concepts, since images can be represented as propositions, so we may as well just talk about propositional structures (e.g. Pylyshyn 1973).

The arguments on both sides can become very sophisticated, far beyond the range of this introduction. However, on the strength of what has been said in this section, we might say that 1 can be true only if 'images' provide an important natural grouping of processes which impose an organization on processing, and 2 is probably true, but may be vacuous if 'images' provide an important natural grouping. Given this approach, our task will be to review the evidence with a view to seeing whether imagery phenomena seem to be distinctive in any way. Similar arguments will be made with respect to the concept of mental models.

## B Visual (imaginal) imagery

The issue of the nature and utility of imagery is an old one in psychology. One of the earliest studies was carried out by Francis

Galton (1880), who studied the abilities of subjects to 'imagine their breakfast tables'. Some subjects claimed to have vivid images in their mind's eye, while others were less confident that they had imagery. As we shall soon see, it is relatively easy to invoke reports of imagery in most people.

The everyday language of imagery is interesting. Typical phrases include 'in my mind's eye', 'clarity of the image', 'reading off from a mental map', and the like. The automatic use of such terms by the man in the street suggests a strong connexion between perception of the visual world and visual imagery. This phenomenological aspect of imagery is not easy to handle within an information-processing framework, although a possibility in this direction will be suggested later. However, it is this aspect which has led some people to suggest a categorical distinction between 'abstract' representations such as propositions, and image-like representations. But, as we have seen, propositional representations are only convenient descriptive devices. There is no necessary conflict between the two description types.

## 1 Demonstrations of imagery during retrieval from memory

The following memory-search task, devised by Roger Shepard (1966), indicates the way in which the use of images seems to be involved in some memory-search tasks. The problem is this:

- Remember the house that you last lived in.
  How many windows did it have?

Most people find that an answer is not immediately forthcoming. Rather, they will describe themselves as 'mentally touring' an image of the house in their mind's eye, counting each window as they come across it. Usually, people 'tour' the inside, but occasionally they 'walk' around the outside! The strong impression of looking at a mental image provides compelling prima facie evidence for something analogous to a sequence of visual scenes in the mind. Meudell (1971) measured the time that it took subjects to answer this question, and found that the time taken increased approximately linearly with the number of windows counted. This result suggests an orderly search, which, while not ruling out non-image explanations, is at least consistent with the idea that an image is being scrutinized.

The potential involvement of imagery in memory retrieval can be found in numerous situations, and the time taken in performing the task often provides evidence consistent with this claim. Consider the following tasks, and how they might contrast:

(i)   List the names of flowers which you know.
(ii)  List the cities of Great Britain.

In the first case, one usually has no organized plan when attempting the task. In fact, it can be characterized fairly closely by a random search through a knowledge base (Bousfield and Sedgewick 1944; Indow and Togano 1970; see also Sanford and Garrod (1981) for an account of the search base). In complete contrast, with task (ii), at some point – probably early on the task – people usually report some sort of 'reading off' relevant cities from a mental map, often from north to south in east–west sweeps. For many people, there is the strong impression that a mental image of a map is being scanned.

It is relatively easy to make predictions about the times people would take to produce successive instances in these two tasks. In reading off from a map, one would expect some variability in the interval between successive instances, but no systematic increase or decrease in mean interval over the period of the whole task. A roughly linear function would be expected, as shown in figure 14-2(a). In contrast, consider a random search of memory.

At a very general level, as memory is searched to begin with, every instance of (say) a flower which is met would be a *new* one, but later on, there will be a high chance that a particular instance newly found would already have been found. Since repetitions are not allowed, search would have to continue. The consequence is that the interval between successive instances named would tend to get longer and longer, the longer one had been working on the task. This too is depicted in figure 14-2. While the organization of memory is such that names are usually retrieved in clusters, rather than individually, so that the function is more bumpy than the ideal, it is always negatively accelerated, and broadly conforms to the random-search equation, and not to the linear function. In fact, when people report using 'maps' to name cities, their functions are roughly linear, and when they do not, they are negatively accelerated (Indow and Togano 1970).

If scanning mental maps is analogous to physically scanning

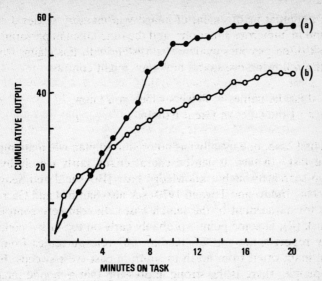

*Figure 14-2.* Data from a subject listing towns and cities in Britain (a), and from a subject listing flowers (b). There is a marked linearity in (a) for the first eight minutes. This subject was especially good at the task, and reported using a 'mental map'. *(Sanford unpublished data.)*

space, then the greater the distance between two elements being successively considered, the longer should be the time taken to carry out the scan. Kosslyn, Ball and Reiser (1978) carried out an experiment to investigate this point. They presented subjects with a map of a fictitious island, containing various landmarks, such as a hut, a tree, and so on. Subjects were trained until they could draw it with great accuracy, from memory. Following this training phase, the subjects took part in a different memory test. They were asked to picture the map mentally and focus on a named object (e.g. 'the tree'). Shortly afterwards, they were asked to focus on a *second* object on the imaginal map. They were asked to press a button when they had found it on their mental maps. The time taken by subjects to press the button depended on how far away (in physical length units) the second object was from the first on the map. In fact, the function was quite linear. It is as though mental scanning of an image is similar to scanning a physical array. Certainly, scanning seems to be a real process, conforming to a rule that whatever the brain's analogy of physical space might be, it takes longer to scan over a greater distance.

## 2 Mental rotation and continuous transformations

Shepard and his colleagues carried out a set of studies which also appear to implicate mental imagery in certain situations. Their now classic work was on mental rotation. Subjects are shown pictures of two objects, which may be identical or different in some respect. In any given case, one of the objects has an orientation which is rotated along one axis with respect to the other. The subject's task is to decide whether the objects are the same or different. A typical example is shown in figure 14-3.

Shepard and Metzler (1971) systematically varied the degree of rotation which would be necessary to exactly align the stimuli. Their results showed a striking linear relationship between the

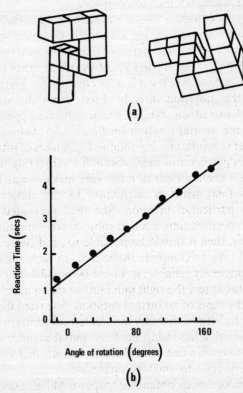

*Figure 14-3.* (a) Typical stimuli used by Shepard and his colleagues. (b) Reaction time as a function of degree of rotation to make a match. *(Adapted from Metzler and Shepard 1974.)*

angle of rotation and the time taken to make a decision, just as though the subjects rotated a mental image of one of the objects (figure 14-3(b)). Similar results are obtained for pairs differing by a rotation in depth. The evidence suggests that when people make such comparisons, they perform some *analogue* of physical rotation itself.

It might be argued that subjects are not performing such a rotation. Just think of what such rotation means – it means continuously reducing the difference in orientation as time spent on the task goes on. But perhaps with widely different orientations it is simply difficult for subjects to establish the similarity between the two patterns, for instance, by comparing different 'features' of the stimuli. With small differences in orientation, it may be simply easier to spot which features to compare.

Two pieces of evidence militate against this alternative. First, subjects typically *report* rotation. Of course, they may simply *infer* rotation, but why infer rotation rather than some other mechanism for doing the task? The second bit of evidence relies on demonstrating that rotation, whatever it is, is *continuous*. Metzler (1973) approached this question directly. First, from the straight-line plots, she calculated the rate at which subjects appeared to be carrying out the mental rotation (in figure 14-3, values would be around 40° per second). Having obtained estimates of rotation rate, she could then predict how much rotation a subject should be able to achieve in a given length of time. Her method was to present *one* stimulus first, with an instruction to the subject to start rotating in a particular direction. She then presented a second stimulus at a specified time later. If subjects *were* rotating the first representation, then it should be possible to predict precisely how long it would take to complete the match. In fact, if the calculations were sufficiently reliable, it should be possible to present the second stimulus at just the right moment, so that a match could be obtained on the basis of no further rotation. She tried this and, for subjects who had low variability in inferred rotation speed, found only a very small relationship between initial angular difference and reaction time. On this basis, Metzler argues that subjects can and do rotate images to make comparisons.

Similar sorts of results obtain for 'paper-folding' tasks, in which subjects have to make judgements of what would happen when paper is folded in various ways. Two problems of this sort are shown in figure 14-4. Shepard and Feng (1972) tried subjects on a

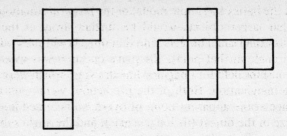

*Figure 14-4.* Mental folding tasks. Can these be folded along the lines to make boxes?

number of more sophisticated puzzles of this general type, and established that the time to make a judgement went up roughly linearly with the number of 'folds' subjects had to imagine in order to do the task.

## 3 Phenomenological studies of imagery

A number of researchers have assumed imagery to be real and important, and to mimic percepts in various ways. Such an assumption enables research into the phenomenal properties of images of things to be carried out. For instance, in looking at a real object, if one moves nearer and nearer to it, it appears to expand until its edges go off the edge of the perceptual field. At the same time, such a 'zoom' process brings the features of the object still in the visual field into clearer detail, and they look larger. It has been argued (e.g. Kosslyn, Pinger, Smith and Shwartz 1981) that if imagery is analogous to perception, then it should display similar properties.

In one study, Kosslyn (1978) used a procedure in which subjects were first asked to imagine line drawings of various things, such as animals. They were asked to imagine each object as if it was a long way off, and then to imagine walking towards it. All subjects claim that the object seemed to loom larger as they 'walked towards it'. Subjects were asked to stop their mental walk when the image loomed so large that it seemed to overflow. They were then asked to estimate the apparent distance which they were from the image. This was done either by verbal estimate, or by moving an apparatus to the same distance from a blank wall. Subjects were evidently able to do this.

On the basis of a simple model of the *physical* situation, one can say that larger objects would be further away at the point of overflow than small objects, and that objects will subtend the same visual angle at that point. Kosslyn's question was whether these relationships held for imagined line drawings which were 'zoomed' in the imagination. Both of the predictions were confirmed. The distance at the apparent point of overflow increased linearly with the size of the object (its longest axis), and the angle subtended at the point of overflow was the same for images of different-sized objects. Furthermore, the same results hold for imagined *lines* of different lengths.

The second part of the story concerns the way that, in perception, zooming brings the details of objects into clearer focus. Would this hold true for visual images? To investigate this, Kosslyn (1975) requested subjects to imagine animals of different subjective sizes. They were instructed to check whether a certain property was present or not by *scrutinizing the image*, and pressing an appropriate button. For instance, if it was a cat, then 'claw' or 'head' might be properties searched for. Subjects often reported having to 'zoom' to see a property, and the smaller the initial image, the longer the questions took to answer. The prediction was thus confirmed.

Now with respect to this, it might be argued that subjects only need to answer the question on the basis of knowledge which can be represented in networks which are unrelated to images (as in chapter 7), and that 'images' have nothing to do with it. Perhaps looking at something in 'more detail' amounts to activating the network from its node at deeper and deeper levels. However, if such a mechanism was implicated, one would expect verification times to depend upon how closely *associated* the property was with the object. This contrasts in an interesting way with the imagery prediction that it should be properties which would *look larger* in the real world which are verified faster. To test this contrast, Kosslyn (1976) partialled the effects of size and associative frequency. When operating under imagery instructions, subjects react faster to properties which are physically larger; when verifying propositions without images, response is faster to highly associated properties. Kosslyn concluded that under image conditions, a mental analogue of size is important.

These data are illustrative of those found in experiments in which people are asked to manipulate images, and suggest that whatever processing is going on when subjects do this, it mimics the world of perception in various ways. One further issue addressed by Kosslyn, Pinger, Smith and Shwartz (1981) are whether images are retrieved from memory as *units*, or as *constructed piecemeal*. Kosslyn (1975) argued that if images of single objects were constructed piecemeal, then larger images, containing more detail, should take longer to form. He found that larger (or more detailed) pictures, which had been previously presented, took longer to form. Similarly, Kosslyn (1980) asked subjects to imagine sets of objects, and found that the time to form an image increased with number of objects. The conclusion reached was that images are formed piecemeal from 'chunks'.

These studies, which rely upon things only the subject can know, are dubbed here 'phenomenological' studies. Altogether, they sound like a substantial demonstration that visual images and imaginary processing are analogous to objects in the world and perceptual processing. Certainly they suggest that when operating under 'imagery instructions', subjects produce behaviour patterns which are constrained in ways similar to the constraints operating upon the physical manipulation of objects in the physical world. This is an important constraint for a number of reasons. But before entering into the significance of all this, we need to touch upon other situations in which visual imagery has been invoked as an explanatory variable.

### 4  The invocation of imagery in reasoning and judgement tasks

Just as subjects seem to use images in some retrieval tasks, and appear to manipulate images in 'rotation' tasks, so they appear to use imagery spontaneously in some ordered reasoning tasks, even though it is in no way demanded by the task that they should. One type of task in which this seems to happen in that of reasoning about linear orderings, sometimes called 'three-term-series' problems. Consider the following:

Tom is taller than Sam.
John is shorter than Sam.
Who is the tallest of the three?

How does one arrive at the solution, *Tom*? Huttenlocher (1968) suggested that one strategy which subjects might use is *imagery*, but of a slightly different type from that considered up to now. Here subjects describe 'arranging' an 'array' of the first two items, either horizontally or vertically in their 'mind's eye'. For vertical arrays, they report starting to build 'from the top', for horizontal arrays, they build 'from the left'. After achieving this representation, they then go on to add the second premise to the array.

Most certainly, subjects do report using imagery in these situations. But one of the interesting features of this account is its similarity to the Johnson-Laird account of mental models for solving syllogisms, discussed in chapter 13. Indeed, in many ways, the imagery account given by Huttenlocher is a precursor of the mental-model notion. In fact, Johnson-Laird (1981) specifically discusses *spatial* inference problems in terms of mental models; we shall return to this shortly.

Imagery has also been involved in the case of making comparative judgements. Consider the following question, and how it is answered: which is larger, an elephant or a horse? (Assume we mean 'prototypical' elephant and horse.) Moyer (1973) asked people to answer a variety of size-comparison queries of this type, and measured the time it took them to answer the questions. Suppose for the moment that whatever process supports discovering the answer to this question, subjects are certain about the answer. If semantic memory had propositional entries for the typical sizes of these and other animals, then there is no reason to suppose that reaction time would depend upon the particular sizes of the animals concerned. However, Moyer (1973) found that the smaller the difference in the sizes of the animals being compared, the larger the reaction time. Indeed, the function relating size difference to reaction time is of the same form as that discussed in connexion with judging which is the 'larger' of two *physical* stimuli (e.g. line length), as discussed in chapter 2, page 30.

This finding is compatible with the idea that the underlying processes are operations on mental images, and that the operations closely resemble the operations of perception.

In a similar vein, Paivio (1978) asked his subjects to compare 'imaginary' clock times, in terms of the angles between the hour and minute hands. A typical problem was of the type 'Which forms the smaller angle, 3.20 or 1.15?'. He found a reliable distance effect, with reaction times being longer for smaller angular differences. His subjects reported constructing and comparing mental images.

Once again, these tasks suggest an *imaginal* comparison process which is analogous to a *perceptual* comparison, generally supporting the view that images are related to objects in the real world, and mental operations with respect to images are related to perceptual processes, in this case. However, it should be pointed out that the symbolic distance effect occurs in situations where visual imagery is not reported. One example has been discussed already (chapter 5, pp. 123–4): judging whether or not two letters of the alphabet are in the correct order (Hamilton and Sanford 1978). The mechanism underlying the comparison process appears to be related to the alphabet being stored as a motor program for saying the alphabet and not to visual imagery. Similar functions even obtain for judging whether pairs of *numbers* are in ascending order (e.g. Moyer and Landauer 1967). In this case, there is no introspective content to processing at all (Fenning and Sinclair 1977). The usual theory of this phenomenon is to suppose that numbers are stored as *analogue* (continuous) representations, among other modes of representation. The idea is that numbers are represented as *values* on a continuum. Numbers close to each other are assumed to have similar values on the continuum.

In a sense, the idea of analogue values is the same as a visual image, yet no imagery is reported. Perhaps this theory is correct; if it is, processes associated with a conscious report of imagery may be part of a more extensive representational mechanism which occasionally gives rise to 'perception-like' impressions. Before discussing the problem associated with all of this, let us turn to a quite different area of psychology in which imagery has been invoked as an explanatory concept.

## C  Imagery and memory

A considerable amount of empirical research has been directed at the relationship between forming images of things and events, and how easy it is to remember those things and events. It is convenient to divide the basic approaches towards the memory-imagery relationship into two sections:

(1)  The effect of instructions to form images of the stimulus material, and the effect that this has on subsequent memory, and

(2)  The effect of stimulus materials themselves – for instance, using material which seems to enable an image to be formed readily, or material which seems to preclude it.

## 1  The effect of stimulus material

It is not unreasonable to suppose that some verbal material (word stimuli) would be more easily translated into images than others. For example, the phrase 'an orange' evokes an image more readily than does the phrase 'a law'. A number of researchers, particularly Alan Paivio in Canada, and John Richardson (Richardson 1980) in the UK, have investigated some of the consequences of this observation. Both found that individual words do vary considerably from one another in terms of how easy subjects feel it is to form an image on the basis of them, and how quickly subjects report forming images of them.

Paivio, Yuille and Madigan (1968) carried out a large-scale study, collecting various ratings for 925 English nouns. Subjects were asked to try to form a visual image of what each noun *denoted*. On the basis of their experience in doing this, the subjects produced ratings for the ease of forming the images. Of course, imageability might well be related to concreteness – the degree to which the words denoted things which could be experienced by the senses. Their subjects were also asked to rate the words in terms of concreteness. In this way, in later experiments, it was possible to partial out the effects of imageability and concreteness.

Using this database, Paivio and his colleagues demonstrated that lists of words which are high on the imagery scale generally gives rise to superior recall in free-recall tasks (Paivio 1968), and in serial-recall tasks (Paivio, Yuille and Rogers 1969). Superior recall was also obtained in paired-associate learning (Paivio, Smythe and Yuille 1968), and in recognition memory (Paivio 1971).

On the basis of these results, Paivio makes the rather simple assumption that high-imagery words are better remembered because they can be stored in memory not just as a 'verbal' code, but also as a mental image of some sort. In contrast, storage of low-imagery words is likely to occur only in 'verbal' mode. This view is termed the *dual-code hypothesis* and, on the face of it, the evidence for it looks strong.

## 2  The effect of instructions to form images

We have already noted that both free-recall efficiency (including serial recall) and paired-associate learning efficiency is enhanced when instructions to form images are used. This would appear to be at least consistent with the dual-coding hypothesis. However, there is evidence that it is a very special kind of image which produces enhanced performance in the paired-associate situation. Bower (1972) compared the incidental learning of pairs of items under two conditions. In one condition, subjects were invited to form *separate* or 'non-interactive' images of two objects – for instance, given the pair 'ball–glass' it is possible to form separate images of a ball and a glass. In the other condition, another group of subjects were invited to form an interacting image, perhaps of a ball *in* a glass.

The results were clear: under the *separate* instructions, there was no real advantage to forming an image; under the *interactive* instructions, there was. His result is interesting, potentially damaging for the dual-code theory, and one that has been amply replicated (cf. Richardson 1980). It implies that it is *setting up relationships between the elements of things to be remembered* which is important, and *not* imagery per se. We might say that the dual-code hypothesis is confounded with what we shall call the *cognitive richness* of the stimuli used in memory experiments. Let us briefly recapitulate some of the experiments which are pertinent to the cognitive richness idea:

(i)   Instructions to use *any* pre-existing memory structures (one is a shoe, two is a . . . etc.) to 'attach' words from a list can result in perfect recall. Related 'images' may simply be attachments of this sort.

(ii)  Processing words in any complex way – utilizing their meanings fully – results in better recall than 'shallow' processing (Craik and Lockhart 1972).

(iii) Complex verbs enable sentences to be recalled more readily if they entail many interconnexions between themselves and the other linguistic entities mentioned in sentences (Gentner 1981).

(iv)  Memory is facilitated if verbal material (sentences) are ordered in such a way as to connect them.

# D   Images, models and introspection

The highpoint of the debate about the role of imagery in thinking occurred in the late nineteenth century, and historical record suggests that the difficulties associated with it were instrumental in the vigour with which behaviourism swept psychology. It is not difficult to appreciate why, looking at the redevelopment of the issue over the past twenty years. First, there is the fact that considerable individual differences exist in the subjective reports of 'having' imagery. For instance, one of my colleagues reports not really having visual imagery – he even dislikes diagrams as an explanatory device. This is quite atypical, of course. But the will o' the wisp subjective impressions which most people have do not readily fit our information-processing conceptions of how the mind might best be modelled.

## 1   Images and models

The philosopher Dennett (1981) calls the group of people who wish to make much of imagery as a phenomenon 'iconophiles', and the group who wish to explain it away as 'iconophobes'. We shall use his terminology. Both groups vary in their arguments, but the typical inconophobe will argue thus: images seem to be associated with a capacity to store spatially describable information, and to manipulate it. However, such storage and manipulations can be handled by representations in terms of propositions and the like, and so supposing that there is more to images tells us nothing. As we pointed out at the start of this chapter, such a statement can be vacuous: it is indeed possible to describe any representation 'propositionally' (cf. Johnson-Laird 1981). The real argument is whether the bunch of activities which we call *imagery* have any special distinctive organizational properties. In the view of the author, they do: they indicate that one of the ways in which data and processing are arranged in the brain is as a *spatial analogue*. Furthermore, when spatial organizational processes are being used, there is at least the *possibility* that impressions of a quasi-perceptual nature seem to occur in people. It seems to me altogether proper that a respectable psychology should at least try to accommodate this fact.

The typical iconophile is much more difficult to grasp: iconophobes accusingly vary their claims about iconophiles from the view that they think images are 'pictures perceived with the mind's eye', which of course they cannot be, to the view that imaginal processing is 'analogue', while propositional representations are 'discrete'. In fact, the data and discussion generated by both sides is where the interest lies – it is probably not even useful to ask questions of whether images are 'real' or 'epiphenomenal' (Dennett 1981).

The evidence suggests that while the phenomena associated with imagery are real processing operations naturally describable by a spatial metaphor, our capacity to carry out quasi-spatial operations is quite limited, and certainly differs from what can be done with a real pictorial display. In addition to the studies described in the preceding sections, consider the following tasks. The first is a very simple test. Form a visual image of the word BEHAVIOUR (if you can). Then read the letters from right to left off your image. Compare the difficulty of the task and the time taken with the ease of reading it in the same way off the page. The second task is described by Simon (1978):

● Do not draw, but instead image a rectangle 2 inches × 1 inch, with a vertical line cutting it into two 1-inch squares. Imagine a diagonal from the upper left-hand corner to the lower right-hand corner of the 2 × 1-inch rectangle. This is diagonal A. Now imagine a second diagonal, B, which starts from the upper right-hand corner, and goes to the lower left-hand corner of the same SQUARE. Consider where diagonal A cuts diagonal B. What is the relationship of the length of B above the cut to the length of B below the cut?

This is a difficult task, and should be compared directly with the process of making the drawing and reading off the answer, which is very much easier indeed. The point of the demonstration is that image construction and manipulation can be quite limited, in much the same way that working memory seems to be limited when carrying out a task like solving a syllogism, for example. Whatever account is given of mental-imagery phenomena, it is necessary to take these limitations into account. This is not as easy as it seems, since there is a tendency to suppose that images are that much 'richer' than non-image representations, and richness is tantamount to a high information content.

Phenomenologically, when one carries out some task using mental imagery – say imagining a house in which one has lived – it seems to be possible to start with some sort of vague image, and then focus on specific details *if required*, just like the 'zooming' phenomena described earlier. If one accepts this, one is forced into the position of speculating about the mechanisms underlying vague images and zooming. There are at least two ways to handle this. One way is to assume that there is some quasi-pictorial representation stored in the brain, rather like a picture. When this representation is required, some search mechanism locates it, perhaps locating it corresponds to getting a 'vague image'. Detailed search within the representation corresponds to 'zooming'. However, there are many problems with this account: there is evidence that visual memory is susceptible to the effects of encoding interpretation, for instance (chapter 6); there is evidence that images are constructed piecemeal (this chapter), and of course, piecemeal constructions *have* to be made if what is being imagined is novel or new.

Another way of handling the problem is to turn to the idea of model construction. When we looked into discourse understanding, problem-solving, and reasoning, we found evidence that in producing a working representation of a problem, subjects used representations which went far beyond the explicit statements provided, necessarily bringing in a great deal of world-knowledge and presupposition, despite having limited working memories. We suggested a way around this apparent dilemma: the limited data structures in working memory include mapping pointers to LTM structures which embodied the extra information. Precisely the same argument could be made for imagery phenomena. The limited range of representations being worked on could be mapped into many more representations which are in LTM and not in working memory. In fact, it is an easy matter to show how model construction brings in extra information (presuppositions) in tasks using spatial reference terms. Johnson-Laird (1983) set a number of people the following problem:

- A is to the left of B; B is to the left of C.
  What relationship holds between A and C?

Most people will answer that A is to the left of C, or at least consider it to begin with. In fact it is undecidable. If one interprets the problem against a *linear* model, then it is true. If one interprets it against a small-circle model, it is false. To appreciate the latter case, suppose that A, B and C are sitting round a small circular café table!

The argument that model construction underlies many kinds of imagery can be made quite easily too. Suppose that one *did* have a rich, quasi-pictorial representation of some object at some level of detail. It would not be much use for imagining the object from a new angle or a new perspective, except in so far as it embodied a set of fixed spatial relationships between different parts of the object. Some process of construction would be required. Another good illustration comes from Johnson-Laird and Wason (1977), devised by Hinton. We are all familiar with cubes, and it is an easy matter to imagine a cube standing flat on a horizontal surface (try it). Now imagine a cube with one corner only touching the horizontal surface, and a diametrically opposed corner vertically above it. Not only is this much harder, but most people do not even know how many corners they would be able to see. Hinton's (unpublished) evidence suggests that for a cube, mental rotation is not really an analogue of real-world rotation, but is dependent upon model construction. Even if quasi-pictorial representations exist, perhaps their utility is easily overrated.

## 2 Models, imagery and introspection

There are two features which make imagery distinctive, whatever the underlying mechanisms which support it. The first is that it is associated with strong introspective impressions of a perceptual kind, and the second is that visual imagery is rich in spatial and other perceptual information. Both of these features imply that it stems from a way in which some mental structures are actually organized.

First consider the perceptual impressions. Although introspection is not always a good guide to process, one has to explain *why* perceptual impressions should be reported. It is possible that imagery reports utilize descriptive terms suited to genuine perception because the procedures used in aspects of perception are also used in imagery. In fact, there is some evidence linking perception with imagery at both a general and a specific level. Thus one aspect of perception is that it is largely modularized by modality. For instance, visual perception interacts only weakly with auditory perception. The same seems to be true of imagery: visual and auditory imagery do not seem to interact. A beautiful illustration of this comes from Brooks (1967; 1968) who showed an independence of visual and auditory memory representations in a short-term memory task. In one task, Brooks presented his subjects with a block letter **E**. The subjects had to look at the letter, and then turn away and hold it as an image. The task was to start at the bottom left-hand corner, and by moving in a clockwise direction, evaluate whether each corner encountered was a top or bottom corner (in which case 'Yes' was the correct reply), or was not ('No'). One group of subjects simply said 'Yes' or 'No' as they did it. A second group was required to go down a checklist of Ys and Ns which were irregularly printed on a response sheet. Performance on this task was consistently more rapid with saying 'Yes' or 'No' than circling Ys and Ns on the checklist. Brooks suggested that the visual scanning involved in looking for Ys and Ns interferes with the visual image. This conclusion appears sound, because in another study, the opposite pattern was found with materials encoded primarily in an articulatory form. Subjects were required to hold in memory sentences like 'A bird in the hand is not in the bush'. The task in this case was to classify each successive word as a noun ('Yes') or not a noun ('No'). In this case, *saying* 'Yes' or 'No' took considerably longer than indicating Ys or Ns on a response sheet. Again, the argument is that the articulatory memory code is interfered with by the act of articulation in saying 'Yes' or 'No'. The experiment shows clear modularity of sensory modality, and implies that a commonality of resources are used for visual search and image search, or for articulatory memory and articulation.

More detailed illustrations come from comparing imagery phenomena with perceptual phenomena. Although some such comparisons are described above (for instance, scanning and zoom effects), it is always possible to argue that subjects in the experiments supporting these phenomena are really only using general, non-perceptual processes to simulate what would happen in a real perceptual case (this is called the 'tacit-knowledge' problem: see Pylyshyn 1981 for details). However, the involvement of perceptual mechanisms could be argued for more strongly if some odd or relatively unknown perceptual phenomenon could be simulated by people carrying out an imaginary perceptual task. Such a study has indeed been carried out by Finke and Schmidt (1977; 1978) which exploits a phenomenon well known only to perception psychologists, called the McCollough Effect (see Favreau and Corballis 1976). In the true perceptual version, subjects are shown patterns of black and red vertical stripes, and black and green horizontal stripes. After looking at these patterns alternately for ten minutes, subjects are presented with test patterns of black and *white* horizontal or vertical stripes. Subjects report seeing *green* on vertical white stripes, and *red* on horizontal white stripes. The Finke–Schmidt procedure is an attempt to discover whether the same effect could be observed using *imagination* as part of the stimulus condition. They showed subjects red and green patches, and asked them to *imagine* black horizontal stripes on the green patch, or black vertical stripes on the red patch. Later, they showed subjects the test patterns, and found that subjects' reports matched the original McCollough Effect (except that the reports were of 'faint' colourings). This experiment is particularly impressive in implicating perceptual machinery in imagery. Perhaps the strong impression of perception which is often a concomitant of imagery tasks results from using some of the same brain mechanisms in the two.

The second point about imagery is that it operates in the same medium as perception. For instance, visual imagery involves the manipulation of spatial knowledge. This is scarcely surprising if one asks what imagery is *for*. Like other acts of thinking, using imagery will be largely to simulate what might happen in the world if one actually acted on the world, but removes the necessity to do it. A good example is placing furniture in a room. Although people will typically go through a good deal of shifting of furniture, there is almost always some planning based upon *imagining* what will fit where, and how it will look. Thus much imagery will be used for *simulation*, and the terms of the simulation must be those which truly exist in the physical world if it is to be of any use. Thus one would expect the mental models used in simulating things relevant to *vision* or *sound* to draw upon knowledge of the physical properties of the visual or acoustic world. In fact, it is a functional necessity that knowledge structures will exist which are general purpose and organized around these properties.

## E  Concluding remarks

Quite obviously, imagery is a complex and contentious topic. Many of the experiments discussed could be described as a methodologist's nightmare, and many results will admit to multiple interpretations. Yet, on phenomenological grounds, imagery, and especially its connexion with perception and perceptual mechanisms, has to be explained. The answer must be yes to the question of whether imagery is worth considering because it reflects something of mental (or brain) organization. Viewed as simulation, imagery is a most important topic; simulation requires constraints which match real-world properties, and in large measure, this seems to be what is behind imagery. However, simulation by imagery, just like the manipulation of less perceptually anchored mental models, is apparently limited computationally, probably through working-memory constraints. Finally, although we have concentrated almost exclusively on visual imagery, other modality-specific simulations are possible: imagining melodies if you are a music lover, imagining new ways of moving if you are a dancer or an athlete, even imagining emotional reactions, all seem to be part of our relatively unexplored world of thought.

# Bibliography

*Where next? Suggested topics for further reading in cognitive science*

This book has been centred on psychology, and the technical experimental literature can be approached both through the references cited, and through the standard journals. Picking one's way through the broader issues of cognitive science can be a little more difficult. Fortunately, a number of compilations and books are available which can provide insights into a variety of important issues.

Of these, the broadest overview is given in D.A. Norman (ed.) (1981), *Perspectives on Cognitive Science*, Erlbaum, Hillsdale, N.J. This contains chapters written by eminent and insightful scientists each giving his own perspective on the subject. One specific topic not addressed in the present book is the relation of cognition to the architecture of the brain: what kind of machine is the brain? Some suggestions are made by Minsky in the book cited above; a much more technical discussion is given in G.E. Hinton and J.A. Anderson (1981), *Parallel Models of Associative Memory*, Erlbaum, Hillsdale, N.J. This is an important technical book, but is difficult. Another issue raised in the book by Norman is that of mental models, a concept we have used throughout the present volume. A key book in this field is P.N. Johnson-Laird (1983), *Mental Models*, Cambridge University Press.

In a search for a general understanding of cognition, it is important to think of the mind in relation to biological systems in general. A biological approach construes the constraints on human information-processing as being forced by man's biological niche. It is difficult to find good technical discussions of this point of view, but for perception, David Marr (1982), *Vision*, W.H. Freeman, San Francisco, provides important hints. Although very beautifully written, this book does assume some familiarity with the literature, and assumes some mathematical knowledge.

This incomplete list of suggestions for broader reading would be yet more incomplete if it included no mention of the philosophical aspects of cognitive science. What are the consequences and problems of the information-processing approach to mind? A good, readable compilation, containing chapters by many important figures, is Haughland (1981), *Mind Design*, MIT Press, Cambridge, Mass.

An earlier volume, again containing seminal and thought-provoking papers, is A.R. Anderson (1964), *Minds and Machines*, Prentice-Hall Inc., Englewood Cliffs, N.J.

University readers will generally be guided by their teachers over the technical background to cognitive science, and the books which help to acquire the appropriate skills. However, for general guidance, I personally find the following useful for students:

(1) *For an overview of logics:*
    J.D. McCawley (1981), *Everything that Linguists Have Always Wanted to Know About Logic'*, Blackwell.
(2) *For an introduction to LISP, a major AI language:*
    (a) P.H. Winston (1977; 1979), *Artificial Intelligence*, Addison-Wesley.
    (b) P.H. Winston and B.K.P. Horn (1981), *LISP*, Addison-Wesley.

In particular, (b) leads the reader easily from desciptions of AI to problems of programming techniques. LISP is not entirely the province of large-memory computers, but also is available in simplified forms on certain micros, such as the Apple.

There are specialist journals associated with the various fields of cognitive science, but among the most important general ones are *Cognitive Science, Brain and Behavioural Science* and *Cognitive Psychology*.

# References

Abelson, R.P. (1972), 'The structure of belief systems', in R.C. Schank and K.M. Colby (eds), *Computer Models of Thought and Language*, Freeman, San Francisco.

Abelson, R.P. (1975), 'Concepts for representing mundane reality in plans', in D.G. Bobrow and A. Collins (eds), *Representation and Understanding*, Academic Press, New York.

Adams, J.K. and Adams, P.A. (1961), 'Realism of confidence judgements', *Psychological Review*, 68, pp. 33–45.

Adamson, R.E. (1952), 'Functional fixedness as related to problem solving: a repetition of three experiments', *Journal of Experimental Psychology*, 44, pp. 288–91.

Allport, D.A., Antonis, B. and Reynolds, P. (1972), 'On the division of attention: a disproof of the single channel hypothesis', *Quarterly Journal of Experimental Psychology*, 24, pp. 225–35.

Anderson, A. (1982), 'Text comprehension – the influence of temporal information on processing and reading rate', unpublished Ph.D. thesis, University of Glasgow.

Anderson, A., Garrod, S.C. and Sanford, A.J. (1983), 'The accessibility of pronominal antecedents as a function of episode shifts in narrative text', *Quarterly Journal of Experimental Psychology*, 35a, pp. 427–40.

Anderson, J.M. (1971), *The grammar of Case: Towards a Localistic Theory*, Cambridge University Press.

Anderson, J.R. and Bower, G.H. (1972), 'Recognition and retrieval processes in free recall', *Psychological Review*, 79, pp. 97–123.

Anderson, R.C. and Pichert, J.W. (1978), 'Recall of previously unrecallable information following a shift in perspective', *Journal of Verbal Learning and Verbal Behavior*, 17, pp. 1–12.

Anderson, R.C., Pichert, J.W., Goetz, E.T., Schallert, D.L., Stevens, K.V. and Trollip, S.R. (1976), 'Instantiation of general terms', *Journal of Verbal Learning and Verbal Behavior*, 15, pp. 667–79.

Andley, R.J. and Pike, A.R. (1965), 'Some alternative stochastic models of choice', *British Journal of Mathematical and Statistical Psychology*, 18, pp. 207–25.

Atkinson, R.C. and Shiffrin, R.M. (1967), 'Human memory: a proposed system and its control processes', in K.W. Spence and J.T. Spence (eds), *The Psychology of Learning and Motivation*, Vol. 2, Academic Press, New York.

Atwood, M.E. and Polson, P.G. (1976), 'A process model for water jar problems', *Cognitive Psychology*, 8, pp. 191–216.

Baddeley, A.D. (1966a), 'Response tendencies in attempts to generate random binary series', *Quarterly Journal of Experimental Psychology*, 18, pp. 119–29.

Baddeley, A.D. (1966b), 'The influence of acoustic and semantic similarity on long-term memory for word sequences', *Quarterly Journal of Experimental Psychology*, 18, pp. 302–9.

Baddeley, A.D. (1976), *The Psychology of Memory*, Harper and Row, New York.

Baddeley, A.D. and Hitch, G. (1974), 'Working memory', in G.H. Bower (ed.), *The Psychology of Learning and Motivation*, Vol. 8.

Baddeley, A.D. and Hitch, G. (1976), 'Recently re-examined', in S. Dornic (ed.), *Attention and Performance VI*.

Baddeley, A.D., Thomson, N. and Buchanan, M. (1975), 'Word length and the structure of short-term memory', *Journal of Verbal Learning and Verbal Behavior*, 14, pp. 575–89.

Baddeley, A.D. and Warrington, E.K. (1970), 'Amnesia and the distinction between long- and short-term memory', *Journal of Verbal Learning and Verbal Behavior*, 9, pp. 176–89.

Baddeley, A.D. and Warrington, E.K. (1973), 'Memory coding and amnesia', *Neuropsychologia*, 11, pp. 159–65.

Ballard, D.H. and Brown, C.M. (1982), *Computer Vision*, Prentice-Hall.

Barret, T.R. and Ekstrand, B.R. (1972), 'Effects of sleep on memory: III. Controlling for time-of-day effects', *Journal of Experimental Psychology*, 96, pp. 321–7.

Bartlett, F.C. (1932), *Remembering*, Cambridge University Press.

Belmont, J.M. and Butterfield, E.C. (1971), 'Learning strategies as determinants of learning deficiencies', *Cognitive Psychology*, 2, pp. 411–20.

Bierswich, M. (1970), 'Semantics', in J. Lyons (ed.), *New Horizons in Linguistics*, Penguin, Baltimore.

Blake, M.J.F. (1971), 'Temperament and time of day', in W.P. Colquhoun (ed.), *Biological Rhythms and Human Performance*, Academic Press, London and New York.

Bobrow, D.G. and Fraser, J.B. (1969), 'An augmented state transition network analysis procedure', 1st IJCAI, pp. 557–67.

Bousfield, W.A. and Sedgewick, C.H.W. (1944), 'The analysis of sequences of restricted associative responses', *Journal of General Psychology*, 30, pp. 149–65.

Bower, G.H. (1972), 'Mental imagery in associative learning', in L.W. Gregg (ed.), *Cognition in Learning and Memory*, Wiley, New York.

Bower, G.H., Black, J.B. and Turner, T.J. (1979), 'Scripts in memory for text', *Cognitive Psychology*, 3, pp. 193–209.

Bransford, J., Barclay, J. and Franks, J. (1972), 'Sentence memory: a constructive versus interpretative approach', *Cognitive Psychology*, 3, pp. 193–209.

Bransford, J.D. and Johnson, M.K. (1973), 'Consideration of some problems of comprehension', in W.G. Chase (ed.), *Visual Information Processing*, Academic Press, New York.

Broadbent, D.E. (1954), 'The role of auditory localisation in attention and memory span', *Journal of Experimental Psychology*, 47, pp. 191–6.

Broadbent, D.E. (1957), 'Immediate memory and simultaneous stimuli', *Quarterly Journal of Experimental Psychology*, 9, pp. 1–11.

Broadbent, D.E. (1958), *Perception and Communication*, Pergamon Press.

Broadbent, D.E. (1967), 'Word-frequency effect and response bias', *Psychological Review*, 74, pp. 1–15.

Broadbent, D.E. (1971), *Decision and Stress*, Academic Press.

Broadbent, D.E. (1973), *In Defence of Empirical Psychology*, Methuen.

Broadbent, D.E. (1975), 'The magic number seven after fifteen years', in A. Kennedy and A. Wilkes (eds), *Studies in Long Term Memory*, Wiley.

Broadbent, D.E. and Broadbent, M. (1973), 'Grouping strategies in short-term memory for alpha-numeric lists', *Bulletin of the British Psychological Society*, 26, p. 135.

Broadbent, D.E. and Gregory, M. (1963), 'Division of attention and the decision theory of signal detection', *Proceedings of the Royal Society*, B, 158, pp. 222–31.

Brooks, D.N. and Baddeley, A.D. (1976), 'What can amnesics learn?', *Neuropsychologia*, 14, pp. 111–22.

Brooks, L.R. (1967), 'The suppression of visualization in reading', *Quarterly Journal of Experimental Psychology*, 19, pp. 288–99.

Brooks, L.R. (1968), 'Spatial and verbal components of the act of recall', *Canadian Journal of Psychology*, 22, pp. 349–68.

Brown, J. (1958), 'Some tests of the decay theory of immediate memory', *Quarterly Journal of Experimental Psychology*, 10, pp. 12–21.

Brown, T.A. and Shufford, E.H. (1973), 'Quantifying uncertainty into numerical probabilities for the reporting of intelligence', Report R-1185-ARPA, RAND Corporation, Santa Monica.

Byrne, R. (1981), 'Mental cookery: an illustration of fact retrieval from plans', *Quarterly Journal of Experimental Psychology*, 33A, pp. 31–8.

Callaway, E. (1965), 'Response speed, the EEG alpha cycle and the autonomic cardiovascular cycle', in A.T. Welford and J.E. Birren (eds), *Behavior, Aging, and the Nervous System*, Charles C. Thomas, Springfield, Illinois.

Carmichael, L., Hogan, H.P. and Walter, A.A. (1932), 'An experimental study of the effect of language on the reproduction of visually perceived form', *Journal of Experimental Psychology*, 15, pp. 73–86.

Carpenter, P.A. and Just, M.A. (1977), 'Reading comprehension as eyes see it', in M.A. Just and P.A. Carpenter (eds), *Cognitive Processes in Comprehension*, Erlbaum, Hillsdale, N.J.

Carroll, J.M., Thomas, J.C. and Malhotra, A. (1980), 'Presentation and representation in design problem solving'. *British Journal of Psychology*, 71, pp. 143–53.

Cattell, J.McK. (1885, 1886), 'The intertia of the eye and brain', *Brain*, 8, pp. 295–312.

Cattell, J.McK. (1885), *Philosophical Studies*, 2, pp. 635–50.

Chapman, L.J. and Chapman, J.P. (1959), 'Atmosphere effect re-examined', *Journal of Experimental Psychology*, 58, pp. 220–6.

Charniak, E. (1972), 'Towards a model of children's story comprehension', Technical Report 266, Artificial Intelligence Laboratory, Massachusetts Institute of Technology.

Chase, W.G. and Ericsson, K.A. (1981), 'Skilled Memory', in J.R. Anderson (ed.), *Cognitive Skills and their Acquisition*, Erlbaum, N.J.

Cherry, E.C. (1953), 'Some experiments on the recognition of speech with one and two ears', *Journal of the Acoustical Society of America*, 25, pp. 975–9.

Chocholle, R. (1940), 'Variation des temps de réaction auditifs en fonction de l'intensité à diverses fréquences', *Année Psychologique*, 41–42, pp. 65–124.

Chomsky, N. (1957), *Syntactic Structures*, Mouton, The Hague.

Clark, H.H. and Clark, E.V. (1977), *Psychology and Language: an Introduction to Psycholinguistics*, Harcourt Brace Jovanich, New York.

Clark, H.H. and Marshall, C.R. (1981), 'Definite reference and mutual knowledge', in A.K. Joshi, B.L. Webber and I.A. Sag (eds), *Elements of Discourse Understanding*, Cambridge University Press.

Cofer, C.N. (1973), 'Constructive processes in memory', *American Scientist*, 61, pp. 537–43.

Cohen, J. and Hansel, C.E.M. (1965), *Risk and Gambling*, Philosophical Library, New York.

Cohen, P.R. (1978), 'On knowing what to say: planning speech acts', unpublished doctoral dissertation, University of Toronto.

Colby, B. (1972), 'A partial grammar of Eskimo folktales', Working paper, School of Social Sciences, University of California, Irvine.

Cole, C. (1975), 'An ethnographic psychology of cognition', in R.W.

Brislin, S. Bochner and W.J. Lonner (eds), *Cross-Cultural Perspectives on Learning 1: Cross-Cultural Research and Methodology*, Halstead Press, New York.

Collins, A.M. and Loftus, E.F. (1975), 'A spreading activation theory of semantic processing', *Psychological Review*, 82, pp. 407–28.

Collins, A.M. and Quillian, M.R. (1969), 'Retrieval time from semantic memory', *Journal of Verbal Learning and Verbal Behaviour*, 8, pp. 240–7.

Collins, A.M. and Quillian, M.R. (1972), 'How to make a language user', in E. Tulving and W. Donaldson (eds), *Organisation and Memory*, Academic Press, New York.

Colquhoun, W.P. (1971), *Biological Rhythms and Human Performance*, Academic Press, London and New York.

Conrad, C. (1972), 'Cognitive economy in semantic memory', *Journal of Experimental Psychology*, 92, pp. 149–54.

Conrad, R. (1964), 'Acoustic confusion in immediate memory', *British Journal of Psychology*, 55, pp. 75–84.

Cox, J.R. and Griggs, R.A. (1982), *Memory and Cognition*, 10, pp. 496–502.

Craik, F.I.M. and Lockhart, R.S. (1972), 'Levels of processing: a framework for memory research', *Journal of Verbal Learning and Verbal Behavior*, 11, pp. 671–84.

Craik, F.I.M. and Tulving, E. (1975), 'Depth of processing and the retention of words in episodic memory', *Journal of Experimental Psychology: General*, 104, pp. 268–94.

Crain, S. and Steedman, M. (1981), 'On not being led up the garden path: the use of context by the psychological parser', paper presented to the Sloan Conference on Modelling Human Parsing, Austin, Texas.

Crowder, R.G. and Morton, J. (1969), 'Precategorical acoustic storage', *Perception and Psychophysics*, 5, pp. 365–73.

Daniel, T.C. (1972), 'Nature of the effect of verbal labels on recognition memory for form', *Journal of Experimental Psychology*, 96, 152–7.

Darwin, C.J., Turvey, M.T. and Crowder, R.G. (1972), 'An auditory analogue of the Sperling partial report procedure: evidence for brief auditory storage', *Cognitive Psychology*, pp. 255–67.

de Groot, A.D. (1965), *Thought and Choice in Chess*, Mouton, The Hague.

de Groot, A.D. (1966), 'Perception and memory versus thought', in B. Kleinmuntz (ed.). *Problem-Solving: Research, Method and Theory*, Wiley.

Dennett, D.C. (1981), 'Two approaches to mental images', in N. Block (ed.), *Imagery*, MIT Press, Cambridge, Mass.

Dent, H.R. (1978), 'Interviewing child witnesses', in M.M. Gruneberg,

P.E. Morris, and R.N. Sykes (eds), *Practical Aspects of Memory*, Academic Press, New York.

Deutsch, J.A. and Deutsch, D. (1963), 'Attention: some theoretical considerations', *Psychological Review*, 70, pp. 80–90.

Dominowski, R.L. and Jenrick, R. (1972), 'Effects of hints and interpolated activity on solution of an insight problem', *Psychonomic Science*, 26, pp. 335–8.

Dooling, D.J. and Christiaansen, R.E. (1977), 'Levels of encoding and retention of prose', in G.H. Bower (ed.), *The Psychology of Learning and Motivation*, Vol. 11, Academic Press, New York.

Dooling, D.J. and Lachman, R. (1971). 'Effects of comprehension on retention of prose', *Journal of Experimental Psychology*, 88, pp. 216–22.

Dooling, D.J. and Mullet, R. (1973), 'Locus of thematic effects in retention of prose', *Journal of Experimental Psychology*, 97, pp. 404–6.

Duffy, E. (1962), *Activation and Behaviour*, Wiley.

Duncker, K. (1945), 'On problem solving', *Psychological Monographs*, 58, 270, pp. 1–113.

Ebbinghaus, H.E. (1885), *Uber das Gedachtuis*, Leipzig: Dunker, translated as *Memory* (C.E. Bussenius, translator), Teachers' College Press, New York, 1913.

Edwards, W. (1968), 'Conservatism in human information processing', in B. Kleinmuntz (ed.), *Formal Representation of Human Judgement*, Wiley, New York.

Eisenstadt, M. and Kareev, Y. (1975), 'Aspects of human problem-solving: the use of internal representations', in D.A. Norman, D.E. Rumelhart and LNR, *Explorations in Cognition*, Freeman, San Francisco.

Eriksen, C.W. and Collins, J.F. (1967), 'Some temporal characteristics of visual perception', *Journal of Experimental Psychology*, 74, pp. 476–84.

Ernst, G.W. and Newell, A. (1969), *GPS: a Case Study in Generality and Problem Solving*, Academic Press, New York.

Eysenck, H.J. (1963), 'Biological basis of personality', *Nature*, 199, pp. 1031–4.

Favreau, D.E. and Corballis, M.C. (1976), 'Negative after effects in visual perception', *Scientific American*, 235, pp. 42–8.

Feller, W. (1968), *An Introduction to Probability Theory and its Applications*, Vol. 1, Wiley, New York.

Fenning, G. and Sinclair, A. (1977), 'The effect of separation on number order decisions', unpublished manuscript, University of Glasgow.

Fillmore, C.J. (1968), 'The case for case', in B. Bach and R.T. Harms (eds), *Universals in Linguistic Theory*, Holt, Rhinehart and Winston, New York.

Finke, R.A. and Schmidt, M.J. (1977), 'Orientation-specific color after effects following imagination', *Journal of Experimental Psychology: Human Perception and Performance*, 3, pp. 599–606.

Fischhoff, B. (1977), 'Perceived informativeness of facts', *Journal of Experimental Psychology: Human Perception and Performance*, 3, pp. 349–58.

Fischhoff, B., Slovic, P. and Lichtenstein, S. (1977), 'Knowing with certainty: the appropriateness of extreme confidence', *Journal of Experimental Psychology: Human Perception and Performance*, 3, pp. 552–64.

Fodor, J.D., Fodor, J.A. and Garrett, M.F. (1975), 'The psychological unreality of semantic representations', *Linguistic Inquiry*, 4, pp. 515–31.

Galton, F. (1880), *Inquiries into Human Faculty and Its Development*, Macmillan.

Garnham, A. (1979), 'Instantiation of verbs', *Quarterly Journal of Experimental Psychology*, 31, pp. 207–14.

Garrod, S.C. and Sanford, A.J. (1982), 'Bridging inferences and the extended demain of reference', in J. Long and A. Baddeley (eds), *Attention and Performance IX*, pp. 311–46.

Garrod, S.C. and Sanford, A.J. (1983), 'Topic dependent effects in language processing', in G.B. Flores D'Arcais and J. Jarvella (eds), *Processes of Language Understanding*, Wiley.

Gentner, D. (1981), 'Verb semantic structures in memory for sentences: evidence for componential representation', *Cognitive Psychology*, 13, 56–83.

Gilliland, T. (1975), *Readability*, Hodder and Stoughton.

Glucksberg, S. and Weisberg, R.W. (1966), 'Verbal behavior and problem solving: some effects of labeling in a functional fixedness problem', *Journal of Experimental Psychology*, 71, pp. 659–64.

Gomulicki, B.G. (1956), 'Recall as an abstractive process', *Acta Psychologica*, 12, pp. 77–94.

Green, D.M. and Swets, J.A. (1966), *Signal Detection Theory and Psychophysics*, Wiley, New York.

Greeno, J.G. (1978), 'Nature of problem solving abilities', in W.K. Estes (ed.), *Handbook of Learning and Cognitive Processes*, Vol. 5, Erlbaum, Hillsdale, N.J.

Grice, G.R. (1968), 'Stimulus intensity and response evocation', *Psychological Review*, 75, pp. 359–73.

Grice, H.P. (1975), 'Logic and conversation', in P. Cole and J.L. Morgan (eds), *Syntax and Semantics, Vol. 3: Speech Acts*, Seminar Press, New York.

Guzman, A. (1968), 'Deomposition of a visual scene into three-dimensional bodies', in Grasseli, A. (ed.), *Automatic Interpretation and Classification of Images*, Academic Press, New York.

Halliday, M.A.K. (1967), 'Notes on transitivity and theme in English', *Journal of Linguistics*, 3, pp. 199–244 and 4, pp. 179–215.

Hamilton, J.M.E. (1980), 'The storage and retrieval of verbal sequences', unpublished Ph.D. thesis, University of Glasgow.

Hamilton, J.M.E. and Sanford, A.J. (1978), 'The symbolic distance effect for alphabetic order judgements: a subjective report and reaction time analysis', *Quarterly Journal of Experimental Psychology*, 30, pp. 33–43.

Hammerton, M. (1973), 'A case of radical probability estimation', *Journal of Experimental Psychology*, 101, pp. 252–4.

Harman, G. (1977), review of J. Bennet, *Linguistic Behavior, in Language*, 53, pp. 417–24.

Harris, Z.S. (1951), *Methods in Structural Linguistics*, University of Chicago Press, Chicago.

Haviland, S.E. and Clark, H.H. (1974), 'What's new?' Acquiring new information as a process in comprehension', *Journal of Verbal Learning and Verbal Behavior*, 13, pp. 512–21.

Hemnon, V.A.C. (1906), 'The time of perception as a measure of differences in sensation', *Archives of Philosophical, Psychological and Scientific Method*, 8.

Henricksen, K. (1971), 'Effects of false feedback and stimulus intensity on simple reaction time', *Journal of Experimental Psychology*, 90, pp. 287–92.

Hinsley, D.A., Hayes, J.R. and Simon, H.A. (1977), 'From words to equations: meaning and representation in algebra word problems', in P.A. Carpenter and M.A. Just (eds), *Cognitive Processes in Comprehension*, Erlbaum, Hillsdale, N.J.

Hornby, P.A. (1972), 'The psychological subject and predicate', *Cognitive Psychology*, 3, 632–42.

Hubel, D.H. and Wiesel, T.N. (1962), 'Receptive fields, binocular interaction, and functional architecture in the cat's visual cortex', *Journal of Physiology*, 160, pp. 106–54.

Hunter, I.M.L. (1964), *Memory*, Penguin.

Hunter, I.M.L. (1978), 'The role of memory in expert mental calculations', in M.M. Gruneberg, P.E. Morris and R.N. Sykes (eds), *Practical Aspects of Memory*, Academic Press, New York.

Huttenlocher, J. (1968), 'Construction of spatial images: a strategy in reasoning', *Psychological Review*, 75, pp. 550–60.

Indow, T. and Togano, K. (1970), 'On retrieving sequence from long-term memory', *Psychological Review*, 77, pp. 317–31.

James, W. (1890), *Principles of Psychology*, Holt, Rinehart and Winston, New York.

Johansson, G. (1973), 'Visual perception of biological motion and its analysis', *Perception and Psychophysics*, 14, pp. 201–11.

Johnson-Laird, P.N. (1975), 'Models of deduction', in R.J. Falmagne (ed.), *Reasoning: Representation and Process in Children and Adults*. Erlbaum, Hillsdale, N.J.

Johnson-Laird, P.N. (1981), 'Mental models in cognitive science', in D.A. Norman (ed.), *Perspectives on Cognitive Science*, Erlbaum, Hillsdale, N.J.

Johnson-Laird, P.N. (1983), *Mental Models*, Cambridge University Press.

Johnson-Laird, P.N., Legrenzi, P. and Sonino-Legrenzi, M. (1972), 'Reasoning and a sense of reality', *British Journal of Psychology*, 63, pp. 395–400.

Johnson-Laird, P.N. and Steedman, M. (1978), 'The psychology of syllogisms', *Cognitive Psychology*, 10, pp. 64–99.

Johnson-Laird, P.N. and Wason, P.C. (1970), 'Insight into a logical relation', *Quarterly Journal of Experimental Psychology*, 22, pp. 49–61.

Johnson-Laird, P.N. and Wason, P.C. (1977), 'A theoretical analysis of insight into a reasoning task', in P.N. Johnson-Laird and P.C. Wason (eds), *Thinking*, Cambridge University Press.

Jones, C.J. and Harris, P.L. (1982), 'Insight into the law of large numbers: a comparison of Piagetian and judgement theory', *Quarterly Journal of Experimental Psychology*, 34A, pp. 479–88.

Kahneman, D. (1973), *Attention and Effort*, Prentice-Hall, Englewood Cliffs, N.J.

Kahneman, D., Slovic, P. and Tversky, A. (1982), *Judgement under Uncertainty: Heuristics and Biases*, Cambridge University Press.

Kahneman, D. and Tversky, A. (1972), 'Subjective probability: a judgement of representativeness', *Cognitive Psychology*, 3, pp. 430–54.

Kaplan, R.M. (1974), 'Transient processing load in relative clauses', unpublished dissertation, Harvard University.

Katona, G. (1940; 2nd edn 1967), *Organizing and Remembering*, Columbia University Press, New York.

Kellas, G., Baumeister, A.A. and Wilcox, S.J. (1969), 'Interaction effects of preparatory intervals, stimulus intensity, and experimental design on reaction time', *Journal of Experimental Psychology*, 80, pp. 311–16.

Kieras, D.E. (1978), 'Good and bad structure in simple paragraphs: effects on apparent theme, reading time, and recall', *Journal of Verbal Learning and Verbal Behavior*, 17, pp. 13–28.

Kinchla, R.A. and Wolf, J. (1979), 'The order of visual processing:

"Top-down", "Bottom-up", or "Middle-out"', *Perception and Psychophysics*, 25, pp. 225–31.

Kinney, G.C., Marsetta, M. and Showman, D.J. (1966), cited in Lindsay and Norman (1977).

Kintsch, W. (1970), *Learning, Memory and Conceptual Processes*, Wiley, New York.

Kintsch, W. (1974), *The Representation of Meaning in Memory*, Lawrence Erlbaum Associates, Hillsdale, N.J.

Kintsch, W. and Keenan, J. (1973), 'Reading rate and retention as a function of propositions in the base structure of sentences', *Cognitive Psychology*, 5, pp. 257–74.

Kintsch, W., Kozminsky, E., Stretby, W.J., McKoon, G. and Keenan, J.M. (1975), 'Comprehension and recall of text as a function of content variables', *Journal of Verbal Learning and Verbal Behavior*, 14, pp. 196–214.

Kintsch, W. and van Dijk, T.A. (1978), 'Toward a model of text comprehension and production', *Psychological Review*, 85, pp. 363–94.

Klemmer, E.T. (1956), 'Time uncertainty in simple reaction time', *Journal of Experimental Psychology*, 51, pp. 179–84.

Koriat, A., Lichtenstein, S. and Fischhoff, B. (1980), 'Reasons for confidence', *Journal of Experimental Psychology: Human Learning and Memory*, 6, pp. 107–18.

Kosslyn, S.M. (1975), 'Information representation in visual images', *Cognitive Psychology*, 7, pp. 341–70.

Kosslyn, S.M. (1976), 'Can imagery be distinguished from other forms of internal representation? Evidence from studies of information retrieval time', *Memory and Cognition*, 4, pp. 291–7.

Kosslyn, S.M. (1978), 'Measuring the visual angle of the Mind's Eye', *Cognitive Psychology*, 110, pp. 356–89.

Kosslyn, S.M. (1980), *Image and Mind*, Harvard University Press, Cambridge, Mass.

Kosslyn, S.M., Ball, T.M. and Reiser, B.J. (1978), 'Visual images preserve metric spatial information: evidence from studies of image scanning', *Journal of Experimental Psychology: Human Perception and Performance*, 4, pp. 47–60.

Kosslyn, S.M., Pinger, S., Smith, G.E. and Shwartz, S.P. (1979), 'On the demystification of Mental Imagery', *Behavioral and Brain Sciences*, 2, pp. 535–81.

LaBerge, D. (1962), 'A recruitment theory of simple behavior', *Psychometrika*, 27, pp. 375–96.

Lacey, J.I. and Lacey, B.C. (1958), 'The relationship of resting autonomic activity to motor impulsivity', in *Brain and Human Behavior*, Vol. 36, Proc. A.R.N.M.D., Williams and Wilkins, Baltimore.

Lakoff, G. (1972), 'Structural complexity in fairy tales', *The Study of Man*, 1, pp. 128–50.

Laming, D.R.J. (1968), *Information Theory of Choice Reaction Times*, Academic Press.

Lawson, E.A. (1966), 'Decisions concerning the rejected channel', *Quarterly Journal of Experimental Psychology*, 18, pp. 260–5.

Lesser, V.R., Fennell, R.D., Erman, L.D. and Reddy, D.R. (1974), 'Organization of the HEARSAY II speech understanding system', Working papers in Speech Recognition III, Carnegie-Mellon University, pp. 11–21.

Levelt, W.J.M., Schreuder, R. and Hoenkamp, E. (1976), 'Structure and use of verbs of motion', in R.N. Campbell and P.T. Smith (eds), *Recent Advances in the Psychology of Language*, Vol. 4B, Plenum Press, New York and London.

Lewis, D.K. (1969), *Convention: a Philosophical Study*, Harvard University Press, Cambridge, Mass.

Lichtenstein, S., Fischhoff, B. and Phillips, L.D. (1982), 'Calibration of probabilities: the state of the art to 1980', in D. Kahneman, P. Slovic and A. Tversky (eds), *Judgement under Uncertainty: Heuristics and Biases*, Cambridge University Press.

Lindsay, P.H. and Norman, D.A. (1977), *Human Information Processing*, Academic Press, New York and London.

Lipton, J. (1977), 'On the psychology of eyewitness testimony', *Journal of Applied Psychology*, 62, pp. 90–5.

Loftus, E.F. and Palmer, J.P. (1974), 'Reconstruction of automobile destruction: an example of the interaction between language and memory', *Journal of Verbal Learning and Verbal Behavior*, 13, pp. 585–9.

Loveless, N.E. and Sanford, A.J. (1974), 'Effects of age on the contingent negative variation and preparatory set in a reaction-time task', *Journal of Gerontology*, 29, pp. 52–63.

Luce, R.D. and Green, R.D. (1972), 'A neural timing theory for response times and the psychophysics of intensity', *Psychological Review*, 79, pp. 14–57.

Luchins, A.S. (1952), 'Mechanizations in problem-solving', *Psychological Monographs*, 54.

Luria, A.R. (1968), *The Mind of a Mnemonist*, Basic Books, New York.

Lyons, J. (1968), *Introduction to Theoretical Linguistics*, Cambridge University Press.

McGeoch, J.A. (1932), 'Forgetting and the law of disuse', *Psychological Review*, 39, pp. 352–70.

McGill, W.J. (1963), 'Stochastic latency mechanisms', in R.D. Luce, R.R. Bush and E. Galanter (eds), *Handbook of Mathematical Psychology*, Vol. 1, pp. 309–61, Wiley, New York.

McKellar, P. (1957), *Imagination and Thinking: a Psychological Analysis*, 1, Academic Press, New York.

McLeod, P. (1977), 'A dual task response modality effect: support for multiprocessor models of attention', *Quarterly Journal of Experimental Psychology*, 29, pp. 651–68.

McLeod, P. (1978), 'Does probe RT measure central processing demand?', *Quarterly Journal of Experimental Psychology*, 30, pp. 83–9.

McNichol, D. (1972), *A Primer of Signal Detection Theory*, Allen and Unwin.

Maier, N.R.F. (1931), 'Reasoning in humans II: the solution of a problem and its appearance in consciousness', *Journal of Comparative Psychology*, 12, pp. 181–94.

Mandler, G. (1967), 'Organization and memory', in K.W. Spence and T.T. Spence (eds), *The Psychology of Learning and Motivation*, Vol. 1, Academic Press, New York.

Manktelow, K.I. and Evans, J.St.B.T. (1979), 'Facilitation of reasoning by realism: effect or non-effect?', *British Journal of Psychology*, 70, p. 477.

Marr, D. (1982), *Vision: a Computational Investigation into the Human Representation and Processing of Visual Information*, Freeman, San Francisco.

Marslen-Wilson, W.D. and Tyler, L.K. (1981), 'Central processes in speech understanding', in *The Psychological Mechanisms of Language*, The Royal Society and the British Academy.

Mason, M. (1975), 'Reading ability and letter search time: effects of arthographic structure defined by single-letter positional frequency', *Journal of Experimental Psychology: General*, 104, pp. 146–66.

Maturana, H.R., Lettvin, J.Y., McCulloch, W.S. and Pitts, W.H. (1960), 'Anatomy and physiology of vision in the frog (*Rana pipiens*)', *Journal of General Physiology*, 43, (Supplement 2, Mechanisms of Vision), pp. 129–71.

Mayzner, M.S. and Tresselt, M.E. (1965), 'Tables of single-letter and digram frequency counts for various word-length and letter-position combinations', *Psychonomic Monograph Supplements*, 1, pp. 13–32.

Melton, A.W. and Irwin, J.M. (1940), 'The influence of degree of interpolated learning on retroactive inhibition and the overt transfer of specific responses', *American Journal of Psychology*, 53, pp. 173–203.

Metzler, J. (1973), 'Cognitive analogues of the rotation of three-dimensional objects', unpublished doctoral dissertation, Stanford University.

Metzler, J. and Shepard, R.N. (1974), 'Transformational studies of the internal representations of three-dimensional objects', in R.L. Solso (ed.), *Theories of Cognitive Psychology: the Loyola Symposium*, Lawrence Erlbaum Associates, Hillsdale, N.J.

Meudell, P.R. (1971), 'Retrieval and representations in long-term memory', *Psychonomic Science*, 23, pp. 295–6.

Meyer, D.E. and Schvaneveldt, R.W. (1971), 'Facilitation in recognising pairs of words: evidence of a dependence of retrieval operations', *Journal of Experimental Psychology*, 90, pp. 227–34.

Meyer, D.E., Schvaneveldt, R.W. and Ruddy, M.G. (1975), 'Loci of contextual effects on visual word-recognition', in P.M.A. Rabbitt and S. Dornic (eds), *Attention and Performance*, V, Academic Press, New York.

Miller, G.A. (1956), 'The magical number seven, plus or minus two: some limits on our capacity for processing information', *Psychological Review*, 63, pp. 81–97.

Miller, G.A. (1962), *Psychology: the Science of Mental Life*, Penguin.

Miller, G.A. (1969), 'The organisation of lexical memory: are word associations sufficient?', in G.A. Talland and E. Martin (eds), *The Pathology of Memory*, Academic Press, New York.

Miller, G.A. (1972), 'English verbs of motion: a case study in semantics and lexical memory', in A.W. Melton and E. Martin (eds), *Coding Processes in Human Memory*, Winston, Washington, D.C.

Miller, G.A., Galanter, E. and Pribram, K.H. (1960), *Plans and the Structure of Behaviour*, Holt, Rinehart and Winston, New York.

Miller, G.A. and Johnson-Laird, P.N. (1976), *Language and Perception*, Harvard University Press, Cambridge, Mass.

Milner, B. (1970), 'Memory and the medial temporal regions of the brain', in K.H. Pribram and D.E. Broadbent (eds), *Biology of Memory*, Academic Press, New York.

Milner, B., Corkin, S. and Teuber, H.L. (1968), 'Further analysis of the hippocampal amnesic syndrome: 14-year follow-up of H.M.', *Neuropsychologica*, 6, pp. 215–34.

Minsky, M. (1975), 'A framework for representing knowledge', in P.H. Winston (ed.), *The Psychology of Computer Vision*, McGraw-Hill, New York.

Mitroff, I.I. and Mason, R.O. (1974), *Management Science*, 20, p. 501.

Moray, N. (1959), 'Attention in dichotic listening: affective cues and the effect of instructions', *Quarterly Journal of Experimental Psychology*, 11, pp. 56–60.

Moray, N. (1967), 'Where is capacity limited? – A survey and a model', *Acta Psychologica*, 27, pp. 84–92.

Moray, N. (1969), *Listening and Attention*, Penguin Books, Baltimore.

Moray, N. (1974), 'A data base for theories of selective listening', in S. Dornic and P. Rabbitt (eds), *Attention and Performance*, V, Academic Press.

Moray, N. and Fitter, M. (1973), 'A theory and the measurement of attention', in S. Kornblum (ed.), *Attention and Performance*, IV, Academic Press, New York.

Moray, N. and O'Brien, T. (1967), 'Signal-detection theory applied to selective listening', *Journal of the Acoustical Society of America*, 42, pp. 765–72.

Morton, J. (1964), 'The effects of context on the visual duration threshold for words', *British Journal of Psychology*, 55, pp. 165–80.

Morton, J. (1969), 'Interaction of information in word recognition', *Psychological Review*, 76, pp. 165–78.

Morton, J. (1970), 'A functional model for memory', in D.A. Norman (ed.), *Models of Human Memory*, Academic Press, New York.

Moyer, R.S. (1973), 'Comparing objects in memory: evidence suggesting an internal psychophysics', *Perception and Psychophysics*, 13, pp. 180–4.

Moyer, R.S. and Landauer, T.K. (1967), 'Time required for judgements of numerical inequality', *Nature*, 215, pp. 1519–20.

Murdoch, B.B. Jr. (1962), 'The serial position effect in free recall', *Journal of Experimental Psychology*, 64, pp. 482–8.

Murray, H.G. (1970), 'Stimulus intensity and reaction time: evaluation of a decision-theory model', *Journal of Experimental Psychology*, 84, pp. 383–91.

Murray, H.G. and Denny, J.P. (1969), 'Interaction of ability level and interpolated activity (opportunity for incubation) in human problem solving', *Psychological Reports*, 24, pp. 271–6.

Mynatt, C.R., Doherty, M.E. and Tweney, R.D. (1977), 'Confirmation bias in a simulated research environment: an experimental study of scientific inference', *Quarterly Journal of Experimental Psychology*, 29, pp. 85–95.

Navon, D. (1977), 'Forest before trees: the precedence of global features in visual perception', *Cognitive Psychology*, 9, pp. 353–83.

Neisser, U. (1963), 'Decision-time without reaction time: experiments in visual scanning', *American Journal of Psychology*, 76, pp. 376–85.

Neisser, U. (1967), *Cognitive Psychology*, Appleton-Century-Crofts, New York.

Neisser, U. and Beller, H.K. (1965), 'Searching through word lists', *British Journal of Psychology*, 56, pp. 349–58.

Neisser, U. and Lazar, R. (1964), 'Searching ten targets simultaneously', *Perceptual and Motor Skills*, 17, pp. 955–61.

Newell, A. (1972), 'You can't play 20 questions with Nature and win', in W.G. Chase (ed.), *Visual Information Processing*, Academic Press, New York.

Newell, A. (1981), 'Physical symbol systems', in D.A. Norman (ed.), *Perspectives on Cognitive Science*, Erlbaum, Hillsdale, N.J.

Newell, A. and Rosenboom, P.S. (1981), 'Mechanisms of skill acquisition and the Law of Practice', in J.R. Anderson (ed.) (1981), *Cognitive Skills and their Acquisition*, Erlbaum, N.J.

Newell, A. and Simon, H.A. (1972), *Human Problem Solving*, Prentice-Hall, Englewood Cliffs, N.J.

Nickerson, R.S. and Adams, M.J. (1979), 'Long-term memory for a common object', *Cognitive Psychology*, 11, pp. 287–307.

Norman, D.A. (1968), 'Toward a theory of memory and attention', *Psychological Review*, 75, pp. 522–36.

Norman, D.A. (1982), *Learning and Memory*, W.H. Freeman, San Francisco.

Norman, D.A. and Bobrow, D.G. (1975), 'On data-limited and resource-limited processes', *Cognitive Psychology*, 7, pp. 44–64.

Norman, D.A., Rumelhart, D.E. and LNR (1975), *Explorations in Cognition*, W.H. Freeman, San Francisco.

Olson, D.R. (1970), 'Language and thought: aspects of a cognitive theory of semantics', *Biological Review*, 77, pp. 257–73.

Pachella, R.G. (1974), 'The interpretation of reaction time in information-processing research', in B.H. Kantowitz (ed.), *Human Information Processing: Tutorials in Performance and Cognition*, Erlbaum, Hillsdale, N.J.

Paivio, A. (1968), 'A factor-analytic study of word attributes and verbal learning', *Journal of Verbal Learning and Verbal Behavior*, 7, pp. 41–9.

Paivio, A. (1971), *Imagery and Verbal Processes*, Rhinehart and Winston, New York.

Paivio, A. (1978), 'Comparisons of mental clocks', *Journal of Experimental Psychology: Human Perception and Performance*, 4, pp. 61–71.

Paivio, A., Smythe, P.C. and Yuille, J.C. (1968), 'Imagery versus meaningfulness of nouns in paired-associate learning', *Canadian Journal of Psychology*, 22, pp. 427–41.

Paivio, A., Yuille, J.C., and Madigan, S. (1968), 'Concreteness, imagery and meaningfulness values for 925 nouns', *Journal of Experimental Psychology*, 76, (1, Part 2).

Paivio, A., Yuille, J.C. and Rogers, T.B. (1969), 'Norm imagery and meaningfulness in free and serial recall', *Journal of Experimental Psychology*, 79, pp. 509–14.

Palermo, D.S. and Jenkins, J.J. (1964), *Word Association Norms*, University of Minnesota Press, Minneapolis.

Penrose, J. (1962), 'An investigation into some aspects of problem solving behaviour', unpublished Ph.D. thesis, University of London.

Peterson, L.R. and Peterson, M.J. (1959), 'Short-term retention of individual items', *Journal of Experimental Psychology*, 58, pp. 193–8.

Pew, R.W. (1969), 'The speed-accuracy operating characteristic', in W.G. Koster (ed.), *Attention and Performance*, II, pp. 16–26, North-Holland, Amsterdam.

Poincaré, H. (1913; 1946), *The Foundations of Science* (G.B. Halsted, translator), Science Press, Lancaster, Penn.

Posner, M.I. (1973), *Cognition: an Introduction*, Scott, Foresman, Glenview, IU.

Postman, L. and Phillips, L.W. (1965), 'Short-term temporal changes in free recall', *Quarterly Journal of Experimental Psychology*, 17, pp. 132–8.

Postman, L. and Ran, L. (1957), 'Retention as a function of the method of measurement', *University of California Publications in Psychology*, 8, pp. 217–70.

Poulton, E.C. (1968), 'The new psychophysics: six models for magnitude estimation', *Psychological Bulletin*, 69, pp. 1–19.

Propp, V. (1968), *Morphology of the Folktale*, University of Texas Press, Austin.

Pylyshyn, Z.W. (1973), 'What the mind's eye tells the mind's brain: a critique of mental imagery', *Psychological Bulletin*, 80, pp. 1–24.

Pylyshyn, Z.W. (1981), 'The imagery debate: analog media versus tacit knowledge', in N. Block (ed.), *Imagery*, MIT Press, Cambridge, Mass.

Quillian, M.R. (1968), 'Semantic memory', in M. Minsky (ed.), *Semantic Information Processing*, MIT Press, Cambridge, Mass.

Rabbitt, P.M.A. and Vyas, S.M. (1970), 'An elementary preliminary taxonomy for some errors in laboratory choice RT tasks', *Acta Psychologica*, 33, pp. 56–76.

Reddy, D.R., Erman, L.D., Fennell, R.D. and Neely, R.B. (1973), 'The HEARSAY speech understanding system: an example of the recognition process', in *Proceedings of the Third International Joint Conference on Artificial Intelligence*, Stanford, California.

Reed, S.K. (1982), *Cognition: Theory and Applications*, Brooks-Cole, Monterey, California.

Reed, S.K., Ernst, G.W. and Banergi, R. (1974), 'The role of analogy in transfer between similar problem states', *Cognitive Psychology*, 6, pp. 436–50.

Reicher, G.M. (1969), 'Perceptual recognition as a function of meaningless stimulus material', *Journal of Experimental Psychology*, 81, pp. 275–80.

Reynolds, A.G. and Flagg, P.W. (1983), *Cognitive Psychology*, Little, Brown and Co., Boston and Toronto.

Richardson, J.T.E. (1980), *Mental Imagery and Human Memory*, Macmillan.

Rips, L.J. and Marcus, S.L. (1977), 'Supposition and the analysis of conditional sentences', in M.A. Just and P.A. Carpenter (eds), *Cognitive Processes in Comprehension*, Erlbaum, Hillsdale, N.J.

Rips, L.J., Shoben, E.J. and Smith, E.E. (1973), 'Semantic distance and the verification of semantic relations', *Journal of Verbal Learning and Verbal Behavior*, 12, pp. 1–20.

Rosch, E. (1973), 'On the internal structure of perceptual and semantic categories', in T.E. Moore (ed.), *Cognitive Development and the Acquisition of Language*, Academic Press, New York.

Rosch, E. (1977), 'Human categorization', in N. Warren (ed.), *Advances in Cross-Cultural Psychology*, Vol. 1, Academic Press.

Rosch, E. and Mervis, C.B. (1975), 'Family resemblances: studies in the internal structure of categories', *Cognitive Psychology*, 7, pp. 573–605.

Roufs, J.A.J. (1963), 'Perception lag as a function of stimulus luminane', *Vision Research*, 3, pp. 81–91.

Rubin, D.C. (1977), 'Very long-term memory for prose and verse', *Journal of Verbal Learning and Verbal Behavior*, 16, pp. 611–21.

Rumelhart, D.E. (1971), *A Multicomponent Theory of the Confusion among Briefly Exposed Alphabetic Characters*, Technical Report 22, Center for Human Information Processing, University of San Diego.

Rumelhart, D.E. (1975), 'Notes on a schema for stories', in D.G. Bobrow and A. Collins (eds), *Representing and Understanding: Studies in Cognitive Science*, Academic Press, New York.

Rumelhart, D.E. (1977), *Introduction to Human Information Processing*, Wiley, New York and London.

Rumelhart, D.E. and Norman, D.A. 'Analogical Processes in Learning', in J.R. Anderson (ed.) (1981), *Cognitive Skills and their Acquisition*, Erlbaum, N.J.

Rumelhart, D.E. and Ortony, A. (1977), 'The representation of knowledge in memory', in R.C. Anderson, R.J. Spiro and W.E. Montague (eds), *Schooling and the Acquisition of Knowledge*, Erlbaum, Hillsdale, N.J.

Ryan, J. (1969), 'Temporal grouping, rehearsal and short-term memory', *Quarterly Journal of Experimental Psychology*, 21, pp. 148–55.

Sachs, J.S. (1967), 'Recognition memory for syntactic and semantic aspects of connected discourse', *Perception and Psychophysics*, 2, pp. 437–42.

Saffran, E.M. and Martin, O.S.M. (1975), 'Immediate memory for word lists and sentences in a patient with deficient short-term memory', *Brain and Language*, 2, pp. 420–33.

Sanford, A.J. (1970), 'Rating the speed of a simple reaction', *Psychonomic Science*, 21, pp. 333–4.

Sanford, A.J. (1971), 'Effects of changes in the intensity of white noise on simultaneity judgements and simple reaction time', *Quarterly Journal of Experimental Psychology*, 23, pp. 296–303.

Sanford, A.J. (1972), 'Loudness and simple reaction time', *Sound*, 6, pp. 92–6.

Sanford, A.J. (1983), *Models, Mind and Man*, Pressgang, Glasgow University.

Sanford, A.J. (1984), 'Processing pronouns with no antecedents', paper delivered at conference on 'Meaning and the Lexicon', Kleves, August, 1983. To be published in proceedings.

Sanford, A.J. and Garrod, S.C. (1981), *Understanding Written Language*, Wiley.

Sanford, A.J. and Garrod, S.C. (1982), 'Towards a psychological model of written discourse comprehension', in J.F. Le Ny and W. Kintsch (eds), *Language and Comprehension: Advances in Psychology*, 9, North-Holland, Amsterdam.

Sanford, A.J. and Leiser, R. (in preparation). Characteristics of scenarios in two probability problems.

Sanford, A.J., Garrod, S.C. and Boyle, J. (1977), 'An independence of mechanism in the origin of reading and classification-based semantic distance effects', *Memory and Cognition*, 5, pp. 214–30.

Sanford, A.J., Garrod, S., Lucas, A. and Henderson, R. (1983), 'Pronouns without explicit antecedents?', *Journal of Semantics*, 2, pp. 303–18.

Sanford, A.J., MacDougall, E. and Simons, J. (1984), 'Gender presupposition and pronoun reference resolution', Unpublished manuscript, Department of Psychology, University of Glasgow.

Schaefer, B. and Wallace, R. (1970), 'The comparison of word meanings', *Journal of Experimental Psychology*, 86, pp. 144–52.

Schank, R.C. (1973), 'Identification of conceptualisations underlying natural language', in R.C. Schank and K.M. Colby (eds), *Computer Models of Thought and Language*, Freeman, San Francisco.

Schank, R. and Abelson, R. (1977), *Scripts, Plans, Goals and Understanding: an Enquiry into Human Knowledge Structures*, Erlbaum, Hillsdale, N.J.

Schiffer, S.R. (1972), *Meaning*, Oxford University Press.

Schlesinger, I.M. (1968), *Sentence Structure and the Reading Process*, Mouton, The Hague.

Scribner, S. (1977), 'Modes of thinking and ways of speaking: culture and logic reconsidered', in P.N. Johnson-Laird and P.C. Wason (eds), *Thinking: Readings in Cognitive Science*, Cambridge University Press.

Selfridge, O. (1959), 'Pandemonium: a paradigm of learning', in *The Mechanization of Thought Processes*, H.M. Stationery Office.

Selfridge, O. and Neisser, U. (1960), 'Pattern recognition by machine', *Scientific American*, 203, pp. 60–8.

Seymour, P.H.K. (1979), *Human Visual Cognition*, Collier Macmillan.

Shadbolt, N. (1983), 'Processing reference', *Journal of Semantics*, 2, pp. 63–98.

Shaffer, L.H. (1975), 'Multiple attention in continuous verbal tasks', in P.M.A. Rabbitt and S. Dornic (eds), *Attention and Performance*, V, Academic Press, New York.

Shallice, T. (1975), 'On the contents of primary memory', in P.M.A. Rabbitt and S. Dornic (eds), *Attention and Performance*, V, Academic Press, New York.

Shepard, R.N. (1966), 'Learning and recall as organization and search', *Journal of Verbal Learning and Verbal Behavior*, 5, pp. 201–4.

Shepard, R.N. (1967), 'Recognition memory for words, sentences, and pictures', *Journal of Verbal Learning and Verbal Behavior*, 6, pp. 156–63.

Shepard, R.N. and Feng, C. (1972), 'A chronometric study of mental paperfolding', *Cognitive Psychology*, 3, pp. 228–43.

Shepard, R.N. and Metzler, J. (1971), 'Mental rotation of three dimensional objects', *Science*, 171, pp. 701–3.

Shiffrin, R.M. and Dumais, S.T. (1981), 'The development of automatism', in J.R. Anderson (ed.), *Cognitive Skills and their Acquisition*, Lawrence Erlbaum Associates, Hillsdale, N.J.

Shiffrin, R.M. and Schneider, W. (1977), 'Controlled and autonomic human information processing: II. Perceptual learning, autonomic attending, and a general theory', *Psychological Review*, 84, pp. 127–90.

Shortliffe, B.H. (1976), *Computer-based Medical Consultations in MYCIN*, Elsevier, New York.

Silver, E.A. (1981), 'Recall of mathematical problem information: solving related problems', *Journal for Research in Mathematics Education*, 12, pp. 54–64.

Silviera, J. (1971), 'Incubation: the effect of interruption, timing, and length on problem solution and quality of problem processing', unpublished dissertation, University of Oregon.

Simon, H.A. (1966), 'Scientific discovery and the psychology of problem solving', in R.G. Colodny (ed.), *Mind, and Cosmos: Essays in Contemporary Science and Philosophy*, University of Pittsburgh Press, Pittsburgh.

Simon, H.A. (1978), 'On forms of mental representation', in C.W. Savage (ed.), *Perception and Cognition: Issues in the Foundation of Psychology*, Vol. IX, Minnesota Studies on the Philosophy of Science, University of Minnesota Press, Minneapolis.

Simon, H.A. and Reed, S.K. (1976), 'Modelling strategy shifts in a problem-solving task', *Cognitive Psychology*, 8, pp. 86–97.

Slovic, P. and Fischhoff, B. (1977), 'On the psychology of experimental surprises', *Journal of Experimental Psychology: Human Perception and Performance*, 3, pp. 544–51.

Smedslund, J. (1963), 'The concept of correlation in adults', *Scandinavian Journal of Psychology*, 4, pp. 165–73.

Smith, E.E., Shoben, E.J. and Rips. L.V. (1974), 'Structure and process in semantic memory: a featural model for semantic decision', *Psychological Review*, 81, pp. 214–41.

Solomon, R.L. and Postman, L. (1952), 'Frequency of usage as a determinant of recognition threshold for words', *Journal of Experimental Psychology*, 43, pp. 195–201.

Sperling, G. (1960), 'The information available in brief visual presentations', *Psychological Monographs*, 74, pp. 1–29.

Sperling, G. (1963), 'A model for visual memory tasks', *Human Factors*, 5, pp. 19–31.

Spoehr, K.T. and Lehmukle, S.W. (1982), *Visual Information Processing*, W.H. Freeman, San Francisco.

Spoehr, K.T. and Smith, E.E. (1975), 'The role of orthographic and phonotactic rules in perceiving letter patterns', *Journal of Experimental Psychology: Human Perception and Performance*, 1, pp. 21–34.

Standing, L. (1973), 'Learning 10,000 pictures', *Quarterly Journal of Experimental Psychology*, 24, pp. 207–22.

Standing, L., Conezio, J. and Haber, R.N. (1970), 'Perception and memory for pictures: single-trial learning of 2560 visual stimuli', *Psychonomic Science*, 19, pp. 73–4.

Stevens, S.S. (1970), 'Neural events and the psychophysical law', *Science*, 170, pp. 1043–50.

Swensson, R.G. (1972), 'The elusive tradeoff: speed versus accuracy in visual discrimination tasks', *Perception and Psychophysics*, 12, pp. 16–32.

Thompson, B. (1962), 'The effect of positive and negative instructions on a simple "find the rule" task', Unpublished paper (see Wason 1968).

Thompson, M.C. and Massaro, D.W. (1973), 'Visual information redundancy in reading', *Journal of Experimental Psychology*, 98, pp. 49–54.

Thorndyke, P.W. (1975), *Cognitive Structures in Human Story Comprehension and Memory*, Technical Report P-5513, The Rand Corporation, Santa Monica.

Thorndyke, P.W. (1976), 'The role of inferences in discourse comprehension', *Journal of Verbal Learning and Verbal Behavior*, 15, pp. 437–46.

Thorndyke, P.W. (1977), 'Cognitive structures in comprehension and memory of narrative discourse', *Cognitive Psychology*, 9, pp. 77–110.

Treisman, A.M. (1960), 'Contextual cues in selective listening', *Quarterly Journal of Experimental Psychology*, 12, pp. 242–8.

Treisman, A.M. (1964), 'Selective attention in man', *British Medical Bulletin*, 20, pp. 12–16.

Treisman, A.M. (1969), 'Strategies and models of selective attention', *Psychological Review*, 76, pp. 282–99.

Treisman, A.M. and Geffen, G. (1967), 'Selective attention: perception or response', *Quarterly Journal of Experimental Psychology*, 19, pp. 1–17.

Tulving, E. (1968), 'When recall is higher than recognition', *Psychonomic Science*, 10, pp. 53–4.

Tulving, E. (1972), 'Episodic and semantic memory', in E. Tulving and W. Donaldson (eds), *Organization of Memory*, Academic Press, New York.

Tulving, E., Mandler, G. and Baumal, R. (1964), 'Interaction of two sources of information in tachistoscopic word recognition', *Canadian Journal of Psychology*, 18, pp. 62–71.

Tune, G.S. (1964), 'Response preferences: a review of some relevant literature', *Psychological Bulletin*, 61, pp. 286–302.

Turing, A.M. (1950), 'Computing machinery and intelligence', *Mind*, 59, pp. 439–42.

Tversky, A. and Kahneman, D. (1971), 'The belief in the law of small numbers', *Psychological Bulletin*, 76, pp. 105–10.

Tversky, A. and Kahneman, D. (1973), 'Availability: a heuristic for judging frequency and probability', *Cognitive Psychology*, 5, pp. 207–32.

Tversky, A. and Kahneman, D. (1974), 'Judgements under uncertainty: heuristics and biases', *Science*, 185, pp. 1124–31.

Tversky, A. and Kahneman, D. (1980), 'Causal schemas in judgements under uncertainty', in M. Fishbein (ed.), *Progress in Social Psychology*, Erlbaum, Hillsdale, N.J.

Tversky, A. and Kahneman, D. (1982), 'Judgements of and by representativeness', in D. Kahneman, P. Slovic and A. Tversky (eds), *Judgement under Uncertainty: Heuristics and Biases*, Cambridge University Press.

Uhr, L. (1963), '"Pattern recognition" computers as models for form perception', *Psychological Bulletin*, 60, pp. 40–73.

Underwood, B.J. (1957), 'Interference and forgetting', *Psychological Review*, 64, pp. 49–60.

Vernon, M.D. (1952), *A Further Study of Visual Perception*, Cambridge University Press, Cambridge.

Vickers, D., Caudrey, D. and Wilson, R.J. (1971), 'Discriminating between the frequency of occurrence of two alternative events', *Acta Psychologica*, 35, pp. 151–72.

Wagenaar, W.A. (1970), 'Subjective randomness and the capacity to generate information', in A.F. Sanders (ed.), *Attention and Performance III*, Acta Psychologica, 33, pp. 233–42.

Wallas, G. (1926), *The Art of Thought*, Harcourt Brace, New York.

Waltz, D.I. (1975), 'Understanding line drawings of scenes with shadows', in P.H. Winston (ed.), *The Psychology of Computer Vision*, McGraw-Hill, New York.

Wanner, E. and Maratsos, M.M. (1974), 'On understanding relative clauses', unpublished manuscript, cited in Rumelhart (1977).

Ward, W.C. and Jenkins, H.M. (1965), 'The display of information and the judgement of contingency', *Canadian Journal of Psychology*, 19, pp. 231–41.

Warrington, E.K. and Shallice, T. (1969), 'The selective impairment of auditory verbal short-term memory', *Brain*, 92, pp. 885–96.

Wason, P.C. (1960), 'On the failure to eliminate hypotheses in a conceptual task', *Quarterly Journal of Experimental Psychology*, 12, pp. 129–40.

Wason, P.C. (1961), 'Response to affirmative and negative binary statements', *British Journal of Psychology*, 52, pp. 133–42.

Wason, P.C. (1968), 'Reasoning about a rule', *Quarterly Journal of Experimental Psychology*, 20, pp. 273–81.

Wason, P.C. (1977), '"On the failure to eliminate hypotheses" ... a second look', in P.N. Johnson-Laird and P.C. Wason (eds), *Thinking: Readings in Cognitive Science*, Cambridge University Press.

Waugh, N.C. and Norman, D.A. (1965), 'Primacy memory', *Journal of Verbal Learning and Verbal Behavior*, 7, pp. 617–26.

Webb, L.W. (1917), 'Transfer of training and retroaction: a comparative study', *Psychological Monographs*, 24, whole number 104.

Weisstein, N. (1973), 'Beyond the yellow-Volkswagen detector and the grandmother cell: a general strategy for the exploration of operations in human pattern recognition', in R.L. Solso (ed.), *Contemporary Issues in Cognitive Psychology: the Loyola Symposium*, Winston and Sons, Washington, D.C.

Weisstein, N. and Harris, C.S. (1974), 'Visual detection of line segments: an object superiority effect', *Science*, 186, pp. 752–5.

Wertheimer, M. (1958), 'Principles of perceptual organisation', in D.C. Beardslee and M. Wertheimer (eds), *Readings in Perception*, Van Nostrand, Princeton.

Wetherick, N.E. (1962), 'Eliminative and enumerative behaviour in a conceptual task', *Quarterly Journal of Experimental Psychology*, 14, pp. 246–9.

Wheeler, D.D. (1970), 'Processes in word recognition', *Cognitive Psychology*, 1, pp. 59–85.

Wickelgren, W.A. (1964), 'Size of rehearsal group and short-term memory', *Journal of Experimental Psychology*, 94, pp. 206–9.

Wiener, N. (1948), *Cybernetics, or Control and Communication in the Animal and the Machine*, Wiley, New York.

Wilding, J.M. (1982), *Perception from Sense to Object*, Hutchinson.

Wilkes, A.L. (1975), 'Encoding processes and pausing behaviour', in A. Kennedy and A. Wilkes (eds), *Studies in Long Term Memory*, Wiley.

Wilkes, A.L., Lloyd, P. and Simpson, I. (1972), 'Pause measures during reading and recall in serial list learning', *Quarterly Journal of Experimental Psychology*, 24, pp. 48–54.

Wilkinson, R.T. (1965), 'Sleep deprivation', in O.G. Edholm and A.L. Bacharach (eds), *The Physiology of Human Survival*, Academic Press.

Wilks, Y. (1976), 'Frames, scripts, stories and fantasies', unpublished paper presented at NATO conference on Psychology of Language, Stirling, 1976.

Winograd, T. (1972), *Understanding Natural Language*, Academic Press, New York.

Winograd, T. (1983), *Language as a Cognitive Process*, Vol. 1: *Syntax*, Addison-Wesley, Reading, Mass.

Winston, P.H. (1970), 'Learning structural descriptions from examples', Report MAC TR-76, Massachusetts Institute of Technology.

Winston, P.H. (1977), *Artificial Intelligence*, Addison-Wesley.

Winzenz, D. (1972), 'Group structure and coding in serial learning', *Journal of Experimental Psychology*, 92, pp. 8–19.

Woods, W.A. (1970), 'Transition network grammars for natural language analysis', CACM, 13, pp. 591–606.

Woodworth, R.S. and Sells, S.B. (1935), 'An atmosphere effect in formal syllogistic reasoning', *Journal of Experimental Psychology*, 18, pp. 451–60.

Yates, F.A. (1962), *The Art of Memory*, Routledge and Kegan Paul.

Yerkes, R.M. and Dodson, J.D. (1908), 'The relation of strength of stimulus to rapidity of habit-formation', *Journal of Comparative and Neurological Psychology*, 18, pp. 459–82.

Zangwill, O.L. (1972), 'Remembering revisited', *Quarterly Journal of Experimental Psychology*, 24, pp. 123–38.

# Author Index

# Subject Index